Lecture Notes in Computer Science 4430

Commenced Publication in 1973
Founding and Former Series Editors:
Gerhard Goos, Juris Hartmanis, and Jan van Leeuwen

T0223179

Christopher C. Yang   Daniel Zeng
Michael Chau   Kuiyu Chang
Qing Yang   Xueqi Cheng   Jue Wang
Fei-Yue Wang   Hsinchun Chen (Eds.)

Intelligence and Security Informatics

Pacific Asia Workshop, PAISI 2007
Chengdu, China, April 11-12, 2007
Proceedings

 Springer

Volume Editors

Christopher C. Yang, The Chinese University of Hong Kong, China
E-mail: yang@se.cuhk.edu.hk

Daniel Zeng, The University of Arizona, USA
E-mail: zeng@eller.arizona.edu

Michael Chau, The University of Hong Kong, China
E-mail: mchau@business.hku.hk

Kuiyu Chang, Nanyang Technological University, Singapore
E-mail: kuiyu.chang@pmail.ntu.edu.sg

Qing Yang, Chinese Academy of Sciences, China
E-mail: qyang@nlpr.ia.ac.cn

Xueqi Cheng,The Chinese Academy of Sciences, China
E-mail: xueqi.cheng@ia.ac.cn

Jue Wang, The Chinese Academy of Science, China
E-mail: jue.wang@mail.ia.ac.cn

Fei-Yue Wang, The Chinese Academy of Science, China
E-mail: feiyue.wang@ia.ac.cn

Hsinchun Chen, The University of Arizona, USA
E-mail: hchen@eller.arizona.edu

Library of Congress Control Number: 2007923593

CR Subject Classification (1998): H.4, H.3, C.2, H.2, D.4.6, K.4.1, K.5, K.6

LNCS Sublibrary: SL 3 – Information Systems and Application, incl. Internet/Web
and HCI

ISSN	0302-9743
ISBN-10	3-540-71548-7 Springer Berlin Heidelberg New York
ISBN-13	978-3-540-71548-1 Springer Berlin Heidelberg New York

Springer is a part of Springer Science+Business Media

springer.com

© Springer-Verlag Berlin Heidelberg 2007
Printed in Germany

Typesetting: Camera-ready by author, data conversion by Scientific Publishing Services, Chennai, India
Printed on acid-free paper   SPIN: 12040827   06/3142   5 4 3 2 1 0

Preface

Intelligence and security informatics (ISI) is concerned with the study of the development and use of advanced information technologies and systems for national, international, and societal security-related applications. The annual IEEE International Conference series on ISI was started in 2003 and the first four meetings were held in the United States. In 2006, the Workshop on ISI (http://isi.se.cuhk.edu.hk/2006/) was held in Singapore in conjunction with the Pacific Asia Conference on Knowledge Discovery and Data Mining, with over 100 contributors and participants from all over the world. These past ISI conferences have brought together academic researchers, law enforcement and intelligence experts, information technology consultants, and practitioners to discuss their research and practice related to various ISI topics including ISI data management, data and text mining for ISI applications, terrorism informatics, deception and intent detection, terrorist and criminal social network analysis, public health and bio-security, crime analysis, cyber-infrastructure protection, transportation infrastructure security, policy studies and evaluation, and information assurance, among others. We continued this stream of ISI conferences by organizing the 2007 Pacific Asia Workshop on ISI (PAISI 2007) to especially provide a stimulating forum for ISI researchers in Pacific Asia and other regions of the world to exchange ideas and report research progress.

PAISI 2007 was hosted by the Chinese Academy of Sciences, the University of Arizona, and the Chinese University of Hong Kong. The one-and-a-half-day program included keynote speeches, a panel, eight refereed paper sessions, and a poster reception. We received 159 papers and selected 42 high-quality papers including 18 long papers, 14 short papers, and 10 posters.

We wish to express our gratitude to all workshop Program Committee members and reviewers, who provided high-quality, valuable, and constructive review comments.

April 2007

Christopher C. Yang
Daniel Zeng
Michael Chau
Kuiyu Chang
Qing Yang
Xueqi Cheng
Jue Wang
Feiyue Wang
Hsinchun Chen

Organization

Organizing Committee

Honorary Co-chairs
Hsinchun Chen, The University of Arizona
Feiyue Wang, Chinese Academy of Sciences

Workshop Co-chairs
Jue Wang, Chinese Academy of Sciences
Daniel Zeng, The University of Arizona
Christopher C. Yang, The University of Hong Kong

Program Co-chairs
Michael Chau, The University of Hong Kong
Kuiyu Chang, Nanyang Technological University
Qing Yang, Chinese Academy of Sciences
Xueqi Cheng, Chinese Academy of Sciences

Program Committee

Clive Best, Joint Research Centre, European Commission, Italy
Robert W.P. Chang, Criminal Investigation Bureau, Taiwan
Patrick S. Chen, Tatung University, Taiwan
Reynold Cheng, Hong Kong Polytechnic University
Yiuming Cheung, Hong Kong Baptist University, Hong Kong
Lee-Feng Chien, Academia Sinica, Taiwan
Ruwei Dai, Chinese Academy of Sciences, China
Vladimir Estivill-Castro, Griffith University, Australia
Uwe Glasser, Simon Fraser University, Canada
Jason Geng, Chinese Academy of Sciences, China
Eul Guy Im, Hanyang University, Korea
Moshe Koppel, Bar-Ilan University, Israel
Kai Pui Lam, Chinese University of Hong Kong, Hong Kong
Wai Lam, Chinese University of Hong Kong, Hong Kong
Mark Last, Ben-Gurion University of the Negev, Israel
Ickjai Lee, James Cook University, Australia
You-lu Liao, National Central Police University, Taiwan
Ee-peng Lim, Nanyang Technological University, Singapore
Duen-Ren Liu, National Chiao-Tung University, Taiwan
Ruqian Lu, Chinese Academy of Science and Fudan University, China
Xin (Robert) Luo, Virginia State University, USA
Anirban Majumdar, University of Auckland, New Zealand
Byron Marshalls, Oregon State University, USA

Table of Contents

Network Security

Short Papers

Data and Text Mining

Cybercrime and Information Access and Security

Intrusion Detection

Network Security

Posters

Terrorism Informatics and Crime Analysis

Network Security and Intrusion Detection

Exploring Extremism and Terrorism on the Web:
The Dark Web Project

Hsinchun Chen

McClelland Professor of Management Information Systems
Director, Artificial Intelligence Lab
Director, NSF COPLINK Center
Management Information Systems Department
Eller College of Management, University of Arizona, USA

Abstract. In this paper we discuss technical issues regarding intelligence and security informatics (ISI) research to accomplish the critical missions of international security and counter-terrorism. We propose a research framework addressing the technical challenges facing counter-terrorism and crime-fighting applications with a primary focus on the knowledge discovery from databases (KDD) perspective. We also present several Dark Web related case studies for open-source terrorism information collection, analysis, and visualization. Using a web spidering approach, we have developed a large-scale, longitudinal collection of extremist-generated Internet-based multimedia and multilingual contents. We have also developed selected computational link analysis, content analysis, and authorship analysis techniques to analyze the Dark Web collection.

Keywords: intelligence and security informatics, terrorism informatics, dark web.

1 Introduction

The tragic events of September 11 and the following anthrax contamination of letters caused drastic effects on many aspects of society. Terrorism has become the most significant threat to national security because of its potential to bring massive damage to our infrastructure, economy, and people. In response to this challenge federal authorities are actively implementing comprehensive strategies and measures in order to achieve the three objectives identified in the "National Strategy for Homeland Security" report (Office of Homeland Security, 2002): (1) preventing future terrorist attacks, (2) reducing the nation's vulnerability, and (3) minimizing the damage and recovering from attacks that occur. State and local law enforcement agencies, likewise, become more vigilant about criminal activities, which can harm public safety and threaten national security.

Academics in the field of natural sciences, computational science, information science, social sciences, engineering, medicine, and many others have also been called upon to help enhance the government's abilities to fight terrorism and other crimes. Science and technology have been identified in the "National Strategy for Homeland Security" report as the keys to win the new counter-terrorism war (Office

C.C. Yang et al. (Eds.): PAISI 2007, LNCS 4430, pp. 1–20, 2007.

of Homeland Security, 2002). Especially, it is believed that information technology will play an indispensable role in making our nation safer (National Research Council, 2002), by supporting intelligence and knowledge discovery through collecting, processing, analyzing, and utilizing terrorism- and crime-related data (Chen *et al.*, 2003a; Chen *et al.*, 2004b). Based on the crime and intelligence knowledge discovered, the federal, state, and local authorities can make timely decisions to select effective strategies and tactics as well as allocate the appropriate amount of resources to detect, prevent, and respond to future attacks.

2 Problems and Challenges

Currently, intelligence and security agencies are gathering large amounts of data from various sources. Processing and analyzing such data, however, have become increasingly difficult. By treating terrorism as a form of organized crime we can categorize these challenges into three types:

- *Characteristics of criminals and crimes.* Some crimes may be geographically diffused and temporally dispersed. In organized crimes such as transnational narcotics trafficking criminals often live in different countries, states, and cities. Drug distribution and sales occur in different places at different times. Similar situations exist in other organized crimes (e.g., terrorism, armed robbery, and gang-related crime). As a result, the investigation must cover multiple offenders who commit criminal activities in different places at different times. This can be fairly difficult given the limited resources intelligence and security agencies have. Moreover, as computer and Internet technologies advance, criminals are utilizing cyberspace to commit various types of cyber-crimes under the disguise of ordinary online transactions and communications.
- *Characteristics of crime and intelligence related data.* A significant source of challenge is information stovepipe and overload resulting from diverse data sources, multiple data formats, and large data volumes. Unlike other domains such as marketing, finance, and medicine in which data can be collected from particular sources (e.g., sales records from companies, patient medical history from hospitals), the intelligence and security domain does not have a well-defined data source. Both authoritative information (e.g., crime incident reports, telephone records, financial statements, immigration and custom records) and open source information (e.g., news stories, journal articles, books, web pages) need to be gathered for investigative purposes. Data collected from these different sources often are in different formats ranging from structured database records to unstructured text, image, audio, and video files. Important information such as criminal associations may be available but contained in unstructured, multilingual texts and remains difficult to access and retrieve. Moreover, as data volumes continue to grow extracting valuable and credible intelligence and knowledge becomes a difficult problem.
- *Characteristics of crime and intelligence analysis techniques.* Current research on the technologies for counter-terrorism and crime-fighting applications lacks a consistent framework addressing the major challenges. Some information technologies including data integration, data analysis, text mining, image and

video processing, and evidence combination have been identified as being particularly helpful (National Research Council, 2002). However, the question of how to employ them in the intelligence and security domain and use them to effectively address the critical mission areas of national security remains unanswered.

Facing the critical missions of national security and various data and technical challenges we believe there is a pressing need to develop the science of "Intelligence and Security Informatics" (ISI) (Chen *et al.*, 2003a; Chen *et al.*, 2004b), with its main objective being the "development of advanced information technologies, systems, algorithms, and databases for national security related applications, through an integrated technological, organizational, and policy-based approach" (Chen *et al.*, 2003a).

3   An ISI Research Framework: Techniques and Caveats

We believe that KDD techniques can play a central role in improving counter-terrorism and crime-fighting capabilities of intelligence, security, and law enforcement agencies by reducing the cognitive and information overload. Knowledge discovery refers to non-trivial extraction of implicit, previously unknown, and potentially useful knowledge from data. Knowledge discovery techniques promise easy, convenient, and practical exploration of very large collections of data for organizations and users, and have been applied in marketing, finance, manufacturing, biology, and many other domains (e.g., predicting consumer behaviors, detecting credit card frauds, or clustering genes that have similar biological functions) (Fayyad & Uthurusamy, 2002). Traditional knowledge discovery techniques include association rules mining, classification and prediction, cluster analysis, and outlier analysis (Han & Kamber, 2001). As natural language processing (NLP) research advances text mining approaches that automatically extract, summarize, categorize, and translate text documents have also been widely used (Chen, 2001) (Trybula, 1999).

Many of these KDD technologies could be applied in ISI studies (Chen *et al.*, 2003a; Chen *et al.*, 2004b). With the special characteristics of crimes, criminals, and crime-related data we categorize existing ISI technologies into six classes: *information sharing and collaboration, crime association mining, crime classification and clustering, intelligence text mining, spatial and temporal crime mining,* and *criminal network mining.* These six classes are grounded on traditional knowledge discovery technologies, but with a few new approaches added, including spatial and temporal crime pattern mining and criminal network analysis, which are more relevant to counter-terrorism and crime investigation. Although information sharing and collaboration are not data mining *per se,* they help prepare, normalize, warehouse, and integrate data for knowledge discovery and thus are included in the framework.

We present in Figure 1 our proposed research framework with the horizontal axis being the crimes types and vertical axis being the six classes of techniques (Chen *et al.*, 2004a). The shaded regions on the chart show promising research areas, i.e., a certain class of techniques is relevant to solving a certain type of crime. Note that more serious crimes may require a more complete set of knowledge discovery techniques. For example, the investigation of organized crimes such as terrorism may depend on criminal network analysis technology, which requires the use of other knowledge discovery techniques such as association mining and clustering. An important observation about this framework is that the high-frequency occurrences and strong association patterns of severe and organized crimes such as terrorism and narcotics present a unique opportunity and potentially high rewards for adopting such a knowledge discovery framework.

Several unique classes of data mining techniques are of great relevance to ISI research. *Text mining* is critical for extracting key entities (people, places, narcotics, weapons, time, etc.) and their relationships presented in voluminous police incident reports, intelligence reports, open source news clips, etc. Some of these techniques need to be multilingual in nature, including the abilities for machine translation and cross-lingual information retrieval (CLIR). *Spatial and temporal mining and visualization* is often needed for geographic information systems (GIS) and temporal analysis of criminal and terrorist events. Most crime analysts are well trained in GIS-based crime mapping tools; however, automated spatial and temporal pattern mining techniques (e.g., hotspot analysis) have not been adopted widely in intelligence and security applications. Organized criminals (e.g., gangs and narcotics) and terrorists often form inter-connected covert networks for their illegal activities. Often referred to as "dark networks," these organizations exhibit unique structures, communication channels, and resilience to attack and disruption. New computational techniques including social network analysis, network learning, and network topological analysis (e.g., random network, small-world network, and scale-free network) are needed for the systematic study of those complex and covert networks. We broadly consider these techniques under *criminal network analysis* in Figure 1.

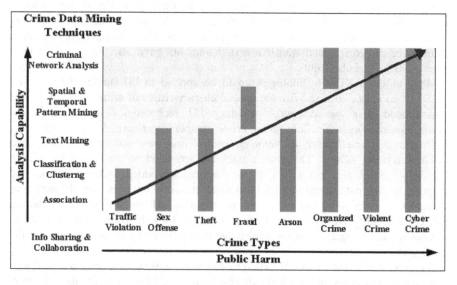

Fig. 1. A knowledge discovery research framework for ISI

Before we review in detail relevant ISI related dada mining techniques, applications, and literature in the next section we wish to briefly discuss the legal and ethical caveats regarding crime and intelligence research.

The potential negative effects of intelligence gathering and analysis on the privacy and civil liberties of the public have been well publicized (Cook & Cook, 2003). There exist many laws, regulations, and agreements governing data collection, confidentiality, and reporting, which could directly impact the development and application of ISI technologies. We strongly recommend that intelligence and security agencies and ISI researchers be aware of these laws and regulations in research. Moreover, we also suggest that a hypothesis-guided, evidence-based approach be used in crime and intelligence analysis research. That is, there should be probable and reasonable causes and evidence for targeting at particular individuals or data sets for analysis. Proper investigative and legal procedures need to be strictly followed. It is neither ethical nor legal to "fish" for potential criminals from diverse and mixed crime, intelligence, and citizen related data sources. The well-publicized Defense Advanced Research Program Agency (DARPA) Total Information Awareness (TIA) program and the Multi-State Anti-Terrorism Information Exchange (MATRIX) system, for example, have recently been shut down by the U.S. Congress due to their potential misuse of citizen data; resulting in impairment of civil liberties (American Civil Liberties Union, 2004).

In an important recent review article by Strickland, Baldwin, and Justsen (Strickland et al., 2005), the authors provide an excellent historical account of government surveillance in the United States. The article presents new surveillance initiatives in the age of terrorism (including the passage of the U.S.A. Patriot Act), discusses in great depth the impact of technology on surveillance and citizen rights, and proposes balancing between needed secrecy and oversight. We believe this is one of the most comprehensive articles addressing civil liberties issues in the context of national security research. We summarize some of the key points made in the article in the context of our proposed ISI research. Readers are strongly encouraged to refer to (Strickland et al., 2005) for more details.

Framed in the context of domestic security surveillance, the paper considers surveillance as an important intelligence tool that has the potential to contribute significantly to national security but also to infringe civil liberties. As faculty of the University of Maryland Information Science department, the authors believe that information science and technology has drastically expanded the mechanisms by which data can be collected, knowledge extracted, and disseminated through some automated means.

An immediate result of the tragic events of September 11, 2001 was the extraordinarily rapid passage of the U.S.A. Patriot Act in late 2001. The legislation was passed by the Senate on October 11, 2001 and by the House on October 24, 2001; and signed by the President on October 26, 2001. But the continuing legacy of the then-existing consensus and the lack of detailed debate and considerations has created a bitter ongoing national argument as to the proper balance between national security and civil liberties. The Act contains ten titles in 131 pages. It amends numerous laws, including, for example, expansion of electronic surveillance of communications in law enforcement cases; authorizing sharing of law enforcement data with intelligence;

expansion of the acquisition of electronic communications as well as commercial records for intelligence use; and creation of new terrorism-related crimes.

However, as new data mining and/or knowledge discovery techniques became mature and potential useful for national security applications, there are great concerns of violating civil liberties. Both the DARPA's TIA Program and the Transportation Security Administration's (TSA) Computer Assisted Passenger Prescreening Systems (CAPPS II) were cited as failed systems that faced significant media scrutiny and public opposition. Both systems were based on extensive data mining of commercial and government databases collected for one purpose and to be shared and used for another purpose; and both systems were sidetracked by a widely perceived threat to personal privacy. Based on much of the debates generated, the authors suggest that data mining using public or private sector databases for national security purposes must proceed in two stages – first, the search for general information must ensure anonymity; second, the acquisition of specific identity, if required, must by court authorized under appropriate standards (e.g., in terms of "special needs" or "probable causes").

In their concluding remarks, the authors cautioned that secrecy in any organizations could pose a real risk or abuse and must be constrained through effective checks and balances. Moreover, information science and technology professionals are ideally situated to provide the tools and techniques by which the necessary intelligence is collected, analyzed, and disseminated; and civil liberties are protected through established laws and policies.

4   University of Arizona Artificial Intelligence Lab Research

In response to the challenges of national security, the Artificial Intelligence Lab and its affiliated NSF (National Science Foundation) COPLINK Center for law enforcement and intelligence research at the University of Arizona has developed many research projects over the past decade to address the six critical mission areas identified in "National Strategy for Homeland Security" report (Office of Homeland Security, 2002): *intelligence and warning, border and transportation security, domestic counter-terrorism, protecting critical infrastructure and key assets, defending against catastrophic terrorism,* and *emergency preparedness and responses.* The main goal of the Arizona lab/center is to develop information and knowledge management technologies appropriate for capturing, accessing, analyzing, visualizing, and sharing law enforcement and intelligence related information (Chen et al., 2003c).

In this paper we present four case studies of relevance to intelligence and warning based on our Dark Web research. In Case Studies 1 and 2, we report the Dark Web Portal project, which collects open source terrorism web site information based on select spidering and portal techniques. A (limited access) web portal has been developed to support retrieval and analysis of these extremist-generated contents. Case Study 3 reports how US domestic extremist groups used the web to disseminate their ideology, recruit members, and support communications. Case Study 4 reports a novel Arabic language model for authorship identification of Dark Web online forums.

Case Study 1: The Dark Web Portal

Because the Internet has become a global platform for anyone to disseminate and communicate information terrorists also take advantage of the freedom of cyberspace and construct their own web sites to propagate terrorism beliefs, share information, and recruit new members. Web sites of terrorist organizations may also connect to one another through hyperlinks, forming a "dark web." We are building an intelligent web portal, called Dark Web Portal, to help terrorism researchers collect, access, analyze, and understand terrorist groups (Chen et al., 2004c; Reid et al., 2004). This project consists of three major components: Dark Web testbed building, Dark Web link analysis, and Dark Web Portal building.

• *Dark Web Testbed Building*:

Relying on reliable governmental sources such as the Anti-Defamation League (ADL), FBI, and United States Committee for a Free Lebanon (USCFL), we identified 224 U.S.A. domestic terrorist groups and 440 international terrorist groups. For U.S.A. domestic groups, group-generated URLs can be found in FBI reports and Google Directory. For international groups, we used the group names as queries to search major search engines such as Google and manually identified the group-created URLs from the result lists. To ensure that our testbed covered major regions in the world, we sought the assistance of language and domain experts in English, Arabic, and Spanish to help us collect URLs in several major regions. All URLs collected were manually checked by experts to make sure that they were created by terrorist groups. After the URL of a group was identified, we used the SpidersRUs toolkit, a multilingual digital library building tool developed by our lab, to collect all the web pages under that URL and store them in our testbed. Table 1 shows a summary of web pages collected from three rounds of spidering (performed bi-monthly).

Table 1. Summary of URLs identified and web pages collected in the Dark Web collection

Region		U.S.A. Domestic			Latin-America			Middle-East		
Batch #		1st	2nd	3rd	1st	2nd	3rd	1st	2nd	3rd
# of seed URLs	Total	81	233	108	37	83	68	69	128	135
	From literature & reports	63	113	58	0	0	0	23	31	37
	From search engines	0	0	0	37	48	41	46	66	66
	From link extraction	18	120	50	0	32	27	0	31	32
# of terrorist groups searched		74	219	71	7	10	10	34	36	36
# of Web pages	Total	125,610	396,105	746,297	106,459	332,134	394,315	322,524	222,687	1,004,785
	Multimedia files	0	70,832	223,319	0	44,671	83,907	0	35,164	83,907

• *Dark Web Link Analysis and Visualization*:

Terrorist groups are not atomized individuals but actors linked to each other through complex networks of direct or mediated exchanges. Identifying how relationships between groups are formed and dissolved in the terrorist group network would enable us to decipher the social milieu and communication channels among terrorist groups across different jurisdictions. Previous studies have shown that the link structure of the web represents a considerable amount of latent human annotation (Gibson *et al.*, 1998). Thus, by analyzing and visualizing hyperlink structures between terrorist-generated web sites and their content, we could discover the structure and organization of terrorist group networks, capture network dynamics, and understand their emerging activities.

- *Dark Web Portal Building*:

Using the Dark Web Portal, users are able to quickly locate specific dark web information in the testbed through keyword search. To address the information overload problem, the Dark Web Portal is designed with post-retrieval components. A modified version of a text summarizer called TXTRACTOR, which uses sentence-selection heuristics to rank and select important text segments (McDonald & Chen, 2002), is added into the Dark Web Portal. The summarizer can flexibly summarize web pages using three or five sentence(s) such that users can quickly get the main idea of a web page without having to read though it. A categorizer organizes the search results into various folders labeled by the key phrases extracted by the Arizona Noun Phraser (AZNP) (Tolle & Chen, 2000) from the page summaries or titles, thereby facilitating the understanding of different groups of web pages. A visualizer clusters web pages into colored regions using the Kohonen self-organizing map (SOM) algorithm (Kohonen, 1995), thus reducing the information overload problem when a large number of search results are obtained. Post-retrieval analysis could help reduce the information overload problem. However, without addressing the language barrier problem, researchers are limited to the data in their native languages and cannot fully utilize the multilingual information in our testbed. To address this problem, we added a cross-lingual information retrieval (CLIR) component into the portal. Based on our previous research, we have developed a dictionary-based CLIR system for use in the Dark Web Portal. It currently accepts English queries and retrieves documents in English, Spanish, Chinese, and Arabic. Another component that will be added to the Dark Web Portal is a machine translation (MT) component, which will translate the multilingual information retrieved by the CLIR component back into the users' native languages.

We show a sample search session in the figures below. Suppose the user is interested in the terrorist group "Ku Klux Klan" and uses it as a search term. Two types of search forms are available: simple search and advanced search (see Figure 2). Our user chose to use simple search at first. The advanced mode gives users more options to refine their search. For example, he can specify that he wants web pages with the exact phrase. In addition, he can restrict the results within a few terrorist categories, or choose to search a particular file type, such as PDF or Word files.

By hitting the "Find Results" button, the top 20 results are displayed (see Figure 3). On the top of the result page it shows a list of "suggested keywords," such as "Aryan Nations" and "David Duke," which help the user to expand or refine his query. Along with the web page result display, our portal also presents the terrorist group name and the corresponding group category. As terrorist group web pages may often disappear,

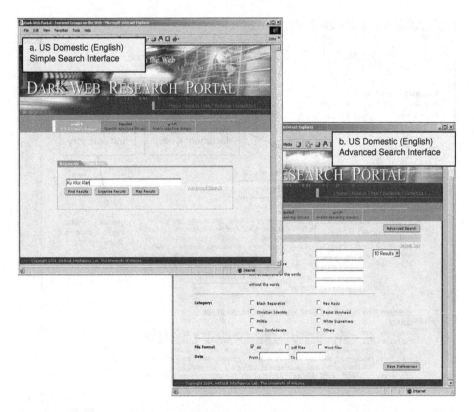

Fig. 2. Dark Web Portal interfaces: simple search and advanced search

"Cached Pages" for each web page collected at different time periods are provided (e.g., 2004/03). Additionally, the user can view web pages, PDF files, or Word files by clicking the corresponding links.

As terrorist groups continue to use the Internet as their communication, recruiting, and propaganda tool, a systematic and system-aided approach to studying their presence on the web is critically needed.

Case Study 2: Jihad on the Web
With weekly news coverage of excerpts from videos produced and webcasted by terrorists, it has become clear that terrorists have further exploited the Internet beyond routine communication and propaganda operations to better influence the outside world (Arquilla & Rondeldt, 1996). Some terrorism researchers posited that terrorists have used the Internet as a broadcast platform for the "terrorist news network," which is an effective tactic because they can reach a broad audience with relatively little chance of detection (Elison, 2000; Tsfati & Weimann, 2002; Weinmann, 2004). Although this alternate side of the Internet, referred to as the "Dark Web" has recently received extensive government and media attention, systematic understanding of how terrorists use the Internet for their campaign of terror is very limited.

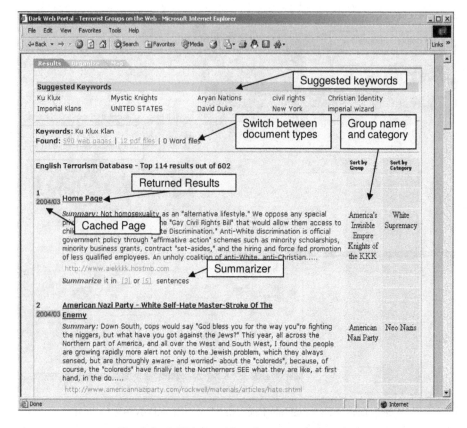

Fig. 3. Dark Web Portal interfaces: returned results

In this study, we explore an integrated computer-based approach to harvesting and analyzing web sites produced or maintained by Islamic Jihad extremist groups or their sympathizers to deepen our understanding of how Jihad terrorists use the Internet, especially the World Wide Web, in their terror campaigns. More specifically, we built a high-quality Jihad terrorism web collection using a web harvesting approach and conducted hyperlink analysis on this collection to reveal various facets of Jihad terrorism web usage. We hope to supplement existing high-quality but manual-driven terrorism research with a systematic, automated web spidering and mining methodology.

- *Building the Jihad Web Collection:*

To guarantee that our collection is comprehensive and representative, we take a three-step systematic approach to construct our collection:

1) Identifying seed URLs and backlink expansion: The first task is to find a small set of high-quality Jihad web sites. To identify terrorist groups, we completely relied on the U.S. Department of State's list of foreign terrorist organizations. In particular, we only selected Middle-Eastern organizations from that list for this study. After identifying the terrorist groups in the Middle-East region, we manually searched major search engines to find web sites of these groups. Our goal here was not to construct a comprehensive list of URLs but merely to compile a small list of high-quality URLs that can serve as the seeds for backlink expansion. The backlinks of these URLs were automatically identified through Google and Yahoo backline search services and a collection of 88 web sites was automatically retrieved.

2) Manual collection filtering: Because bogus or unrelated terrorist sites can make their way into our collection, we developed a manual filtering process based on evidence and clues in the web sites. Aside from sites which explicitly identify themselves as the official sites of a terrorist organization or one of its members, a web site that contains praise of or adopts ideologies espoused by a terrorist group is included in our collection.

3) Extending search: To ensure the comprehensiveness of our collection we augment the collection by means of expanded searches. Based on the 26 web sites identified in the previous step, we constructed a small lexicon of commonly-used Jihad terms with the help of Arabic language speakers. Examples of highly relevant keywords included in the lexicon are: "حرب صليبية" ("Crusader's War"), "المجاهدين" ("Moujahedin"), "الكفار" ("Infidels"), etc. This lexicon is utilized to perform expanded searches. The same rules used in the filtering process are used here to discern fake and unrelated web sites. As a result, our final Jihad web collection contains 109,477 Jihad web documents including HTML pages, plain text files, PDF documents, and Microsoft Word documents.

- *Hyperlink Analysis on the Jihad Web Collection:*

We believe the exploration of hidden Jihad web communities can give insight into the nature of real-world relationships and communication channels between terrorist groups themselves (Weimann, 2004). Uncovering hidden web communities involves calculating a similarity measure between all pairs of web sites in our collection. We define similarity as a function of the number of hyperlinks in web site "A" that point to web site "B," and vice versa. In addition, a hyperlink is weighted proportionally to how deep it appears in the web site hierarchy. The similarity matrix is then used as input to a Multi-Dimensional Scaling (MDS) algorithm (Torgerson, 1952), which generates a two dimensional graph of the web sites. The proximity of nodes in the graph reflects their similarity level.

As shown in Figure 4, domain experts recognized six clusters representing hyperlinked communities in the network. On the left side of the network resides the Hizbollah cluster. Hizbollah is a Lebanese militant organization. Established in 1982 during the Israeli invasion of Lebanon, the group routinely attacked Israeli military personnel until their pullout from south Lebanon in 2000. A cluster of web sites of Palestinian organizations occupies the bottom-left corner of the network, including: Hamas, Al-Aqsa Martyr's Brigades, and the Palestinian Islamic Jihad. An interesting observation here is the close link between the Hizbollah community and the Palestinian militant groups' community. Hizbollah has traditionally sympathized with the Palestinian cause.

On the top-left corner sits the Hizb-ut-Tahrir cluster. Hizb-ut-Tahrir is a political party with branches in many countries over the Middle-East and in Europe. Although the group is believed to be associated with Al-Qaeda, an apparent relation between

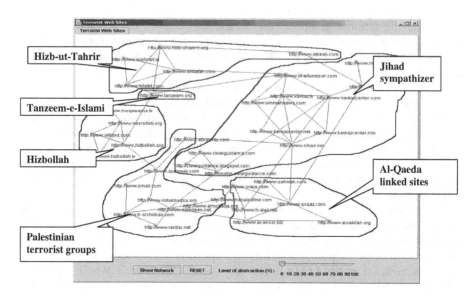

Fig. 4. The Jihad terrorism web site network visualized based on hyperlinks

the two groups has not been proven. Looking at the bottom-right corner one can see a cluster of Al-Qaeda affiliated sites. This cluster has links to two radical Palestinian web sites. Al-Qaeda sympathizes with Palestinian groups and some Palestinian Islamist groups like Hamas and Islamic Jihad share the same Salafi ideology with Al-Qaeda. In the top-right corner, the Jihad Sympathizers web community includes web sites maintained by sympathizers of the Global Salafi movement. For example, "kavkazcenter.net" and "clearguidance.com" are two web sites maintained by sympathizers of the Chechen rebels. As expected the sympathizers community does not have any links to Hezbollah's community as they follow radically different ideologies.

Visualizing hyperlinked communities can lead to a better understanding of the Jihad web presence. Furthermore, it helps foretell likely relationships between terrorist groups.

Case Study 3: US Domestic Extremist Groups on the Web

Although not as well-known as some of the international terrorist organizations, the extremist and hate groups within the United States also pose a significant threat to our national security. Recently, these groups have been intensively utilizing the Internet to advance their causes. Thus, to understand how the domestic extremist and hate groups develop their web presence is very important in addressing the domestic terrorism threats. This study proposes the development of systematic methodologies to capture domestic extremist and hate groups' web site data and support subsequent analyses. In this study, we aim to answer the following research questions: What are the most appropriate techniques for collecting high-quality web pages of domestic extremist and hate groups? What are the systematic procedures for analyzing and visualizing the content of individual these web sites?

We propose a sequence of semi-automated methods to study domestic extremist and hate group content on the web. First, we employ a semi-automatic procedure to harvest and construct a high quality domestic terrorist web site collection. We then perform hyperlink analysis based on a clustering algorithm to reveal the relationships between these groups. Lastly, we conduct an attribute-based content analysis to determine how these groups use the web for their purposes. Because the procedure adopted in this study is similar to that reported in Case Study 3, Jihad on the Web, we only summarize selected interesting results below.

- *Collection Building:*

We manually extracted a set of URLs from relevant literature. In particular, the web sites of the "Southern Poverty Law Center" (SPLC, www.splcenter.org), and the Anti-Defamation League (ADL, www.adl.org) are authoritative sources for domestic extremists and hate groups. A total of 266 seed URLs were identified in SPLC and the ADL web sites as well as in the "Google directory". A backlink expansion of this initial set was performed and the count increased to 386 URLs. The resulting set of URLs is validated through an expert filtering process. A total of 97 URLs were deemed relevant. We then spidered and downloaded all the web documents within the identified web sites. As a result, our final collection contains about 400,000 documents.

- *Hyperlink Analysis:*

Using the MDS algorithm (Torgerson, 1952), we visualize the hidden hyperlinked communities among 44 web sites randomly retrieved from our collection. Three communities are identified in the network shown in Figure 5. The left side of the network shows the "Southern Separatists" cluster, which mainly consists of the web sites of new confederate organizations in the Southern states. They espouse a separatist ideology, promoting the establishment of an independent state in the south. In addition, they share elements of white-supremacy ideas with other non-neo-confederate racist organizations such as the KKK. A cluster of web sites of white supremacists occupies the top-right corner of the network, including: Stormfront, White Aryan Resistance (www.resist.com), etc. Neo-nazis groups occupy the bottom portion of Figure 5.

- *Content Analysis:*

We asked our domain experts to review each web site in our collection and record the presence of low-level attributes based on an eight-attribute coding scheme: Sharing Ideology, Propaganda (Insiders), Recruitment and Training, Command and Control, Virtual Community, Propaganda (Outsiders), Fundraising, and Communications. For instance, the web page of "Nation of Islam" contains recordings of the organization's leaders (for their followers). The presence of these recordings contributes to the web site's content richness and is coded under the "Propaganda (Insiders)" attribute. Our web coding scheme is similar in nature to the one developed by Demchak et al. (2000) for coding government web site characteristics.

The manual coding of the attributes in a web site takes about 45 minutes. After completing coding for the web sites in our collection, we compared the content of each of the six domestic extremist and hate groups as shown in Figure 6. "Sharing Ideology" is the attribute with the highest frequency of occurrence in these web sites. It encapsulates all communication media devoted to portraying the goals of the

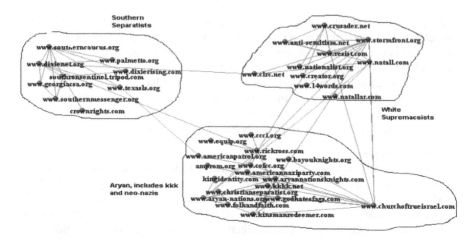

Fig. 5. Web community visualization of selected domestic extremist and hate groups

terrorist group, defining its general policies, and presenting the foundational ideology. In addition, "Propaganda (Insiders)" and "Recruitment and Training" are widely used by all groups on their web sites.

Another interesting observation is the low presence of "Propaganda (Outsiders)," with the exception of Eco-terrorism/Animal Rights groups, which are considered to have a much wider audience than the racist groups, who have a more targeted audience. Much research is still needed for the systematic understanding of how domestic extremist and hate groups use the web to promote their causes.

Figure 7-4. Content analysis of web sites of domestic extremist and hate groups.

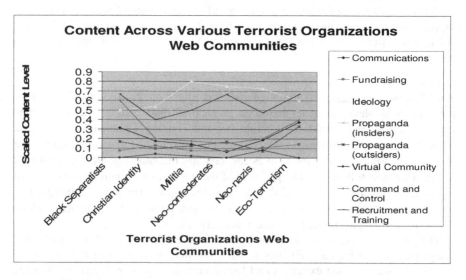

Fig. 6. Content coding for various terrorist organizations web communities

Case Study 4: Developing an Arabic Authorship Model for Dark Web Forums
The evolution of the Internet as a major international communication medium has spawned the advent of a multilingual dimension. Application of authorship identification techniques across multilingual web content is important due to increased globalization and the ensuing security issues that are created.

Arabic is one of the six official languages of the United Nations and the mother tongue of over 300 million people. The language is gaining interest due to its socio-political importance and differences from Indo-European languages. The morphological challenges pertaining to Arabic pose several critical problems for authorship identification techniques. These problems could be partially responsible for the lack of previous authorship analysis studies relating to Arabic.

In this study we apply an existing framework for authorship identification to Arabic web forum messages. Techniques and features are incorporated to address the specific characteristics of Arabic, resulting in the creation of an Arabic language model. We also present a comparison of English and Arabic language models.

Most previous authorship studies have only focused on English, with a few studies done on Greek and Chinese. Stamamatos et al. applied authorship identification to a corpus of Greek newspaper articles (Stamamtos et al., 2001). Peng et al. conducted experiments on English documents, Chinese novels, and Greek newspapers using an n-gram model (Peng et al., 2003). Zheng et al. performed authorship identification on English and Chinese web forum messages (Zheng et al., 2003). In all previous studies, English results were better than other languages. Applying authorship identification features across different languages is not without its difficulties. Since most writing style characteristics were designed for English, they may not always be applicable or relevant for other languages. Structural and other linguistic differences can create feature extraction nightmares.

Arabic is a Semitic language, meaning that it belongs to the group of Afro-Asian languages which also includes Hebrew. It is written from right to left with letters in the same word being joined together, similar to English cursive writing. Semitic languages have several characteristics that can cause difficulties for authorship analysis. These challenges include properties such as inflection, diacritics, word length, and elongation.

- *Inflection:*

Inflection is the derivation of stem words from a root. Although the root has a meaning, it is not a word but rather a class that contains stem instances (words). Stems are created by adding affixes (prefixes, infixes, and suffixes) to the root using specific patterns. Words with common roots are semantically related. Arabic roots are 3-5 letter consonant combinations with the majority being 3-letters. Al-Fedaghi and Al-Anzi believe that as many as 85% of Arabic words are derived from a tri-lateral root, suggesting that Arabic is highly inflectional (Al-Fedaghi & Al-Anzi, 1989). Inflection can cause feature extraction problems for lexical features because high levels of inflection increase the number of possible words, since a word can take on numerous forms.

- *Diacritics:*

Diacritics are markings above or below letters, used to indicate special phonetic values. An example of diacritics in English would be the little markings found on top of the letter "e" in the word résumé. These markings alter the pronunciation and meaning of the word. Arabic uses diacritics in every word to represent short vowels, consonant lengths, and relationships between words.

• *Word Length:*
Arabic words tend to be shorter than English words. The shorter length of Arabic words reduces the effectiveness of many lexical features. The short-word count feature; used to track words of length 3-letters or smaller, may have little discriminatory potential when applied to Arabic. Additionally, the word-length distribution may also be less effective since Arabic word length distributions have a smaller range.

• *Elongation:*
Arabic words are sometimes stretched out or elongated. This is done for purely stylistic reasons using a special Arabic character that resembles a dash ("-"). Elongation is possible because Arabic characters are joined during writing. Table 2 shows an example of elongation. The word MZKR ("remind") is elongated with the addition of four dashes between the "M" and the "Z." Although elongation provides an important authorship identification feature, it can also create problems.

Table 2. An Arabic elongation example

Elongated	English	Arabic	Word Length
No	MZKR	مذكر	4
Yes	M----ZKR	مـــذكر	8

Our test bed consisted of English and Arabic datasets. The English dataset was adapted from Zheng et al.'s study and consists of messages from USENET newsgroups (Zheng et al., 2003). The dataset identifies 20 authors engaged in potentially illegal activities relating to computer software and music sale and trading. The data consists of 20 messages per author for a total of 400 messages. The Arabic dataset was extracted from Yahoo groups and is also composed of 20 authors and 20 messages per author. These authors discuss a broader range of topics including political ideologies and social issues in the Arab world. Based on previous studies, there are numerous classification techniques that can provide adequate performance. In this research, we adopted two popular machine learning classifiers; ID3 decision trees (called C4.5) and Support Vector Machine (SVM). The Arabic feature set was modeled after the English feature set. It includes 410 features, with the key differences highlighted in Table 3.

The results for the comparison of the different feature types and techniques are summarized in Table 4 and Figure 7. In both datasets the accuracy kept increasing with the addition of more feature types. The maximum accuracy was achieved with the use of SVM and all feature types for English and Arabic. Using all features with the SVM classifier, we were able to achieve an accuracy level of 85.43% for the Arabic data set; a level lower than the 96.09% achieved for the English data set.

A comparison of C4.5 and SVM revealed that SVM significantly outperformed the decision tree classifier in all cases. This is consistent with previous studies that also

Table 3. Differences between English and Arabic feature sets

Feature Type	Feature	English	Arabic
Lexical, F1	Short Word Count	Track all words 3 letters or less	Track all words 2 letters or less
	Word Length Distribution	1-20 letter words	1-15 letter words
	Elongation	N/A	Track number of elongated words
Syntactic, F2	Function Words	150 words	250 words
	Word Roots	N/A	30 roots
Structural, F3	No Differences	-	-
Content Specific, F4	Number of words	11	25

Table 4. Accuracy for different feature sets across techniques

Accuracy (%)	English Dataset		Arabic Dataset	
Features	**C4.5**	**SVM**	**C4.5**	**SVM**
F1	86.98%	92.84%	68.07%	74.20%
F1+F2	88.16%	94%	73.77%	77.53%
F1+F2+F3	88.29%	94.11%	76.23%	84.87%
F1+F2+F3+F4	89.31%	**96.09%**	81.03%	**85.43%**

showed SVM to be superior. The difference between the two classifiers was consistent across English and Arabic, with English accuracies being about 10% higher.

In the future we would like to analyze authorship differences at the group-level within a specific language. Identification of unique writing style characteristics for speakers of the same languages across different geographic locations (e.g., Iraq vs. Palestine), cultures (e.g., Sunni vs. Shiite), and interest (e.g., terrorist) groups could prove to be an interesting endeavor.

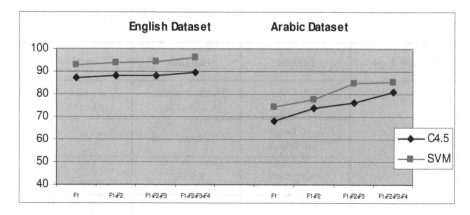

Fig. 7. Authorship identification accuracies for different feature types

5   Conclusions and Future Directions

In this paper we discuss technical issues regarding intelligence and security informatics (ISI) research to accomplish the critical missions of international security. We propose a research framework addressing the technical challenges facing counter-terrorism and crime-fighting applications with a primary focus on the knowledge discovery from databases (KDD) perspective. We also present several Dark Web related case studies for open-source terrorism information collection, analysis, and visualization. As this new ISI discipline continues to evolve and advance, several important directions need to be pursued, including technology development, testbed creation, and social, organizational, and policy studies. We hope active ISI research will help improve knowledge discovery and dissemination and enhance information sharing and collaboration among academics, local, state, and federal agencies, and industry, thereby bringing positive impacts to all aspects of our society.

Acknowledgement

The Dark Web research has been partially supported by the National Science Foundation Digital Government Program, the Intelligence Technology Innovation Center (ITIC)/CIA Knowledge Discovery and Dissemination Program, and the Department of Homeland Security BorderSafe Program.

References

Adderley, R., & Musgrove, P. B. (2001). Data mining case study: Modeling the behavior of offenders who commit serious sexual assaults. In F. Provost & R. Srikant (Eds.), *Proceedings of the 7th ACM SIGKDD International Conference on Knowledge Discovery and Data Mining* (pp. 215-220). New York: Association for Computing Machinery.

Al-Fedaghi Sabah S. and Al-Anzi, F. (1989) A new algorithm to generate Arabic root-pattern forms. Proceedings of the 11th National Computer Conference, King Fahd University of Petroleum & Minerals, Dhahran, Saudi Arabia, (pp. 4-7).

American Civil Liberties Union. (2004). *MATRIX: Myths and reality.* Retrieved July 27, 2004, from the World Wide Web: http://www.aclu.org/Privacy/Privacy.cfm?ID=14894&c=130

Arquilla, J. & Ronfeldt, D. F. Advent of Netwar. (1996). *Rand Report,* http://www.rand.org/.

Chen, H., Miranda, R., Zeng, D. D., Demchak, C., Schroeder, J., & Madhusudan, T. (Eds.). (2003a). *Intelligence and Security Informatics: Proceedings of the First NSF/NIJ Symposium on Intelligence and Security Informatics.* Berlin: Springer.

Chen, H., Moore, R., Zeng, D., & Leavitt, J. (Eds.). (2004b). *Intelligence and Security Informatics: Proceedings of the Second Symposium on Intelligence and Security Informatics.* Berlin: Springer.

Chen, H., Qin, J., Reid, E., Chung, W., Zhou, Y., Xi, W., et al. (2004c). The Dark Web Portal: Collecting and analyzing the presence of domestic and international terrorist groups on the Web. In *Proceedings of the 7th Annual IEEE Conference on Intelligent Transportation Systems (ITSC 2004).*

Chen, H. & Xu, J. (2005) Intelligence and security informatics for national security: a knowledge discovery perspective, In B. Cronin (Ed.), *Annual Review of Information Science and Technology (ARIST),* Volume 40. Information Today, Inc., Medford, New Jersey.

Cook, J. S., & Cook, L. L. (2003). Social, ethical and legal issues of data mining. In J. Wang (Ed.), *Data mining: Opportunities and challenges* (pp. 395-420). Hershey, PA: Idea Group Publishing.

Elison, W. (2000) Netwar: Studying Rebels on the Internet. *The Social Studies* **91,** 127-131.

Fayyad, U. M., Djorgovshi, S. G., & Weir, N. (1996). Automating the analysis and cataloging of sky surveys. In U. Fayyad, G. Piatetsky-Shapiro, P. Smyth & R. Uthurusamy (Eds.), *Advances in knowledge discovery and data mining* (pp. 471-493). Menlo Park, CA: AAAI Press.

Fayyad, U. M., & Uthurusamy, R. (2002). Evolving data mining into solutions for insights. *Communications of the ACM, 45*(8), 28-31.

Gibson, D., Kleinberg, J., & Raghavan, P. (1998). Inferring Web communities from link topology. In R. Akscyn, D. McCracken, & E. Yoder (Eds.), *Proceedings of the 9th ACM Conference on Hypertext and Hypermedia* (pp. 225-234). New York: Association for Computing Machinery.

Han, J., & Kamber, M. (2001). *Data mining: Concepts and techniques.* San Francisco, CA: Morgan Kaufmann.

Office of Homeland Security. (2002). National Strategy for Homeland Security. Washington D.C.: Office of Homeland Security.

O'Hara, C. E., & O'Hara, G. L. (1980). *Fundamentals of Criminal Investigation* (5th ed.). Springfield, IL: Charles C. Thomas.

Reid, E. O. F., Qin, J., Chung, W., Xu, J., Zhou, Y., Schumaker, R., et al. (2004). Terrorism Knowledge Discovery Project: A knowledge discovery approach to address the threats of terrorism. In H. Chen, R. Moore, D. Zeng & J. Leavitt (Eds.), *Proceedings of the Second Symposium on Intelligence and Security Informatics (ISI'04)* (pp. 125-145). Berlin: Springer.

Stamatatos, E., Fakotakis, N., & Kokkinakis, G. (2001). Computer-based authorship attribution without lexical measures. Computers and the Humanities, 35(2), (pp. 193-214).

Strickland, L. S., Baldwin, D. A., & Justsen, M. (2005) Domestic security surveillance and civil liberties, In B. Cronin (Ed.), *Annual Review of Information Science and Technology (ARIST),* Volume 39. Information Today, Inc., Medford, New Jersey.

Tolle, K. M., & Chen, H. (2000). Comparing noun phrasing techniques for use with medical digital library tools. *Journal of the American Society for Information Science, 51*(4), 352-370.

Torgerson, W. S. (1952). Multidimensional scaling: Theory and method. *Psychometrika, 17,* 401-419.

Trybula, W. J. (1999). Text mining. In M. E. Williams (Ed.), *Annual Review of Information Science and Technology (ARIST)* (vol. 34, pp. 385-419). Medford, NJ: Information Today, Inc.

Tsfati, Y. & Weimann, G. www.terrorism.com: Terror on the Internet. *Studies in Conflict & Terrorism,* **25,** 317-332 (2002).

Weimann, G. (2004). www.terrorism.net: How Modern Terrorism Uses the Internet. *Special Report* 116, U.S. Institute of Peace.

Zheng, R., Qin, Y., Huang, Z., & Chen, H. (2003). Authorship analysis in cybercrime investigation. In H. Chen, R. Miranda, D. Zeng, C. Demchak, et al. (Eds.), *Proceedings of the First NSF/NIJ Symposium on Intelligence and Security Informatics (ISI'03)* (pp.59-73). Berlin: Springer.

Analyzing and Visualizing Gray Web Forum Structure

Christopher C. Yang[1], Torbun D. Ng[1], Jau-Hwang Wang[2],
Chih-Ping Wei[3], and Hsinchun Chen[4]

[1] Department of Systems Engineering and Engineering Management
The Chinese University of Hong Kong
[2] Central Police University, Taiwan
[3] Institute of Technology Management
National Tsing Hua University, Hsinchu, Taiwan
[4] Department of Management Information Systems
University of Arizona

Abstract. Web is a platform for users to search for information to fulfill their information needs but it is also an ideal platform to express personal opinions and comments. A virtual community is formed when a number of members participate in this kind of communication. Nowadays, teenagers are spending extensive amount of time to communicate with strangers in these virtual communities. At the same time, criminals and terrorists are also taking advantages of these virtual communities to recruit members and identify victims. Many Web forum users may not be aware that their participation in these virtual communities have violated the laws in their countries, for example, downloading pirated software or multimedia contents. Police officers cannot combat against this kind of criminal activities using the traditional approaches. We must rely on computing technologies to analyze and visualize the activities within these virtual communities to identify the suspects and extract the active groups. In this work, we introduce the social network analysis technique and information visualization technique for the Gray Web Forum – forum that may threaten public safety.

Keywords: Gray Web forum, social network analysis, information visualization, security informatics, information extraction.

1 Introduction

A Web forum is a virtual platform for expressing personal and communal opinions, comments, experiences, thoughts, and sentiments. In general, a Web forum has less factual content than other general Web sites. Nonetheless, a Web forum bears strong factual connections between its members. To someone who is outside or new to this Web forum, this human-emphasized feature raises the interest of understanding the influential status of different members as well as the influential relationships between them. An outside observer may want to have a higher confidence in trusting the information in a message by knowing its authoritativeness. A newcomer may treat messages from more influential members more seriously.

C.C. Yang et al. (Eds.): PAISI 2007, LNCS 4430, pp. 21–33, 2007.
© Springer-Verlag Berlin Heidelberg 2007

The degree of influence of a member may come from being a leader, a contributor or a facilitator of discussed topics in a Web forum. A leader initiates and leads topics of discussion. A contributor provides supporting details and arguments to enrich discussed topics. A facilitator provides content and person references to the forum with the knowledge and experience of the subject matter and the forum itself. In practice, the roles of members evolve throughout the growth of a Web forum. Moreover, these roles can be easily recognized by experienced members in a particular forum. However, such roles may be difficult to be recognized or understood by outsiders or newcomers.

1.1 Definition and Related Work on Gray Web Forum

A forum is defined as the computer-mediated medium for the open discussion of subjects of public interest [7]. Internet forums are virtual communities that build on top of the Internet technologies for their members to share information without face-to-face contact with others. Such environment is ideal for criminals to conduct or encourage crimes because their identities are easy to be discovered. The *Gray Web Forum* is defined as the virtual community formed through Internet forums, which focused on topics that might potentially encourage biased, offensive, or disruptive behaviors and may disturb the society or threaten the public safety. Wang et al. [7] have identified several *Gray Web Forums* in the topics of gambling, pirated CDs, spiritualism and sentimentalism.

There are usually three types of operations when a member login to a forum: (1) Start a new thread of discussion, (2) View an existing posting, (3) Reply to an existing posting. A posting is a message sent to a forum for public view by a forum member. A group of postings related to a specific topic is called a thread. There are usually four types of forum members: (1) initiators, (2) followers, (3) active members and (4) inactive members. Initiators are members who frequently creating new threads for discussion but seldom response to other threads. Followers are members who frequently responding to postings but seldom create new threads. Active members are members who frequently create new threads and reply to postings. Inactive members are members who have only participated in the forum a few times.

Among all Web forums in the Internet, Gray Web Forums are of particular interest to law enforcement and security agencies because of their discussions in some gray areas having potential to post different levels of threats to some communities or an entire society. With today's tools in text indexing, searching and classification, it is possible to identify Gray Web Forums based on certain criteria from textual content analysis. However, the textual analysis does not provide automatic means to facilitate the identification of roles of different subscribers in those Web forums. In this work, we introduce the social network analysis technique to provide a means to re-create a communication network from threads in a Web forum to represent the Web forum structure. Web forum structure analysis will provide the structural context of an entire forum and the statistical relationships between members based on their posted messages according to different threads in the forum. However, the massive quantity of messages and links between them easily complicates the Web forum structure and hardens the task to identify a few relatively more important members in the Web forum. Hence, we introduce information visualization technique to investigate Web forums with different levels of abstraction.

2 Forum Social Network

Social network is a representation of social entities such as people in an organization known as actors and their relationships and interactions in a structure of network (or graph). Each node (or vertex) represents an actor and each link (or arc) represents one or more than one relationship or interaction. The link can be a directed link or undirected link depending on the relationship or interaction that it is representing. For example, node A and node B represent two persons and the link between A and B represents that there are a relationship between A and B. A is a classmate of B and they participate in the computing competition. In this case, the link is undirected because the relationship is mutual. In the example of Web forum, node A and node B represent two members participating in a Web forum. A directed link from B to A represents that B has posted a message replying to a message posted by A earlier.

In a forum social network, each node represents a member who has posted at least one message in the forum and each link represents that there are at least one message that is posted by the starting node and replying to the message posted by the ending node some time earlier. In our earlier work on terrorist social network [10], each link has a weight to represent the association strength between the corresponding nodes. The weight is determined by the number and types of relationships existing between the corresponding nodes. For example, two terrorists can be related by multiple types of relationships such as acquaintance, friends, relatives, nuclear family member, teachers, and religious leader. The weight is computed based on a formulation in terms of the importance of the relationship and number of relationship between two terrorists. In a forum social network, the link represents the interactions from a forum member to another forum member. The association strength is measured by the frequency of interactions between two forum members and the total number of postings across all threads.

Given that A has created a number of threads in a forum, B posts one or more message replying to A's message among all the posting in the thread. The weight of the directed link from B to A representing the association strength is computed as

$$w_{BA} = \sum_{\substack{\text{All threads} \\ \text{created by} A}} \frac{\text{Number of messages posted by } B \text{ in } A\text{'s thread}}{\text{Total number of messages in } A\text{'s thread}}$$

w_{BA} is normalized by the largest weight in the network.

A Web forum social network is formally represented as a weighted graph $G = (V, E; w)$, where V corresponds to the set of nodes (forum members), E is the set of links, w is a function mapping each directed link $(u,v) \in E$ to a weight w_{uv} in the range $[0,1]$ that indicates the strength of association from u to v.

2.1 Social Network Analysis

Social network analysis is a strategy for investigating social structures, which draws significant attention in the recent years, especially in the area of Web structure mining. Applications of social network analysis can be found in publication and citation network analysis, collaboration structure analysis, social interaction network analysis, hyperlink analysis, and terrorist social network analysis. Wetherell et al. [8] describes social network analysis as conceptualizes social structure as a network with ties connecting members and channeling resources, focuses on the characteristics of ties rather than on the characteristics of the individual members, and views communities networks of individual relations that people foster, maintain, and use in the course of their daily life.

Many algorithms have been developed in particular for hyperlink analysis in the recent years due to the popularity of World Wide Web and Internet search engines [3]. Hyperlink analysis supports Internet search engines to rank the Web pages in terms of their popularity or their authority in the topics that the user is searching. Hyperlink analysis augments the typical information retrieval techniques which only measure the relevance between Web pages and user query based on the keyword analysis. In hyperlink analysis, it is assumed that a hyperlink from Web page A to Web page B is a recommendation of B by the author of A. It is also assumed that A and B might be on the same topic. However, there are some hyperlinks that are created only for the purpose of navigation within or across Web sites.

The hyperlink analysis for ranking Web pages can be divided into two schemes [3]: query-independent scheme and query-dependent scheme. Query-independent ranking scheme assign a score to a Web page by analyzing the whole network for all queries. Query-dependent ranking scheme conducts a hyperlink analysis for each query. PageRank algorithm [2,6] is the most prominent query-independent ranking scheme, which is now used in Google search engine. HITS algorithm [4] ranks the Web pages in neighborhood graph expanded by the seed pages collected from search engines in terms of two scores: authority score and hub score. A Web page with high authority score has many hyperlinks from the good hubs. On the other hand, a Web page with high hub score has hyperlinks to many good authoritative pages. In a forum social network, the links are not exactly hyperlinks as discussed in the hyperlink analysis although forum messages and Web pages are both available on the World Wide Web and using the Web standards. A link in the forum social network represents a message is posted to response to a message posted earlier. It does not mean that it is recommended by the author of a later message but the topic of both messages is the same.

To conduct analysis on forum social networks, we shall investigate several other methodologies and formulations in general social network analysis such as centrality and prestige [8]. Important actors in a forum social network are those that are linked or involved with many other actors extensively. A central actor is a member who involved in many ties. Centrality of a node can be measured by degree centrality, closeness centrality, or between centrality.

The degree centrality is defined as the out-degree of a node normalized with the maximum out-degree of a network. Given a social network with n nodes, the degree centrality formulation is

$$degree\ centrality(u) = \frac{out-degree\ of\ u}{n-1}$$

The closeness centrality is measured by the distance from a node to all other nodes. Let the shortest distance of a directed path from u to v be $d(u,v)$. The closeness centrality formulation is

$$closeness\ centrality(u) = \frac{n-1}{\sum\limits_{v=1}^{n} d(u,v)}$$

The betweenness centrality measures the control of a node over other pairs of nodes in a social network. Let p_{uv} be the number of shortest paths between u and v. The betweenness of w is defined as the number of shortest paths that pass w $(p_{uv}(w))$ normalized by the number total number of shortest paths of all pairs of nodes not including w. The betweenness centrality formulation is

$$betweenness\ centrality(w) = \frac{\sum\limits_{u<v} p_{uv}(w) / p_{uv}}{(n-1)(n-2)}$$

The prestige measure focuses on the in-degree of a node rather than the in-degree that is used in centrality measure. Prestige of a node can be measured by degree prestige or proximity prestige.

Degree prestige is measured by the in-degree of a node divided by the total number of nodes in the network subtracted by 1.

$$degree\ prestige(v) = in-degree\ of\ v / n-1$$

The proximity prestige generalizes the prestige measurement by considering nodes that are directly and indirectly linked to the node v, which means all nodes that have a directed path to v. Considering C_v is the set of nodes that have directed path to v, the proximity is measuring the distance of the nodes in C_v to u. The proximity prestige formulation is

$$proximity\ prestige(v) = \frac{|C_v| / n-1}{\sum\limits_{u \in C} d(u,v) / |C_v|}$$

3   Visualizing Forum Social Network

Given a forum social network with several hundreds of nodes (i.e. forum participants), the network is so busy that it is extremely difficult to identify any particular participant and visualize his/her relationship with other participants. In order to optimize the use of the two-dimensional space for presenting the network, we have adopted the spring embedder algorithm to initialize the coordinates of the nodes in the network [10]. Such algorithm optimizes the distances between nodes to fully utilize the two-dimensional space. The lengths of links reflect the association strength between the corresponding ending nodes.

We have also implemented two visualization tools, fisheye view and fractal view, to provide interactive visualization by selecting focus points. Using fisheye view, region

Fig. 1. Terrorist social network after applying spring embedder algorithm

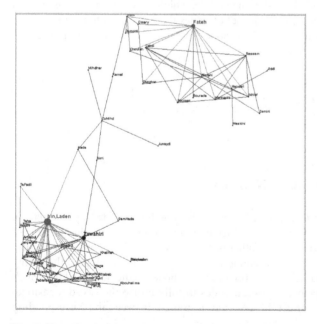

Fig. 2. Terrorist social network after applying fisheye view and fractal view. The focus nodes are "bin Laden" and "Fateh".

of interest is enlarged but other regions are diminished. Such technique allows users to explore the local details in the region of interest while maintaining the global structure of the network. Using fractal view, users may filter less relevant nodes and links by adjusting the degree of abstraction. The remaining subgraph contains the nodes and edges that are most relevant to the focus of interest.

Multiple focus points can also be applied on the visualization techniques. Nodes that are most relevant to all focuses will be identified. That means gateways between important members and active sub-community with a few members as leaders can be extracted.

Figure 1 shows the terrorist social network after applying the embedder algorithm to initialize the coordinates of the nodes. The length of links reveals the association strength between the corresponding terrorists. We can see four subgroups formed naturally in the whole social network. Figure 2 shows the subgraph of the terrorist social network after applying fisheye view and fractal view with "bin Laden" and "Fateh" as focuses. Bin Laden and

Fateh are both terrorist leaders. Applying such interactive visualization technique, the connections between the two leaders become obvious.

3.1 Extracting Active Sub-graph from Forum Social Network

In this study, we have investigated two Gray Web Forums in Taiwan using the social network structural analysis technique and the interactive visualization technique. The first Gray Web Forum is 櫻桃城 (http://bbs.a35.info/thread.php?fid=529) which is a forum related to pirated CDs. The second Gray Web Forum is 萬善堂 (http://oie.idv.tw/cgi-bin/bbs/forums.cgi?forum=1) which is a forum related to gambling. Both forums are considered crime related because pirated CDs and gambling are illegal in Taiwan. Information posted on these two forums is very likely violating the local laws. Analysis of these forums will support the police investigators to identify the suspects and extract their community.

Figure. 4 shows the 櫻桃城 social network and Fig. 4 shows the distributions of in-degree and out-degree of the network. There are 83 nodes totally. The nodes with in-degree equal to zero represent members who have never posted any new thread. There are 43% of the members in 櫻桃城 whose in-degree equal to zero. The nodes

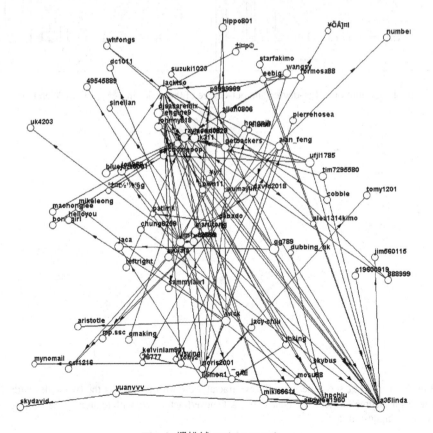

Fig. 3. 櫻桃城 social network

with out-degree equal to zero represent members who have never reply to postings. That means these members only create new threads. There are 52% of the members in 櫻桃城 who have out-degree equal to zero. Given these statistics, there are only 5% of the members who have created threads and responded to other threads since it is impossible for a node to have both in-degree and out-degree equal to zero in a forum social network. The roles of most of the members in 櫻桃城 are very clear and extreme. They are either initiators or followers.

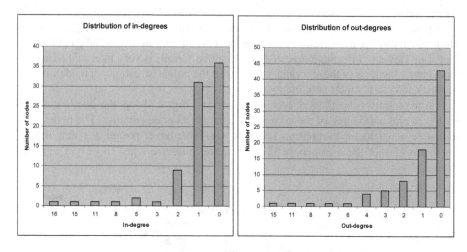

Fig. 4. Distributions of in-degree and out-degree of the nodes in 櫻桃城 Gray Web Forum

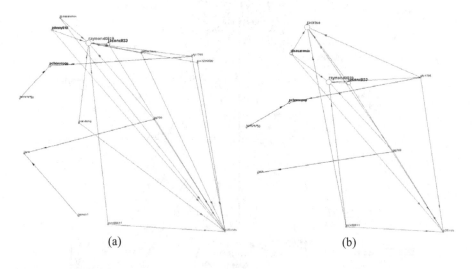

Fig. 5. (a) 櫻桃城 social network fisheye/fractal view with focuses as the two nodes with the highest in-degree, (b) 櫻桃城 social network fisheye/fractal view with focuses as the three nodes with the highest in-degree

We also found that 48% of the nodes have their in-degree equal to either 1 or 2. That means among the members who have posted at least a thread (57%), 84% of them receive only 1 or 2 responses. There are only a few of them who have relatively large responses. The interactions in櫻桃城 are not very active.

In our visualization tools, users may use any centrality and prestige measurements to select the focus nodes. In the following illustrations, we are using the degree centrality and degree prestige.

Figure 5(a) shows the fisheye and fractal view of 櫻桃城 social network with two and three focus nodes. These focus nodes are the nodes with the highest in-degree (degree centrality). Given these views, we can identify the members who are actively replying to these popular threads.

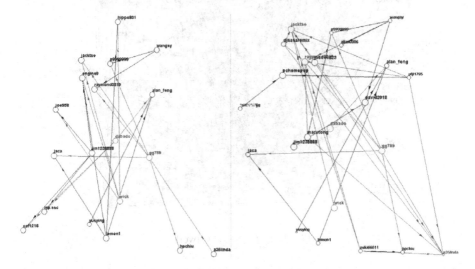

Fig. 6. (a) 櫻桃城 social network fisheye/fractal view with focuses as the three nodes with the highest out-degree (b) 櫻桃城 social network fisheye/fractal view with focuses as the three nodes with the highest in-degree and the two nodes with the highest out-degree

Figure 6 (b) shows the fisheye and fractal view of 櫻桃城 social network with five focus nodes. Three of these focus nodes are the nodes with the highest in-degree. Other two of these focus nodes are the nodes with the highest out-degree. Given these views, we can extract the sub-community of 櫻桃城 that members are actively creating threads or actively responding to the popular threads.

Figure 6 (a) shows the fisheye and fractal view of 櫻桃城 social network with three focus nodes. These three focus nodes are the nodes with the highest out-degree (degree prestige). Given these views, we can identify the threads that these active followers are actively replying to.

Figure 7 shows the萬善堂 social network and Figure 8 shows the distributions of in-degree and out-degree of the network. The萬善堂 social network is much bigger than the櫻桃城 social network. There are 335 nodes. There characteristics of the 萬善堂

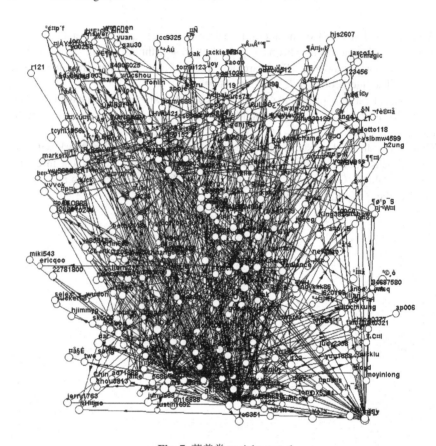

Fig. 7. 萬善堂 social network

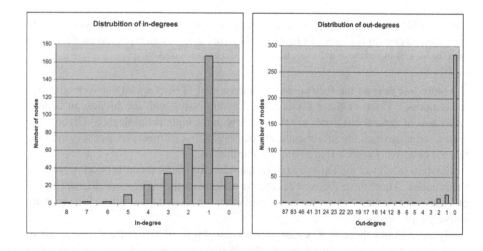

Fig. 8. Distributions of in-degree and out-degree of the nodes in 萬善堂 Gray Web Forum

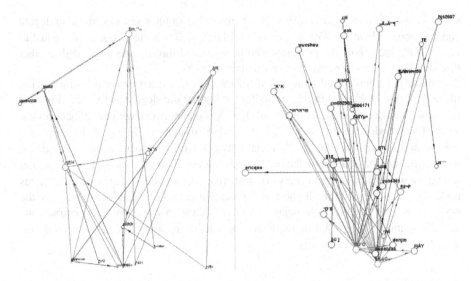

Fig. 9. (a)萬善堂 social network fisheye/fractal view with focuses as the three nodes with the highest in-degree, (b) 萬善堂 social network fisheye/fractal view with focuses as the two nodes with the highest out-degree

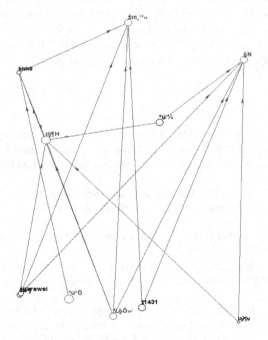

Fig. 10. 萬善堂 social network fisheye/fractal view with focuses as the three nodes with the highest in-degree and the two nodes with the highest out-degree

social network is also slightly different. There are 9% of the members whose in-degree equal to zero. There are 85% of the members in萬善堂 who have out-degree equal to zero. There are 6% of the members who have created threads and responded to other threads. That means most members are active initiators.

Similarly, we have used fisheye and fractal view to extract active sub-graph using the nodes with the highest in-degree and/or the highest out-degree as focuses. Figure 9 (a) shows the fisheye and fractal view of 萬善堂 social network with three focus nodes. These focus nodes are the nodes with the highest in-degree. Figure 9 (b) shows the fisheye and fractal view of 萬善堂social network with two focus nodes. These two focus nodes are the nodes with the highest out-degree. Figure 10 shows the fisheye and fractal view of 萬善堂 social network with five focus nodes. Three of these focus nodes are the nodes with the highest in-degree. Other two of these focus nodes are the nodes with the highest out-degree. Given these views, we can extract the sub-community of 萬善堂 that members are actively creating threads or actively responding to the popular threads.

4 Conclusion

In this work, we have introduced the social network analysis technique and the information visualization technique to analyze and visualize the Gray Web forum. The social analysis technique identifies the nodes with the highest centrality and prestige. The interactive fisheye and fractal views support the exploration of the network and the extraction of active sub-group within the community. We have presented two case studies on two Taiwan Gray Web forums -櫻桃城 and 萬善堂.

References

1. B. Amento, L. Terveen, and W. Hill, "Does Authority Mean Quality? Predicting Expert Quality Ratings of Web Documents," *Proceedings of 23rd International ACM SIGIR Conference Research and Development in Information Retrieval*, ACM Press, New York, 2000, pp.296-303.
2. S. Brin and L. Page, "The Anatomy of a Large-Scale Hypertextual Web Search Engine," *Proceedings of Seventh International World Wide Conference*, New York, 1998, pp.107-117.
3. M. R. Henzinger, "Hyperlink Analysis for the Web," *IEEE Internet Computing*, January/February, 2001, pp.45-50.
4. J. Kleinberg, "Authorative Sources in a Hyperlinked Environment," *Proceedings of Ninth Annual ACM-SIAM Symposium on Discrete Algorithms*, ACM Press, New York, 1998, pp.668- 677.
5. E. Otte and R. Rousseau, "Social Network Analysis: A Powerful Strategy, also for the Information Sciences," *Journal of Information Sciences*, 29(6), 2002, pp.441-453.
6. L. Page et al., "The PageRank Citation Ranking: Bringing Order to the Web," *Standford Digital Library Technologies*, Working Paper 1999-0120, Standford University, Palo Alto, CA, 1998.

7. J. Wang, T. Fu, H. Lin, H. Chen, "A Framework for Exploring Gray Web Forums: Analysis of Forum-Based Communities in Taiwan" *Proceedings of IEEE International Conference on Intelligence and Security Informatics,* San Diego, CA, May, 2006, pp.498-503.

8. S. Wasserman and K. Raust, *Social Network Analysis,* Cambridge University Press, 1994.

9. C. Wetherell, A. Plakans, and B. Wellman, "Social Networks, Kinship, and Community in Eater Europe," *Journal of Interdisciplinary History,* 24, 1994, pp.639-663.

10. C. C. Yang, N. Liu, and M. Sageman, "Analyzing the Terrorist Social Network with Visualization Tools," *Proceedings of IEEE International Conference on Intelligence and Security Informatics,* San Diego, CA, May, 2006, pp.331-342.

11. Y. Zhou, E. Reid, J. Qin, G. Lai, and H. Chen, "U.S. Domestic Extremist Groups on the Web: Link and Content Analysis," *IEEE Intelligent Systems,* 20(5), 2005, pp.44-51.

An Empirical Analysis of Online Gaming Crime Characteristics from 2002 to 2004

Yungchang Ku[1], Ying-Chieh Chen[2], Kuo-Ching Wu[3], and Chaochang Chiu[1]

[1] Department of Information Management, Yuan Ze University,
135, Far-East Rd., Chung-Li, Taoyuan, Taiwan
unicon@mail.cpu.edu.tw, imchiu@saturn.yzu.edu.tw
[2] Department of Information Management, National Police Agency,
No. 7, Sec. 1, Jhongsiao E. Rd., Jhongjheng District, Taipei, Taiwan
bomy@npa.gov.tw
[3] Department of Information Management, Central Police University,
56, Shu-Ren Rd., Ta-Kang, Taoyuan, Taiwan
wkc@mail.cpu.edu.tw

Abstract. Along with the rapid development of online gaming worldwide, online games have become the very successful and outstanding industry in recent years, especially in Massive Multiplayer Online Role-Playing Games (MMORPGs). Cyber-criminal activity arising from online games is increasing at an alarming rate. Further, online gaming crimes have turned out the most serious cybercrime in many countries, such as Taiwan, South Korea, China, Hong Kong, and so on. According to our analysis of online gaming characteristics in Taiwan from the year of 2002 to 2004, the majority of online gaming crime is theft and fraud, but fraud gets higher from 20% to 36%. Identity theft and social engineering are the major criminal means. The offenders are mainly male and always proceed alone. The age of offenders is low (average over 60% in the age range of 15-25). The offenders are mostly students, workers and the unemployed, most of them not having criminal records. The type of game giving rise to most of the criminal cases is still Lineage Online, but other games are getting higher from 0.8% to 28.4%. The value of the online gaming loss over $1500 U.S. dollars is getting higher from 3.8% to 9.9%. In this paper, we present an empirical analysis of online gaming criminal activity from the year of 2002 to 2004 in Taiwan and suggest ways to combat the criminal activity.

Keywords: online gaming crime; MMORPG; cybercrime; virtual property.

1 Introduction

Along with the fast-pace development of the Internet, various network applications have been very successful, including online gaming, electronic commerce, online banking, and so on. Within these industries, the development of online gaming has met with the most success. A new report from DFC Intelligence forecasts that the worldwide market for online games will reach US $9.8 billion in 2009. This represents

C.C. Yang et al. (Eds.): PAISI 2007, LNCS 4430, pp. 34–45, 2007.

a 410% increase over 2003 revenue of $1.9 billion [1]. In 2009, the largest market for online games is expected to be the Asia-Pacific region with $4.2 billion in revenue.

Online gaming (or massively multiplayer online role-playing game, MMORPG) is a form of computer entertainment played by one or more persons over the Internet. Online gaming is indeed an explosive industry and has recently been very successful. Many online gaming companies are not surviving but thriving. For instance, the online gaming "Lineage", which was developed by NCSoft.com of South Korea, has more than 2.3 million players in South Korea in 2003 and more than 2.5 million players in Taiwan in 2004 [2]. The number of Lineage users is almost one-fourth of all network users of both countries.

Globally, online gaming has rapidly grown across different generations. No matter male or female, young or old, white or blue collar, poor or rich, all of them indulge in this novel form of entertainment. The success of online gaming changes the software business model, and makes the related industry have a prosperous growth, for example, virtual property auction, broadband provider, multimedia designer, online payment, internet café, network security, programmer, and advertising, by providing high quality and plentiful experience. Policies for developing the digital content industry have been the key driving force for economic development in which online gaming plays an important and principal role [2]. Furthermore, many vendors from Asia target their products towards North America, Europe, etc., and we can see that online gaming is beginning to take off and thrive in many countries. Nevertheless, what we are concerned about the accompanying negative influence of on e-society.

However, virtual properties in the virtual society may have a very high value. For instance, a virtual character with level 57 ranger values $2000 U.S. dollars in ebay auction website [3]. As another example, consider Korea's Lineage game, the virtual currency exchange rate was 2500:1 (2500 virtual currency can be converted to 1 US dollar) during 2002. Many players are willing to pay real money to buy virtual property in order to upgrade their virtual characters. These have led many players to attempt to benefit from the illegal use of online virtual properties through online cheating, theft, robbery, and so on. Unfortunately, with the growth of online gaming, there has been an amazing growth in the online gaming-related crimes (mostly in the age range of 15-25) especially in MMORPG series. Such cyber-criminal activity within online games is increasing at an alarming rate. In 2002, the number of thefts, fraudulent activities, robberies, counterfeited documents, assault and batteries, threats and illegal gambling cases from online games has increased to 1300 cases from 55 only 2 years earlier. Furthermore, online gaming-related crime has become the most serious problem within all cyber-criminal cases in Taiwan.

In our previous research, we illustrated the online gaming crime and security problems [4], analyzed the influence of online gaming crime [5], gave a thorough taxonomy for a variety of criminal behaviors [6], and briefly analyzed the characteristics of online gaming crime [7]. Since there is little published research in this area, in this paper, we gather 2179 criminal cases during the year of 2002 to 2004 from Taiwan related to the online gaming crime, and analyze them for: reasons for prosecution, offender's gender and age range, criminal method, crime scene, time, and the market value of virtual property for each case, etc. The sources for this research are Taiwan's judicial documents. This paper is intended to provide a complete and thorough illustration of online gaming crimes and security problems as well as countermeasures for them.

The remainder of this paper is organized as follows. In section 2, the statistics of online gaming crime is analyzed along with the criminal cases themselves. To further describe the criminal behavior, we categorize the approaches used in the commission of these crimes in section 3. In section 4, we present possible suggestions and methods of prevention to solve these problems. We give our conclusions in section 5.

2 Statistics of Online Gaming Crimes

We randomly chose 2179 online gaming criminal cases as examples. The cases occurred during the year of 2002 to 2004 in Taiwan. First, we will give a definition on online gaming crime and analyze them for special features focusing on the tendency for online gaming crime, examining related prosecutions, offenders, victims, and criminal methods. These criminal cases are from official criminal reports, from different judicial or investigative authorities.

2.1 Online Gaming Crime Definition

Online gaming crime comprises a criminal activity in which an individual, a computer and a network game are the key entities involved. Some online gamers use illegal or immoral means to gain advantage in their online games. Exactly which of these means is illegal varies greatly by province/state, territory, and country. Examples of online gaming crime are: theft, fraud, robbery, kidnapping, threat, assault and battery, destruction of property, counterfeiting, receipt of stolen property, privacy violations, software piracy, extortion, gambling, and so on. Most of the cases can be attributed to theft and fraud; nevertheless, we list some of the possible derivative crimes.

2.2 Case Analysis

Using the above-mentioned criminal cases, we first analyze their distribution with respect to different attributes of prosecution including: type of crimes, time of occurrence, date, crime scene, and monetary value.

(1) Type of Crimes: Theft and Fraud are the major type of online gaming crimes. Table 1 depicts that most of cases were charged with theft, but the cases have dropped from 73.7% to 60.5%. Fraud has been increased from 20.2% to 36.01%.

Table 1. Frequency of occurrence of different types of crime from 2002 to 2004

Measure	Value	Frequency (Percentage)		
	Year	2002	2003	2004
Type of Crimes	Theft	452(73.7%)	470(63.17%)	498(60.58%)
	Fraud	124(20.2%)	183(24.60%)	296(36.01%)
	Conversion	9(1.5%)	8(1.08%)	8(0.97%)
	Reception of Stolen Property	2(0.3%)	2(0.27%)	2(0.24%)
	Others	26(4.2%)	11(1.48%)	18(2.19%)
Total		613(100.0%)	744(100.0%)	822(100.0%)

(2) Type of Online Games: Table 2 shows that the majority of the criminal cases happened on Lineage online game, but it had decreased from 93.3% to 69.9%. Crimes on other games were getting higher from 0.8% to 28.47%.

Table 2. Frequency of crimes based for different online games from 2002 to 2004

Measure	Value	Frequency (Percentage)		
	Year	2002	2003	2004
Type of Online Games	Lineage	572(93.3%)	521(70.03%)	575(69.90%)
	JinYong Online	23(3.8%)	26(3.49%)	7(0.80%)
	Stone Age	10(1.6%)	2(0.27%)	3(0.40%)
	CrossGate	3(0.5%)	6(0.81%)	3(0.40%)
	Others	5(0.8%)	189(25.4%)	234(28.47%)
Total		613(100.0%)	744(100.0%)	822(100.0%)

(3) Time of Crime Distribution: Table 3 shows that there is not distinct difference for the time of crime.

Table 3. Time of crime occurrence distribution from 2002 to 2004

Measure	Value	Frequency (Percentage)		
	Year	2002	2003	2004
Time	0-2	53(8.6%)	65(8.74%)	75(9.12%)
	2-4	60(9.8%)	62(8.33%)	73(8.88%)
	4-6	48(7.8%)	52(6.99%)	70(8.52%)
	6-8	49(8.0%)	53(7.12%)	61(7.42%)
	8-10	58(9.5%)	56(7.53%)	71(8.64%)
	10-12	26(4.2%)	42(5.65%)	56(6.81%)
	12-14	73(11.9%)	67(9.01%)	81(9.85%)
	14-16	54(8.8%)	62(8.33%)	73(8.88%)
	16-18	55(9.0%)	74(9.95%)	73(8.88%)
	18-20	33(5.4%)	63(8.47%)	56(6.81%)
	20-22	47(7.7%)	76(10.22%)	61(7.42%)
	22-24	57(9.3%)	72(9.68%)	72(8.76%)
Total		613(100.0%)	744(100.0%)	822(100.0%)

(4) Crime Scene Distribution: Table 4 shows that most criminal activities were committed in Internet cafés, but they were dropped from 54.8% to 43.4%. In addition, many offenders also used their home network to commit the crime.

Table 4. Crime scene distribution from 2002 to 2004

Measure	Value	Frequency (Percentage)		
	Year	2002	2003	2004
Crime Scene	Internet café	336(54.8%)	352(47.31%)	357(43.4%)
	Offender's dwelling	189(30.8%)	165(22.18%)	223(27.1%)
	Victim's dwelling	22(3.6%)	68(9.14%)	96(11.6%)
	School	4(0.7%)	7(0.94%)	7(1.0%)
	Others	62(10.1%)	152(20.43)	139(16.9%)
Total		613(100.0%)	744(100.0%)	822(100.0%)

(5) Market Value of Each Case Distribution: In cases, the average value of the online gaming crime loss is about $459 U.S. dollars. The value of the online gaming loss over $1500 U.S. dollars is getting higher from 3.8% to 9.9%. Table 5 depicts the distribution of the criminal cases based on lost value.

Table 5. Market value of each case distribution from 2002 to 2004

Measure	Value	Frequency (Percentage)		
	Year	2002	2003	2004
Market Value of Each Case (U.S. dollars)	No Record	111(18.1%)	293(39.38%)	366(44.53%)
	<100	96(15.7%)	67(9.01%)	41(4.97%)
	100-300	210(34.3%)	115(15.46%)	85(10.34%)
	301-500	48(7.8%)	87(11.69%)	88(10.74%)
	501-700	54(8.8%)	52(6.99%)	57(6.96%)
	701-900	34(5.5%)	25(3.36%)	33(3.98%)
	901-1100	10(1.6%)	42(5.65%)	47(5.77%)
	1101-1300	20(3.3%)	13(1.75%)	23(2.78%)
	1301-1500	7(1.1%)	3(0.40%)	0(0.00%)
	>1500	23(3.8%)	47(6.32%)	82(9.94%)
Total		613(100.0%)	744(100.0%)	822(100.0%)

2.3 Offender Analysis

In this section, we analyze the distribution of online gaming crime cases based on the different attributes of offenders including: offender's gender, age, profession, whether the offender had a criminal record, and whether the offender colluded with others.

(1) Gender: In average, there are over 90% male offenders within whole cases.

Table 6. Offenders' gender distribution from 2002 to 2004

Measure	Value	Frequency (Percentage)		
	Year	2002	2003	2004
Gender	Male	587(95.8%)	637(85.62%)	752(91.50%)
	Female	26(4.2%)	107(14.38%)	70(8.50%)
Total		613(100.0%)	744(100.0%)	822(100.0%)

(2) Age: Table 7 shows that young offenders between 15 and 20 years old have the highest number in 2002, but it has dropped to 28.5% in 2004. In 2003 and 2004, the majority of offenders' age is between 21 and 25.

Table 7. Offenders' age distribution from 2002 to 2004

Measure	Value	Frequency (Percentage)		
	Year	2002	2003	2004
	<14	52(8.5%)	0(0.0%)	2(0.20%)
	15-20	388(63.3%)	32(4.30%)	234(28.50%)
	21-25	135(22.0%)	506(68.01%)	381(46.40%)
Age	25-30	26(4.2%)	155(20.83%)	119(14.50%)
	31-35	10(1.6%)	31(4.17%)	36(4.40%)
	36-40	0(0.0%)	13(1.75%)	44(5.30%)
	>40	2(0.3%)	7(0.94%)	6(0.70%)
Total		613(100.0%)	744(100.0%)	822(100.0%)

(3) Profession: Table 8 shows that most of the offenders are students in 2002, but it has been dropped to 17.6% in 2004. Workers who committed online gaming crime are getting higher. The main professions of the offenders include students, workers, and military. The unemployed make up one-fourth of all offenders.

Table 8. Distribution of offenders' profession from 2002 to 2004

Measure	Value	Frequency (Percentage)		
	Year	2002	2003	2004
	Student	286(46.66%)	131(17.61%)	145(17.60%)
	Unemployed	147(23.98%)	191(25.67%)	191(23.20%)
	Worker	78(12.72%)	195(26.21%)	232(28.20%)
Profession	Military	44(7.18%)	84(11.29%)	74(9.00%)
	Business	9(1.47%)	28(3.76%)	53(6.50%)
	IT	2(0.33%)	4(0.54%)	12(1.40%)
	Others	47(7.67%)	111(14.92%)	116(14.10%)
Total		613(100.0%)	744(100.0%)	822(100.0%)

(4) Have Criminal Record: Table 9 indicates that most of offenders had no criminal records.

Table 9. Have criminal record distribution from 2002 to 2004

Measure	Value	Frequency (Percentage)		
	Year	2002	2003	2004
Have criminal record?	Yes	111(18.1%)	198(26.61%)	173(21.00%)
	No	502(81.9%)	546(73.39%)	649(79.00%)
Total		613(100.0%)	744(100.0%)	822(100.0%)

2.4 Criminal Method Analysis

In order to analyze online gaming crime, we categorize the 18 criminal methods into 5 categories, which are identity theft, social engineering, hacking tools or system weakness, and force or revenge. Table 10 depicts the criminal methods with corresponding number of criminal cases and percentages. We bypassed 643 cases from our official report that had no mention of the exact criminal methods used.

Table 10. Criminal method distribution from 2002 to 2004

Criminal Methods	ValueFrequency(Percentage)		
	2002	2003	2004
1. Identity Theft	159(25.94%)	298(40.05%)	341(41.52%)
2. Social Engineering	161(26.26%)	229(30.78%)	209(25.44%)
3. Hacking Tools or System Weakness	43(7.01%)	40(5.38%)	40(4.81%)
4. Force or Revenge	3(0.49%)	1(0.13%)	2(0.24%)
5. Unrecognized	247(40.29%)	176(23.66%)	230(27.99%)
Total	613(100%)	744(100%)	822(100%)

3 Criminal Behavior Analysis

3.1 Why MMORPGs Are Attractive to Players and Criminals

There are a number of reasons why MMORPGs are attractive to both players and criminals alike.

(1) Attractive as a good challenge; also there is a large community of players.
(2) Desire to gain rare virtual property or virtual money.
(3) One can accumulate virtual fortune gradually and in the cases of some games, it can be converted into cash.
(4) Represents great amusement.
(5) There is a challenge in moving their virtual character to a higher level.

(6) Criminals find the lack of authentication/security schemes make it easy to profit by illegal means.
(7) Some virtual properties are highly valuable in marketplace.
(8) There is a market for virtual property because sufficient numbers of people would rather pay money for virtual property rather than the energy, skill, or time to work within the game.
(9) The trade and exchange of virtual property has become prevalent.
(10) The perception of MMORPGs has changed to the point where many people now think they are making money instead of just for entertainment.
(11) It is apparent that the different business model for MMORPGs in Asia (as opposed to North America) leads to higher MMORPG crime rate [5].

3.2 Criminal Behavior Analysis

In this Section, we first analyze the main reasons for some online gaming crimes, and then summarize a variety of criminal behaviors.

As we have described, over 70% of criminal cases happened within the Lineage online game. We give the following analysis:

(1) Lineage is the earliest and biggest online game in terms of market scale. During 2002 to 2004, it claimed over 2.5 million memberships in Taiwan.
(2) Many virtual properties in Lineage have a higher value in the real market than other games.
(3) Gamania Corp., the source of Lineage, provides more detailed log record information with which investigators can easily trace criminal footprints as evidence. Thus, information on Lineage criminal activity is more complete, leading to more criminal cases identified with Lineage. On the other hand, most other vendors lack adequate audit schemes or cooperative strategies with enforcement authorities. Therefore, for these vendors, the enforcement authorities could not execute their investigations or were prohibited by limited evidence.

Different online gaming vendors may have different administrative mechanisms; for instance, some vendors can record and audit details regarding virtual property trading, transference, dropping, processing, etc., but others may only record little information about logon and/or logoff. Once a dispute happens, it may be difficult to distinguish who is right or wrong. If a vendor is lacking a scheme for auditing and tracing of record information, it would lead to problems in carrying out prosecution.

4 Suggestions and Preventions

In this section we suggest potential approaches for dealing with the rising incidence of gaming crime.

4.1 Preventing Identity Theft

Identity theft is a key problem area. Some approaches to preventing criminal activity in this area include:

(1) Use of virus and Trojan scanning software: for instance, the online gaming service provider could run this as part of its operation for all client software.

(2) Online tests of the username password efficacy: at enrollment, the online gaming service would check the effectiveness of a selected username and password.

(3) Requiring changes of username/password: every few weeks the gaming service would require the user to change the username/password to new ones.

(4) Detection of suspicious activity: the online gaming service would detect when there is more than one instance of a supposedly unique player being online in order to detect sharing of username/password.

(5) Use of Digital Certificates: players would be required to apply for certificates from a certification authority (CA) in advance. Unfortunately, players may find this procedure complicated. The need to have the digital certificate at hand is considered inconvenient, may hamper mobility and thus would affect the players' interest in the game.

(6) Smart Card to identify users: while effective for authenticating users, it unfortunately adds to the cost of the game, and would require a card reader.

(7) Biometric Authentication: such as fingerprint verification, hand geometry, iris scanning, retina scanning, voice recognition, signature verification or facial recognition. These authentication mechanisms all need particular devices or readers to function. Players may feel uncomfortable and find them too complicated for everyday use.

(8) Password Transmitted via Cell Phone: gaming authentication servers use related definitions and calculations to produce random passwords and then transmit them to players through cell phones. Due to the prevalence of cell phones, this authentication mechanism could provide an effective and secure scheme, but cost considerations would be a big issue. Also, players must have cell phones. Furthermore, unless the message has been appropriately encrypted, cellular transmissions could be intercepted.

(9) Dynamic Password Authentication: known as One-time Password Generators; this is similar to traditional static passwords since a password is used in conjunction with a UserID. They are limited to one time use [8]. The advantage of this technique is preventing the replay of a compromised password.

4.2 Other Protective Measures

Other protective measures include the following:

(1) Use insurance to protect virtual property. While not preventing the crime, it would compensate for loss. Systemically, insurers may require online gaming service providers to maintain certain security standards.

(2) Deploy built-in cheating detection mechanisms. The major objective for this measure is to reduce the modification of game software and use of fraudulent means so as to shrink the possibility of criminal activities. Such a system would detect or discover unusual activities or modifications, and produce related alarms. Some online gaming vendors, such as Joe Wilcox, have developed similar mechanisms [9].

(3)   Advise the vendor's customers exactly what information the vendor will, and will not ask for on websites or via e-mail. If personal, financial or sensitive information must be exchanged, the vendor must clearly indicate under what conditions that exchange will occur.

(4)   Build up an instant response/report platform. Using this platform, vendors can instantly provide essential information or case study with their customers on investigating or reporting suspicious/illegal means or circumstances. Effectively this would be a call centre focused on dealing with potentially illegal behavior.

(5)   Be the first to establish similar website domain URLs. For example, www.google.com will still take users to the proper web address, www.google.com. The idea behind this is to help prevent fake websites.

(6)   Register the user's identity in environments such as Internet cafés as far as possible. Internet cafés and other public places providing online gaming should record their customers' identities, time period of online use, and other data to support the investigation of criminal activities.

(7)   Record complete audit data and keep it at least three months. Online gaming vendors need to enhance their auditing systems, as well as record and store important information such as a record of virtual property transferred, for tracing or investigating by an enforcement authority.

(8)   Improve related legal education. According to our statistics, most of offenders were under 25 years old, in this age bracket, people easily breach the law and lack legal or moral education. Teachers and parents should learn and understand the negative influence of online gaming on their students or children.

(9)   Educate players to keep their UserIDs and passwords secret, and let them know that this is their responsibility.

(10)   Establish safe trading schemes or channels. Players should be very careful during online trading. Exchanging, selling, or purchasing virtual properties via a trusted third party can provide a safer environment than trading in private.

(11)   Deploy rights management mechanisms to lock virtual property for use by only those authorized.

(12)   Law enforcement authorities can employ "honey pots" to lure and capture online gaming offenders; online gaming honey pots are fake online gaming systems that act as decoys to collect data on criminal activity [10].

5 Conclusion

In this paper, we gathered and analyzed 2179 criminal cases of online gaming crimes that happened in Taiwan during the year of 2002 to 2004. We can imagine that the upcoming online gaming crimes and cheating cases will undermine the development of the online gaming industry. Furthermore, these crimes not only influence the players' mental addiction but also may lead to other societal problems. Although these crime problems are not as serious as conventional violent crimes, people need to be aware of the problems arising from online gaming, especially since the age of online gaming offenders is going down. Entertainment should be entertainment, and not become a dark corner of the Internet corrupted with criminal issues. In addition to pursuing profits, the vendors need to be educators and to a certain respect, enforcers of appropriate behavior in the playing of these online games. We hope that the online gaming-related issues identified here will be noticed by many so that these problems may be solved through education, laws and appropriate technologies. It is clear that implementing measures to mitigate crime is necessary. In this paper we also have provided some suggestions and prevention approaches to help deal with criminal activity.

References

1. The Online Game Market, DFC Intelligence 2004, Game Industry Report by GITISS 2004.
2. The collision of new industry – Taiwan online games are getting stronger, Digital content promotion website, Available: http://www.nmipo.org.tw/files/3-2/6/6-4.pdf.
3. Lineage 2 Kain Lvl 57Silver Ranger, Accessed June 20, 2004, Available: http://cgi.ebay.com/ws/eBayISAPI.dll?ViewItem&item=8113549502&indexURL=0&photoDisplayType=2#ebayphotohosting.
4. Chen Y. C., Lin S. K., and Hwang J. J.,: The influence of computer crime in online gaming on E-society - taking example for Taiwan in 2002, *International Conference on Innovative Information Technology Policy and E-Society*, National Cheng-Chi University, Taiwan, 2003.
5. Chen Y. C., Chen P. S., Song R., and Korba L.,: Online Gaming Crime and Security Issues – Cases and Countermeasures from Taiwan, *PST 2004 Conference, Fredericton*, Canada, 2004.
6. Chen Y. C., Chen P. S., Song R., Yee G., and Korba L.,: Classification of Online Gaming Crime and Security, Submitted to *IRMA 2005 International Conference*, San Diego, California, USA, 2005.
7. Chen Y. C., Chen P. S., Hwang J. J., Korba L., Song R., Yee G.,: An Analysis of Online Gaming Crime Characteristics, *Journal of Internet Research*, 2005.
8. "Best Practices - User Authentication Mechanisms", retrieved June 20, 2004, from:http://www.itsc.state.md.us/oldsite/info/InternetSecurity/BestPractices/Authentic.htm.
9. Unreal Playground, "Exclusive Interview with Dr. Sin of Epic Games", October, 2002, retrieved June 20, 2004, from: http://www.unrealplayground.com/inter view.php?id=1.
10. W.Martin, "Honey Pots and Honey Nets – Security through Deception", May, 2001, retrieved Sept. 27, 2004, from: http://www.sans.org/rr/papers/4/41.pdf.

Yungchang Ku is a police officer working in Curriculum Section, Academic Affairs, Central Police University (CPU), Taiwan. He received the B.S. degree from CPU in 1996, the M.S. degree from National Central University (NCU) in 2001, and now in doctoral program of Information Management at Yuan Ze University. His research interests are Data mining, Criminal Linguistics Profiling, and Crime Analysis.

Ying-Chieh Chen is a police officer working in Information Office, National Police Agency, Taiwan. He is also a Ph.D. Candidate in the Information Management Department at the National Chiao-Tung University (NCTU), Taiwan. Since 1997, he has also been a police officer as cybercrime investigator in Taipei County Police Bureau, Taiwan, where he works as the manager of the cybercrime unit.

Kuo-Ching Wu is a professor and chairperson in the Information Management Department at the Central Police University (CPU), Taiwan. His research interests include object-oriented programming design and data mining of computer crime and law enforcement capability of police.

Chaochang Chiu is a Professor of Information Management and the Associate Dean of the R&D Division at Yuan Ze University, Taiwan. He is the Associate Editor of International Journal of Electronic Commerce. His current research interests are in the areas of forecasting and resources allocation optimization under uncertainty.

Detecting Cyber Security Threats in Weblogs Using Probabilistic Models

Flora S. Tsai and Kap Luk Chan

School of Electrical & Electronic Engineering,
Nanyang Technological University, Singapore, 639798
fst1@columbia.edu

Abstract. Organizations and governments are becoming vulnerable to a wide variety of security breaches against their information infrastructure. The magnitude of this threat is evident from the increasing rate of cyber attacks against computers and critical infrastructure. Weblogs, or blogs, have also rapidly gained in numbers over the past decade. Weblogs may provide up-to-date information on the prevalence and distribution of various cyber security threats as well as terrorism events. In this paper, we analyze weblog posts for various categories of cyber security threats related to the detection of cyber attacks, cyber crime, and terrorism. Existing studies on intelligence analysis have focused on analyzing news or forums for cyber security incidents, but few have looked at weblogs. We use probabilistic latent semantic analysis to detect keywords from cyber security weblogs with respect to certain topics. We then demonstrate how this method can present the blogosphere in terms of topics with measurable keywords, hence tracking popular conversations and topics in the blogosphere. By applying a probabilistic approach, we can improve information retrieval in weblog search and keywords detection, and provide an analytical foundation for the future of security intelligence analysis of weblogs.

Keywords: cyber security, weblog, blog, probabilistic latent semantic analysis, cyber crime, cyber terrorism, data mining.

1 Introduction

Cyber security is defined as the intersection of computer, network, and information security issues which directly affect the national security infrastructure [15]. Cyber security problems are frequent, serious, and global in nature. The number of cyber attacks by persons and malicious software are increasing rapidly. Many cyber criminals or hackers may post their ongoing achievements in weblogs, or blogs, which are websites where entries are made in a reverse chronological order. In addition, weblogs may provide up-to-date information on the prevalence and distribution of various cyber security incidents and threats.

Weblogs range in scope from individual diaries to arms of political campaigns, media programs, and corporations. Weblogs' explosive growth is generating large volumes of raw data and is considered by many industry watchers one of the top

C.C. Yang et al. (Eds.): PAISI 2007, LNCS 4430, pp. 46–57, 2007.

ten industry trends [3]. Blogosphere is the collective term encompassing all blogs as a community or social network. Because of the huge volume of existing weblog posts and their free format nature, information in the blogosphere is rather random and chaotic, but immensely valuable in the right context. Weblogs can thus potentially contain usable and measurable information related to cyber security threats, such as malware, viruses, cyber blackmail, and other cyber crime.

With the amazing growth of blogs on the web, the blogosphere affects much in the media. Studies on the blogosphere include measuring the influence of the blogosphere [6], analyzing the blog threads for discovering the important bloggers [11], determining the spatiotemporal theme pattern on blogs [10], focusing the topic-centric view of the blogosphere [1], detecting the blogs growing trends [7], tracking the propagation of discussion topics in the blogosphere [8], and searching and detecting topics in corporate blogs [16].

Existing studies have focused on analyzing forums and news articles for cyber threats [12,18,19], but few have looked at weblogs. In this paper, we focus on analyzing cyber security weblogs, which are blogs providing commentary or analysis of cyber security threats and incidents.

In our work, we analyzed various weblog posts to detect the keywords of various topics of the blog entries, hence tracking the trends and topics of conversations in the blogosphere. Probabilistic Latent Semantic Analysis (PLSA) was used to detect the keywords from various cyber security blog entries with respect to certain topics. By using PLSA, we can present the blogosphere in terms of topics with measurable keywords.

The paper is organized as follows. Section 2 reviews the related work on intelligence analysis and extraction of useful information from weblogs. Section 3 describes an overview of the Latent Semantic models such as Latent Semantic Analysis and Probabilistic Latent Semantic Analysis model for mining of weblog-related topics. Section 4 presents experimental results, and Section 5 concludes the paper.

2   Review of Related Work

This section reviews related work in intelligence analysis and extraction of useful information from weblogs.

2.1   Intelligence Analysis

Intelligence analysis is the process of producing formal descriptions of situations and entities of strategic importance [17]. Although its practice is found in its purest form inside intelligence agencies, such as the CIA in the United States or MI6 in the UK, its methods are also applicable in fields such as business intelligence or competitive intelligence.

Recent works related to security intelligence analysis include using entity recognizers to extract names of people, organizations, and locations from news articles, and applying probabilistic topic models to learn the latent structure behind the named entities and other words [12]. Another study analyzed the evolution of terror attack incidents from online news articles using techniques related to temporal and event relationship mining [18]. In addition, Support Vector Machines were used for improving document classification for the insider threat problem within the intelligence community by analyzing a collection of documents from the Center for Nonproliferation Studies (CNS) related to weapons of mass destruction [19]. These studies illustrate the growing need for security intelligence analysis, and the usage of machine learning and information retrieval techniques to provide such analysis. However, much work has yet to be done in obtaining intelligence information from the vast collection of weblogs that exist throughout the world.

2.2   Information Extraction from Weblogs

Current weblog text analysis focuses on extracting useful information from weblog entry collections, and determining certain trends in the blogophere. NLP (Natural Language Processing) algorithms have been used to determine the most important keywords and proper names within a certain time period from thousands of active weblogs, which can automatically discover trends across blogs, as well as detect key persons, phrases and paragraphs [7]. A study on the propagation of discussion topics through the social network in the blogophere developed algorithms to detect the long-term and short-term topics and keywords, which were then validated with real weblog entry collections [8]. On evaluating the suitable methods of ranking term significance in an evolving RSS feed corpus, three statistical feature selection methods were implemented: χ^2, Mutual Information (MI) and Information Gain (I), and the conclusion was that χ^2 method seems to be the best among all, but full human classification exercise would be required to further evaluate such method [14]. A probabilistic approach based on PLSA was proposed in [10] to extract common themes from blogs, and also generate the theme life cycle for each given location and the theme snapshots for each given time period. PLSA has also been previously used for weblog search and mining of corporate blogs [16].

Our work differs from existing studies in two respects: (1) We focus on cyber security weblog entries which has not been studied before in the context of intelligence analysis (2) We have used probabilistic models to extract popular keywords for each topic in order to detect themes and trends in cyber threats and terrorism events.

3   Latent Semantic Models

This section reviews the latent semantic models used for this work, which involve latent sematic analysis and extending probabilistic latent semantic analysis for topic detection in weblogs.

3.1   Latent Semantic Analysis

Latent Semantic Analysis (LSA) [4] is a well-known technique for information retrieval and document classification. LSA solves two fundamental problems in natural language processing: synonymy and polysemy:

- In synonymy, different words may have the same meaning. Thus, a person issuing a query in a search engine may use a different word from what appears in a document, and may not retrieve the document.
- In polysemy, the same word can have multiple meanings, so a searcher can get unwanted documents with the alternate meanings.

LSA solves the problem of lexical matching methods by using statistically derived conceptual indices instead of individual words for retrieval [2]. LSA uses a term-document matrix (TDM) which describes patterns of term (word) distribution across a set of documents.

LSA then finds a low-rank approximation which is smaller and less noisy than the original term-document matrix. The downsizing of the matrix is achieved through the use of singular value decomposition (SVD), where the set of all the terms is then represented by a vector space of lower dimensionality than the total number of terms in the vocabulary. The consequence of the rank lowering is that some dimensions get "merged".

In LSA, each element of the $n \times m$ term-document matrix reflects the occurrence of a particular word in a particular document, i.e.,

$$\mathbf{A} = [a_{ij}], \tag{1}$$

where a_{ij} is the number of times or frequency in which term i appears in document j. As each word will not usually appear in every document, the matrix $\mathbf{A}$ is typically sparse with rarely any noticeable nonzero structure [2].

The matrix $\mathbf{A}$ is then factored into the product of three matrices using SVD. Given a matrix $\mathbf{A}$, where rank($\mathbf{A}$) = r, the SVD of $\mathbf{A}$ is defined as:

$$\mathbf{A} = \mathbf{U}\mathbf{S}\mathbf{V}^T. \tag{2}$$

The columns of $\mathbf{U}$ and $\mathbf{V}$ are referred to as the left and right singular vectors, respectively, and the singular values of $\mathbf{A}$ are the diagonal elements of $\mathbf{S}$, or the nonnegative square roots of the n eigenvalues of $\mathbf{A}\mathbf{A}^T$.

As defined by Equation (2), the SVD is used to represent the original relationships among terms and documents as sets of linearly-independent vectors. Performing truncated SVD by using the k-largest singular values and corresponding singular vectors, the original TDM can be reduced to a smaller collection of vectors in k-space for conceptual query processing [2].

3.2   Probabilistic Latent Semantic Analysis for Weblog Mining

Probabilistic Latent Semantic Analysis (PLSA) [9] is based on a generative probabilistic model that stems from a statistical approach to LSA [4]. PLSA is able to capture the polysemy and synonymy in text for applications in the information retrieval domain. Similar to LSA, PLSA uses a term-document matrix which describes patterns of term (word) distribution across a set of documents (blog entries). By implementing PLSA, topics are generated from the blog entries, where each topic produces a list of word usage, using the maximum likelihood estimation method, the expectation maximization (EM) algorithm.

The starting point for PLSA is the *aspect model* [9]. The aspect model is a latent variable model for co-occurrence data associating an unobserved class variable $z_k \in \{z_1, \ldots, z_k\}$ with each observation, an observation being the occurrence of a keyword in a particular blog entry. There are three probabilities used in PLSA:

1. $P(b_i)$ denotes the probability that a keyword occurrence will be observed in a particular blog entry b_i,
2. $P(w_j|z_k)$ denotes the class-conditional probability of a specific keyword conditioned on the unobserved class variable z_k,
3. $P(z_k|d_i)$ denotes a blog-specific probability distribution over the latent variable space.

In the collection, the probability of each blog and the probability of each keyword are known, while the probability of an aspect given a blog and the probability of a keyword given an aspect are unknown. By using the above three probabilities and conditions, three fundamental schemes are implemented:

1. select a blog entry b_i with probability $P(b_i)$,
2. pick a latent class z_k with probability $P(z_k|b_i)$,
3. generate a keyword w_j with probability $P(w_j|z_k)$.

As a result, a joint probability model is obtained in asymmetric parameterization:

$$P(b_i, w_j) = P(b_i)P(w_j|b_i), \tag{3}$$

$$P(w_j|b_i) = \sum_{k=1}^{K} P(w_j|z_k)P(z_k|b_i) \tag{4}$$

After the aspect model is generated, the model is fitted using the EM algorithm. The EM algorithm involves two steps, namely the expectation (E) step and the maximization (M) step. The E-step computes the posterior probability for the latent variable, by implying Bayes' formula, so the parameterization of joint probability model is obtained as:

$$P(z_k|b_i, w_j) = \frac{P(w_j|z_k)P(z_k|b_i)}{\sum_{l=1}^{K} P(w_j|z_l)P(z_l|b_i)} \tag{5}$$

The M-step updates the parameters based on the expected complete data log-likelihood depending on the posterior probability resulted from the E-step. Hence the M-step re-estimates the following two probabilities:

$$P(w_j|z_k) = \frac{\sum_{i=1}^{N} n(b_i, w_j)P(z_k|b_i, w_j)}{\sum_{m=1}^{M} \sum_{i=1}^{N} n(b_i, w_m)P(z_k|b_i, w_m)} \qquad (6)$$

$$P(z_k|b_i) = \frac{\sum_{j=1}^{M} n(b_i, w_j)P(z_k|b_i, w_j)}{n(b_i)} \qquad (7)$$

The EM iteration is continued to increase the likelihood function until the specific conditions are met and the program is terminated. These conditions can be a convergence condition, or a cut-off point, which is specified for reaching a local maximum, rather than a global maximum.

In short, the PLSA model selects the model parameter values that maximize the probability of the observed data, and returns the relevant probability distributions by implying the EM algorithm. Word usage analysis with the aspect model is a common application of the aspect model. Based on the pre-processed term-document matrix, the blogs are then classified onto different aspects or topics. For each aspect, the keyword usage, such as the probable words in the class-conditional distribution $P(w_j|z_k)$, is determined. Empirical results indicate the advantages of PLSA in reducing perplexity, and high performance of precision and recall in information retrieval [9].

4   Experiments and Results

We have used latent semantic models to analyze weblogs related to cyber security threats and incidents, and applied probabilistic models for weblog analysis on our dataset. Dimensionality reduction was performed with latent semantic analysis to show the similarity plot of weblog terms. We extract the most relevant categories and show the topics extracted for each category. Experiments show that the probabilistic model can reveal interesting patterns in the underlying topics for our dataset of security-related weblogs.

4.1   Data Corpus

For our experiments, we extracted a subset of the Nielson BuzzMetrics weblog data corpus[1] that focuses on blogs related to cyber security threats and incidents related to cyber crime and terrorism. The original dataset consists of 14 million weblog posts collected by Nielsen BuzzMetrics for May 2006. Although the blog entries span only a short period of time, they are indicative of the amount and variety of blog posts that exists in different languages throughout the world.

Blog entries in the English language related to cyber security threats such as malware, cyber crime, and terrorism were extracted and stored for use in our analysis. Figure 1 shows an excerpt of a weblog post related to cyber blackmail.

---

[1] http://www.icwsm.org/data.html

Cyber blackmail is on the increase ... Criminal gangs have moved away from the stealth
use of infected computers ... to direct blackmailing of victims. ... Cyber blackmailing
is done ... by encrypting data or by corrupting system information. The criminal then
demands a ransom for its return to the victim. ...

Fig. 1. Excerpt of weblog post related to cyber blackmail and ransom

There are a total of 5493 entries in our dataset, and each weblog entry is saved
as a text file for further text preprocessing. For the preprocessing of the blog
data, HTML tags were removed and lexical analysis was performed by removing
stopwords, stemming, and pruning using the Text to Matrix Generator (TMG)
[20]. The total number of terms after pruning and stopword removal is 797. The
term-document matrix was then input to the LSA and PLSA algorithms.

4.2   Semantic Detection of Terms

We used the LSA model [4] for analyzing semantic detection of terms, as LSA is
able to consider weblog entries with similar words which are semantically close.
The results of applying LSA on this term-document matrix (with $k=2$) is shown
in Figure 2.

The plot shows the similarity in two-dimensional space of the terms in the
weblog entries. Although many terms are not visible because of the large number
of words, there are a few groupings evident from the graph. Some of the visible
terms include the grouping of *spyware*, *malware*, and *software* at the top center
of the plot. Another group visible at the right include *Iraq*, *war*, *Bush*, and

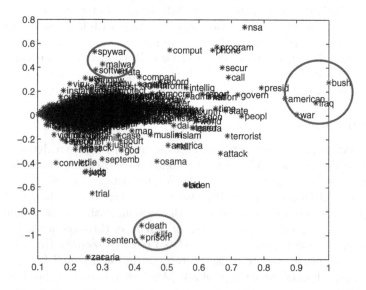

Fig. 2. Two-dimensional plot of terms for weblog entries using LSA

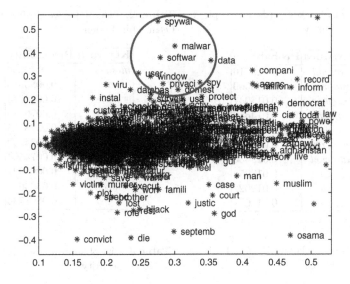

Fig. 3. Zoomed-in graph of Figure 2

American. Yet another grouping include the terms *death, prison,* and *life* at the bottom of the graph. Zooming into the large cluster from Figure 2, Figure 3 shows a subset of the big cluster of keywords. A larger group of keywords (*spyware, malware, software, data, user, window, privacy, spy, domestic*) can be identified, thus showing the ability descend through a hierarchical grouping of keywords. The implications of the graphs demonstrate the possibility to visualize closely-related terms in two-dimensional space. Although the two-dimensional graphs may be an over-simplification of the dimensionality reduction that takes place, the plot can help to visualize the terms and relate to the topics produced for the weblogs.

4.3 Results for Weblog Topic Analysis

We conducted some experiments using PLSA for the weblog entries. Tables 1-4 summarizes the keywords found for each of the four topics (Computer Security, Osama bin Laden, Iraq War, and US National Security).

By looking at the various topics listed, we are able to see that the probabilistic approach is able to list important keywords of each topic in a quantitative fashion. The keywords listed can relate back to the original topics. For example, the keywords detected in the Computer Security topic features items such as computers, spyware, software, and internet.

Figure 4 shows the graph of the topic-document distribution of the weblog entries by date. Some of the topics have a higher density of documents distributed around certain dates. This can be used to match certain events in each topic to the weblog entries. For example, the heavy clustering of documents for Topic 4 (US National Security) indicate that there was an increase on the weblog

Table 1. List of keywords for Topic 1: Computer Security

Keyword	Probability
comput	0.023716
malwar	0.020509
spywar	0.018047
softwar	0.014650
secur	0.014257
window	0.013527
internet	0.013436
http	0.013266
web	0.012022
user	0.011651

Table 2. List of keywords for Topic 2: Osama bin Laden

Keyword	Probability
moussaoui	0.0170900
don	0.0083916
life	0.0083244
bin	0.0079485
laden	0.0078515
osama	0.0074730
prison	0.0074594
peopl	0.0064921
death	0.0063618
god	0.0061734

Table 3. List of keywords for Topic 3: Iraq War

Keyword	Probability
iraq	0.0134810
war	0.0089393
islam	0.0087796
zarqawi	0.0086076
militari	0.0073831
muslim	0.0073576
afghanistan	0.0072725
iran	0.0070231
qaeda	0.0069711
iraqi	0.0065779

Table 4. List of keywords for Topic 4: US National Security

Keyword	Probability
nsa	0.0142720
bush	0.0127100
phone	0.0121350
program	0.0099155
presid	0.0098480
cia	0.0093545
american	0.0088027
record	0.0086708
call	0.0086591
administr	0.0084607

conversations in this topic around the middle of May 2006. This can be due to US President Bush's comment on May 11, 2006 about a USA Today report on a massive NSA database that collects information about all phone calls made within the United States [5]. This is one example of an event that can trigger much conversation in the blogosphere.

For the topic of Computer Security, we further decompose into separate subtopics, two of which are shown in Tables 5-6. Malware, which includes computer viruses, worms, trojan horses, spyware, adware, and other malicious software, is the topic derived from examining the keywords in Subtopic 1. Subtopic 2 is classified as Macintosh, and reflects the increasing reports of cyber attacks affecting Macintosh computers. Therefore, we can classify and decompose the topics into a hierarchy of subtopics, which may be useful for examining larger data sets.

The power of PLSA in cyber security applications include the ability to automatically detect terms and keywords related to cyber security threats and terror events. By presenting blogs with measurable keywords, we can improve

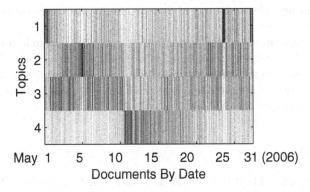

Fig. 4. Topic by document distribution by date

Table 5. List of keywords for Subtopic 1: Malware

Keyword	Probability
spywar	0.0174610
trojan	0.0117580
adwar	0.0092120
scan	0.0088160
anti	0.0087841
free	0.0074914
spybot	0.0074895
remov	0.0072834
download	0.0069242
viru	0.0068496

Table 6. List of keywords for Subtopic 2: Macintosh

Keyword	Probability
mac	0.0078348
secur	0.0056874
appl	0.0054443
microsoft	0.0041262
attack	0.0041169
system	0.0039921
report	0.0037533
cyber	0.0037227
crime	0.0036151
comput	0.0035352

our understanding of cyber security issues in terms of distribution and trends of current threats and events. This has implications for security agencies wishing to monitor real-time threats present in weblogs or other related documents.

5 Conclusions

In this paper, we analyzed weblog posts for various categories of cyber security threats related to the detection of cyber security threats, cyber crime, and cyber terrorism. To our knowledge, is the first such study focusing on cyber security weblogs. We use latent semantic analysis to illustrate similarities in terms distributed across all the terms in the weblog dataset. Our experiments on our dataset of weblogs demonstrate how our probabilistic weblog model can present the blogosphere in terms of topics with measurable keywords, hence tracking popular conversations and topics in the blogosphere. By applying a probabilistic approach, we can improve information retrieval in weblog search and keywords detection, and provide an analytical foundation for the future of security intelligence analysis of weblogs.

Potential applications of this stream of research may include automatically monitoring and identifying trends in cyber terror and security threats in weblogs. This can have some significance for government and intelligence agencies wishing to monitor real-time potential international terror threats present in weblog conversations and the blogosphere.

References

1. Avesani, P., Cova, M., Hayes, C., Massa, P.: Learning Contextualised Weblog Topics. WWW '05 Workshop on the Weblogging Ecosystem: Aggregation, Analysis and Dynamics (2005)
2. Berry, M., Dumais, S. and O'Brien, G.: Using linear algebra for intelligent information retrieval. SIAM Review, 37(4):573–595 (1995).
3. Columbus, L.: Blog Mining Gets Real. CRM Buyer (2005).
4. Deerwester, S., Dumais, S., Landauer, T., Furnas,G., Harshman, R.: Indexing by latent semantic analysis. In Journal of the American Society of Information Science, 41(6) (1990) 391–407
5. Diamond, J.: NSA has massive database of Americans' phone calls. In USA Today (May 10, 2006)
6. Gill, K.E.: How Can We Measure the Influence of the Blogosphere? WWW '04 Workshop on the Weblogging Ecosystem: Aggregation, Analysis and Dynamics (2004)
7. Glance, N.S. Hurst, M. Tomokiyo, T: BlogPulse: Automated Trend Discovery for Weblogs. WWW '04 Workshop on the Weblogging Ecosystem: Aggregation, Analysis and Dynamics (2004)
8. Gruhl, D. Guha, R.,Liben-Nowell, D., Tomkins, A.: Information Diffusion Through Blogspace. WWW '04 (2004)
9. Hofmann, T.: Probabilistic Latent Semantic Indexing. SIGIR'99 (1999)
10. Mei, Q., Liu, C., Su, H., Zhai, C.: A Probabilistic Approach to Spatiotemporal Theme Pattern Mining on Weblogs. WWW '06 (2006)
11. Nakajima, S., Tatemura, J., Hino,Y., Hara,Y., Tanaka, K.: Discovering Important Bloggers based on Analyzing Blog Threads. WWW '05 Workshop on the Weblogging Ecosystem: Aggregation, Analysis and Dynamics (2005)
12. Newman, D., Chemudugunta, C., Smyth, P., Steyvers, M.: Analyzing Entities and Topics in News Articles Using Statistical Topic Models. ISI '06 (2006)
13. Pikas, C.K.: Blog Searching for Competitive Intelligence, Brand Image, and Reputation Management. Online. 29(4) (2005) 16–21
14. Prabowo, R., Thelwall, M.: A Comparison of Feature Selection Methods for an Evolving RSS Feed Corpus, Information Processing and Management, 42 (2006) 1491–1512
15. Tsai, F.S., Chan, C.K. (eds): Cyber Security, Pearson Education, Singapore (2006)
16. Tsai, F.S., Chen, Y., Chan, K.L.: Probabilistic Latent Semantic Analysis for Search and Mining of Corporate Blogs (2007)
17. Wikipedia contributors: Intelligence Analysis. In: Wikipedia, The Free Encyclopedia, http://en.wikipedia.org/wiki/Intelligence_analysis. (accessed Nov 7, 2006).

18. Yang, C.C., Shi, X., Wei, C.-P.: Tracing the Event Evolution of Terror Attacks from On-Line News. ISI '06 (2006)
19. Yilmazel, O., Symonenko, S., Balasubramanian, N., Liddy, E.D.: Leveraging One-Class SVM and Semantic Analysis to Detect Anomalous Content. ISI '05 (2005)
20. Zeimpekis, D., Gallopoulos, E.: TMG: A MATLAB Toolbox for generating term-document matrices from text collections. Grouping Multidimensional Data: Recent Advances in Clustering. Springer (2005) 187–210

What-if Emergency Management System: A Generalized Voronoi Diagram Approach

Ickjai Lee, Reece Pershouse, Peter Phillips, and Chris Christensen

School of Math, Physics & IT,
James Cook University, Douglas Campus,
Townsville, QLD4811, Australia

Abstract. As witnessed in many recent disastrous events, emergency management is becoming more and more important to prevent hazards, plan for actions, quickly respond to minimize losses, and to recover from damages. In this paper, we propose the complete higher-order Voronoi diagram based emergency management system for what-if analysis which is particularly useful in highly dynamic environments. This system is based on a unified order-k Delaunay triangle data structure which supports various topological and regional queries, and what-if analysis. The proposed system encompasses: 1) what-if scenarios when new changes are dynamically updated; 2) what-if scenarios when order-k generators (disasters or professional bodies) or their territorial regions are of interest; (3) what-if scenarios when ordered order-k generators or their territorial regions are of interest; 4) what-if scenarios when k-th nearest generators or their territorial regions are of interest; 5) what-if scenarios with mixtures of the above.

1 Introduction

As witnessed in many recent catastrophes, intelligent emergency management is becoming an increasingly important issue for our health and safety. Never-ending natural hazards are constantly occurring and highly devastating man-made threats are frequently happening. Our daily life has been endangered by these disastrous activities and intelligent emergency management systems are in great demand. Timely and effective emergency management can reduce human casualties, structural damages, prevent secondary disasters, and minimizes economic losses and social disruption [1].

Geographic Information Systems (GIS) have been one of the popular tools and have been widely used in various aspects of emergency management [2,3,4,5,6,7]. They support features such as data capturing, structuring, preprocessing, mapping, visualization, and also zonal and focal analysis. However, most of them are limited to producing cartographic mappings, basic simulations and visualization rather than emergency planning, preparedness and predictive modelling [8]. One of the intrinsic properties of disastrous activities is of their inherent dynamic nature. They are active and unpredictable. What-if analysis for various scenarios is of great importance to the understanding of their dynamics and to emergency planning. For instance, in a situation where several professional bodies

C.C. Yang et al. (Eds.): PAISI 2007, LNCS 4430, pp. 58–69, 2007.

are required to collaborate to recover damaged areas to minimize losses when a disaster occurs, government agencies would be interested in which area is covered by a certain set of professional bodies, how many bodies must be involved in the recovery, what happens when the first few nearest bodies are engaged in other disaster recoveries and so forth.

Current GIS provide limited functions enabling what-if analysis, and thus computer software simulating various scenarios for what-if analysis is in great demand [8,9]. There exist several emergency management simulators [1,10,11,12]. They provide tools to model movement and behavior of people, and help people systematically respond when a disaster occurs. However, they fail to provide a general purpose what-if analysis toolbox handling various scenarios for timely and well-informed decision makings in highly dynamic environments.

What-if analysis is exploratory and interactive [13]. It explores scenarios as soon as changes are suggested. Thus, a computer system providing what-if analysis is typically equipped with a data structure supporting fast local updates and consistent spatial tessellations. The Voronoi diagram and its dual Delaunay triangulation provide a robust framework for exploring various scenarios for what-if analysis, and have been widely applied to many aspects of geospatial analysis [14]. The Voronoi diagram provides consistent natural neighboring information overcoming the inconsistent modelling of traditional raster and vector models [15]. Its dual triangulation provides a robust data structure framework for dynamic local updates. In addition, there exist many generalizations on the Voronoi diagram supporting what-if analysis. Several attempts [9,13] have been made to employ the flexibility (generalizability) of Voronoi tessellation for what-if analysis. However, they are limited to certain environments requiring extreme and confined generalizations, and as such are not general enough to cover various scenarios for managing emergencies in highly dynamic environments.

In this paper, we propose a generalized Voronoi diagrams based emergency management system for what-if analysis particularly useful in highly dynamic environments. It builds a unified order-k Delaunay triangle data structure from which users can derive the complete order-k Voronoi diagrams, the complete ordered order-k Voronoi diagrams and the complete k-th nearest Voronoi diagrams. Note that emergency planning and recovery are based on the scale of the disaster. These generalized Voronoi diagrams provide useful information to situations where more than k professional bodies are required to get involved in a recovery. The proposed system supports: 1) what-if scenarios when new changes (disasters or professional bodies) are dynamically updated; 2) what-if scenarios when order-k generators or their Voronoi regions are of interest; (3) what-if scenarios when ordered order-k generators or their Voronoi regions are of interest; 4) what-if scenarios when k-th nearest generators or their Voronoi regions are of interest; 5) what-if scenarios with mixtures of the above.

The rest of paper is organized as follows. Section 2 defines the higher order Voronoi diagrams and k-th nearest Voronoi diagram. It also investigates their interrelationships and algorithmic procedures. Section 3 discusses the working principle of our proposed system. It provides an algorithmic procedure of

Voronoi-based what-if emergency management system, and explores its capabilities. Section 4 draws concluding remarks.

2   Modelling with Generalized Voronoi Diagrams

The ordinary Voronoi diagram of a set $P = \{p_1, p_2, \ldots, p_n\}$ of generators in a study region S tessellates it into mutually exclusive and collectively exhaustive regions. Each region has a generator closest to it. This geospatial tessellation provides natural neighbor relations that are crucial for many topological queries in geospatial modelling and analysis, whilst its dual graph, the Delaunay triangulation, provides a robust framework for structural arrangements of the Voronoi diagram. This geospatial tessellation has many generalizations and this flexibility provides a robust framework for what-if and what-happens modelling and analysis [9]. Higher order Voronoi diagrams are natural and useful generalizations of the ordinary Voronoi diagram for more than one generator [14]. They provide tessellations where each region has the same k (ordered or unordered) closest sites for a given k. These tessellations are useful for situations where more than one location of interest are not functioning properly (engaged, busy, closed or fully scheduled) or several locations are required to work together.

The order-k Voronoi diagram $\mathcal{V}^{(k)}$ is a set of all order-k Voronoi regions $\mathcal{V}^{(k)} = \{V(P_1^{(k)}), \ldots, V(P_n^{(k)})\}$, where the order-$k$ Voronoi region $V(P_i^{(k)})$ for a random subset $P_i^{(k)}$ consisting of k points out of P is defined as follows:

$$V(P_i^{(k)}) = \{p | \arg\max_{p_r \in P_i^{(k)}} d(p, p_r) \leq \arg\min_{p_s \in P \backslash P_i^{(k)}} d(p, p_s)\}. \tag{1}$$

In $\mathcal{V}^{(k)}$, k generators are not ordered, however in some emergency management situations an ordered set would be of interest. This ordered set can be modelled by the ordered order-k Voronoi diagram $\mathcal{V}^{<k>}$. It is defined as $\mathcal{V}^{<k>} = \{V(P_1^{<k>}), \ldots, V(P_n^{<k>})\}$, where the ordered order-k Voronoi region $V(P_i^{<k>})$ is defined as

$$V(P_i^{<k>}) = \{p | d(p, p_{i1}) \leq \ldots \leq d(p, p_{ik}) \leq d(p, p_j), p_j \in P \backslash \{p_{i1}, \ldots, p_{ik}\}\}. \tag{2}$$

One generalized variant of the ordinary Voronoi diagram similar to $\mathcal{V}^{(k)}$ is the k-th nearest Voronoi diagram. This is particularly useful when users are interested in only k-th nearest region. The k-th nearest Voronoi diagram $\mathcal{V}^{[k]}$ is a set of all k-th nearest Voronoi regions $\mathcal{V}^{[k]} = \{V^{[k]}(p_1), \ldots, V^{[k]}(p_n)\}$, where the k-th nearest Voronoi region $V^{[k]}(p_i)$ is defined as

$$V^{[k]}(p_i) = \{p | d(p, p_i) \leq d(p, p_j), \ p_j \in P \backslash \{k \text{ nearest points to } p_i\}\}. \tag{3}$$

Several algorithmic approaches [16,17,18,19] have been proposed to efficiently compute higher order diagrams in the computational geometry community. Dehne [18] proposed an $O(n^4)$ time algorithm that constructs the complete $\mathcal{V}^{(k)}$. Several other attempts [16,17,19] have been made to improve the computational time requirement of Dehne's algorithm. The best known algorithm for the order-k Voronoi diagram is $O(k(n - k) \log n + n \log^3 n)$ [20]. Thus, the complete $\mathcal{V}^{(k)}$ requires $O(k^2(n - k) \log n + kn \log^3 n)$ time.

Our system builds a unified Delaunay triangle data structure that enables us to derive the complete $\mathcal{V}^{(k)}$, $\mathcal{V}^{<k>}$ and $\mathcal{V}^{[k]}$ for various what-if analysis. The Delaunay triangle based data structure well supports various geospatial topological queries including natural neighbor and region queries. We implement $\mathcal{V}^{(k)}$ based on Dehne's algorithm and extend it to include the complete $\mathcal{V}^{<k>}$ and $\mathcal{V}^{[k]}$ based on the fact that $\mathcal{V}^{<k>} = \bigcup \mathcal{V}^{(k)}$ and $\mathcal{V}^{[k]} = \mathcal{V}^{(k-1)} \cup \mathcal{V}^{(k)}$.

3   Voronoi-Based What-if Emergency Management System

3.1   Complete Order-k Delaunay Triangle Data Structure

A flexible data structure supporting multiple models for diverse what-if scenarios is a must for highly dynamic emergency management systems. The data structure needs to efficiently support rapid transits from model to model, and effectively manage various models. Our proposed system is based on a unified triangle based data structure that robustly supports all $\mathcal{V}^{(k)}$, $\mathcal{V}^{<k>}$ and $\mathcal{V}^{[k]}$. The unified data structure stores all order-k Delaunay triangles to efficiently support the complete $\mathcal{V}^{(k)}$, $\mathcal{V}^{<k>}$ and $\mathcal{V}^{[k]}$ spontaneously. Table 1 depicts the complete order-k Delaunay triangle data structure. It stores the complete order-k

Table 1. Complete order-k Delaunay triangle data structure

Order-k Delaunay triangle $\triangle$	Inpoint
Order-0 Delaunay triangle $\triangle p_a p_b p_c$	$\emptyset$
...	$\emptyset$
Order-1 Delaunay triangle $\triangle p_i p_j p_k$	$p \in P$
...	...
...	...
Order-$(n - 3)$ Delaunay triangle $\triangle p_q p_r p_s$	$P \setminus \{p_q, p_r, p_s\}$
...	...

Delaunay triangles and consists of two fields: order-k triangle and inpoints. Here, a triangle $\triangle p_l p_m p_n$ becomes an order-k triangle if its circumcircle contains k other points (inpoints) within it. For instance, the lowest degree triangles, order-0 Delaunay triangles, do not contain any other points within their circumcircles whilst the highest degree triangles, order-$(n - 3)$ triangles, contain all points in P except three points forming the triangles. An algorithmic procedure of our system based on this data structure is described in the following subsection.

3.2 Algorithm and Analysis

Our system takes a set P of generators as an input and builds a unified order-k Delaunay triangle data structure from which the complete $\mathcal{V}^{(k)}$, $\mathcal{V}^{<k>}$ and $\mathcal{V}^{[k]}$ can be derived. The pseudo-code of our proposed system is as follows.

Algorithm. **Voronoi-based What-if Emergency Management System**
     Input: A set $P = \{p_1, p_2, \ldots, p_n\}$ of generators;
     Output: Unified order-k Delaunay triangle data structure (DS), and
            complete $\mathcal{V}^{(k)}$, $\mathcal{V}^{<k>}$ and $\mathcal{V}^{[k]}$;
  1) **begin**
  2) $DS \Leftarrow$ `BulkLoad`(P);
  3) `DrawDiagrams`(DS);
  4) **do**

  5) $\begin{cases} DS \Leftarrow \texttt{DynamicUpdate}(p); \\ \texttt{Retrieve}(p); \end{cases}$

  6)   `DrawDiagrams`(DS);
  7) **while** the user exits;
  8) `Save`(DS);
  9) **end**

Initially, `BulkLoad`(P) loads a dataset and builds DS to begin with. This step builds an entire set of order-k Delaunay triangles as a unified data structure for the complete $\mathcal{V}^{(k)}$, $\mathcal{V}^{<k>}$ and $\mathcal{V}^{[k]}$. Since every possible triangle $\triangle p_i p_j p_k$ needs to be tested for which order-k triangle it belongs to, this step requires $O(n^4)$ time. In the next step, `DrawDiagrams`(DS) derives and draws $\mathcal{V}^{(k)}$ and $\mathcal{V}^{<k>}$ (for $1 \leq k \leq n-1$), and $\mathcal{V}^{[k]}$ (for $1 \leq k \leq n$) at the user's choice of k. Note that, multiple k can be chosen in multiple windows. This step implements [18] for the derivation of the complete $\mathcal{V}^{(k)}$ from DS. Our system derives $\mathcal{V}^{<k>}$ from $\mathcal{V}^{<k>} = \bigcup \mathcal{V}^{(k)}$ whilst it derives $\mathcal{V}^{[k]}$ from $\mathcal{V}^{[k]} = \mathcal{V}^{(k-1)} \cup \mathcal{V}^{(k)}$.

In Step 5), users can have two different modes: edit and retrieval. In edit mode (`DynamicUpdate`(p)), users can either add a new generator p or remove it from P. This update consists of two substeps. First it needs to go though every order-k triangle in DS to check if its circumcircle contains p or not. If it does, then it is marked as an order-$(k+1)$ triangle, otherwise it is left unchanged. Second, the dynamic update step will create new order-k triangles $\triangle p_i p_j p$ with $p_i, p_j \in P$. Deletion is implemented in a similar way. Both substeps require $O(n^3)$, thus `DynamicUpdate`(p)) requires cubic time. In retrieval mode, users are able to retrieve topological information for a given location p (mouse click) from the complete $\mathcal{V}^{(k)}$, $\mathcal{V}^{<k>}$ and $\mathcal{V}^{[k]}$. Retrievable topological information includes ordered and unordered k-nearest neighbors to p, Voronoi regions ($V^{(k)}(p)$, $V^{<k>}(p)$ and $V^{[k]}(p)$) and their perimeters and areas, and their topologically adjacent Voronoi neighbors. Step 6 requires $O(n^3)$ time, thus our proposed system requires $O(n^4)$ time.

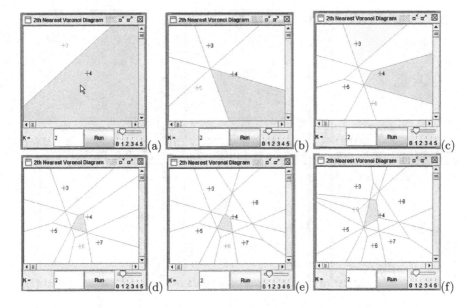

Fig. 1. 2nd Nearest Voronoi diagrams with dynamic updates: $2 \leq |P| \leq 7$

3.3 What-if with Dynamic Updates

Dynamic updates (Step 5 of the algorithm in Section 3.2) allow users to explore what-if scenarios to help them make prompt decisions in constantly changing environments. Figure 1 depicts $\mathcal{V}^{[2]}$ when P varies from $\{p_3, p_4\}$ to $\{p_3, p_4, p_5, p_6, p_7\}$. Shaded Voronoi regions are highlighted regions when a location is mouse clicked (shown in Fig. 1(a)) in retrieval mode. Also, their corresponding 2nd nearest generators are highlighted in green. A series of dynamic updates shown in Fig. 1 is particularly useful for planning in highly active environments as the interactivity allows the planner to visually inspect and make decisions based on an easily digested representation. Let us consider an evacuation management system, and assume P represents a set of evacuation places and the clicked location is of the user's interest. Figure 1 shows the second nearest evacuation place and its territories from the clicked location as the number of evacuation places vary. This is of particular interest when the first evacuation place is fully booked or roads to it are not accessible. Hence we can determine and visualize very quickly alternative evacuation plans as our environmental factors come into play.

3.4 What-if with Homogeneous Voronoi Diagrams

In many emergency management situations, several professional bodies are required to cooperate to aid with recovery and restoration. This is particularly the case when disasters are severe, meaning rapid action is essential to minimize the damage. For example, many different fire departments may need to work together

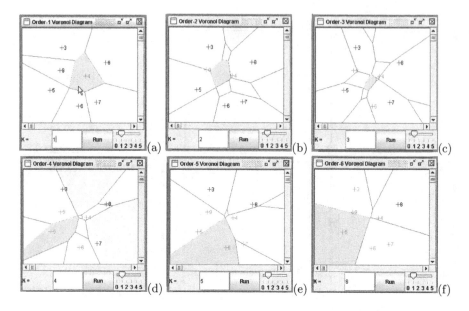

Fig. 2. The complete order-k Voronoi diagrams with $|P| = 7$: (a)$\mathcal{V}^{(1)}$; (b)$\mathcal{V}^{(2)}$; (c)$\mathcal{V}^{(3)}$; (d)$\mathcal{V}^{(4)}$; (e)$\mathcal{V}^{(5)}$; (f)$\mathcal{V}^{(6)}$

to extinguish a large forest fire. Figure 2 shows the complete $\mathcal{V}^{(k)}$ with the same P as in Fig. 1(f). Highlighted points and regions are order-k neighbors and their corresponding Voronoi regions when the same point as in Fig. 1(a) is clicked. If we assume that a forest fire starts in the clicked location, then this figure provides answers to questions such as which k professional bodies must be involved in the recovery or what are their Voronoi regions. In this particular example, the order-3 Voronoi region of the clicked location gives the smallest area.

3.5   What-if with Dynamic Updates in Heterogeneous Voronoi Diagrams

Emergency management systems must be able to handle complex and unpredictable environments. A combination of dynamic updates and order-k Voronoi diagrams, the ordered order-k Voronoi diagrams and the k-th nearest Voronoi diagrams can be used to explore these complex what-if scenarios. Figure 3 depicts such scenarios.

3.6   What-if Emergency Management with Real Datasets

This section examines the complete $\mathcal{V}^{(k)}$, $\mathcal{V}^{<k>}$ and $\mathcal{V}^{[k]}$ of real datasets from 217 urban suburbs of Brisbane, the capital city of Queensland, Australia. The study region is highly dynamic and active. It continues to experience significant and sustained population growth and various criminal activities [21]. Figure 4 shows

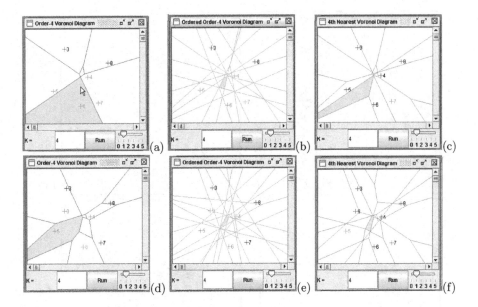

Fig. 3. $\mathcal{V}^{(4)}$, $\mathcal{V}^{<4>}$ and $\mathcal{V}^{[4]}$ of $P = \{p_3, \ldots, p_8\}$ and those of $\hat{P} = P \cup \{p_9\}$: (a)$\mathcal{V}(P^{(4)})$; (b)$\mathcal{V}(P^{<4>})$; (c)$\mathcal{V}(P^{[4]})$; (d)$\mathcal{V}(\hat{P}^{(4)})$; (e)$\mathcal{V}(\hat{P}^{<4>})$; (f)$\mathcal{V}(\hat{P}^{[4]})$

a dataset within the study region and various Voronoi diagrams. Figure 4(a) depicts 25 murder incidents (red crosses) that occurred in the study region in the year of 1998 with two police departments (blue houses).

Scenario 1
Assumption: Each police department is involved in the same number (k) of nearest crime investigations.
Task: Covering all the crimes with the introduction of an additional department within the study region while minimizing k.

This scenario is of particular interest when crime incidents are excessive to deal with, and each police station has limited resources (policemen and patrol cars etc) thus are unable to handle all existing crime incidents. The complete order-k $\mathcal{V}^{(k)}$ provides a solution to this scenario. Users need to explore the entire spectrum of order-k $\mathcal{V}^{(k)}$ to find a large enough k covering $P' \subset P$ and leaving $P - P'$ to be covered by the additional department. Figure 4(b) shows the $\mathcal{V}(P^{(10)})$. Here, $V^{(10)}$ of two police departments are green shaded and their 10 nearest murder incidents are highlighted in thick black crosses. Note that, some murder incidents are covered by both departments' 10 nearest crime incidents. In this case, both police departments will cooperate in the investigation. There are 11 incidents not covered by either department when k is 10. These uncovered incidents are scattered around the study region and we cannot easily spot a candidate location within the study region for the additional police department that will cover the other incidents. Figure 4(c) shows the $\mathcal{V}(P^{(15)})$ where each police

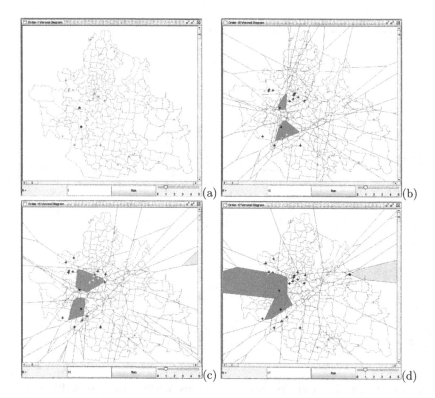

Fig. 4. A set P of murder incidents that occurred in 1998 and 2 police departments in 217 urban suburbs of Brisbane, Australia ($|P| = 25$): (a) The study region with P and 2 police departments; (b) $\mathcal{V}(P^{(10)})$; (c) $\mathcal{V}(P^{(15)})$; $\mathcal{V}(P^{(17)})$

department investigates 15 murder incidents at the same time. In this case, 7 murder cases are left uncovered with 2 cases in the north, 2 in the east and 3 in the south. An order-15 Voronoi region shaded in yellow in the eastern part of Fig. 4(c) covers the 7 remaining incidents. However, this region falls outside of the study region. Figure 4(d) shows the $\mathcal{V}(P^{(17)})$ which does not improve the coverage of existing police departments. There are still 7 incidents uncovered. However, there exists a $V(P^{(17)})$ (shaded in yellow) which covers the 7 remaining incidents and falls within the study region. This suggests that the minimum k would be 17 and the possible location of the additional department would be the intersection area of the study region and the yellow shaded $V(P^{(17)})$ as shown in Fig. 4(d).

Scenario 2
Assumption: Each department investigates incidents in the following order: the nearest murder first, the second next and so on so forth up to k.
Task: Relocating police departments without affecting the order of k investigations.

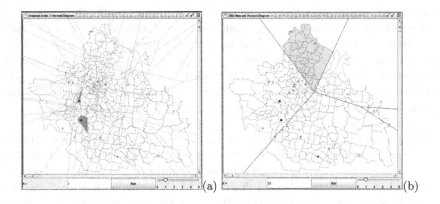

Fig. 5. Ordered order-k and k-th nearest Voronoi diagrams of P: (a) $\mathcal{V}(P^{<3>})$; (b) $\mathcal{V}(P^{[25]})$

This scenario is particularly useful when locations of target interest (police stations in this example) are constantly changing. This task can be modelled by the ordered order-k Voronoi diagrams. Figure 5(a) shows $\mathcal{V}(P^{<k>})$ when k is 3. The shaded Voronoi regions represent areas where police stations can move around without affecting the order of investigations.

Scenario 3
Assumption: Families of murder victims want to relocate to another place within the study region.
Task: Relocating family of murder victim to another place within the study region having the corresponding murder case as the k-the nearest.

Murder is one of the worst crime types and families of murder victims may want to move to a new location to start a new life away from the constant reminders of the criminal act. In this case, they may want to move as far away as possible from their corresponding incident(s). Here we consider a family moving within the defined geographical boundaries. Note that, $\mathcal{V}(P^{<k>})$ becomes the farthest Voronoi diagram when $k = |P|$. Thus, this scenario can be modelled by the k-th nearest Voronoi diagram. Figure 5(b) shows $\mathcal{V}(P^{<25>})$. The shaded areas are suburbs where the family of the murdered individual could move to, considering that the incident is at the southern part of the study region (marked $+$) hence they can relocate having the incident as the farthest point in the study region. This type of planning could speed up the time taken for individuals and families to integrate back into their communities.

4   Final Remarks

In this paper, we introduce a robust framework for what-if emergency management systems. It enables the user to explore the complete order-k, ordered order-k and k-th nearest Voronoi diagrams that provide on-the-fly information for various what-if scenarios. We present several scenarios for how it can be used for various stages of emergency management. Undoubtedly, it can be used for the four phases (mitigation, preparedness, response and recovery) of emergency management [22]. It needs to build a unified order-k Delaunay triangle data structure to start with. Once constructed, it can process various topological and region queries in diverse situations, and support dynamic updates for interactive emergency analysis.

Our system can be extended to include more what-if scenarios in parallel with other Voronoi diagram generalizations. In some situations, professional bodies or disasters may have different weights (resources, impacts or damages). These can be modelled by weighted Voronoi diagrams. In some evacuation situations, the "crow-flies-distance" may not be the right choice since obstacles may block roads to evacuation places and simply roads are not straight. The constrained Delaunay triangulation seems to be a solid candidate for these scenarios. A further study is required to extend our data structure to handle all these scenarios.

References

1. Balasubramanian, V., Massaguer, D., Mehrotra, S., Venkatasubramanian, N.: Drill-Sim: A Simulation Framework for Emergency Response Drills. In Mehrotra, S., Zeng, D.D., Chen, H., Thuraisingham, B.M., Wang, F.Y., eds.: Proceedings of the IEEE International Conference on Intelligence and Security Informatics. Lecture Notes in Computer Science 3975, San Diego, CA, Springer (2006) 237–248
2. Chang, N.B., Wei, Y.L., Tseng, C.C., Kao, C.Y.J.: The Design of a GIS-based Decision Support System for Chemical Emergency Preparedness and Response in an Urban Environment. Computers, Environment and Urban Systems 21(1) (1997) 67–94
3. Dymon, U.J., Winter, N.L.: Evacuation Mapping: The Utility of Guidelines. Disasters 17 (1993) 12–24
4. Goodchild, M.F.: Gis and disasters: Planning for catastrophe. Computers, Environment and Urban Systems 30 (2006) 227–229
5. Kevany, M.J.: GIS in the World Trade Center Attack - Trial by Fire. Computers, Environment and Urban Systems 27 (2003) 571–583
6. Montoya, L.: Geo-data Acquisition through Mobile GIS and Digital Video: An Urban Disaster Management Perspective. Environmental Modelling & Software 18 (2003) 869–876
7. Salt, C.A., Dunsmore, M.C.: Development of a Spatial Decision Support System for Post-Emergency Management of Radioactively Contaminated Land. Journal of Environmental Management 58(3) (2000) 169–178
8. Zerger, A., Smith, D.I.: Impediments to Using GIS for Real-time Disaster Decision Support. Computers, Environments and Urban Systems 27 (2003) 123–141
9. Gahegan, M., Lee, I.: Data Structures and Algorithms to Support Interactive Spatial Analysis Using Dynamic Voronoi Diagrams. Computers, Environments and Urban Systems 24(6) (2000) 509–537
10. AEA Technology: EGRESS. http://www.aeat-safety-and-risk.com/html/egress.html (Accessed in 2006)
11. CrowdDynamics: Myriad II. http://www.crowddynamics.com (Accessed in 2006)

12. IES: Virtual Environment. http://www.iesve.com (Accessed in 2006)
13. Lee, I., Gahegan, M.: Interactive Analysis using Voronoi Diagrams: Algorithms to Support Dynamic Update from a Generic Triangle-Based Data Structure. Transactions in GIS 6(2) (2002) 89–114
14. Okabe, A., Boots, B.N., Sugihara, K., Chiu, S.N.: Spatial Tessellations: Concepts and Applications of Voronoi Diagrams. Second edn. John Wiley & Sons, West Sussex (2000)
15. Gold, C.M.: Problems with Handling Spatial Data - The Voronoi Approach. Canadian Institute of Surveying and Mapping Journal 45(1) (1991) 65–80
16. Aurenhammer, F., Schwarzkopf, O.: A Simple On-Line Randomized Incremental Algorithm for Computing Higher Order Voronoi Diagrams. In: Proceedings of the Symposium on Computational Geometry, North Conway, NH, ACM Press (1991) 142–151
17. Chazelle, B., Edelsbrunner, H.: An Improved Algorithm for Constructing kth-Order Voronoi Diagrams. IEEE Transactions on Computers 36(11) (1987) 1349–1354
18. Dehne, F.K.H.: On $O(N^4)$ Algorithm to Construct all Voronoi Diagrams for K-Nearest Neighbor Searching in the Euclidean plane. In Díaz, J., ed.: Proceedings of the International Colloquium on Automata, Languages and Programming. Lecture Notes in Artificial Intelligence 154, Barcelona, Spain, Springer (1983) 160–172
19. Lee, D.T.: On k-Nearest Neighbor Voronoi Diagrams in the Plane. IEEE Transactions on Computers 31(6) (1982) 478–487
20. Berg, M., Kreveld, M., Overmars, M., Schwarzkoph, O.: Computational Geometry: Algorithms and Applications. Second edn. Springer-Verlag, West Sussex (2002)
21. Murray, A.T., McGuffog, I., Western, J.S., Mullins, P.: Exploratory Spatial Data Analysis Techniques for Examining Urban Crime. British Journal of Criminology 41 (2001) 309–329
22. Haddow, G.D., Bulldock, J.A.: Introduction to Emergency Management. Butterworth-Heinemann (2003)

Agent Based Framework for Emergency Rescue and Assistance Planning*

Yujun Zheng[1,2], Jinquan Wang[1], and Jinyun Xue[2]

[1] Systems Engineering Institute of Engineer Equipment, Beijing 100093, China
yujun.zheng@computer.org
[2] Institute of Software, Chinese Academy of Sciences, 100080 Beijing, China

Abstract. Under the difficult circumstances such as catastrophic terrorism, emergency rescue and assistance planning (ERAP) always involves complex sets of objectives and constraints. We propose a multi-agent constraint programming framework which is aimed to tackling complex operations problems during the emergency response processes. The framework employs the component-based agent model to support ERAP problem specification, solving, composition/decomposition, feedback and dynamic control. A typical emergency response system is composed of seven types of top-level agents, which are further composed of sub-agents at lower levels of granularity. In particular, agents that play key roles in task control and problem solving are based on asynchronous team (A-Team) in which sub-agents share a population and evolve an optimized set of solutions. A case study is presented to illustrate our approach.

1   Introduction

An integrated emergency response system is a decision support system that supports the emergency manager in planning, coordinating, and implementing rescue and assistance and other support operations during the response processes. Due to the increasing threats including terrorism, infectious diseases, catastrophes and war, today's emergency rescue and assistance planning (ERAP) not only involves more and more complex sets of objectives and constraints, but also needs to take multi-incident [1] and dynamic functionalities (including real-time monitoring and coordination, resource redeployment, etc.) into consideration.

Despite this, most researches on emergency response systems (e.g., [2,3,4,5]) still focus on the narrow use of single approaches such as expert conversation, mathematical programming, case based reasoning (CBR) and rule based reasoning (RBR), which have serious limitations in defining weights, expressing relationships and tradeoffs between the objectives, and changing the relative importance of different objectives [6] for ERAP problems, and typically result in a large monolithic model that is difficult to solve, understand, and maintain.

---

* Supported in part by grants from NNSF (No. 60573080) and NGFR 973 Program (No. 2003CCA02800) of China.

C.C. Yang et al. (Eds.): PAISI 2007, LNCS 4430, pp. 70–81, 2007.

Constraint programming is a widely used paradigm for declarative description and effective solving of constraint satisfaction problems (CSP) especially in areas of planning and scheduling [7]. In recent years, constraint programming has integrated many artificial intelligence (AI) techniques to enhance its capability to represent and automatically enforce diverse and complex constraints inherent in real-world applications [8]. Focusing on developing a method that allows each agent to be specialized to a single constraint or objective, [9] proposes the asynchronous team (A-Team), in which individual agents exchange results to produce a set of non-dominated solutions that show the tradeoffs between objectives, and evolve a population of solutions towards a Pareto-optimal frontier.

The paper proposes a multi-agent constraint programming framework which is aimed to tackling complex ERAP operations problems during the emergency response processes. It employs a component-based agent model which consists of seven types of top-level agents, and the agents that play key roles in response programming and planning are further composed of asynchronous teams of sub-agents. Section 2 briefly introduces the preliminary of the A-Team, sufficient to understand the paper. Section 3 describes the fundamental architecture of the framework in detail. Section 4 presents a case study of problem-solving that addresses a chemical emergency. Section 5 concludes with some discussion.

2   A-Team

An A-Team consists of a population of candidate solutions and multiple problem solving methods (agents). It enables us to easily combine disparate problem solving strategies, each in the form of an agent, and enables these agents to cooperate to improve the quality and diversity of the resulting solutions [10]. Agents in an A-Team are composed of the following four components that enable them to participate into the teams and assist in the population evolution:

- A *requester* that requests notification of system events and determines if the agent has become relevant to the current situation.
- A *selector* that picks zero or more solutions as input to the optimization operator.
- An *operator* that runs and produces zero or more result solutions and passes them to the distributor.
- A *distributor* that filters the results and adds them to the output population.

The selection of agents to run and some of the algorithms used by the agents are probabilistic. The key to getting good results is to select a divers set of algorithms and to run the A-Team until the marginal rate of improvement falls below a threshold or the available time has been exhausted. Although the results can not be guaranteed theoretically, empirical results suggest that this approach produces [6].

The A-Team initially proposed in [9] just defines four types of agents, and is subject to special limitations such as inefficient heuristics and insufficient information about tradeoffs between the objectives and constraints. In [11] we extend the A-Team by adding CSP-specific agents, explicitly defining solution states and their transition rules, and enabling solution decomposition/composition in the framework, and therefore improve its modularity, scalability, and effectiveness for constraint programming significantly.

3   Architecture

Our framework employs the component-based agent model [12,13] to support specification, solving, composition/decomposition, feedback and dynamic control of ERAP problems. That is, an emergency response system can be constructed by composing a group of top-level agents, which are further composed of sub-agents at lower levels of granularity. Sub-agents can be further divided into lower levels, and new agents can be integrated into the framework at different levels of granularity. Agents, sub-agents and agent components can be optional and distributed across the networks including WAN, LAN, PAN, and BAN. As shown in Fig. 1, a typical emergency response system consists of the following seven types of top-level agents:

- *Receivers*: the agents that receive ERAP tasks from the command center or other information systems.
- *Decision-Makers*: the agents that analyze the tasks and generate ERAP solutions to support the emergency manager.
- *Senders*: the agents that assign sub-tasks to appropriate emergency responders (including human and other software systems/agents).
- *Solvers*: the agents that use hybrid reasoning and/or operations algorithms to work out concrete ERAP solutions.
- *Data-Managers*: the agents that manage the database of ERAP-related resources and provide required data for problem-solving.

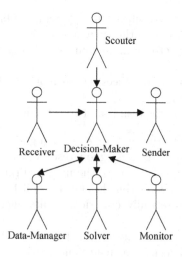

Fig. 1. Top-level agents in the the fundamental architecture

- *Monitors*: the agents that monitor the process of response tasks performed and receive feedback information from the emergency responders.
- *Scouters*: the agents that detect the changes of the response environment.

3.1   Decision-Maker Agents

Each *Decision-Maker* Agent is an A-Team shown in Fig. 2, where all ERAP tasks assigned are placed in the population, and the following sub-agents cooperate to generate optimal solutions for the tasks:

- *Analyzers*: the agents that analyze the tasks assigned, identify task properties, obtain task-related data through *Inquirers*, and put the tasks into the population. They also analyze information provided by *Monitors* and/or *Scouter*, and then modify the relevant task properties.
- *Inquirers*: the agents that inquire data required by *Analyzers* from *Data-Managers*.
- *Updaters*: the agents that update data through services of *Data-Managers* when tasks consume the resources or environment changes.
- *Specializers*: the agents that distill and normalize the problems, employ *Solvers* to solve them, and return feasible solutions to the population.
- *Decomposers*: the agents that decompose specific ERAP problems and transfer the result sub-tasks to *Senders*.

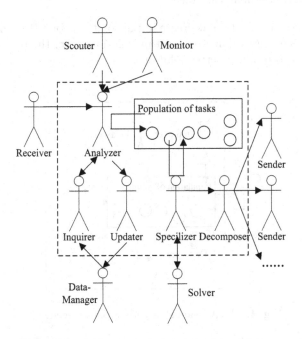

Fig. 2. The A-Team structure of *Decision-Maker* agent

In perspective of a *Decision-Maker*, an ERAP task in its population has four states: *unactuated, pending, acting,* and *ended,* as shown in Fig. 3. In detail, An *unactuated* task is an initial CSP created by the *Analyzer.* Afterward, different *Specializers* try to distill sub-problems with objectives, variables and constraints fall into their knowledge domains, and find an adequate *Solver* to solve the sub-problem. If there is any sub-problem either unsolved or unassigned (by a *Sender*) to another *Decision-Maker*, the task is in its *pending* state; else all its sub-solutions (except those assigned out) are synthesized to a full solution which can be sent to the emergency manager for implementation, and the task becomes an *acting* one. When the task is completed or canceled, it is *ended* and can be removed from the population by the *Analyzer.*

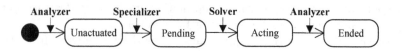

Fig. 3. The state diagram of ERAP tasks in *Decision-Maker*

3.2   Solver Agents

Each *Solver* Agent is an A-Team shown in Fig. 4, where all ERAP operations problems assigned are placed in the population, and the following sub-agents cooperate to evolve optimal solutions:

- *Constructors*: the agents that create initial solutions for ERAP problems.
- *Improvers*: the agents that take existing solutions from the population and modify them to produce better solutions.

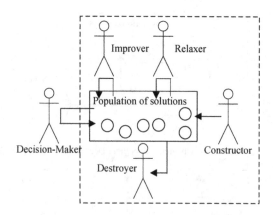

Fig. 4. The A-Team structure of *Solver* agent

- *Relaxers*: the agents that take infeasible, objective-sensitive, constraint-sensitive, or over-complicated solutions from the population and relax some constraints for the problem.
- *Destroyers*: the agents that remove low quality or redundant solutions from the population and keep the size of the population in check.

In perspective of a *Solver*, a CSP solution has five states during its problem solving process, as illustrated in Fig. 5. First, a ERAP sub-problem (or a *pending* solution) is put into the solution population by a *Specializer* of the *Decision-Maker*. A *Constructor* takes it from the population and tries to work out an initial *concrete* solution, whose objective functions will then be continually improved by *Improvers* until it becomes an *optimal* solution[1]. Here the global optimization is achieved mainly by constraint propagation [14], feasibility reasoning and optimality reasoning [15]. Problem-solving and relaxing tactics are further discussed in the following two subsections.

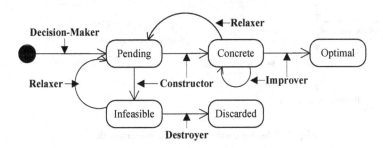

Fig. 5. The state diagram of ERAP solutions in Solver agents

3.3 Problem Solving Tactics and Predefined Libraries

In a *Solver*, a *Constructor* agent is also composed of four sub-agents: *Searcher*, *Reasoner*, *Selector*, and *Algorithm*. Dealing with a problem, the *Searcher* first searches a most similar solution in the predefined ERAP solution library; if successfully, the *Reasoner* then reuses an existing solution or works out a new solution for the problem by hybrid CBR and RBR [16] and constraint-based reasoning [17]; else the *Selector* selects an algorithm from the algorithm library by estimating the constraint complexity and strength and objective complexity of the CSP. *Constructor* then builds or reuses an *Algorithm* agent that encapsulates the algorithm to solve the problem.

Figure 6 shows a typical operations algorithm library that we implement for the framework. It is organized with a taxonomic tree [18], which contains three top-level tactics including mathematical programming, global search, and local search. In particular, global search and local search do not always guarantee the

---

[1] *concrete* and *optimal* solutions are both feasible solutions, but the latter is non-dominated, i.e., no feasible solution is better than it in the set in all the objectives.

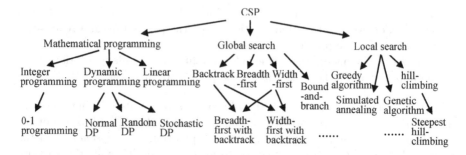

Fig. 6. The organization of the operations algorithm library

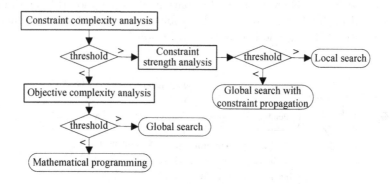

Fig. 7. The heuristic algorithm selection flow

optimal solutions since their main concern is to quickly find an acceptable, sub-optimal solution for combinatorial problems in reasonable time. Figure 7 gives the accompanied algorithm selection flowchart for the *Selector* agents.

If a CSP is identified by the *Constructor* as unsolvable, or it could not be solved using applicable algorithms in limited time, the problem is regarded as having an *infeasible* solution.

3.4 Solution Relaxing

According to problem characteristics and user preferences, *Relaxers* may relax constraints on both *infeasible* and *concrete* solutions. In [11] we propose a typical policy for CSP relaxation, which is summarized as follows:

– When proposing an ERAP problem, the *Decision-Maker* may explicitly add a mark *RelaxLevel* (ranging from 0 to 2) to the *pending* solution that states the level of permitted constraint relaxation.
– For an *infeasible* solution whose *RelaxLevel* is 1 or 2, the *Relaxer* heuristi-cally violates some problem constraints based on the constraint sensitivity

analysis, increases its *RelaxCount*, and sends it back to the population. Here the solution becomes *pending*.

- For a *concrete* solution whose *RelaxLevel* is 2, the *Relaxer* tries to violate some problem constraints and tests the result: if slight violation(s) will yield significant improvement on some objectives, increases its *RelaxCount*, and sends it back to the population; otherwise remains the solution unchanged.
- For a *concrete* solution whose *RelaxLevel* is 1 and *RelaxCount* > 0, the *Improver* tries to remove the constraint violations through iterative repair[19].
- For an *infeasible* solution whose *RelaxLevel* is 0, or whose *RelaxCount* exceeds a pre-defined limit, the *Destroyer* removes it from the population, that is, the solution is *discarded*.

3.5   Performance Evaluation

Using a simple client-agent-server model and 29 case problems, we conduct a comparative evaluation for four prototype systems: A implements our framework, B implements the original A-Team framework [20], C is an object-oriented constraint programming system [21], and D a knowledge-based reasoning system. The experimental result is briefly summarized as follows:

- All cases are resolvable in A and B, but A achieves an average 69% performance improvement over B.
- 23 cases are resolvable C, on which A achieves an average 370% improvement over C.
- Only 6 cases are resolvable in D, though it achieves an average 35% improvement over A.

4   Case Study

To illustrate the agent behavior in our framework, here we present a case study which comes from the use cases of a chemical emergency response information system. In this scenario, a terrorism attack causes a chemical fire at the first target (namely A_8), and the emergency manager is requested to send 5 rescue teams and 150 units of chemical retardants to the scene. As shown in the urban network of Fig. 8, there are two emergency medical centers (located at H_1 and H_2) that have 4 and 8 chemical rescue teams respectively, and two warehouses (located at S_1 and S_2) that have 300 and 400 units of retardants respectively.

After receiving the task and querying the related data, the *Decision-Maker* creates an initial problem, which is then separated into six sub-CSP by its *Specializers*. The objectives of the first four sub-CSP, namely P_1, P_2, P_3 and P_4, are to find shortest paths from H_1, H_2, S_1, and S_2 to A_8 respectively. The other two sub-CSP that deal with team and retardant allocation respectively, are defined in Table 1, where R is the amount of resource required, S the amount supplied, T the time consumed, c the length of network edges (labeled in the figure), and constraint C_3 sets the maximum time within which the resource must be arrived.

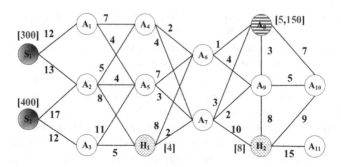

Fig. 8. The urban transportation network of the problem

Table 1. Allocation sub-problems P_5 and P_6

CSP	P_5	P_6
ORTHOGONALIZING	$P_1: c_{11}\#P_1.OBJ(0)$	$P_3: c_{11}\#P_3.OBJ(0)$
	$P_2: c_{12}\#P_2.OBJ(0)$	$P_4: c_{12}\#P_4.OBJ(0)$
VARIABLES	$R = 5, S_i, T_i, c_{ij}$	$R = 30, S_i, T_i, c_{ij}$
OBJECTIVES	MIN: $f_1 = |R - \sum_i S_i|$	MIN: $f_1 = |R - \sum_i S_i|$
	MIN: $f_2 = \sum_i S_i \times T_i$	MIN: $f_2 = \sum_i S_i \times T_i$
CONSTRAINTS	$C_1 : S_1 \leq 4$	$C_1 : S_1 \leq 300$
	$C_2 : S_2 \leq 8$	$C_2 : S_2 \leq 400$
	$C_3 : MAX_i(T_i) \leq 30$	$C_3 : MAX_i(T_i) \leq 60$
	$C_4 : \forall(i)S_i \geq 0$	$C_4 : \forall(i)S_i \geq 0$

Although dealing with multi-objective optimizations, it is not very difficult for *Solvers* with operations algorithm such as Dijkstra and simplex algorithms to work out the whole solution as follows:

- P_1: MIN-$PATH(H_1, A_8) = 5$ $(H_1 - A_7 - A_8)$
- P_2: MIN-$PATH(H_2, A_8) = 11$ $(H_2 - A_9 - A_8)$
- P_3: MIN-$PATH(S_1, A_8) = 21$ $(S_1 - A_2 - A_4 - A_6 - A_8)$
- P_4: MIN-$PATH(S_2, A_8) = 22$ $(S_2 - A_3 - H_1 - A_7 - A_8)$
- P_5: MIN-$f_1 = 0, MIN-f_2 = 31$ $(S_1 = 4, S_2 = 1)$
- P_6: MIN-$f_1 = 0, MIN-f_2 = 3150$ $(S_1 = 150, S_2 = 0)$

Suppose the solution is approved by the emergency manager. When the *acting* task is being performed, two other incidents of chemical fire at A9 and A11 are concurrently reported to the command center: A9 needs 6 rescue teams and 200 units of retardants, and A11 needs 3 rescue teams and 100 units of retardants.

Receiving the new two tasks, the *Decision-Maker* queries the feedback information from the *Monitor* of the previous task, which shows that one rescue team has arrived at the scene A8, one on the way from A7 to A8, and the others are still in preparation, meanwhile the 150 units of retardants is now arrived at A4.

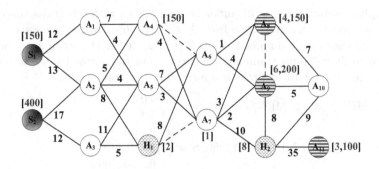

Fig. 9. The updated transportation network

At the same time, a *Scouter* reports that the streets from A4 to A6 and from H1 to A7 are both in heavy traffic jam. That is, the path (A4,A6), (H1,A7), and (A8,A9), as well as the node A9 are failed in the network, as shown in Fig. 9.

For the new CSP, all its shortest-path sub-problems need to be resolved, and the resource allocation sub-problems now become much more complicated, as illustrated in Table 2.

Table 2. Updated allocation sub-problems P_{16} and P_{17}

CSP	P_{16}	P_{17}
ORTHOGONALIZING	$P_1: c_{11}\#P_1.OBJ(0)$	$P_7: c_{11}\#P_7.OBJ(0)$
	$P_2: c_{12}\#P_2.OBJ(0)$	$P_8: c_{12}\#P_8.OBJ(0)$
	$P_3: c_{13}\#P_3.OBJ(0)$	$P_9: c_{13}\#P_9.OBJ(0)$
	$P_4: c_{21}\#P_4.OBJ(0)$	$P_{10}: c_{21}\#P_{10}.OBJ(0)$
	$P_5: c_{22}\#P_5.OBJ(0)$	$P_{11}: c_{22}\#P_{11}.OBJ(0)$
	$P_6: c_{23}\#P_6.OBJ(0)$	$P_{12}: c_{23}\#P_{12}.OBJ(0)$
		$P_{13}: c_{31}\#P_{13}.OBJ(0)$
		$P_{14}: c_{32}\#P_{14}.OBJ(0)$
		$P_{15}: c_{33}\#P_{15}.OBJ(0)$
VARIABLES	$R_i, S_{ij}, T_{ij}, c_{ij}$	$R_i, S_{ij}, T_{ij}, c_{ij}$
OBJECTIVES	MIN: $f_1 = \sum_i \lvert R - \sum_j S_{ij} \rvert$	MIN: $f_1 = \sum_i \lvert R - \sum_j S_{ij} \rvert$
	MIN: $f_2 = \sum_i \sum_j S_{ij} \times T_{ij}$	MIN: $f_2 = \sum_i \sum_j S_{ij} \times T_{ij}$
CONSTRAINTS	$C_1: \sum_j S_{1j} \leq 2$	$C_1: \sum_j S_{1j} \leq 150$
	$C_2: \sum_j S_{2j} \leq 8$	$C_2: \sum_j S_{2j} \leq 400$
		$C_3: \sum_j S_{3j} \leq 150$
	$C_3: MAX_j(T_{1j}) \leq 15$	$C_4: MAX_j(T_{1j}) \leq 45$
	$C_4: MAX_j(T_{2j}) \leq 30$	$C_5: MAX_j(T_{2j}) \leq 60$
	$C_5: MAX_j(T_{3j}) \leq 30$	$C_6: MAX_j(T_{3j}) \leq 60$
	$C_6: \forall(ij)S_{ij} \geq 0$	$C_7: \forall(ij)S_{ij} \geq 0$

Now there are not enough rescue teams to support all of the emergency operations; based on a predefined solution of resource allocation, a *Solver* uses hybrid CBR and RBR to work out the team allocation sub-solution for P_{16}. However, the supply of retardants is still sufficient, so a *Solver* with constraint reasoning finds that only the transportation from A4 to A11 could satisfy the constraint C_6 of P_{17}, and therefore 100 units at A4 is first allocated to the scene A11; another *Solver* with dynamic programming then works out the optimal sub-solution for P_{17}. The result of shortest-paths is omitted here for conciseness.

- P_{16}: MIN-$f_1 = -2$, MIN-$f_2 = 168$, $S = \begin{pmatrix} 2 & 0 & 0 \\ 1 & 4 & 3 \end{pmatrix}$

- P_{17}: MIN-$f_1 = 0$, MIN-$f_2 = 12250$, $S = \begin{pmatrix} 0 & 150 & 0 \\ 150 & 0 & 0 \\ 0 & 50 & 100 \end{pmatrix}$

Furthermore, our use cases have imposed more variations and constraints on the problem, including the failure to organize some rescue teams because of the lack of medics or equipment, the reinforcement of new rescue teams, roads with one-way traffic and speed limits, the rated capacity of the vehicles, etc. The experimental result shows that our approach is capable of working out optimal solutions (whenever existing) even in the most complex cases, which are not covered due to length limitations.

5   Conclusion

The paper reports an multi-agent framework for solving complex, particularly combinatorial, rescue and assistance planning problems under emergency conditions. It is based on the component-based agent model in which multiple problem solving agents cooperate with each other by exchanging results to produce a set of non-dominated solutions. An integrated emergency response system can be constructed by composing distributed sub-systems and agents, which are further compose of distributed sub-agents at lower levels of granularity. Our framework has been successfully implemented in the emergency response information systems for engineering and anti-chemical forces, and demonstrated its contribution to the significant improvement of the ERAP efficiency and effectiveness. Ongoing research will focus on the learning and other adaptive behaviors of the agents.

References

1. Chen, R., Sharman, R., Rao, H.R., and Upadhyaya, S.J.: Design Principles of Coordinated Multi-incident Emergency Response Systems. Lecture Notes in Computer Science, vol. 3495 (2005) 81-98
2. Li, Y.D., He, H.G., Xiao, B.H., Wang, C.H., and Wang F.Y.: CWME: A Framework of Group Support System for Emergency Responses. Lecture Notes in Computer Science, vol. 3975 (2005) 706-707
3. Luo, J.W., Liu Z.M., and Shi, Z.Z.: Analysis and Implementation of Expert System KCExpert. Computer Engineering, vol. 32, no. 2 (2006) 232-233, 259
4. Yao, Y.Y., Wang, F.Y., Wang, J., and Zeng, D.: Rule + Exception Strategies for Security Information Analysis. IEEE Intelligent Systems, vol. 20, no. 5, (2005) 52-57

5. Turoff, M., Chumer, M., Walle, B.V., and Yao, X.: The Design of a Dynamic Emergency Response Management Information System (DERMIS). The Journal of Information Technology Theory and Application, vol. 5, no. 4 (2004) 1-35
6. Akkiraju, R., Keskinocak, P., Murthy, S., and Frederick, W.: An Agent-Based Approach for Scheduling Multiple Machines. Applied Intelligence, vol. 14, no. 2 (2001) 135-144
7. Bistarelli, S.: Semirings for Soft Constraint Solving and Programming. Lecture Notes in Computer Science, vol. 2962 (2004) 1-20
8. Alguire, K.M. and Gomes, C.P.: Technology for Planning and Scheduling under Complex Constraints. Proceedings of Society for Optical Engineering, Boston, USA (1997) 101-107
9. Talukdar, S.N., Baerentzen, L., Gove, A., and Souza, P.D.: Asynchronous Teams: Cooperation Schemes for Autonomous Agents. Journal of Heuristics, vol. 4, no. 4 (1998) 295-321
10. Rachlin, J., Goodwin, R., Murthy, S., Akkiraju, R., Wu, F., Kumaran, S., and Das R.: A-Teams: An Agent Architecture for Optimization and Decision-Support. Lecture Notes in Computer Science, vol. 1555 (2000) 261-276
11. Zheng, Y.J., Wang L. L., and Xue J.Y.: An A-Team Based Architecture for Constraint Programming. Lecture Notes in Computer Science, vol. 4088 (2006) 552-557
12. Skarmeas, N. and Clark, K.L.: Component Based Agent Construction. International Journal on Artificial Intelligence Tools, vol. 11, no. 1 (1999) 139-163
13. Brazier, M.T., Jonker, C.M., and Treur, J.: Principles of Component-Based Design of Intelligent Agents. Data Knowledge Engineering, vol. 41, no. 1 (2002) 1-27
14. Pepper, P. and Smith, D.R.: A High-level Derivation of Global Search Algorithms (with Constraint Propagation). Science of Computer Programming. vol. 28, special issue on FMTA (Formal Methods: Theory and Applications) (1996) 247-271
15. Focacci, F., Lodi A., and Milano, M.: Optimization-Oriented Global Constraints. Constraints, vol. 7, no. 3-4 (2002) 351-365
16. Yasunobu, C., Yamada, H., Genta, S., and Kamada, Y.: An integrating method for rule-based reasoning and case-based reasoning. Journal of Japanese Society for Artificial Intelligence, vol. 7, no. 6 (1992) 1087-1095
17. Barbuceanu, M. and Lo, W.K.: Integrating Conversational Interaction and Constraint Based Reasoning in an Agent Building Shell. Lecture Notes in Computer Science, vol. 1887 (2001) 144-156
18. Smith, D.R.: Toward a Classification Approach to Design. Lecture Notes in Computer Science, vol. 1101 (1996) 62-84
19. Zweben, M., Daun, B., Davis, E., and Deale, M.: Scheduling and rescheduling with iterative repair. Intelligent Scheduling (eds. Zweben, M. and Fox, M.S.), Morgan Kaufman (1994) 241-255
20. Zheng, Y.J., Li, H.Y., and Xue, J.Y.: Multi-agent based materiel-support decision support system. Computer Research and Development, vol. 43, sl. no. 8 (2006) 480-485
21. Zheng, Y.J., Wang, L.L., and Xue, J.Y.: A Constraint Programming Framework for Integrated Materiel Logistic Support. Journal of Nanjing University, vol. 40, sl. no. 10 (2005) 30-35

Object Tracking with Self-updating Tracking Window[*]

Huimin Qian[1], Yaobin Mao[1], Jason Geng[2], and Zhiquan Wang[1]

[1] School of Automation, Nanjing University of Sci. & Tech.
Nanjing, P.R. China, 210094
[2] IEEE Intelligent Transportation Systems Society, U.S.A
qhmin0316@163.com

Abstract. A basic requirement for a practical tracking system is to adjust the tracking model in real time when the appearance of the tracked object changes. However, since the scale of the targets often varied irregularly, systems with fixed-size tracking window usually could not accommodate to these scenarios. In present paper, a new multi-scale information measure for image was introduced to probe the size-changes of tracked objects. An automatic window-size updating method was then proposed and integrated into the classical color histogram based mean-shift and particle filtering tracking frameworks. Experimental results demonstrated that the improved algorithms could select the proper size of tracking window not only when the object scale increases but the scale decreases as well with minor extra computational overhead.

1 Introduction

As an active research branch in computer vision, visual surveillance in dynamic scenes has found broad applications in security guard for important sites, traffic surveillance on expressways, detection of military targets, etc. The observation of a person or other interested targets is a typical application in visual surveillance, in which object tracking is a key and rudimental technique for further processes, for instance, classification, recognition and behavior understanding. Since tracking algorithms are often integrated with other processes, several basic requirements such as computational efficiency, precision, adaptability to scale changes and realtime processing are needed. It's not an easy task to meet all above requirements, therefore many existing tracking algorithms did not work efficiently. In recent years, there are two excellent algorithms, namely mean-shift [1] and particle filtering [2] having been widely adopted in object tracking. In both approaches, statistics are used. For the mean-shift technique, a nonparametric statistical method in seeking the nearest mode of a point sample distribution [3] is employed, by which the efficiency of mode search is highly improved. While, the particle filtering technique [13,14] that is based on Monte Carlo simulation,

---

[*] This work was partially supported by National Science Foundation of Jiangsu Province under grant BK2004421.

uses point mass (or "particle") to represent a probability density that applied to any state-space model for non-linear and non-Gaussian estimation problems generally appeared in target tracking.

The original mean-shift algorithm was first adopted as an efficient technique for appearance-based blob tracking [1], but the algorithm only used a fixed-size tracking window. To increase the adaptivity of the algorithm, other improvements in [4,5,6,7,8,11,12] have selected the scale of the mean-shift kernel to directly determine the size of the tracking-window. [11] used the moments of the sample weighted image to compute target scale and orientation. However, this approach is only appropriate if there was merely a single foreground object existing on the scene. In [4], the original window together with its 10 percent increment and decrement was subject to test to find which one was best matched the given target in terms of Bhattacharyya coefficient. Experiments have indicated that this method was encouraging to the scenario where target diminishes while discouraging to target enlarges. In [12], methods for adaptive kernel size selection were explored in the context of clustering point sample distributions for image segmentation, however these methods are too computationally expensive to apply to real-time tracking. In [5] the kernel bandwidth was updated by an affine model through the estimation calculated by the vertex match of the objects between two successive frames. Since the algorithm is relied on vertex match, it's not applicable to nonrigid object. Model updating methods via estimating object kernel histogram by Kalman filtering were proposed in [6] and [7]. Although these algorithms were robust against the influence of occlusion, illumination changes and object scale varying, similar to [4], the updating methods were also discouraging to the targets with increasingly changed scales. In [8] the theory of feature scale selection based on local maxima of differential scale-space filters was adapted to the determination of the kernel scale in mean-shift tracking. However, the algorithm has heavy computational overload meanwhile the mean-shift iteration is equivalent to seeking the average of the scale-space with given position space when the Epanechuikov has constant differential coefficient. For particle filter based tracking algorithms, few attention was put onto the scale-updating of tracking window. The algorithm proposed in [2] updated the scale of target window only by adding disturbances on scale parameters during the particle renewal, whereas experiments have showed its unsatisfactory results.

Since either mean-shift based or particle filtering based tracking algorithms rely on a feather matching process, the size of tracking window would significantly affect the precision of target matching and position, which consequently determines the whole tracking precision. If the tracking window is much larger than the size of tracked object, there would be more background pixels contained in the window. As a result, the correlation value between the testing target and the target template would be reduced. Actually, a too large window would also cause the tracker to become more easily distracted by background clutter. Whereas, if the window size is too small, the feature of the tracked object would not be fully obtained in a tracking window, which leads to the lost of target. This case often appears when we track an augmented object. Many existing tracking algorithms including above mentioned ones adopt the fixed-size tracking window or dissatisfactory window-updating strategies, and it is difficult for them to catch effectually an object with distinct scale change.

In this paper, a multi-scale image information measure (MSIIM) has been introduced into object tracking systems to tackle the problem of window size selection and updating. Inspired by [9], where a multi-scale image information measuring method indicates that image information in scale-space is in inverse proportion to the image scale. We found that the distance between the observer and the object was also reflected by the MSIIM. The scale changes of the moving target in video can be regarded as the distance changes between the observer and the target in real scene. Therefore we associated the scale changes with the MSIIM, and used it to determine the size changes of the tracking window. The main contribution of the paper is that we have suggested a new definition of two kinds of feature points to define the MSIIM, and have proposed an automated updating mechanism for tracking window. We also have integrated the proposed method into the classical color based mean-shift and particle tracking frameworks. Experimental results showed that the performance of the modified mean-shift and particle tracking algorithms had been significantly improved.

The remainder of the paper is organized as follows. After describing the definition of the multi-scale image information measure in section 2, we present object tracking methods with self-updating window that use MSIIM in section 3. Then, in section 4, experimental results are reported. Finally we conclude the paper in section 5.

2   Multi-scale Image Information Measure

It is well-known that the perception of human vision exhibits a scale effect, i.e., the closer one sees an image, the more details he observes. The scale effect also holds true in object tracking where the tracked object has more information in large scale than in small scale. Therefore, if there exists a method being able to measure the quantity of information and sequentially distinguish the object's scale, the tracking window size could be selected according to the information changes. Here we present a measure named Multi-Scale Image Information Measure to achieve the goal.

2.1   Two Kinds of Image Feature Points

In Marr's Theory [10], visual processing could be divided into three steps, namely the primal sketch, the 2.5 D sketch, and the 3D representation. The primal sketch is the first representation inferred from the image brightness changes, and its elements directly reflect the physical existence. So the number of the elements extracted in the primal sketch can be used as a measure for image information. Here we define two kinds of image feature points and use the number of feature points to measure multi-scale image information.

Suppose a point, P is a pixel in an image plane, $f(x, y)$, and its 8 nearest-neighbors are denoted as $N_l(P)$ (shown in Fig. 1), where $l = 1 \sim 8$. If we use a polar vector (P, l), $l \in L$, $L = \{k\pi/4, k = -4, \ldots, 0, \ldots, 3, k \in Z\}$, to represent one neighbor point of P, then the mathematical description of the 8 nearest-neighbors is given as follows:

$$f_l(x) = \begin{cases} f(x - \sin l, y + \cos l) & l = n\pi/2 \\ f(x - \sqrt{2}\sin l, y + \sqrt{2}\cos l) & l = n\pi/4 \text{ and } l \neq n\pi/2 \ . \end{cases} \tag{1}$$

where $n \in Z$. Along arbitrary direction of 8 polar angles, l, the directional

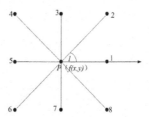

Fig. 1. Relationship between pixel P and its 8 nearest-neighbors, $N_l(P)$

differential operator can be defined as:

$$\nabla_l f(x, y) = \frac{f_l(x, y) - f(x, y)}{\Delta h} = f_l(x, y) - f(x, y) \ . \tag{2}$$

where $\Delta h = 1$ is the sample step. The central-difference of image $f(x, y)$ is defined as:

Definition 1. *Suppose area $[0, X] \times [0, Y]$ is on a discrete image $f(x, y)$, the central-difference image sequence $\{g_k(x, y)\}$ of $f(x, y)$ is defined as:*

$$g_k(x, y) = \begin{cases} f(x, y) & x = 0, X \text{ or } y = 0, Y \\ f_l(x, y) - f_{l-\pi}(x, y) & 0 < x < X \text{ and } 0 < y < Y \ . \end{cases} \tag{3}$$

where $l = k\pi/4, 0 \leq k \leq 3, k \in Z$.

Based on formula(2) and (3), in terms of local extremum of differential operator, the two kinds of feature points defined in [9] could be uniformly redefined as follows:

Definition 2. *Let $f(x, y)$ be a 2D discrete image, and $P(x, y)$ be a pixel on it. If $\forall l_1 \in L_0$, $l_2 = l_1 - \pi$, $\nabla_{l_1} f(x, y) \cdot \nabla_{l_2} f(x, y) > 0$, where $L_0 = k\pi/4, k = 0, 1, 2, 3$, then pixel P is called the first-class feature point.*

Definition 3. *Let $f(x, y)$ be a 2D discrete image, $P(x, y)$ be a pixel on it, and $\{g_t(x, y)\}$ is a central-difference image sequence. If $\forall l_1 \in L_0, l_2 = l_1 - \pi$, $\nabla_{l_1} g_k(x, y) \cdot \nabla_{l_2} g_k(x, y) > 0$, where $L_0 = k\pi/4, k = 0, 1, 2, 3$, then pixel P is called the second-class feature point.*

The intuitional explanation of above two definitions is straightforward: the first-class feature points are the extremum points in an image; the second-class feature points are the points whose neighbors have extrema along certain directions. More detailed explanation can be depicted as follows: suppose a point P_k, who is one of the 8 neighbor points of P in image $f(x,y)$, is in the central-difference image sequence $\{g_k(x,y)\}$. If for all $k(0 \leq k \leq 3,\ k \in Z)$, P_k is the extremum of $g_k(x,y)$ along the direction $l = k\pi/4$, then the point P would be taken as a second-class feature point.

| (a) original image | (b) first class feature points image | (c)second class feature points image |

Fig. 2. Original image and the relevant feature points figures

Both the first and the second class feature points have represented certain important information for an image. As shown in Fig. 2, the two classes of feature points have figured out the silhouettes of the alarm clock, book and the picture frame.

2.2   Information Measure of Images

Since in Marr's view, both the first and the second class feature points are basic elements in low level vision, we use **Definition 4** to aggregate them to measure the information contained in a discrete gray-scale image. For color images, the information measure is the summation of three color channels.

Definition 4. *For a gray-scale image $f(x,y)$, if the number of the first-class feature points on the image is I_1, and the number of the second-class feature points is I_2, then the information measure of the image is defined as the sum of I_1 and I_2.*

Human visual system is of multi-scale feature, thus a video segment in which the scene zooms in or zooms out can consist of a multi-scale space. If we set the distance d between the observer and the scene as a scale factor, then the small-sized object corresponds to the d with big value, whilst, the big-sized object corresponds to the d with small value. Denote arbitrary an image in multi-scale space as $f(X,d)$, where $X = (x,y)$ is the plane coordinate, and the information measure of its corresponding image is denoted as I_d, $I_d = I[f(X,d)], d \geq 0$.

Following experimental results will demonstrate that similar to Gaussian scale-space, the information measure defined in **Definition 4** is proportional to the object size in video, therefore the aforementioned information measure is a multi-scale image information measure (MSIIM).

From far to near, we continuously took a series of 45 pictures on a cactus. We computed the MSIIM on each picture to get an information change versus cactus's size curve, which is presented in Fig. 3 (a). The x-axis in Fig. 3 (a) representing object's height is in unitary height, and the y-axis is in unitary MSIIM. As the figure shows, when the size of the cactus increases gradually, the distance d decreases, and the corresponding MSIIM increases as well. We also have calculated the information ratio S_I and the height ratio S_H between two successive pictures, and the error $e = 1 + \lg(S_I) - S_H$ was derived which is shown in Fig. 3 (b). Since the error approaches zero, an experiential relationship between the information ratio and the object size was derived: $H \approx H_0(1 + \lg(S_I))$, where H_0 is the object size in previous picture, and H is the size in current picture.

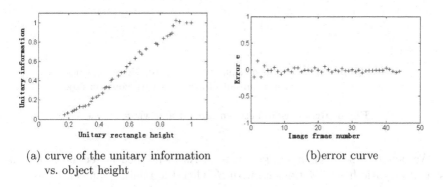

(a) curve of the unitary information   (b) error curve
vs. object height

Fig. 3. Experimental result on the cactus picture sequence

Through above analysis, it can be seen that the MSIIM can be used for differentiating the object size in a video sequence, thus, it is possible to select the size of tracking window according to the changes of the measure.

3   Object Tracking with Self-updating Tracking Window

As mentioned in section 1, the size of the tracking window significantly affects the algorithm's performance. For an overexpanded tracking window, the super-abundant background region would reduce the correlation between the object and the object template, and for multi-object tracking, several objects' tracking windows may be overlapped thus interfere with each other. While for an over-deflated tracking window, the loss of information would make the tracking ineffectual. In this section, an automatic scale updating method based on the MSIIM is proposed, and is integrated into mean-shift [1] and particle filtering [2] tracking frameworks.

3.1 Scale Updating Algorithm of Tracking Window

The main idea of the scale updating process is described as follows: calculate the tracked object's MSIIM every N frames, then update the size of the tracking window according to the change of the MSIIM. Here the interval N is dependent on the scale changing velocity that ultimately determined by the scene of the video. Suppose now a tracker is working on the n-th frame, we first calculate the MSIIM, I_1 on the current tracking window, then multiply a factor of $1 + \alpha$ and a $1 - \alpha$ on the window size respectively to calculate two new MSIIM, I_2 and I_3. The same process is also performed on the $n + N$-th frame to obtain another three MSIIMs, I_4, I_5 and I_6. The corresponding relationship between MSIIM and window scale is illustrated in Fig. 4, where the background was ignored.

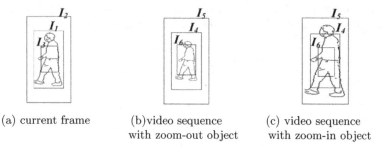

(a) current frame   (b)video sequence   (c) video sequence
                         with zoom-out object   with zoom-in object

Fig. 4. Relationship between MSIIM and window scale

We denote a scale changing factor as S. As mentioned in section 2, the information ratio has a relationship with S. Then the relationship can be used to determine the trend of object changing as well as to update the tracking window. If $I_5 - I_2 \geq 0$, it's reasonable to guess that the scale of the object is increasing, then we can use formula (4) to update S. Otherwise, if $I_5 - I_2 < 0$, the object's scale may decrease, then S will be updated by formula (5).

$$S = \begin{cases} \lg(\beta \cdot \frac{I_5 - (I_2 - I_1)}{I_1}) & I_5/I_4 > I_2/I_1 \\ 0 & others \ . \end{cases} \tag{4}$$

$$S = \begin{cases} \beta \cdot \lg(I_4/I_1) & I_1 \cdot 0.95 > I_4 \\ 0 & others \ . \end{cases} \tag{5}$$

Both in formula (4) and (5), parameter β is used to eliminate the influence of background, and is determined by video content. Once the scale factor S is gotten, the height H and width W of the tracking window can be updated according to formula (6).

$$\begin{cases} H = H \cdot (1 + S) \\ W = W \cdot (1 + S) \ . \end{cases} \tag{6}$$

The whole process of the scale updating algorithm was summarized as follows:

(1) Set frame number $n = 0$, scale factor $S = 0$, and the processing interval to N;
(2) Fetch a video frame, and set $n = n + 1$. If $n = 1$, initialize the tracker and the height H and width W of the tracking window; otherwise, go to next step;
(3) If frame number n is a multiple of N, then go to step (4), or else, set $S = 0$, and go directly to (5);
(4) Calculate three MSIIMs, $I_1(n), I_2(n), I_3(n)$ respectively on the current frame, then according to the information change to determine the object change tendency, and accordingly use formula (4) or (5) to work out the scale factor S;
(5) Use formula (6) to update the height and width. Go back to step (2) if the video does not finish yet, otherwise exit the algorithm.

Our scale updating algorithm is different from the one reported in [4], where the kernel-window of mean-shift is modified. In [4], the author chose the best tracking window from three candidates including the original window, and the windows with ±10% increment over the original. The substance of that algorithm is to make several hypothetical guesses first, then select the one with the best result. But the result it got usually is not the best, for the algorithm is not based on the actual scale changes of the object. While our algorithm updates the tracking window in the light of the visual information changes of the object during the tracking, and it also updates the kernel histogram of the object. Therefore, the proposed algorithm can efficiently track the object not only with decreasing scale but also with increasing scale.

4   Experimental Results

In this section, we will show tracking results using the improved mean-shift and the particle filtering algorithms by our automatic window-size selection

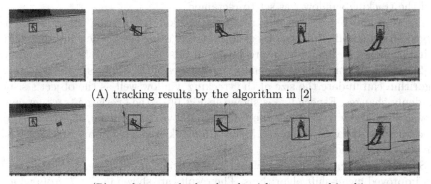

(A) tracking results by the algorithm in [2]

(B) tracking results by the algorithm proposed in this paper

Fig. 5. Tracking results by particle filtering algorithms for scale increasing targets

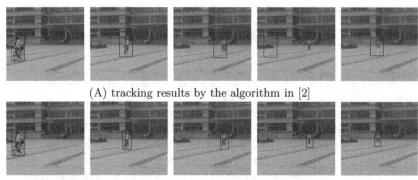

(A) tracking results by the algorithm in [2]

(B) tracking results by the algorithm proposed in this paper

Fig. 6. Tracking results by the particle filtering algorithms for scale decreasing targets

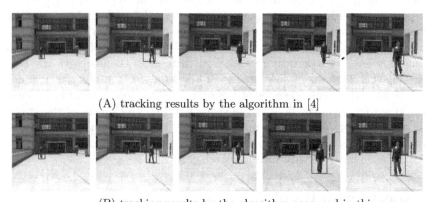

(A) tracking results by the algorithm in [4]

(B) tracking results by the algorithm proposed in this paper

Fig. 7. Tracking results by mean-shift algorithms for scale increasing targets

approach. In our experiments three segments of videos were subjected to test, and the tracking window was set to rectangle.

Figure 5 and Fig. 6 have illustrated the tracking results for videos with enlarged object and diminished object respectively using the particle filtering algorithm proposed in [2] and its improvement in this paper. Figure 5 shows method in [2] cannot accommodate effectually the changes of the object's scale, while our algorithm can update the size of the tracking window well as the object's scale suddenly changes. Especially, as shown in Fig. 6(a), the overlarge tracking window has made the tracker lose the target. In above experiments, the parameters used for scale updating are $\alpha = 0.5, \beta = 1.6$ for skier video and $\alpha = 0.5, \beta = 0.85$ for bike-woman video.

Similar experiments have been performed using original mean-shift [4] and our improved mean-shift algorithms. The results are shown in Fig. 7, from which we find the original algorithm reported in [4] could not be expanded effectively

Table 1. Tracking performance evaluation in terms of AR and CR for enlarging target

tracking algorithm	scale-updating method	video segment	Area Rate	Cover Rate
particle filtering	in [4]	skier	0.3105	0.2785
		walkinggirl2	0.5062	0.3911
		motorclist	0.2680	0.2124
	ours	skier	1.0626	0.7553
		walkinggirl2	1.2574	0.9745
		motorclist	1.4362	0.9264
mean shift	in [2]	walkinggirl1	0.8184	0.5723
		bicyclist4	0.7413	0.5184
		walkingman	0.8752	0.6111
	ours	walkinggirl1	1.4858	0.9174
		bicyclist4	1.2917	0.9671
		walkingman	1.4075	0.9369

Table 2. Tracking performance evaluation in terms of AR and CR for diminishing target

tracking algorithm	scale-updating method	video segment	Area Rate	Cover Rate
particle filtering	in [4]	bicyclist1	3.9110	0.6751
		walkingboy2	4.2513	0.9983
		walkingwoman	2.3247	0.9925
	ours	bicyclist1	1.3456	0.9859
		walkingboy2	1.1402	0.9877
		walkingwoman	1.0724	0.9722
mean shift	in [2]	walkingboy1	1.2864	0.8716
		bicyclist2	0.7514	0.5962
		bicyclist3	0.8144	0.7093
	ours	walkingboy1	1.1687	0.9768
		bicyclist2	1.2185	0.8857
		bicyclist3	1.1745	0.9802

especially in the scenarios of the object's scale increasing, while our developed algorithm can solve the problem well. The parameters used in above experiments are $\alpha = 0.5, \beta = 1$ for the size-increasing girl video.

To further evaluate the efficiency of our improved tracking algorithms, it is necessary to define quantitative measures. Here two measures, namely Area-Rate (AR) and Cover-Rate (CR) are defined. The former is used to evaluate the correctness of the tracking window's change, while the later indicates the availability of the tracking algorithm. It is obvious that both values are expected to be 1. Suppose the total pixels in the area of tracking window is denoted as set A_1, the total pixels in target region is set A_2, and an intersection set of A_1 and A_2 is B. N_1, N_2, and N_B are the number of pixels in set A_1, A_2 and B respectively. Then the definitions of AR and CR are given in equation (7) and (8) respectively:

$$AR = N_1/N_2 \qquad (7)$$
$$CR = B/N_2. \qquad (8)$$

Table 1 and 2 have separately listed the comparison results in the context of the enlarging target and the diminishing target. It's clear that for both instances our improved particle filtering algorithm is surpassing to the one in [4] in terms of both AR and CR. As for mean shift, our improved algorithm also has better tracking efficiency than the original one reported in [2] because the size change of the tracking window in [2] is jumping while it is smooth in this paper.

5   Concluding Remarks

Visual surveillance in dynamic scenes is an active and important research area, strongly driven by many potential and promising applications, such as access control, personnel identification, abnormal detection [15], and terroristic behavior analysis. As an unbreakable part, object tracking has played an important role in visual surveillance systems and is the foundation of many advanced analysis like behavior understanding and event detection.

In this paper, we have presented an effectual tracking algorithm with adaptability to scale changes and realtime processing. The multi-scale image information measure method on still-image [9] was extended to video sequence, and an automatic tracking window selection algorithm based on the MSIIM was provided. The proposed algorithm has been integrated with the classical mean-shift based and particle filtering based tracking frameworks, and achieved encouraging results. Since the scale updating process of our algorithm is of low computational complexity, and the operation is only restricted in the region of the tracking window, the computational overhead is slight and either the improved mean-shift based tracker or particle filtering based tracker could work in real-time. Because the scale-updating process reported in this paper will not affect the structure of original trackers, it can act as an universal algorithm to be integrated with many existing tracking frameworks.

References

1. Comaniciu D., Ramesh V., Meer P.: Real-time tracking of non-rigid objects using mean shift. In: Werner B, ed. *IEEE Int'l Proc. of the Computer Vision and Pattern Recognition*. Stoughton: Printing House. **2** (2000) 142–149
2. Nummiaro K., Koller-Meier E., Van Gool L.: An adaptive color-based particle filter. *Image and Vision Computing*. **21** (2003) 99–110

3. Cheng,Y.Z.: Mean shift, mode seeking, and clustering.*IEEE Trans.on Pattern Analysis and Machine Intelligence*. **17** (1995) 790–799
4. Comaniciu D., Ramesh V., Meer P.: Kernel-Based object tracking. *IEEE Trans. on Pattern Analysis and Machine Intelligence*. **25** (2003) 564–575
5. Peng NS, Yang J, Liu Z, Zhang FC.: Automatic selection of kernel-bandwidth for Mean-Shift object tracking. *Journal of Software*. **16** (2005) 1542–1550 (In Chinese)
6. Peng NS, Yang J, Liu Z.: Mean Shift blob tracking with kernel histogram filtering and hypothesis testing. *Pattern Recognition Letters*. **26** (2005) 605–614
7. Peng NS, Yang J, Zhou DK, Liu Z.: Mean-Shift tracking with adaptive model update mechanism. *Journal of Data Acquisition & Processing*. **20** (2005) 125–129 (In Chinese)
8. Collins RT.: Mean-Shift blob tracking through scale space. In: Danielle M, ed. *IEEE Int'l Conf. on Computer Vision and Pattern Recognition*. Baltimore: Victor Graphics. **2** (2003) 234–240
9. Wang ZY, Cheng ZX, Tang SJ.: Information measures of scale-space based on visual characters. *Chinese Journal of Image and Graphics*. **10** (2005) 922–928 (In Chinese)
10. Milan S., Vaclav H., Roger B.: Image processing, analysis, and machine vision(second Edition). *Thomson Learning and PT Press*. (2003)
11. Bradski G. R., Clara S.: Computer vision face tracking for use in a perceptual user interface. *Intelligence Technology Journal*. (1998) 1–15
12. Comaniciu D., Ramesh V., Meer P.: The variable bandwidth mean shift and data-driven scale selection. *Proc. of the IEEE Int'l Conf. on Computer Vision*. (2001) 438–445
13. Sanjeev M., Maskell S., and Gordon N.: A tutorial on particle filters for online nonlinear/non-Gaussian Bayesian tracking. *IEEE Trans on Signal Processing*. **50** (2002) 174–188
14. Doucet A., Godsill S., and Andrieu C.: On sequential monte carlo sampling methods for Bayesian filtering. *Statistic and Computing*. **10** (2000) 197–208
15. Xiaolei Li, Jiawei Han, Sangkyum Kim.: Motion-alert: automatic anomaly detection in massive moving objects. *Proc. of the 2006 IEEE Intelligence and Security Informatics Conference*. San Diego, CA. (2006) 166–177

A Case-Based Evolutionary Group Decision Support Method for Emergency Response*

Jidi Zhao, Tao Jin, and Huizhang Shen

Department of Information Systems, Shanghai Jiao Tong University, Shanghai, 200052, China
{judyzhao33,jint,hzshen}@sjtu.edu.cn

Abstract. According to the characters of emergency decision-making in crisis management, this paper proposes a special decision-making method to deal with the inadequate information, uncertainty and dynamical trend. This CBR-based decision support method retrieves similar cases from Case Base and forecasts the prior distribution of absent feature values using Bayesian Dynamic Forecasting Model. Then the result is put into Markov-based state transition matrix to order suggested solutions by suitability and assist consensus achieving among decision makers. This novel method is suitable to emergency decision making as it provides support for the dynamic and evolutionary character of emergency response.

Keywords: Emergency Response, CBR, GSS, Bayesian Dynamic Forecasting.

1 Introduction

The quick response and decision-making for emergencies has attracted lots of research to resolve this problem by refining reaction strategy or designing preventive plan previously. Most of those researches describe a decision-making process with single decision maker. However, it is seldom that single person can own comprehensive understanding of all phases of emergency and the limitation of personal ability is more likely to be the bottleneck of crisis management. Therefore, further research is needed to improve the effectiveness and efficiency of Emergency Decision-Making (EDM) but we are disappointed to find out that there are few such researches. Generally speaking, how to use modern information and network technology, involve multiple subjects in the decision-making process, and then construct special GSS for EDM are the critical issues when researching EDM theory and technique.

EDM in crisis management is a typical unstructured problem with complex structure and unexpected progress. Meanwhile, when faced with emergency, the decision makers are usually disturbed by the incomplete and disordered information. The GSS for EDM, as a result, should not only provide recommendable solutions, but also simulate the evolution of emergency and assist the process of dynamic decision-making and consensus achievement. From this perspective, techniques including

---

* This research is supported by NSFC(70671066).

C.C. Yang et al. (Eds.): PAISI 2007, LNCS 4430, pp. 94–104, 2007.

Case-Based Reasoning (CBR), Bayesian Dynamic Fore-casting and Markov State Transition Matrix show their suitableness.

Typically, there are no explicit rules or widely suitable solutions that can be used as reference in process of EDM. The final decision, to a great extent, is made based on previous experience of domain experts. CBR is inspired by the way through which human-beings analyze and process problems. It adopts analogical reasoning [1] and resolves problems based on past experience of similar situation. There are two assumptions which support the theory of CBR [2]:

- Reusable: the same or similar problems have the same or similar solutions;
- Recurable: the same or similar problems would recur sometime later.

Under these assumptions, CBR uses past experience to solve current problems. This approach has many advantages over the rule-based reasoning (RBR), especially in unstructured environments. CBR uses snippets of knowledge which contain implicit rules to replace structured, explicit rules, thus avoiding perplexing task of rule extraction. Moreover, CBR retains recently solved problems as well as their solutions into the case base as new cases and passes over the knowledge update and maintenance in RBR systems [2].

The focus of this paper is to propose a feasible and effective decision mode and support methodology for EDM. Firstly, we analyze the special character of EDM so as to clarify the requirement of EDM on decision support tools (Section 2 & 3). Then we give a brief introduction of related theory and techniques which are used in our method (Section 4 & 5). Finally, we explain how the proposed method and system work in Section 6.

2 Special Requirements of EDM

Currently, prevalent method used to support EDM is based on Continuous Plan or Disaster Recovery Plan (DRP). But in fact, decision makers of EDM would usually find out that it's really hard to choose a proper predefined reaction plan as:

- they may be not sure about the real situation of the scene of emergency;
- they are forced to draw the conclusion within strict time limitation; and
- they should be responsible for the consequence of decision.

The particularity of EDM makes plan-based method doomed to fail sometimes and researches on EDM should approach the problem from the aspect of special character of EDM.

2.1 Low Success Rate of Matching to Existing DRP

Almost all the DRPs are defined based on generative logical rules, namely if-then rules. This kind of method firstly describes a scenario and then gives the reactive activities. Once accidents happen, plans whose scenario matching to the real situation would be chosen and its recommendation will be followed.

The fact, on the other hand, is not so optimistic. No same thing happens again. A tiny difference in detail may lead the whole event to the opposite direction. So before making decision, decision makers need to consider differentiations between real situation and predefined plans on various facets, including emergency itself, environment, resource restriction, etc. Consequently, the measurement of plan suitability becomes the bottleneck of EDM and the scientificalness of plan-based methods is questionable.

For example, the west coast area of both Pacific and Atlantic suffer from the disaster of Typhoon (i.e. Hurricane). Whether a DRP designed for typhoon hit in west coast of Pacific (e.g. Wenzhou city of southeast China's Zhejiang Province) is suitable to deal with Hurricane Katrina hit in New Orleans? Consider following problems,

- The average altitude of Wenzhou is above sea level with no big lake in its neighborhood, whereas New Orleans was located to the south of Lake Pontchartrain, a large water mass above the city;
- China's main power to deal with emergencies is national military forces and local officials should obey arrangement of central or superior government. But neither U.S. Army nor U.S. National Guard was responsible for the emergency response and received no relevant trainings;
- The living standard in the two countries has significant difference, so process of evacuation may require differently on the public assistance and resource.

Obviously, because of the differences in both natural and political environments, the DRP designed for Wenzhou is not that suitable to New Orleans. As similar situations will happen to any DRPs, direct reuse seems not feasible and predefined plans should be used as references.

2.2 Inadequate, Disordered and Evolutionary Emergency Information

Emergency response is an evolutionary process. At any moment, the event could be led to different directions by different conditions. If all possibilities are taken into account, an event will be demonstrated as a tree structure. Usually, predefined reaction plans consider only several branches which have high possibility so as to be feasible and cost-efficiency and previous cases are only the solutions to single branch.

In other words, such static decision method, namely the plans and cases, are based on certain and adequate information, which would definitely result as low suitability as they have already defined the scenario. Their solutions and recommendations cannot fulfill the requirement of dynamic real events, let alone common situation that decision makers cannot have enough information about emergency. Furthermore, because the information collecting channels are also faced with risk, the information qualify has little assurance and they may arrive disorderly.

All above factors have great impact on EDM process. So when decision makers trying to looking for suitable plans or similar previous cases, they may find:

- They don't have a clear view about the emergency;
- They cannot find a satisfactory result as no case matches the situation;
- Emergency is going on and supplementary information arrives continuously.

Since the static decision methods are helpless to resolve above problems, a novel decision support method is needed to support dynamic events and inadequate information. This paper approaches the problem by analyzing the character of event evolution. By taking the external interferer and limited information into account, this paper creates status transfer model, forecasts every possibility, calculates respective probability, and then builds the special framework for dynamic EDM. By this way, the restriction of static methods can be broken and the support method will be more valuable.

3   GSS for EDM

Designing a special Group Support System (GSS) is a recommendatory method. GSS provides support to both discussion and consensus achievement [3]. Typically, decision makers participate in the computer-mediated decision process anonymously and enjoy equal status. The responsibility of process control and facilitation lies on the GSS. Therefore, parameterizing for GSS, e.g. task category, decision objective, etc. is critical to its effectiveness and efficiency [4][5][6].

GSS for EDM should be designed to fulfill the special requirement of EDM. To deal with poor quality and inadequacy of decision information, GSS should pro-vide recommendations based on limited information. To respond to the evolutionary process of emergency, GSS should support the forecasting of event evolution and dynamic decision process. To comply with the strict time restriction, GSS should limit the interferer into discussion and automatically assist achieving consensus. Furthermore, to involve decision makers in group decision process within short time, GSS should be built based on distributed structure.

4   CBR and Related Techniques

Although predefined DRPs and previous solutions of similar cases have limitation when adopting them by simply reuse, they are still of great value. Presenting those solutions to decision makers will significantly improve the effectiveness and efficiency. CBR system is suitable for both predefined plans and previous cases. Its output provides primary support to the EDM process.

4.1   Case Base Generation

The generation of case base and design of index system is the foundation of CBR. Usually, domain experts create case base by analyzing previous events and referring to relevant predefined planes. Then analysis result is used to design normalized description method and formalized represent framework for cases. Thus, previous events can be formalized and case base is simultaneously generated. Technically, all descriptive features of a case are indices of case base.

4.2   Case Retrieve

It is an N-ary task to retrieve case in case base. The k-nearest neighbor (k-NN) method is the common way to complete N-ary task [7]. k-NN is a kind of lazy learning algorithm. It retrieves the k least distant (i.e., most similar) cases of a given query. The quality of k-NN therefore depends on which cases are deemed least distant, which is determined by its distance function.

The general process of k-NN can be described as follows [8]:

The process inputs a query case **q** and outputs a set of cases similar to **q**. Each case $x = \{x_1, x_2, ..., x_{|F|}\}$ is a point in multidimensional space defined by a feature set **F**. k-NN computes the distance $d(x, q)$ of **q** to each $x \in X$ using:

$$d(x,q) = (\sum_{f \in F} w(f) \cdot \delta(x_f, q_f)^r)^{\frac{1}{r}}. \tag{1}$$

where k-NN defines $r = 2$ (i.e., Euclidean distance), function $\delta()$ defines how values of a given feature f differ and $w(f)$ defines the feature weighting function. Then, the cases whose distance to **q** is less than distance threshold are presented to decision makers, i.e.

$$Output = \{x_i | x_i \in X, d(x_i, q) < vt\}. \tag{2}$$

Where vt is the similarity threshold defined by domain experts according to the character of emergency.

4.3 Measure of Feature Similarity

From equation (1), we can find out the performance of k-NN is highly sensitive to the definition of distance function, i.e., the measurement of how cases differ on various features and the weighting method among features.

When measuring feature similarity (i.e. defining function $\delta()$), both numerical and nominal features should be taken into account. At the same time, since it is not infrequent that people are not sure about feature value, both certain feature value and fuzzy feature value should be considered. Thus, all the case features can be classified into the following four categories [9].

- Crisp numeric feature (CN): its value can be either continuous or discrete, e.g. $500, 1.35, etc.
- Crisp symbolic feature (CS): its value is usually a certain term, e.g. Rainy.
- Fuzzy linguistic (FL): its value can be treated as a linguistic variable, e.g. Medium, Large, and Very Large.
- Fuzzy numeric and fuzzy interval (FNI): its value is usually an uncertain number or an interval with no clarified boundary, e.g. around 200, 300~500.

For different categories, there are different methods to deal with the similarity.

Although fuzzy linguistic and fuzzy numeric can be represent with Gauss Function, the process of Gauss Function is over complicated. This paper adopts trapezium-based fuzzy set to simulate the fuzzy features [10].

If some of the features of query case **q** are absent, just put them aside and measure the similarity on existing features. Therefore, the similarity threshold vt will depend on the integrality of query case **q**. The more features **q** has, the lower vt is. But the change range should be carefully controlled.

4.4 Weighting Method Based on Similarity Rough Set

The weight of attributes is pivotal to the case retrieve when measuring case similarity using k-NN rule. k-NN's sensitive to its distance function can be reduced by parameterizing the distance function with feature weights. Many weighting methods have been proposed and an overview can be found in [8].

Rough set theory (RST) [11][12]is a mathematical tool used for dealing with vagueness, imprecise and uncertainty of data and now widely used in the areas of AI and cognitive sciences. It can be applied to select the most relevant condition features to the final decision [13].

However, all continuous features have to be discretized prior to using rough set, which is facing with risk of losing precious information. In paper [14], we pro-posed a weighting method based on an extension of standard RST call similarity-based rough set (SRS) [15][16]. This algorithm uses similarity relation instead of indiscernibility relation so as to avoid the discretization. Feature weights were calculated by Similarity-Based Discernibility Matrix. As long as feature similarity threshold was given, Results can be generated automatically by computer.

The RSR-based weighting method assigns heavier weights on features having greater contribution to case differentiation. It observes the appearance of each feature in Core, Reduct, and other entries in matrix. Features in Core own heaviest weights, while features appear in neither Core nor Reduct and arise infrequently in matrix have lighter weights.

The most obvious advantage of this algorithm is its lower compute complication and easiness to realization by computer program. The result of experiment comparison shows that it achieve similar classification accuracy with traditional RST-based weighting methods, i.e. feature dependency, and even better performance on some datasets.

5 Bayesian Dynamic Forecast Model

Forecasting the value of absent features for query case q is important to EDM as the improvement in information richness would of great help to EDM.

Dynamic model [17] is one of key means of Bayesian Forecasting. It treats forecasting distribution as conditional probability distribution. The forecasting process based on Bayesian Dynamic Model is shown in Figure 1.

In Figure 1, θ_t is the set of evaluation-needed parameters of target model at Time T. $\theta_t \in R^{nt}$, R^{nt} is parameter space. D_t is the information set of Time T and all previous time. Thus, D_0 is the initial information set when T=0. y_t is observa-tion vector. $p(\theta_t)$ is prior distribution while $p(\theta_t | y_t)$ is posterior distribution.

The forecasting process starts from age T-1. Once actual test result (θ_{t-1}, D_{t-1}) are obtained, the posterior distribution is derived as $p(\theta_{t-1} | D_{t-1})$. At this stage, this information can be used to update a prior distribution for θ_t. That is $p(\theta_t | D_{t-1})$. At this point, one-step ahead forecasting at time T can be implement-ed. Upon

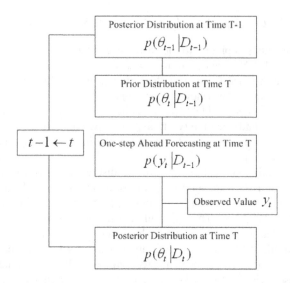

Fig. 1. Recursive Algorithm of Bayesian Dynamic Forecasting

availability of information (y_t) at Time **T**, posterior distribution at Time **T** can be calculated by Bayes' Formula and it is also the prior distribution at Time **T+1**. Thus, the Bayesian Forecasting operates in a recursive way.

6 CBR-Based Decision Mode for EDM

Traditional CBR consists of 4Rs, i.e. Retrieve, Revise, Reuse, and Retain. But actually, the revise, namely case adaptation, is still a problem awaits suitable resolution. Common methods include revising previous solution based on expert experience or adopting revise rules generated from previous similar actions.

However, these means are not that suitable to EDM. Decision makers cannot be sure about the emergency for the inadequate information. They are unable to gain a clear view of the emergency as well as its development trend. Moreover, emergency has great negative impact on society stabilization and security of civilian. The heavy responsibility on the shoulder forces decision makers to make every decision prudentially.

Since we have already ascertained that the key barricade to EDM is the inadequacy and disorder of information, a useful EDM support tool should enable to assist decision makers forecasting event trend within strictly time limit. In other words, EDM support tool is expected to help decision makers estimate the value of absent features and predict development roadmap for emergent events.

Figure 2 demonstrates the iterative CBR-based decision mode for EDM. The support system presents decision makers with recommendations based on limited information at first. Then, by the interaction between experts and system, this tool estimates the value of critical absent features by Bayesian Dynamic Forecasting Model. Then, with estimating result taken into account, the system sorts solutions by its suitability to real situation. Once supplementary information or feedback of reaction arrives, the new information would initiate another round of decision making. Detailed process of the mode is described as follows.

Step1. Case retrieve based on limit information

When emergency happens, decision makers firstly collect relevant information. With aid of the case normalized description method and formalized represent framework, new event was represented as a query case.

Then, as what is explained in Section **V**, decision makers retrieve similar cases or predefined plans in Case Base. If such cases exist, support system returns single or a set of similar cases according to the similarity threshold. The solutions of these cases are preparative material for the following decision activities. In case the return is NULL, go to Step 5.

Step2. Differentiation Analysis

Since case retrieve process is based on the inadequate information. The Similarity, on this level of information richness, is not that reliable. The feasibility of reusing their solutions is also questionable.

Therefore, when given with a series of similar cases and their solutions, decision makers need to conduct the differentiation analysis so as to gain insight in character of each solution. Only when decision makers know well about the suitability and relatively advantage and disadvantages of each solution, can they choose the right one.

At this step, decision makers should achieve consensus about what additional information is needed to make further decision and this is exactly what need to be estimated in the following steps.

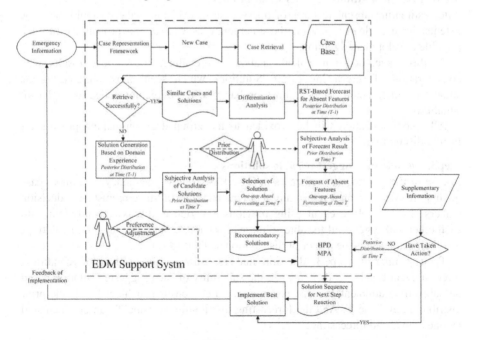

Fig. 2. The iterative CBR-based decision mode for EDM

Step3. Forecasting of absent features

The absence of emergency features leads to the insufficient condition to make decision. However, the time limitation of EDM is extremely strict. It is impossible to wait for supplementary information. So, reasonable forecasting is necessary.

We forecast absent feature value by Bayesian Dynamic Forecasting Model. This means makes full use of historical information while taking factors of people into account. Decision makers are also responsible for the forecasting and should provide information.

If the evaluation-need feature is inside the case representation framework, it can be estimated through Rough Set based method, using existing features. Here, the absent feature is treated as Decision Attribute (**D**) and all existing features are treated as Condition Attributes (**C**). Then, an Information System (**S**) can be constructed. From **S**, we build up Discernibility Matrix, calculate Core set and Re-duct set based on the matrix, and define reasoning rules by relational operation. For example, a typical rule could be $a1b3 \Rightarrow d2$ which means if feature **a** equal to 1 and feature **b** equal to 3, the decision feature **d** is 2. More detailed introduction about rough set can be find in [11][12]. This result is concluded based on the previous experience and it is a value of the highest probability, i.e. the posterior distribution at Time (**T-1**).

Then, support system interacts with decision makers by human-machine dialogue. By combining posterior distribution and subjective judgment, the prior distribution of evaluation-needed features at Time **T** can be defined. Then, make one-step ahead forecasting at Time **T** using the properties of beta distribution and result as a forecasting distribution of evaluation- needed features at Time **T**.

Step4. Present solutions in order of suitability

After estimating absent features of query case q, decision makers should, to some extents, have a clearer view of the emergency as well as the probability of each possible development direction.

At this stage, decision makers analyze and evaluate the retrieve results with consideration of forecasting result. Solutions which seem most suitable to the situation which could happen most probably will be recommended in order of suitability.

All recommendation will be provided to the group decision-making process for further discussion.

Step5. Discuss and suggest feasible solutions

In case of there is no matched cases in Case Base to new emergency, i.e., query case q, support system cannot return any recommendation. In this circumstance, decision makers should analyze event using previous experience, discuss the problem with each other and suggest all feasible solutions for choice. Thus, the suggested solutions and their sequence is the posterior distribution at Time (**T-1**).

Then, similar to step 3, decision makers estimate absent decision condition, forecast event trend, and then analyze the suitability of each suggested solution based on subjective judgment and discussion. Once a consensus is achieved, it is the prior distribution at Time **T**. And the forecasting distribution at Time **T** can be calculated by one-step ahead forecasting.

The difference between this stage to step 3 is that step 3 uses Bayesian Model to forecast the distribution of absent feature value whereas in this stage the model is used to forecast the suitability of different suggested solutions.

Step6. Make decision with aid of Markov-based GSS
Although all recommendatory solutions are ordered by suitability, there still may be dissidence. A GSS process is introduced in this stage so as to achieve consensus among all decision makers.

We proposed a novel GSS approach in another paper [18]. By analyzing the preference sequence of each decision maker as well as its connotative character, the approach assists consensus achieving by Markov-based state transition matrix. It can be proved that this approach can, in limit steps, achieve a consensus identical to the final steady result of infinite rounds of discussion. In other words, it greatly improves the consensus achieving efficiency with no sacrifice of effectiveness.

When consensus is achieved, the first solution in the queue was adapted as the next step reaction.

Step7. The stochastic sequential decision-making for EDM
During the process of making decision or implementing solutions, there should be new information about the emergency arriving in succession. They can be observation result, and feedback of the previous step decision. All of them can be treated as input of further step of decision-making.

If new information arrives before the implementation of decision of Time T, this information is treated as the observe result at Time T. By using Bayes' Formula, we can calculate the posterior distribution at Time T (see Figure 1). The result is again put into Markov state transition matrix and the solution sequence may be updated.

On the other hand, if the new information arrives after the implementation of decision, the information will, together with the feedback of decision, initiate another round of EDM.

7 Conclusion

This paper proposed an evolutionary group decision support method for dynamic emergency. Decision makers firstly retrieve previous similar cases and predefined emergency recovery plans in CBR system. In order to select suitable action plans, absent decision condition, namely absent case features, are carefully estimated using rough set theory and Bayesian dynamic forecasting model. Then, with both candidate solutions and forecasting result taken into account, consensus among decision makers are achieved by Markov state transition matrix based GSS and all solutions are ordered by suitability. During the process of decision-making and implementation, supplementary information as well as decision feedback arrives successively, initiating new rounds of decision. Thus, the interaction and cooperation with experts and machine put dynamic evolution of emergency under control and such sequential decision process would significantly improve the effectiveness and efficiency of EDM in crisis management.

References

1. Mantaras, R. L. D., Mcsherry, D., Bridge, D., et, al. Retrieval, reuse, revision, and retention in case-based reasoning[J]. The Knowledge Engineering Review, 2005; 00(1-2)
2. Shi, Z.Z. Knowledge Discovery[M]. Beijing: Tsinghua University Press. 2002: pp.85~105 in Chinese
3. Jessup, L. M. and Valacich, J. S. Group Support Systems: New Perspectives, Macmillan, New York, NY, 1993.
4. Huang, W., Wei, K.K., and Lim, J. Using GSS to Support Global Virtual Team-building: A Theoretical Framework, International Journal of Global Information Management, Jan.-Mar. 2003, 11 (1), pp. 72-89.
5. Galegher, J. and Kraut, R.E. Technology for intellectual teamwork: perspectives on research and design. In Galegher, J., Kraut, R.E. and Egido, C. (Eds.) Intellectual Teamwork: Social and Technological Foundations of Cooperative Work. Lawrence Erlbaum Associates, Publishers, USA, 1990, pp.1-20.
6. Huang, W., Raman, K.S., and Wei, K.K., Impact of GSS and Task Type on Social Influence in Small Groups, IEEE Transactions on Systems, Man, and Cybernetics, Sept. 1997, 27 (5), pp. 578-587.
7. Dasarathy, B. V. (Ed.). Nearest neighbor(NN) norms: NN pattern classification techniques[M]. Los Alamitos, CA: IEEE Computer Society Press. 1991
8. Wettschereck, D., Aha, D.W., Takao, M.. A Review and Empirical Evaluation of Feature Weighting Methods for a Class of Lazy Learning Algorithms[J]. Artificial Intelligence Review, 1997, 11(1-5): 273□314
9. Pal, K., Campell, J.A. A hybrid system for decision-making about assets in English divorce case[A]. Proc of First United Kingdom Workshop on CBR[C], Salford, UK, 1995, 152-156
10. Zhang, B.S., Yu, Y.L. Hybrid Similarity Measure for Retrieval in Case-based Reasoning System[J]. System Engineering Theory and Practice. No. 3, 2002, pp: 131-136 in Chinese
11. Pawlak, Z. Rough sets[J]. International Journal of Information and Computer Science. 1982; 11: pp.341~356
12. Pawalk, Z. Rough Sets: Theoretical Aspects of Reasoning about Data[M], Dordrecht: Kluwer Academic Publishers. 1991.
13. Gupta K.M., Moore, P.G., Aha, D.W., Pal, S.K. Rough Set Feature Selection Methods for Case-Based Categorization of Text Documents[C]. In S.K. Pal et al. (Eds.): PReMI 2005, LNCS 3776. Springer–Verlag Berlin Heidelberg, 2005: pp.792~ 798
14. Tao, J., Shen, H.Z. Feature Selection and weighting method based on Similarity Rough Set for CBR[C]. Proc. of the 2006 IEEE International Conference on Service Operations, Logistics, and Informatics. Shanghai, China, 2006: 948-952
15. Slowinski, R., Vanderpoonten, D. Similarity relation as a basis for rough approximations[J]. Advances in Machine Intelligence and Soft Computing 1997:4, pp.17~33
16. Stepaniuk, J. Similarity Based Rough Sets and Learning[C]. Proceedings of the 4th International Workshop on Rough Sets, Fuzzy Sets, and Machine Discovery. Tokyo, Japan. November 6-8, 1996: pp.18~22
17. Harvey, A.C., Forecasting, Structural Time Series Models and the Kalman Filter, Cambridge, 1990.
18. Shen, H.Z., Zhao, J.D. How to efficiently achieve consensus in group decision-making of Emergency Response to Crisis Management – Research on a Stochastic Approach. Working paper.

Lightweight Anomaly Intrusion Detection in Wireless Sensor Networks

Haiguang Chen[1,2], Peng Han[2], Xi Zhou[2], and Chuanshan Gao[2]

[1] Mathematic and Science College, Shanghai Normal University
Shanghai, P.R. China, 200234
chhg@shnu.edu.cn
[2] Dept. of Computer Science and Engineering, Fudan University
Shanghai, P.R. China, 200433
{hgchen,041021070,zhouxi,cgao}@fudan.edu.cn

Abstract. Wireless Sensor Networks (WSNs) have an excellent application to monitor environments such as military surveillance and forest fire. However, WSNs are of interest to adversaries in many scenarios. They are susceptible to some types of attacks because they are deployed in open and unprotected environments. The WSNs are constituted of scarce resource devices. These security mechanisms which used for wired networks cannot be transferred directly to wireless sensor networks. In this paper we propose lightweight anomaly intrusions detection. In the scheme, we investigate different key features for WSNs and define some rules to building an efficient, accurate and effective Intrusion Detection Systems (IDSs). We also propose a moving window function method to gather the current activity data. The scheme fits the demands and restrictions of WSNs. The scheme does not need any cooperation among monitor nodes. Simulation results show that we proposed IDSs is efficient and accurate in detecting different kinds of attacks.

Keywords: Anomaly intrusion, Wireless sensor network, Key feature, IDSs, Security.

1 Introduction

Wireless sensor networks have wide applications due to these sensor nodes ease of deployment, particularly in remote areas. WSNs serve to collect data and to monitor and detect events. However, these sensor nodes are deployed in open and unprotected environments and these inherent characteristics of a sensor network limit its performance. In particular, the WSNs node was exposed to all kinds of attacks from physical layer to transport layer. As a result, it is crucial important for the practical implementation of WSNs to determine how well a wireless sensor network can perform its given task in open field and out of human control. And how to detect anomaly intrusion is a critical issue for WSNs.

Intrusion detection can be defined as a process of monitoring activities in a system, which can be done by a monitor node or network system. The mechanism is called intrusion detection systems (IDSs). IDSs collect activity information and then analyze these data to determine whether there are any activities that violate the security rules.

C.C. Yang et al. (Eds.): PAISI 2007, LNCS 4430, pp. 105–116, 2007.

Once IDSs determines that an unusual activity or an activity that is known to be an attack occurs, then it generates an alarm.

Although, there have existed several intrusion detection techniques developed for wired networks, they are not suitable for wireless sensor networks and cannot be transferred directly to WSNs due to the strict resource restriction. Therefore, these techniques must be modified or new techniques must be developed to make intrusion detection work effectively in WSNs.

In this paper, we propose a lightweight anomaly intrusion detection scheme for WSNs. The scheme uses rules and key features application to detect attacks. The main contributions in our paper are listed as follows:

- Rules application can detect known attacks fast in WSNs.
- Key features used to characterize the WSNs behaviors, and potentially applicable to detect previously unseen attacks.
- Propose a dynamic way to collect message data for IDSs to analyzes these data and determine the intrusion behavior of the nodes.

The rest of the paper is organized as follows. Section 2 briefly describes the related work about IDSs. Section 3 describes the problem and network model for WSNs used in our paper .Section 4 presents key features and rules for us to detect intrusion in WSNs. Section 5 describes our scheme in detail. Section 6 describes IDSs simulator and the simulative attacks. Section 7 gives the simulation results with our scheme. Finally, the summary and conclusions of our work are given in section 8.

2   Related Works

IDSs are important security tools in computer networks. Many solutions have been proposed to traditional networks [11, 12, 13, 14], but because the WSNs resources are so restricted in energy, storage and capability of computation that make direct application of these solutions inviable.

In recent year, Ad-hoc and WSNs security has been studied in a number of proposals. Zhang and Lee [1] are among the first to study the problem of intrusion detection in wireless Ad-hoc networks. They proposed architecture for a distributed and cooperative intrusion detection system for Ad-hoc networks, their scheme based on statistical anomaly detection techniques. But the scheme need much time, data and traffic to detect intrusion. In WSNs, the nodes cannot afford the cost.

Mishra, et al. [2] proposed a review of intrusion detection in wireless Ad-hoc networks, but did not discuss the actual detection techniques.

Bhargav et al. [3] proposed an intrusion detection and response model to enhance security in AODV. Marti et. al. [4] proposed two techniques: watchdog and pathrater that improve throughput in Ad-hoc network. We have used a similar idea in this paper. As we will see, the monitor node watches its neighbors and also knows what each one of them will do with the messages which receive from another neighbor. If the neighbor of the sensor nodes changes, delays, replicates, or simply keeps the message data that ought to be retransmitted, the monitor gets the current state of the neighbor node and maybe gets intrusion detection in WSNs. This technique can also be used to detect other types of attacks.

Yu and Xiao [5] proposed detecting selective forwarding attacks in WSNs, which based on a multi-hop acknowledgement technique to launch alarms by obtaining responses from intermediate nodes. But the scheme can only discriminate abnormal packet loss from channel error packet loss at a high ratio.

Hu et al. [6] proposed a method for detecting wormhole attacks in Ad-hoc networks. The scheme evaluated the time spend on the transmission of packets between nodes in the WSNs. The work used two protocols: Slot authenticates MAC and TIK. But both protocols need synchronization of the network trusted time. As we know, in WSNs, that it is very hard to keep nodes strict synchronized.

Pires et al [7] proposed a scheme through comparing the power of the received signal with the power of the observed signal in the network to detect such as wormhole and HELLO flood attacks in WSNs. The scheme proposed in [7] for WSNs still can be used as one special of the rules in our IDSs. But our scheme work proposes a wider solution for attacks, and capable of detecting several types of intruders and attacks in WSNs.

3   Problem Statement and Network Model

3.1 Problem Statement

We study the problem of enabling the monitor nodes of WSNs to detect the malicious behavior of the attacks nodes. In this paper, we consider lightweight anomaly intrusion detection in the context of the following design goals: (a) resource efficiency and detect known attacks fast, (b) decentralized implementation, (c) accuracy in high ratio of networks error.

3.2 Network Model

Network generation: We assume that the network consists of a set of scarce resource sensor nodes N. Each sensor can connect through a wireless link to any other sensor located within a certain radio transmission range r, thus r is the maximal range allowed by power constraints nodes. A set of specially equipped nodes M we call monitors. The radio transmission range of monitor is R. The monitor node uses its radio in a promiscuous mode, storing relevant information and processing it according to selected rules which we will describe later. We assume that all network nodes include monitors are deployed randomly in a specific network region of area, A. To model this, we use a Poisson point process [8] over area, A, with constant density. The random deployment of the monitors M with a density $p_M = \dfrac{|M|}{A}$ ($|\bullet|$ is the cardinality of a set).and the sensor nodes N with the density, $p_s = \dfrac{|N|}{A}$.

Let SHB_m denote the set of sensor nodes heard by a monitor m, the probability that m hears exactly k sensor nodes is equal to the probability that sensor nodes are deployed within an area of size πR^2. Since sensor nodes and monitors deployment follows a spatial Poisson process [8].

$$p(|SHB_m| = k) = \frac{(p_m \pi R^2)^k}{k!} e^{-p_m \pi R^2} \tag{1}$$

Let *SHBs* denote the set of sensor nodes heard by another sensor node s. The probability that node s has k' neighbor nodes is:

$$p(|SHBs| = k') = \frac{(p_s \pi r^2)^{k'}}{k'!} e^{-p_s \pi r^2} \tag{2}$$

Using (1), we compute the probability that every monitor hears at least k sensor nodes. Because we use the random sensor deployment model which implies statistical independence in the number of sensor nodes heard by each monitor sensor and hence:

$$p(|SHM_m| \geq k, \forall m \in M) = p(|SHM_m| \geq k)^{|M|} = (1 - p(|SHM_m| < k))^{|M|}$$
$$= (1 - \sum_{i=1}^{k-1} \frac{(p_m \pi R^2)^k}{k!} e^{-p_m \pi R^2})^{|M|} \tag{3}$$

Using (2), we can get probability that every sensor nodes has at least k' neighbor nodes.

$$p(|SHS_s| \geq k', \forall s \in N) = p(|SHS_s| \geq k')^{|N|} = (1 - p(|SHS_s| < k'))^{|N|}$$
$$= (1 - \sum_{i=1}^{k'-1} \frac{(p_s \pi r^2)^{k'}}{k'!} e^{-p_s \pi r^2})^{|N|} \tag{4}$$

And the probability of each sensor node has no more than k'' neighbor nodes.

$$p(|SHS_s| \leq k'', \forall s \in N) = p(|SHS_s| \leq k'')^{|N|} = (\sum_{i=1}^{k''} \frac{(p_s \pi r^2)^{k''}}{k''!} e^{-p_s \pi r^2})^{|N|} \tag{5}$$

WSNs initialization: We assume that sensor nodes and monitors use key predistribution scheme [9, 10] and get the shared keys among WSNs before deployment. The attackers cannot get the plaintext of the message.

As we know, the WSNs are base on a certain kind of application. Different applications for sensor networks have different requirements such as maximum/minimum packets per second in sending or receiving, maximum/minimum computation. We will describe in detail later.

Sensor Network Attacks Model: Before the description of network attacks model, a few assumptions listed as follows:

a)   The message was sent from one node to another node, the message data was cryptograph [15], and the attacks cannot get the plaintext of message data.

b)   There is no data fusion or aggregation by other sensor nodes when generated by the original node. The message payload is the same along the path from its origin to the destination.

c)   No any new sensor nodes were added into the target WSNs and the sensor nodes are static in the networks.

d)   Each node has only one next forward node to transmit messages in its route table.

We briefly describe DoS attacks from physical layer to transport layer, this will be used in section 4,5,6,7. A more detail study conducted by Wood and Stankovic [16].

Physical layer: a) Physical attacks, the sensor node may destruct by attacks or replace some import part by intruder. b) Radio jamming interferes, the attacker jam the WSNs with the radio frequencies the nodes are using.

Data link layer: a) Collisions, a type of link layer jamming. It is usually by full-time jamming of the channel. b) Exhaustion of battery attacks. The attacker often attempt repeated retransmission even after unusually late collisions.

Network layer: a) Selective forwarding. The attacker may choose not to forward some selected packets and drop them. b) Sybil attack. The attackers do it by having a malicious node present multiple identities to the network and confuse the routing protocols. c) Wormholes attack. The adversary tunnels messages received in one part of the network over a low latency link, to another part of the network where the messages are then replayed. An attacker disrupt routing by creating well positioned wormholes that convince nodes multiple hops from the destination that they are only a couple of hops away through the wormhole. d) Hello flood. This attack can also be thought of as a type of broadcast wormhole. The attacker high powered antenna can convince every node in the network that it is their neighbor. e) Sinkhole. Sinkhole attack is to lure traffic to a malicious part of the network and usually be done by advertising high quality routes i.e.

Transport layer: a) Desychronisation attacks. The attackers forge or modify control flags and sequence numbers between two nodes. Let the sensor nodes lost control synchronization and lead to an infinite cycle that waste energy. b) Flood attacks. The attacker's goal is to exhaust memory resources of a victim node. The attacker sends many connection establishment requests, and forces the victim node to allocate memory in order to maintain the state for each connection.

4   Key Features and Rules

We use two methods to analyze the intrusion in WSNs. For each event happened in the WSNs. We use the rules method and key features method to decide the behavior of the node whether is an intrusive or normal event. At first, we use rules method, if this way can't work then we use key features to judge the behavior.

Key features: This method to analyze the performance of a node to decide if the node is being attacked. We calculate several current state values of the node, if one of the values exceed the allowed bound, then we consider attacker is being active. This way use much computation but it works perfect, and can detect more efficiency than rules methods. Before we describe the key features of the WSNs, we suppose: a) the probability of incoming packets per second of the node is P_{mean} , according to our assumptions. The probability of out-coming packets are the same as incoming packets, P_{mean} . Because the target WSNs is for a special application, so it is reasonable using this assumption. b) The minimum neighbor number and maximum neighbor number are k', k'' .c) the average computation time for a packet in a node is t .d) the average storage space for a packet in a node is ss . e) Energy consume ratio is pu per packet. Then we give a few key features listed as follows:

a) *Packet throughout probability:* in the radio range of a node, r .Using formula (4) and formula (5) we get the probability for minimum total traffic packets are

$$P_{mitraf} = (1 - \sum_{i=1}^{k'-1} \frac{(p_s \pi r^2)^{k'}}{k'!} e^{-p_s \pi r^2})^{|N|} P_{mean} \tag{6}$$

The probability for maximum total traffic packets are

$$P_{matraf} = (\sum_{i=1}^{k''} \frac{(p_s \pi r^2)^{k''}}{k''!} e^{-p_s \pi r^2})^{|N|} P_{mean} \tag{7}$$

b) *Number of neighbors:* when the sensor nodes was deployed in the target area, the number neighbors of a node is decrease and cannot increase for some of its neighbors will use out its battery.

c) *Change ratio of Route table:* In our assumption, because the node of our target networks is static and no new node was added into the network, the route table cannot change too fast, so the route table is steady for a period of time.

d) *Computation:* the Max compute time for a node is:

$((k''-1)p_{mean} + \Delta n)t$, where Δn is a parameter $\tag{8}$

e) *Storage:* the max storage space for a node when each of its neighbor send packet to it. The value is $(k''-1)p_{mean} + \Delta n$ $\tag{9}$

f) *Energy:* the max energy used is $((k''-1)p_{mean} + \Delta n)pu$ $\tag{10}$

We have defined six key features for a special target network, but if every time we use these six features to decide if there is an intrusion, it is not economical. So we will describe other rules used in anomaly intrusion detection. If these rules cannot detect intrusion then combine with key features. In our simulation results, we will see the Sybil attack and selective forward attack can detect by key features.

Rules for detection

a) *Max repeat time for a message:* The same message can be retransmitted by the same neighbor must lower than the excepted times. Desychronisation and Flood attacks can be detected by this rule.

b) *Radio transmission range:* All messages was transmitted to the neighbor nodes by a node must use its own radio range, and originated (previous hop) from one of its neighbors. Attacks like Radio jamming, Wormhole and Hello flood, where the intruder sends messages to a far located node using a more powerful radio, can be detected by this rule.

c) *Collision in a node:* the max message number of collisions must be lower than the expected number in the network. Radio jamming and Flood attacks can detected by using this rules.

d) *Integrity of a message:* the message data must be the same along the path from its source node to the destination node, for there is no message data aggregation in our target networks. If a message was modified by the attacker, this rule can detect the intruder.

e) *Interval time for message:* the time between two consecutive messages for the receiver node cannot larger or smaller than the allowed limits. Several attacks such as Hello flood and Flood attack can be detect by this rule.

5 A Lightweight IDSs Scheme

Our proposed algorithm was divided into the following three phases, we show it in figure 1: a) data collection: in this phase, the monitor nodes using a window classify function in a promiscuous mode to collect messages within its radio range. And the important information is filtered and classified before being stored, for subsequent analysis. b) Rules application and instruction detection: in this phase, the rules are applied to the stored data. If the messages do not obey the rules and a failure is raised, we can detect an intrusion. If there are no any rules to match the left data then we use the following phase. c) Key features application and intrusion detection: in b), some of the messages cannot be recognized by rules, and then we use relevant key features to detect the behavior of these nodes. Such as Physical attack, Selective forwarding attack and Sybil attack can be detect in this phase.

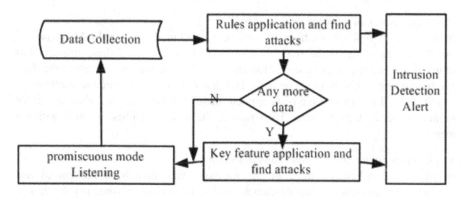

Fig. 1. The architecture of IDSs

Data collection
In this phase, messages are listened in promiscuous mode by the monitor mode and the important information is filtered, classified and stored for future analysis. The Important information includes some important behavior of the sensors message data which will be used for rules application and key features application.

The amount of the collect messages was decided by the window function. The time is divided into slices, the window function takes several slices time, the window function is dynamic and the time decided by the results of IDSs. In Algorithm 1, we give the technique described above.

Algorithm 1. Adjust window function with detection history

With initialization MT the Monitor nodes do

$$Current_{MT} = MT$$

For all neighbors do

For all rules and key features do

If $Current_{MT} < \max_{MT}$ then

If detected unknown message data then

$$Current_{MT} = Current_{MT} + \Delta T$$

Else if ($Current_{MT} > MT$) then

$$Current_{MT} = Current_{MT} - \Delta T$$

End if

End if

End for

End for

From Algorithm 1, we can see if find any unknown message data, the monitor node need more message data to decide whether it is a normal data or abnormal data.

Rules application and instruction detection:
In data collection phase, we have got some classified message data. In this phase, we use these data apply to the rules. If a message fails in one of these rules, at this moment, the message can be discarded and no other rule will be applied to the data. We have adopted this strategy due to the fact that WSNs have resource restrictions.

When of all our rules have been applied, there still have message data left in the monitor mode's storage space. Then we use the following phase to deal with the message.

Key features application and intrusion detection:
In the rules application, most of the message data have been recognized and discarded. In this phase we use the remains of the data to extract some key features of these data. If a message data fails in one of these key features, at this moment, as in rules application phase, the message will be discarded.

After using our key features, if there still has some message data. It means that we cannot recognize these data for a limited data, so we need to gather more data to detect these data. We just leave these data for next turn to detect. As show in algorithm 1, we need more time to gather data.

6 IDSs Simulator and Attacks

There have existed several simulators developed or adapted for WSNs, such as SensorSim [17], TOSSIM, Power TOSSIM [18] and WiSNAP [19]. But, unfortunately, none of them are appropriate for our purpose. Then we have developed our own WSNs simulator using C++ and Matlab 7. We use C++ to implement Physical layer and   Data link layer. Network layer and Transport layer were implemented using Matlab 7.

Our simulator is composed of the following modules: WSNs, message data, sensor node, monitor node, intruder node, events and attacks generator, IDSs and reporter. In our simulator, we use 200 sensor nodes, 20 monitor nodes, 4 intruders. The monitor node only monitors all of the neighbors within its radio range.

In our networks, two types of occasional network failures, eleven types of intruder attacks from Physical layer to Transport layer that we have describe in section 3.2. The two types of failures: 1) Packet collision: a packet is lost while being transmitted and its source node detects the loss due to a collision.2) packet loss: a packet sent by a node is lost while being transmitted and its source node is not known of the loss event. Occasional network errors follow a probabilistic model, which takes place with a message is sent by a node. All these occasional networks errors are from 5% to 25% in our simulator. The initial window size for data collection is 5T (T is the unit of time), ΔT is 2T. And the rules and key features application time for monitor node is 2T, at this moment, the monitor node does not listening the channel.

7 Simulation Results

Some types of attack not related to network occasional error such as packet collision and packet loss. We classify these attacks into three types.1) not related with network errors 2) related with packet collision 3) related with packet loss. And the results are shown from Figure 2 to Figure 5.

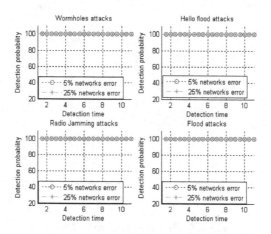

Fig. 2. Four kinds of attacks with IDSs

Wormhole attack, Hello attack, Radio Jamming and flood attacks. These attacks are not mistaken with any kind of occasional networks errors, so the detection probability is not influenced by the probability of occasional errors and detection time. That means all these attacks can be detected by rules application.

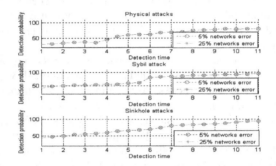

Fig. 3. Three kinds of attacks with IDSs

Physical attacks, Sybil attacks, Sinkhole attacks are not influenced by networks errors, all these attacks not easy been detected by rules application. From the Figure 3, we can see that we need much more data and longer data collection time for our scheme to analyze these kinds of attacks. In physical attacks, some of sensor nodes maybe apart from networks by intruders. Rules application is not easy to detect the attackers, we use key features application to detect the attackers, and find the numbers of neighbor and route table changed. Sybil attacks usually let the neighbors of node to be changed, and Sinkhole attacks can be detected by route table.

Collision attack can be confused with the message collision occasional failure. From the result we can know it is one of the attacks with better detection results, i.e.,

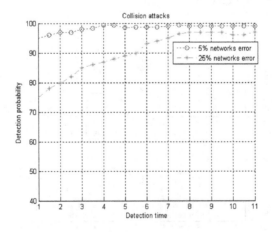

Fig. 4. Collision attacks with IDSs

with 5% network error, it can detect almost 100% in simulation run time. And with 25% network error, it can detect more than 90% intrusion for a period of run time. Because in our schemes, we need longer data collection time to get more data for us to detect this kind of attack.

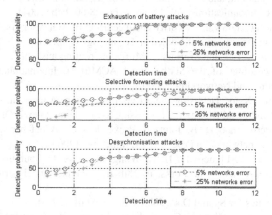

Fig. 5. Three kinds of attacks with IDSs

Exhaustion of battery attacks, Selective forward attacks and desychronisation attacks are related with network errors. Exhaustion of battery attacks is not much sensitive with network errors. This kind of attack can let sensor repeat send packets or let these nodes to use much energy sources to compute. The simulation results show that our scheme can detect this attack for a period of time. And almost 100% attacks can be detected. Selective Forward attack are sensitive with network errors, from the results we can see the network with 5% error, at the first period of time, only 80% attacks can be detected, but later, it can detect almost 100% of the attacks. The Desychronisation attacks usually are confused by packet loss. With network error, at the fist time, it can only detect lower than 50% attacks. But for a period of run time, the monitor node gather more message data, the monitor node can more effectively detected this kind of attack.

8 Conclusion

An important issue for security in WSNs is how to detect attacks in an accurate and suitable time. In this paper, we have made three important contributions to this work. First, we have presented an intrusion detection scheme for sensor networks, which uses rules application to detect these known attacks. Second, we have identified a general set of key features that can be used to characterize the WSNs behaviors in a network for intrusion detection, and are potentially applicable to detect unknown attacks. Third, we have proposed a dynamic technique to gather the amount of message data for IDSs. With the growing importance of sensor network applications, our scheme helps to provide a more accurate guarantee of the actual time to detect the intrusion in WSNs.

References

1. Y. Zhang and W. Lee. Intrusion Detection in Wireless Ad-Hoc Networks. In Proc. ACM MobiCom, pages 275-283,(2000).
2. A. Mishra, K. Nadkarni, and A. Patcha, "Intrusion detection in wireless ad hoc networks", IEEE Wireless Communications, vol. 11, no. 1, pp. 48-60, Feb (2004).
3. S. Bhargava and D. Agrawal, "Security enhancements in AODV protocol for wireless ad hoc networks", in Proceedings of Vehicular Technology Conference, (2001).
4. S. Marti, T. Giuli, K. Lai, and M. Baker, "Mitigating routing misbehavior in mobile ad hoc networks", Proceedings of the Sixth annual ACM/IEEE International Conference on Mobile Computing and Networking, (2000)..
5. Bo Yu and Bin Xiao. Detecting Selective Forwarding Attacks in Wireless Sensor Networks. In Parallel and Distributed Processing Symposium, 2006. IPDPS (2006).
6. Y.-C. Hu, A. Perrig, and D. B. Johnson, Packet leashes: A defense against wormhole attacks in wireless networks, in Proc of IEEE Infocomm (2003).
7. W. R. Pires, T. H. P. Figueiredo, H. C. Wong,and A. A. F. Loureiro, Malicious node detection in wireless sensor networks, in 18th Int'l Parallel and Distributed Processing Symp, (2004).
8. N. Cressie, Statistics for Spatial Data, John Wiley & Sons, (1993).
9. Laurent Eschenauer and Virgil D. Gligor. A keymanagement scheme for distributed sensor networks. In Proceedings of the 9th ACM Conference on Computer and Communication Security, pages 41–47,November (2002).
10. Wenliang Du, Jing Deng, Yunghsiang S. Han, Shigang Chen and Pramod Varshney. A Key Management Scheme for Wireless Sensor Networks Using Deployment Knowledge. In Proceedings of the IEEE INFOCOM'04, March 7-11, 2004, Hongkong. Pages 586-597
11. K. Ilgun, R. A. Kemmerer, and P. Porras, State transition analysis: A rule-based intrusion detection approach, IEEE Trans on Software Engineering, 21 (1995), pp. 181–199.
12. K. Ilgun, Ustat: A real-time intrusion detection system for unix, in Proc of IEEE Computer Society Symp on Research in Security and Privacity, May (1993).
13. V. Paxon, Bro: A system for detecting network intruders in real-time, in Proc of USENIX, USENIX Security, (1998).
14. P. A. Porras and P. G. Neumann, Emerald: Event monitoring enabling responses to anomalous live disturbances, in Proc of 20th NIST-NCSC Nat'l Info Systems Security Conf, 1997, pp. 353–365.
15. Haiguang Chen, Peng Han ,Bo Yu, Chuanshan Gao A New Kind of Session Keys Based on Message Scheme for Sensor Networks   The Seventeenth Asia Pacific Microwave Conference (APMC 2005 Dec. 4-7, (2005) Suzhou , China
16. A. D.Wood and J. A. Stankovic, "Denial of service in sensor networks," Computer,vol. 35, no. 10, pp. 54–62, (2002).
17. S. Park, A. Savvides, and M. B. Srivastava, Sensorsim: A simulation framework for sensor networks, in Proc of the 3rd ACM Int'lWorkshop on Modeling, Analysis and Simulation of Wireless and Mobile Systems, (2000), pp. 104–111.
18. V. Shnayder, M. Hempstead, B. rong Chen,G. W. Allen, and M. Welsh, Simulating the power consumption of large-scale sensor network applications, in Proc of the 2nd Int'l Conf on Embedded Networked Sensor Systems, (2004), pp. 188–200.
19. Stephan Hengstler and Hamid Aghajan, WiSNAP: A Wireless Image Sensor Network Application Platform. In Proc. of 2nd Int. IEEE/Create-Net Conf. on Testbeds and Research Infrastructures for the Development of Networks and Communities, Barcelona, Spain Mar. (2006).

ASITL: Adaptive Secure Interoperation Using Trust-Level

Li Jin and Zhengding Lu

Department of Computer Science & Technology,
Huazhong University of Science & Technology, Wuhan 430074, China
jessiewelcome@126.com

Abstract. The development of network and distributed computing has aroused more and more information exchange between far away servers and clients. Many traditional access control systems based on certificates or predefined access control policies are insufficient to deal with abnormal access requests or hidden intrusions. A flexible and efficient mechanism is needed to support open authentication and secure interoperations. In this paper, we address this issue by proposing an Adaptive Secure Interoperation system using Trust-Level (ASITL), which involves a statistical learning algorithm to judge an access request event, an adaptive calculating algorithm to dynamically adjust a user's trust-level and a self-protecting mechanism to prevent the system from potential risks. In particular, we also presented examples to demonstrate the secure working flow of ASITL.

Keywords: Access Control; Secure Interoperation; Trust-level.

1 Introduction

The development of network has made it necessary to extend access to distributed areas. How to share information without sacrificing the privacy and security has become an urgent need. Many kinds of protection devices have come into being, such as firewall, intrusion detection system and access control system. Traditional protecting technology is defined as granting or denying requests to restrict access to sensitive resources [1, 2], the central thrust of which is preventing the system from ordinary mistakes or known intrusions.

The emergence of trust-oriented access control technologies has promised a revolution in this area. With the wide spread of large-scale decentralized systems, more and more researchers have introduced the concept of "trust" to improve a system's security degree. It always involves risk-evaluation for a network activity or a user's historical reputation. For a secure interoperation system, a simple decision of "trust" or not is too insufficient to deal with the following security problems:

- *Dishonest network activities*: A user may have behaved honestly until he is regarded as a "trust" one, then he starts to do malicious activities.
- *Identity spoofing*: A dangerous user may steal validity certificates to replace the real "trust" host to receive services which he does not have privilege.

C.C. Yang et al. (Eds.): PAISI 2007, LNCS 4430, pp. 117–128, 2007.
© Springer-Verlag Berlin Heidelberg 2007

- *Authentication risk*: The underlying assumption of an authentication-based interoperation system is that users already know each other in advance. However, interoperations often take place between strangers, even between different security domains. Users from different domains who don't know each other need to exchange large amount of information every day.

How to maintain the largest compatible security without sacrificing local autonomy is the main challenge for each secure interoperating system. There are many researchers who have amply discussed the importance of "trust" in a dynamic access control system and reached many achievements. However, how to change an abstract concept of "trust" into a numeric value was insufficiently discussed. For an application-oriented secure model, it is more important than the concept to realize a secure interoperation. The activation of this paper is drawn by this idea, as well as the following issues: establishment of "trust" is not permanent, adaptive secure interoperation needs fine-grained abnormal judging strategies, and sensitive information exchanging should be related with the trust degree of the requestor.

To solve these problems, we introduced a new quantitative concept "trust-level" to access control policies and developed a novel Adaptive Secure Interoperation System using Trust-Level (ASITL). To realize a real-time protection for the system, ASITL enhances the accuracy of abnormal events judging mechanism with a statistical learning algorithm, automatically adjusts trust-level for the current user, and finally makes decision according to the trust-level. In Section 2, we discuss some related achievements of secure interoperation and trust management in recent years. We describe the whole architecture and working flow of the ASITL in Section 3. The trust evaluation module which involves abnormal judging mechanism and trust-level calculating algorithm is discussed in Section 4. Concluding remarks is added in Section 5.

2   Related Works

Several research efforts have been devoted to the topic of trust strategies in secure interoperations and trust management.

Ninghui Li and John C. Mitchell proposed RT, which combines the strengths of Role-based access control and Trust-management systems [3]. It constructed a logic trust management framework that followed role-based access control strategies, without special statements for "trust".

Similarly, "trust" in [4] was not described as a security evaluating feature. They mainly discussed the delegation depth control and proposed RT_{+0} , which is a significant improvement for RT_0 in a trust-management system.

Some trust services, such as trust establishment, negotiation, agreement and fulfillment were reported in [5], [6] and [7]. Although they concluded many security factors that might influence the trust degree of an interoperation, they did not propose a formulized metric to quantize it.

Furthermore, Elisa B. et al. discussed secure knowledge management, focusing on confidentiality, trust, and privacy [8] and Kilho S. et al. presented a concrete protocol for anonymous access control that supported compliance to the distributed trust management model [9], both of which represented novel achievements in this area.

As mentioned above, our framework which integrates access control, statistical learning and trust-level evaluating leads to a number of advantages in a secure interoperation environment.

- A dishonest user can not deceive the authentication server to reach his true intention. Once a dishonest network activity is detected, the user's trust-level will be decreased and he will not be granted any further privileges. Therefore, many potential risks can be efficiently forbidden.
- To get a higher trust-level, a user seeking to any advanced service has to submit correct certificate and obey rules all the time.
- With a statistical learning algorithm, event a new intrusion or an unknown event can also be learned and added into the abnormal events DB.
- A valid user from a different domain, who does not have a local identity, also can take part in an authentication and ask for corresponding services.

3 An Overview of ASITL Framework

ASITL system is distributed into three parts: user domain, trust authentication domain and service domain. The trust authentication domain is the kernel of the system. The main secure interoperation is processed in it. To enhance the efficiency, the authentication server responds to a valid user and directly transfers his requests to a corresponding application server. Otherwise, if the authentication server receives any unconventional requests or suspicious certificates, such as a non-local user's requests or an intrusion behavior, Trust Evaluating Module will be triggered at once. During the whole process of secure interoperation, Trust Evaluating Module constantly updates the trust-level with the results of abnormal judging mechanism and trust-level calculating algorithm.

3.1 Components

Figure 1 shows the architecture of ASITL that integrates both abnormal judging mechanism and trust-level calculating algorithm. Moreover, self-adaptability is always supported for abnormal events or unexpected situations. ASITL consists of eight components as follows:

Application server. It supplies corresponding service to valid users who can pass trust authentication.

Authentication server. With the results of Certificate Authentication, Access control policies, and if necessary, Trust-level Evaluation Module, it decides whether or not grant a request of current user.

Certificate authentication. It verifies the validity of certificates submitted by a requestor.

Certificates DB, which stores and manages privilege certificates.

Access control policies, which defines access control rules for the system.

Abnormal judging mechanism. As a part of Trust Evaluating Module, it involves a self-adaptive statistical learning algorithm which uses a probability method to define class for an abnormal event.

Trust-level calculating algorithm, which is the center algorithm of trust evaluating module. It defines a mathematic model to calculate trust-level value with an abnormal event's kind and its occurrence number.

Trust evaluation module. This module involves above two parts: Abnormal judging mechanism and trust-level calculating algorithm. When the authentication server receives an unqualified certificate or other abnormal data, Trust Evaluating Module can deal with mistakes at a tolerance degree and forbid malicious users. The detail discussion will be presented in Section 4.

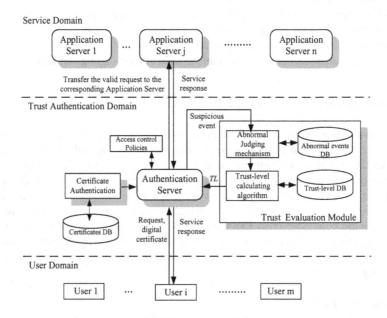

Fig. 1. ASITL system architecture

3.2 Working Flow

A typical session involving a trust interoperation working flow is described as follows:

1. A user sends a request to the authentication server.
2. According to user's request and access control policies, the authentication server asks for some necessary certificates.
3. The user submits some needed certificates:
   (1) If the certificates can satisfy the policies, the user's request will be transmitted to the corresponding application servers. In this case, the request is valid and the authentication server will transfer the responding service from the application server to the user. A secure interoperation is finished.

    (2) Otherwise, the authentication server sends further authentication requirements to the user and Trust Evaluation Module starts to work at once.
4. The user sends other certificates once more to further proof his identity.
5. The authentication server continues to authenticate the current user. Trust Evaluation Module real-time verifies abnormal events and updates the trust-level for the user.
    (1) If the user's trust-level is beyond the system's threshold value, the current session will be canceled and the user will be banned in the system for a predefined time-out period.
    (2) Otherwise, the user has to continue to submit some more certificates to verify his identity until his certificates satisfy the request and access control policies.

4 Trust Evaluation Module

Unlike a traditional access control model, which has to define policies for all possible requests in advance, the ASITL provides adaptive access control policies to enhance the flexibility of the system. It not only can satisfy ordinary users, but also can deal with the unpredictable situations, such as an accident mistake or a potential intrusion. Moreover, trust evaluation module has self-adaptability. When there are not available certificates for an authentication, the authentication server asks for further proofs and the trust evaluation module starts to work at once. In order to maintain consistency and simplicity, authentication server generates a user ID and maintains a history record for each user. A user ID is generated by an encrypting algorithm that combines the user's IP address and MAC address.

Generally, a trust observation period is a fixed interval of time, i.e., a threshold defined by system, or a period between two audit-related events. Firstly, abnormal judging mechanism uses a statistical learning algorithm to verify the kind of an abnormal event. Secondly, trust-level calculating algorithm updates the current trust value with the abnormal event kind and the occurrence number. Thirdly, an updated trust-level is returned to the authentication server. Finally, authentication server makes decision of granting or denying a privilege.

4.1 Abnormal Judging Mechanism

Ordinarily, a network event involves a set of intrinsic features, such as timestamp, req_IP, dst_IP, service, and so on. It is difficult to distinguish a normal event from an abnormal one with a single feature. In order to enhance adaptability and accuracy of this module, we apply a statistical learning algorithm which is based on multi-feature. Before describing the algorithm in detail, we define two concepts of *feature* and *class* for it.

Definition 1. Every network event contains a set of intrinsic features. When we analysis a network event, some of these features are essential, some of them are irrelevant. We call those essential features as key feature, named *feature*.

Definition 2. A feature can be divided into a mixture one or more topic kinds, named *classes*, which are associated with different kinds of network events.

Theorem 1. Supposing that

1. An event E in the abnormal events DB can be described with a feature set F ;
2. All features $f \in F$ are mutually exclusive and are associated with one or more of a set of classes C_k ;

3. A suspicious event E_i is observed by a feature set $F_J = \{f_1, f_2, ..., f_j, ... f_J\}$;

Then the index I of the most probable event E_i is given by

$$I = \arg\max_i \sum_J \left(\log p(C_{f(j)} \mid E_i) - \log p(C_{f(j)}) \right) \tag{1}$$

$p(X)$ denotes the probability of event X and $C_{f(j)}$ is the class that feature f_j is assigned.

Proof

Through the feature set, we can judge an event kind using Bayes algorithm:

$$p(E_i \mid F_J) = \frac{p(E_i)p(F_J \mid E_i)}{p(F_J)} \tag{2}$$

As the features are independent, we can induce that

$$p(E_i \mid F_J) = \frac{p(E_i)\prod_J p(f_j \mid E_i)}{\prod_J p(f_j)} \tag{3}$$

Assume that features are initiated by one of an equiprobable set of events $E_1, E_2, ..., E_m$ then

$$p(E_i \mid F_J) = \frac{1}{p(E_i)^{J-1}} \prod_J p(E_i \mid f_j) \tag{4}$$

Given a set of observed feature set F_J , we should calculate the value of $p(E_i \mid f_j)$. Let a feature is classified by one or more class C_k with probability $p(C_k \mid f_j)$, the relationship between C_k and E_i can be described as follows:

$$p(E_i \mid F_j) = \sum_K p(E_i \mid C_k)p(C_k \mid f_j) \tag{5}$$

According to the independency of features, we have

$$p(E_i \mid F_J) = \frac{1}{p(E_i)^{J-1}} \prod_J \sum_K p(E_i \mid C_k)p(C_k \mid f_j) \tag{6}$$

The training set can provide an estimate of $p(C_k \mid E_i)$, then by Bayes algorithm

$$p(E_i \mid C_k) = \frac{p(E_i)p(C_k \mid E_i)}{p(C_k)} \tag{7}$$

Therefore,

$$p(E_i \mid F_J) = \frac{1}{p(E_i)^{J-1}} \prod_J \sum_K \frac{p(E_i)p(C_k \mid E_i)}{p(C_k)} p(C_k \mid f_j)$$

$$= p(E_i) \prod_J \sum_K \frac{p(C_k \mid E_i)}{p(C_k)} p(C_K \mid f_j) \tag{8}$$

The index I of the most probable event E_i is given by $I = \arg\max\limits_i p(E_i \mid F_J)$

$$I = \arg\max\limits_i \left(p(E_i) \prod_J \sum_K \frac{p(C_k \mid E_i)}{p(C_k)} p(C_K \mid F_j) \right) \tag{9}$$

If a feature can be uniquely assigned to a single class and $C_{f(j)}$ is the class that feature f_j is assigned, then

$$p(E_i \mid F_J) = p(E_i) \prod_J \frac{p(C_{f(j)} \mid E_i)}{p(C_{f(j)})} \tag{10}$$

We use log formula in (10) then

$$I = \arg\max\limits_i \sum_J \left(\log p(C_{f(j)} \mid E_i) - \log p(C_{f(j)}) \right) \tag{11}$$

Theorem 1 is an improved statistical self-learning algorithm which based on a probability method to define the class of a suspicious event. With this machine learning algorithm, the whole flow chart of the abnormal judging module is given in Figure 2.

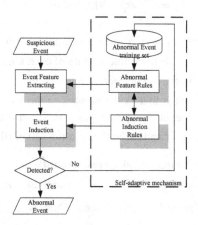

Fig. 2. Flow chart of abnormal judging mechanism

We realize the self-adaptability of this mechanism as follows:

Step 1: Initialize the events training set by extracting general features from large amount of abnormal events and learning to deduce some basic rules from current abnormal feature set.

Step 2: Receive an abnormal event which is needed to be classified.

Step 3: Extract the features and send them to the Event Induction module.

① If it can be divided into a known class, its abnormal kind will be transferred to the trust-level calculating module.

② Otherwise, the unknown features are sent back to the training set and update the current feature rules for next judging process.

4.2 Trust-Level Calculating Algorithm

With determinations made by the abnormal judging module, trust-level calculating algorithm updates the current user's trust-level and feeds back a quantitative "trust" value to the authentication server.

The trust-level evaluating module records the user ID and assigns trust-level according to the authentication server's request. The validity period of current trust-level is from user's login to logout. That is to say, a user's trust-level is valid during current interoperation. When an interoperation is finished or early cancelled, the finally trust-level of current user will be recorded in trust-level DB as a history record for next access request.

We use an adaptive evaluating algorithm to calculate the current user's trust-level. The output value changes according to the current user's activities. Once trust evaluating module receives an abnormal event, which can be specified by abnormal judging module, the interoperating user's trust-level will be changed.

Definition 3. A user's trust-level is defined as follows:

$$T_u = \frac{1}{k} \sum_{k=1}^{m} \alpha_k^{l_k} \quad (1 \le k \le m) \tag{12}$$

T_u denotes the trust-level of user u. m is the amount of abnormal events kinds as described in Section 4.1. α_k is the influence rate of each kind of event - a real number in the interval $[0,1]$. l_k is the occurrence number of event k. Consequently, T_u is in the range of $[0, 1]$. It is noted that as the number or the kinds of abnormal behaviors increases, the user's trust-level, T_u, approaches to 0. l_k starts as 0 to reflect there is no prior interaction between user and the authentication server (that is, unknown users).

Example 1. There are 3 kinds of abnormal event E_1, E_2, E_3 and their trust rates are α_1 =0.9, α_2 =0.7, α_3 =0.5. l_1, l_2, and l_3 denotes the occurrence number of E_1, E_2, E_3. Table1 shows T_u's going trend when E_1 events are detected. Table2 shows T_u's going trend when both E_1 and E_2 events are detected. Table3 shows T_u's going trend when all the kind of events are detected. We assume that l_1, l_2, and l_3 all follow the same increasing rate. *With the increasing of event kinds, the larger l_k, the faster the T_u decreases.*

Table 1. T_u on E_1 increasing

l_1	l_2	l_3	T_u
0	0	0	1.0000
3	0	0	0.9097
5	0	0	0.8635
7	0	0	0.8261
9	0	0	0.7958
11	0	0	0.7713
13	0	0	0.7514
15	0	0	0.7353

Table 2. T_u on E_1 and E_2 increasing

l_1	l_2	l_3	T_u
0	0	0	1.0000
3	3	0	0.6907
5	5	0	0.5862
7	7	0	0.5202
9	9	0	0.4759
11	11	0	0.4445
13	13	0	0.4213
15	15	0	0.4035

Table 3. T_u on E_1, E_2 and E_3 increasing

l_1	l_2	l_3	T_u
0	0	0	1.0000
3	3	3	0.3990
5	5	5	0.2633
7	7	7	0.1895
9	9	9	0.1432
11	11	11	0.1114
13	13	13	0.0880
15	15	15	0.0702

Example 2. Assuming there is a file access control system. With the sensitivity S of files, all files can be divided into three classes A, B, and C ($S_A > S_B > S_C$). To maintain secure levels of this system, we defines three different certificates C_1, C_2 and C_3 ($C_3 > C_2 > C_1$). A single certificate or certificate combinations grant different privileges. Furthermore, access control policies are defined in Table 4.

Table 4. File access control policies

File	Trust-level	Certificates	History Records
A	$0.7 \leq TL < 1.0$	C_1, C_2, C_3	$0.7 \leq AVG_{TL}$
B	$0.4 \leq TL < 0.7$	C_1, C_2	$0.4 \leq AVG_{TL}$
C	$0.1 \leq TL < 0.4$	C_1	$0.1 \leq AVG_{TL}$

There are three kinds of abnormal events E_1, E_2, E_3 and access control policy defines the lowest threshold of T_u, named T_{uT}, is 0.1000. Furthermore, E_1, E_2, E_3 and their trust rate α_1, α_2, α_3 are described as follows:

Certificate_Error_Event: a user presents a needless certificate. Although it is valid, it is not the right one that authentication server needed. This event may indicate a certificate mistake of the user. The trust influence rate of this event is α_1 =0.9.

Certificate_Invalidation_Event: a user presents an expired, damaged or revoked certificate. This event may indicate an attempt to a network fraud. The trust influence rate of it is α_2 =0.7.

Request_Overflow_Event: a user sends abnormally large amounts of requests. This event may indicate an attempt to a Dos attack or a virus intrusion. The trust influence rate of this event is α_3 =0.5.

Jimmy wants to access some files and sends a request with his identity certificate to the authentication server. The authentication server receives the request and certificates. But the server also detects some abnormal events. According to access control policies, Jimmy should submit more certificates to confirm a needed access privilege. Therefore, the authentication server returns a request for further proofs and starts Trust Evaluating module. This module firstly generates a user ID for Jimmy, secondly initializes a trust-level for him and then starts to monitor all network activities of him. To demonstrate the secure mechanism of ASITL, we assume three different possible results:

Jimmy is a malicious intruder: He does not have a valid certificate at all. From the beginning, he sends expired or damaged certificates to the authentication server continually. *Certificate_Invalidation_Event* is detected constantly and the occurrence number of it increases fast. When the occurrence number reaches a threshold amount, a new abnormal event—— *Request_Overflow_Event* may be detected. Once Jimmy's *TL* is below 0.1, he will be forbidden by the system. And the final *TL* with his ID will be recorded in the history record. If this result continually takes place more than five times, the user ID will be recorded in the Black List.

Jimmy is a potentially dangerous user: He only has a valid certificate C_1, so his privilege only can access the files of Class C. But his true intention is the more sensitive files of Class A or Class B. In order to accumulate a good reputation, he maintains a high *TL* ($0.4 \leq TL < 1.0$) and AVG_{TL} ($0.4 \leq AVG_{TL}$) by validly accessing Class C files with certificate C_1. In order to access more sensitive files, he presents an expired certificate C_2 or a fake certificate C_3. The abnormal event of *Certificate_Invalidation_Event* is trigged and his *TL* decreases fast. Without the valid certificates, he neither can access the wanted files nor maintain a high *TL*. Although Jimmy has owned a high *TL* and a good history record by dealing with less sensitive files C, his potential intention of more sensitive files A or B can never be reached.

Jimmy is a normal user: He sends file request and corresponding valid certificate to the authentication server. If his certificate is suited to the privilege of the request, his *TL* and history records can satisfy the access control policies, he will pass the authentication and his request will be responded by the application server.

5 Conclusions and Future Work

To supply secure interoperations for different security domains, we have proposed ASITL, an Adaptive Secure Interoperation system using Trust-level. The development of ASITL was guided by a set of desiderata for achieve a fine-grained access control system that maintains the most compatible security without sacrificing local privacy, including the necessary of a self-learning judging mechanism to adapt to unexpected or unconventional occasions that beyond access control definition, the ability of automatically evaluating user's trust degree by the real-time authentication activities and the support of tolerating all kinds of intrusions. "Trust-level" is a variable value which can efficiently reflect a user's trust degree by judging the behavior kinds and counting the occurrence number. Based on trust-level value, ASITL provably judges the validity of a new suspicious event, dynamically evaluates the user's trust degree and makes responds to the requestors. Furthermore, ASITL can be sure that all secure measures have been completed before sensitive information is exchanged.

There are many areas that need future work. First, we need to develop the ability and efficiency of the learning mechanism to shorten the responding period. For example, neural network algorithm or a similar method can also be used to abnormal judging mechanism. Moreover, we need design a comprehensive lifecycle for a secure interoperation. Second, we will further optimize the cooperating abilities among modules in the system to enhance the performance of the system. Finally, besides calculating a user's trust-level, trust evaluating for the authentication server will also be taken into account and users' privacy issues need to be investigated.

Acknowledgments. This paper is supported by the National Nature Science Foundation of China, Project Nos.60403027, 60502024, the Innovation Fund for Technology Based Firms of Ministry of Science and Technology of China under Grant No.04C26214201284, Nature Science Foundation of HuBei, Project No.2005ABA258.

References

1. Park, J., Sandhu, R.: RBAC on the Web by smart certificates. In: Endler, M., Schmidt, D. C., (eds.): Proceedings of 4th ACM Workshop on Role-Based Access Control, ACM Press, Fairfax, VA(1999)1-9
2. Bonatti, P., Vimercati, S., Samarati, P.: A modular approach to composing access control policies. In: Sushil, J., Pierangela, S., (eds.): Proceedings of 7th ACM Conference on Computer and Communication Security, ACM Press, Athens, Greece (2000) 164-173

3. Li, N., Mitchell, J., Winsborough, W.: RT: A role-based trust-management framework. In: Bemmel, J., McCray, A., (eds.): Proceedings of 3rd DARPA Information Survivability Conference and Exposition (DISCEX III). IEEE Computer Society Press, Washington (2003) 201-212

4. Fan, H., Xian, Z., Shaobin, W.: Delegation Depth Control in Trust-management System. In: Shih, T., Shibata Y., (eds.): Proceedings of 19th International Conference on Advanced Information Networking and Applications, Vol.2. IEEE Computer Society Press, Taiwan (2005) 411-414

5. Xiong, L., Ling, L.: PeerTrust: Supporting Reputation-Based Trust for Peer-to-Peer Electronic Communities. IEEE Transactions on Knowledge and Data Engineering, Vol.16, No.7 (2004) 843-857

6. Bhavani, T.: Trust Management in a Distributed Environment. In: Bilof, R., (ed.): Proceedings of the 29th Annual International Computer Software and Application Conference, Vol.2. IEEE Computer Society Press, Edinburgh, Scotland (2005) 561-562

7. Nathan, D., Andras, B., David, E.: Using Trust and risk in Role-based Access Control Policies. In: Trent, J., Elena, F., (eds.): Proceedings of the 9th ACM Symposium on Access Control Models and Technologies, ACM Press, New York (2004) 156-162

8. Kilho, S., Hiroshi, Y.: Provably Secure Anonymous Access Control for Heterogeneous Trusts. In: Anderson, S., Felici, M., (eds.): Proceedings of the 1st International Conference on Availability, Reliability and Security. IEEE Computer Society Press, Vienna, Austria (2006) 24-33

9. Bertino, E., Khan, L., Sandhu, R.: Secure Knowledge Management: Confidentiality, Trust, and Privacy. IEEE Transactions on Systems, man, and Cybernetics. Vol. 36, No.3 (2006) 429-438

A RT0-Based Compliance Checker Model for Automated Trust Negotiation*

Zhensong Liao and Hai Jin

Services Computing Technology and System Lab
Cluster and Grid Computing Lab
School of Computer Science and Technology
Huazhong University of Science and Technology, Wuhan, 430074, China
hjin@mail.hust.edu.cn

Abstract. Compliance checker is an important component for *automated trust negotiation* (ATN) to examine whether the credentials match the access control policies. A good design for compliance checker helps to speed up trust establishment between parties during the negotiation, and can also improve negotiation efficiency. Unfortunately, it has been noted that compliance checker has got little attention in design and implementation. On the contrary, more work has been spent on the algorithms on how to protect sensitive information. A RT_0 based compliance checker (RBCC) model for ATN is presented in this paper. We give its architecture and workflow, and illustrate how it works through a practical example. The case study shows that the model satisfies compliance checker's basic requirements and provides good information feedback mechanism to protect sensitive information.

1 Introduction

Exchange of attribute credentials is an important means to establish mutual trust between strangers who wish to share resources or conduct business transactions. ATN [1][2][3] provides an approach to regulate the flow of sensitive attributes during such an exchange. In every ATN system, there is a vital component called compliance checker. Compliance checker aims at examining whether the user's digital credentials satisfy local resource's access control policies.

Compliance checker must satisfy the basic requirements before it can serve for ATN. The requirements of compliance checker in ATN are listed as follows [2] (Suppose Alice is a resource provider, while Bob is a user).

a. Compliance checker modes. There are two distinct compliance checker modes. The first is the traditional way a compliance checker plays in the *trust management* (TM) environment. The compliance checker produces a Boolean result indicating whether or not the credentials satisfy the policy. PolicyMaker adopts this way and returns a justification when the access is denied [4]. The

---

* The paper is supported by National Natural Science Foundation of China under grant No.90412010.

C.C. Yang et al. (Eds.): PAISI 2007, LNCS 4430, pp. 129–140, 2007.

second is required when some sensitive policies are disclosed. For example, suppose Alice wants to deny Bob's access to a sensitive resource because Bob presents insufficient credentials. Rather than simply throw "access denied", Alice will give a hint to guide the negotiation to a successful conclusion.

b. Credential validity. During trust negotiation, Alice's runtime system must validate the credentials Bob discloses. It is required that the integrity of the credential contents should be verified using the digital signature of the credential to guard against forgery. Thereto, the verifier should know the credential issuer's public key of the root credential in the chain. Moreover, if a policy states that the credential cannot be revoked, the runtime system must know how to carry out this examination.

c. Credential ownership. Usually, Alice's policy requires that Bob be the owner of the credential he submits, i.e., the owner of the leaf credential of a chain, or some other subjects mentioned in the chain. To accomplish this, Alice's runtime system requires Bob to prove ownership of the private key.

d. Credential chain discovery. Often, the prerequisite credentials in a trust negotiation may not be readily available locally. Compliance checker should provide a mechanism to solve distributed credential chain discovery problem.

Compliance checker plays a key role for ATN. A well-designed compliance checker has many properties such as: (1) Supporting disclosure of sensitive information. Sensitive information includes secret credentials and important access control policies. Compliance checker can provide a secure mechanism to gradually disclose credentials and access control policies by using efficient policy languages, or effective communication protocols. (2) Protecting sensitive policy. Compliance checker can prevent information leakage and purposive attacks by adopting particular techniques, such as hidden credentials [5], OSBE [6]. (3) Popular feedback approach. If a compliance checker makes use of well-defined feedback mechanism, it helps to improve successful negotiation rate. For instance, *Know* [7] is a good example to make feedback come true. If *Know* is introduced to compliance checker, it makes ATN better.

In this paper, a *RT$_0$-Based Compliance Checker* (RBCC) model for ATN is proposed. RBCC adopts *ordered binary decision diagram* (OBDD) [7] as its policy tree to provide disclosure and protection of sensitive information, and uses improved feedback mechanism based on *Know* to provide justification. Generally, our work has the contributions as follows:

a. It is the first time to make much emphasis on design and implementation of compliance checker. Early work has a default idea that compliance checker just goes on a match between credentials and access control policies, while ignores that compliance checker has a great impact on negotiation efficiency and successful negotiation rate.

b. It is the first time to introduce role-based trust management (RT) policy language to implement a compliance checker model. RT_0 is easy to understand and convenient in expression, which is adequate to meet the requirements of compliance checker.

c. For the first time we add well-defined feedback mechanism to compliance checker, which improves resource's access availability.

The reminder of this paper is organized as follows. Section 2 discusses the related work about compliance checker. Since RBCC is based on RT_0, so we give a simple overview of RT and RT_0 in Section 3. In Section 4, we present the detailed description of RBCC, including its architecture, workflow and implementation. In Section 5, we use a practical example to show how RBCC works. Section 6 summarizes the features of RBCC. Section 7 concludes the paper.

2 Related Work

Since compliance checker is used to check whether the revealed credentials satisfy access control policies or not, the notion of compliance checker appears when TM becomes an issue to be studied. PolicyMaker [4] uses the traditional compliance checker mode to realize the match between credentials and policies, and returns a justification when access is denied so as to guide access to success. KeyNote [8] adopts a modified compliance checker mode, which especially supports the specification of a user-defined justification whenever the result is false. During trust negotiation, KeyNote determines whether to grant access to a sensitive service or to disclose a sensitive credential or policy. M. Blaze et al [9] propose a network layer security architecture, where the compliance checker determines how an action requested by principals should be handled, given a policy and a set of credentials. As a matter of fact, these work emphasized on the mode.

Recently, much attention is paid on some components and requirements of compliance checker. For one thing, to meet the requirement of credential validity, various types of credentials are designed and developed due to different applications. X.509 [13] and PGP [14] are typical identity credentials, while SPKI/SDSI [15] serves as attribute credentials. To meet the requirement of credential ownership, many digital signature algorithms of high secure level appear to prove ownership of the private key associated with the public key used to identify the subject in the credential, such as RSA [16]. To meet the requirement of credential chain discovery, N. Li et al present lot of efficient algorithms to solve this problem [10].

On the other hand, much work focuses on how to protect sensitive information during the match between credentials and access control policies. N. Li et al [1] present TTG protocol and ACK policy to achieve the goal. J. E. Holt et al [5] propose hidden credentials to ensure the security of credentials and policies. OACerts [11] is another important means to avoid leakage of sensitive information. Similar techniques are discussed in [2]. However, these techniques just serve for some components of compliance checker, and the global notion of compliance checker becomes more and more oblivious.

We design a model for compliance checker according to its requirements. Compliance checker has four basic requirements. We have a modification towards the traditional mode and adopt RT_0 to satisfy the other three requirements. Our work differs from early work as follows:

a. We design a compliance checker model according to the basic requirements, which accomplishes and unifies the functionalities. Researchers have realized almost all of the functions of compliance checker, but they do not integrate the functions into a unified compliance checker.

b. We enrich the functions of compliance checker, which help to guide the trust negotiation to success. In our model, we adopt 0-1 table [3] to check the policy consistency. We add a feedback component to handle the failure negotiation. If the access is denied, the feedback component is triggered to guide the negotiation process.

c. Our model has the property of protecting sensitive information. We use a certain strategy to ensure that both parties cannot get more information from the negotiation. Users do not need to disclose more credentials than they can access the resource.

3 An Overview of RT_0

RT_0, presented in [10], is a popular and most basic language in the RT family of TM languages. In RT family, there are four classes of languages. RT_0 defines the basic roles, RT_1 adds the parameters for roles, RT^T supports *Separation of Duty (SoD)*, and RT^D works for delegation of role activations. In this section we focus on RT_0.

3.1 The Basic Knowledge of RT_0

The basic constructions of RT_0 include entities and role names. Entities are also called principals, which are used to identify credentials. Policy statements take the form of role definitions. A role definition contains a head and a body. RT_0 has four common types and two extensible types:

- Simple Member: $A.r \leftarrow B$. This credential means A defines B to be a member of A's r role, i.e., $B \in members(A.r)$.
- Simple Containment: $A.r \leftarrow B.r_1$. This credential means A defines its r role to include all members of B's r_1 role, i.e., $members(B.r_1) \subseteq members(A.r)$.
- Linking Containment: $A.r \leftarrow A.r_1.r_2$. $A.r_1.r_2$ is called a linked role. This means $members(A.r_1.r_2) = \cup_{B \in members(A.r1)} members(B.r_2 \subseteq members(A.r)$.
- Intersection Containment: $A.r \leftarrow B_1.r_1 \cap ... \cap B_k.r_k$. This defines $A.r$ to contain the intersection of all roles $B_1.r_1, ..., B_k.r_k$.
- Simple Delegation: $A.r \Leftarrow B:C.r_2$. This means A delegates its authority over r to B, and B can delegate it to $C.r_2$. It equals to $A.r \leftarrow B.r \cap C.r_2$.
- Linking Delegation: $A.r \Leftarrow B.r_1:C.r_2$. This means A delegates its authority over r to members of $B.r_1$, and the delegation is restricted to members of $C.r_2$.

3.2 Support for Compliance Checker

In [12], K. E. Seamons et al had a detailed analysis and overview of policy languages, including RT_0. Trust negotiation has a lot of requirements towards policy languages, such as well-defined semantics authentication. RT_0 has a good semantic foundation. In RT_0, policy statements are translated into DATALOG rules, which guarantee that the semantics is precise and algorithmically tractable. Besides, RT_0 has a good support for vocabulary agreement, which makes RT_0 overwhelming and distinguished from others. In short, RT_0 meets the requirements of credential validity, credential ownership, distributed credential chain discovery, sensitive policies, which ensures that RBCC is secure enough to protect the transmitting message.

3.3 Relevant Illumination

Usually, access control policy has two types: simple policy and complex policy [5]. Simple policy is the basic expressive unit, also called meta-policy, while complex policy consists of many simple policies. RBCC adopts three types of operations to decompose complex policy into simple ones:

- *AND*: to incorporate policies into a uniform one. For instance, *Policy=(P₁ AND P₂)* means P_1 and P_2 are both required to be satisfied.
- *OR*: to select one from the policy expression. For instance, *Policy=(P₁ OR P₂)* means only one of P_1 and P_2 is required to be satisfied.
- *MofN(m, P₁, P₂, ..., Pₙ)*: to choose *m* policies from *n* policies. For instance, *Policy=MofN(2, P₁, P₂, P₃)* means arbitrary two policies in {P_1, P_2, P_3} are required to be satisfied, the policy-set could be {P_1, P_2}, {P_1, P_3} or {P_2, P_3}.

Additionally, RBCC introduces a feedback mechanism to assist trust negotiation when the access is denied. RBCC uses OBDD to construct policy graph. OBDD is a canonical form representation for Boolean formulas where two restrictions are placed on binary decision diagrams: the variables should appear in the same order on every path from the root to a terminal, and there should be no isomorphic subtrees or redundant vertices in the diagram. Fig. 1 is an example of OBDD expression. From Fig. 1, we can see that OBDD depends on the numbers and the order of variables.

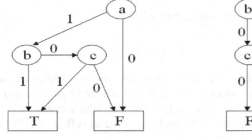 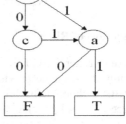

(a)OBDD in the order of a,b,c: a∧(b∨c)   (b) OBDD in the order of b,c, a : a∧(b∨c)

Fig. 1. OBDD example in different order for a∧(b∨c)

4 RT₀-Based Compliance Checker

In this section, we will give the detail description of RBCC, including the architecture, the workflow, and the simple implementation.

4.1 The Architecture of RBCC

Fig. 2 shows the architecture of RBCC based on the goal and functionality of compliance checker. RBCC consists of four components as follows:

- Consistency Checker: to detect whether there exists a conflict in resource's access control policies. This guarantees that every input access control policy is valid and effective, and avoids unwanted negotiation failure.

- Validity Checker: to examine the validity of users' disclosed local credentials. In order to prevent unauthorized access to resource, the goal of validity checker is to filtrate all invalid or spurious credentials, and helps to clear up illegal access.
- Matching Service: as the main component to check whether the disclosed local credentials fit for resource's access control policies. In addition, the matching service must ensure that the important content of user's credentials should not be leaked so that users' privacy can be effectively protected.
- Feedback Service: as a user-oriented interface by returning justification to indicate what credentials a user should submit to gain access. It is triggered when the access is denied. It gives hints to users while sensitive policies are hidden.

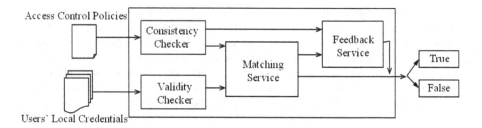

Fig. 2. The architecture of RBCC

4.2 The Workflow of RBCC

For the purpose of general use, RBCC can be realized as a secure middleware. Before trust negotiation, the resource provider should edit access control policies and input them into RBCC. Since RBCC is designed for ATN, which requires that the insensitive access control policies should be published. The workflow of RBCC is as follows:

a. Consistency Checker receives access control policies and has an examination of polices' consistency. First, consistency checker decomposes the input policy into many meta-policies. Then, consistency checker uses 0-1 table to analyze all possible results. In 0-1 table, 0 represents *False*, while 1 stands for *True*. Later, consistency checker summarizes the 0-1 results and classifies the policies into three types: 1) Incompatible policy, i.e., the access control policy has conflicts, and the results are all *False*. For example, suppose complex policy P can be expressed as $P=P_1 \wedge P_2$, where $P_1=P_0$, $P_2= \neg P_0$, then $P \equiv False$ and is incompatible. 2) Acceptable policy, i.e., the results include some *True* and some *False*. 3) Non-recommended policy, i.e., there exists no conflicts in the complex policy, but all the results are *True*. When a policy is a non-recommended one, the trust negotiation is always successful even if the user does not disclose any credential. Non-recommended policy means that the complex policy is of no effect and deserves not being recommended.

b. Validity Checker receives a user's local credentials, including identity credentials and attribute credentials, and uses a certain algorithm to identify whether the user is the ownership of the credentials.

c. Matching Service takes the parameters of access control meta-policies and credentials. Matching service lists all the possible credential-sets, which meet the requirement of policy, and uses the credentials to match the credential-sets. If it returns *True*, we say that the credentials satisfy the requirement of the policy, and the trust is established. Otherwise, the access is not granted and the feedback service will be triggered.

d. Feedback service is invoked to provide feedback to users about why the access is denied. The feedback service constructs a policy graph using OBDD and gives justifications according to self-defined rules so as to protect sensitive information.

4.3 The Implementation of RBCC

In this section, we will give the detail description on how to implement the components of RBCC.

4.3.1 0-1 Table for Consistency Checker

0-1 table [3] is an effective method to list all the possible results of a policy expression. For instance, the policy "The high performance computers of CGCL lab provide open cluster computing. Everyone who is a professor, a teacher or a PhD can use it directly. Otherwise, if a user is a graduate (Ms) and also a team-leader, he can use it too." can be expressed as: $Policy=(P_1 \ OR \ P_2 \ OR \ P_3 \ OR \ (P_4 \ AND \ P_5))$, where P_i can be satisfied by C_i and C_1: $CGCL.Professor \leftarrow User$, C_2: $CGCL.Teacher \leftarrow User$, C_3: $CGCL.PhD \leftarrow User$, C_4: $CGCL.Ms \leftarrow User$, C_5: $CGCL.Teamleader \leftarrow User$. The corresponding 0-1 table can be expressed as Table 1. Table 1 shows that CGCL policy is an acceptable one, and tells us the basic satisfied credential-sets are $\{C_1\}$, $\{C_2\}$, $\{C_3\}$ and $\{C_4, C_5\}$.

Table 1. 0-1 table for CGCL policy

P_1	P_2	P_3	P_4	P_5	Policy
1	X	X	X	X	1
X	1	X	X	X	1
X	X	1	X	X	1
X	X	X	1	1	1
0	0	0	0	X	0
0	0	0	X	0	0

(Note: 0 represents False, 1 represents True, X represents 0 or 1)

4.3.2 Signature Check Technique to Realize Validity Checker

Every credential has a pair of public key and private key. The public key is open and used as an identifier or a principle of a credential, while the private key is kept secret. The goal of validity checker is to identify whether the user has the private key corresponding to the public key. RBCC adopts an oblivious signature algorithm to handle it. The checking process is as follows:

a.   To check the validity of the received credentials. RBCC proposes a checking function: $Verify_{PK}[M, s]$, where, $Verify$ is the name of function, PK is the credential's public key, M is the content of the credential, s is the signature and $s=sig_{PK}(M)$. If $Verify_{PK}[M, s]=True$, the credential is valid and legal.

b.   To ensure that the user has the corresponding private key. The system administrator randomly picks a string a, encrypts it with PK, and gets $E_{PK}(a)$. He passes it to the user. If the user possesses the private key, he can decrypt it and get a'. Then he sends a' back. If $a=a'$, the user holds the credentials.

The above process guarantees non-forgery and integrity of credentials, which meets the requirements of credential validity and ownership.

4.3.3   Credential-Set Comparison for Matching Service

Consistency Checker adopts 0-1 table to confirm coherence of access control policies, and it also generates the basic credential-sets for the policy. Matching service reuses the credential-sets to check whether the disclosed digital credentials satisfy the policy. RBCC provides a series of functions to deal with it.

- *PolicyToCredential(Policy)*: To map meta-policy to their credential. Since each meta policy has a corresponding credential, this function is to generate the credential of *Policy*, i.e., $PolicyToCredential:P_i{\rightarrow}C_i$.
- *GenerateCredentialset(Policy)*: To generate basic credential-sets for complex policy. The function scans the 0-1 table and produces basic credential-sets according to the policy's *True* results.
- *MatchCredential(Cred, Credential-set)*: To examine whether a credential-set belongs to user's submitted credentials *Cred*. For instance, the CGCL policy's basic credential-set can be expressed as $Credential\text{-}set_{CGCL} =\{\{C_1\}, \{C_2\}, \{C_3\}, \{C_4,C_5\}\}$. If $\exists c{\subseteq}Credential\text{-}set_{CGCL}$, and $c{\subseteq}Cred$, then the user's credentials meet the requirement of the access control policy.

4.3.4   Rules for Feedback Service

If the access is denied by matching service, it means the user has not disclosed enough credentials or relevant ones. Feedback service guides user to attain successful access through providing feedback according to man-made rules based on *Know* [7]. The rules should be effective and able to protect sensitive information.

- **Rule 1.** Feedback is hierarchical

Different users have various feedbacks. For example, a professor and a PhD access the same secret system, the professor may get "Non-work period, please change another time", while the PhD may get "Sorry, your permission is limited, please change your role and try again".

- **Rule 2.** Shift of roles is much difficult than shift of contents

Usually, every user has a fixed role in a period. In this case, asking the user to change his role means the failure of such trust negotiation. The rule tries to ensure that the user can use his current role to grant access as possible.

- **Rule 3.** Feedback should not involve sensitive information

ATN discloses its access control policy before the negotiation process. Often, released policy is not sensitive. If the policy is somehow sensitive, its disclosure will only happen when trust relationship comes to a certain level. This rule prevents information leakage and unauthorized attack.

As far as the cost to carry out the rules is concerned, the cost depends on the practical applications. The feedback mechanism is based on *Know* and uses OBDD to provide hints. In [7], the authors evaluate *Know*, and specify that OBDD is just a representation of the access control policy, it can be constructed ahead of time and only need to be re-computed if the policy is changed. The runtime overhead to find the suggestion is negligible – in the order of milliseconds, i.e., the implementation of the rules had no performance overhead on successful requests.

5   A Case Study for RBCC

Suppose there is a scenario described as follows: CGCL provides online high performance cluster computing. Everyone who is a professor, a teacher or a PhD can use it directly. Or, if a user is a graduate (Ms) and also a team-leader, he can use it too. Otherwise, if the user satisfies arbitrary two items in {principal granted, user from HP, scientific project}, the access is allowed.

This policy can be expressed as:

$$Policy=(P_1 \ OR \ P_2 \ OR \ P_3 \ OR \ (P_4 \ AND \ P_5) \ OR \ MofN(2, \ P_6, \ P_7, \ P_8))$$

In *Policy*, C_1: *CGCL.Professor←User*, C_2: *CGCL.Teacher←User*, C_3: *CGCL.PhD ←User*, C_4: *CGCL.Ms←User*, C_5: *CGCL.Teamleader←User*, C_6: *CGCL.Principal-granted←User*, C_7: *HP.clerk←User*, C_8: *Project.Class←Science*.

When CGCL's policy is input into consistency checker, it will generate the policy's basic credential-set. *Credential-set={{C_1}, {C_2}, {C_3}, {C_4, C_5}, {C_6, C_7}, {C_6, C_8}, {C_7, C_8}}*.

Suppose Tom to be a clerk and programmer from Lenovo. He wants to have an image-searching test. That is, he has a credential set *Cred*, including at least: C_A: *lenovo.clerk←Tom*, C_B: *lenovo.programmer←Tom*, C_C: *Test.Class←Science*, i.e., C_A, C_B, $C_C \in Cred$. He submits *Cred* to request for cluster computing. CGCL server checks *Cred*, matches it with *Credential-set* and finds that only C_C is acceptable and can be treated as C_8. Then the access is denied.

Feedback service analyzes *Cred*, considers Tom's identity and makes suitable feedback. The feedback can be expressed as Fig. 3, in which 3(a) shows the policy decomposition; 3(b) gives the OBDD graph. Since Tom is a user of Lenovo, so meta-policy P_7 should not be revealed so as to avoid unauthorized inference. (If P_7 reveals, Tom would like to think that CGCL and HP might have a cooperation or business transaction.) Based on this consideration, 3(b) ignores the node for P_7.

Turn to this scenario. Tom proposes *Cred*, including C_A, C_B and C_C. To take three rules into account, the feedback information will be "Your access is not allowed. You are welcome if you get CGCL principal's authorization". The feedback tells Tom why his access is denied and how to attain the access. Here illustrates how the rules play. Since Tom is not a member of CGCL, so the feedback information comes from the right subtree. In order to protect sensitive information, it cannot reveal "You are welcome if you are a member of HP". Meanwhile, Tom may have some difficulty in changing his role so that it needs not to show "Please change your identity to a role of CGCL".

Cluster : Policy
Policy ↔ $P_A \vee P_B$
P_A ↔ User $\in$ CGCL $\wedge$ ($P_1 \vee P_2 \vee P_3 \vee (P_4 \wedge P_5)$)
P_1 ↔ User.role=Professor
P_2 ↔ User.role=Teacher
P_3 ↔ User.role=PhD
P_4 ↔ User.role=Ms
P_5 ↔ User.role=Teamleader
P_B ↔ User $\notin$ CGCL $\wedge$ (($P_6 \wedge P_7) \vee (P_6 \wedge P_8) \vee (P_7 \wedge P_8$))
P_6 ↔ Principal.granted=True
P_7 ↔ User.role=HP
P_8 ↔ Project.Class=Science
Meta-policy:
P_7 : false

(a) Policy decomposition

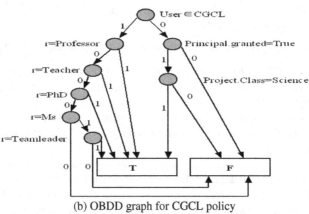

(b) OBDD graph for CGCL policy

Fig. 3. Feedback expression example

6 Features of RBCC

From the above description, RBCC has features as follows:

a. Meeting all the requirements of compliance checker. In RBCC, validity checker is used to meet the requirements of credential validity and credential ownership. RBCC adopts RT_0 to support credential chain discovery.

b. Supporting consistency of access control policy. In order to avoid negotiation failure derived from the conflicts of access control policy, RBCC designs a component, consistency checker, to ensure the policy's validity. Meanwhile,

0-1 table provides an effective and efficient method to generate policy path, which greatly improves searching efficiency.

c. Protection of sensitive information. During the policy decomposition, the sensitive policies are hidden. The OBDD graph prevents sensitive information from revealing so that each negotiator can get nothing during the negotiation process.

d. Flexible feedback mechanism. The feedback mechanism of RBCC is based on *Know* [7], which is successfully implemented and applied in some access control systems. RBCC improves *Know* by modifying the cost function and rules to generate flexible feedback.

e. Easy to extend and migrate. From Fig. 2 and the above description, we can see that when designing user-defined interfaces to RBCC, for example, letting users draw access control policy, allowing editing feedback and so forth, RBCC can be integrated as a secure middleware for ATN. It shows that RBCC can be easily extended and migrated.

7 Conclusions

Compliance checker plays a key role in ATN. In this paper, we design and implement a RT_0-based compliance checker model for ATN. We propose the architecture and workflow of RBCC, and illustrate how to implement every component in RBCC. We adopt 0-1 table to examine whether the access control policies are valid, which can avoid unwanted failing trust negotiation from the start. We add a component to check the legitimacy of the digital credentials. We also introduce a flexible feedback component to cooperate the parities.

References

[1] W. H. Winsborough and N. Li. Towards practical automated trust negotiation. In *Proceedings of the 3rd International Workshop on Policies for Distributed Systems and Networks*. IEEE Computer Society Press, 2002, pp.92-103.

[2] Z. Liao, H. Jin, C. Li, and D. Zou. Automated trust negotiation and its development trend. *Journal of Software*. 2006, Vol.17, No.9, pp.1933-1948 (in Chinese with English abstract).

[3] H. Jin, Z. Liao, D. Zou, and W. Qiang. A new approach to hide policy for automated trust negotiation. In *Proceeding of the 1st International Workshop on Security (IWSEC'06)*. Springer Press, LNCS, Vol.4266, 2006, pp.168-178.

[4] M. Blaze, J. Feigenbaum, and M. Strauss. Compliance checking in the PolicyMaker Trust Management System. *Financial Cryptography 1998*, pp.254-274.

[5] J. E. Holt, R. Bradshaw, K. E Seamons, and H. Orman. Hidden credentials. In *Proceedings of 2nd ACM Workshop on Privacy in the Electronic Society*. ACM Press, 2003, pp.1-8.

[6] N. Li, W. Du, and D. Boneh. Oblivious signature-based envelope. In *Proceeding of the 22nd ACM Symposium on Principles of Distributed Computing*. ACM Press, 2003, pp.182-189.

[7] A. Kapadia, G. Sampemane, and R. H. Campbell. *Know*: Why Your Access Was Denied: Regulating Feedback for Usable Security. In *Proceeding of the 22nd ACM Symposium on Computer and Communication Security*. ACM Press, 2004, pp.74-84.

[8] M. Blaze, J. Feigenbaum, J. Ioannidis, and A. D. Keromytis. The KeyNote Trust-Management System. *RFC 2704*, September 1999.

[9] M. Blaze, J. Ioannidis, and A. D. Keromytis. Trust Management and Network Layer Security Protocols. In *Proceedings of ACM Transactions on Information and System Security*. ACM Press, 2002, pp.95-118.

[10] N. Li, W. H. Winsborough, and J. C. Mitchell. Distributed credential chain discovery in trust management. *Journal of Computer Security*, 2003, 11(1):35-86.

[11] J. Li and N. Li. OACerts: Oblivious Attribute Certificates. In *Proceeding of 3rd Conference on Applied Cryptography and Network Security*. ACM Press, 2003, pp. 108-121.

[12] K. E. Seamons, M. Winslett, T. Yu, B. Smith, E. Child, J. Jacobson, H. Mills, and L. Yu. Requirements for Policy languages for Trust Negotiation. In *Proceeding of 3rd IEEE Intel Workshop on Policies for Distributed Systems and Networks*. IEEE Computer Society Press, 2002, pp.68-79.

[13] International Telecommunication Union. Recommendation X.509 – Information Technology – Open System Interconnection – The Directory: Authentication Framework. Aug, 1997.

[14] S. Capkun, L. Buttyan, J. P. Hubaux. Small worlds in security systems: an analysis of the PGP certificate graph. In *Proceeding of the 2002 Workshop on New Security Paradigms*. IEEE Computer Society Press, 2002, pp.187-201.

[15] D. Clarke, J. E. Elien, C. Ellison, M. Fredette, A. Morcos, and R. L. Rivest. Certificate chain discovery in SPKI/SDSI. *Journal of Computer Security*. 9(4):285-322, 2001.

[16] R. L. Rivest, A. Shamir, and L. M. Adleman. A method for obtaining digital signatures and public key crytosystems. *Communications of the ACM*. ACM Press, 1978, pp. 120-126.

TCM-KNN Algorithm for Supervised Network Intrusion Detection

Yang Li[1,2], Bin-Xing Fang[1], Li Guo[1], and You Chen[1,2]

[1] Institute of Computing Technology, Chinese Academy of Sciences, Beijing China, 100080
[2] Graduate School of Chinese Academy of Sciences, Beijing China, 100080
liyang@software.ict.ac.cn

Abstract. Intrusion detection is a hot topic related to information and national security. Supervised network intrusion detection has been an active and difficult research hotspot in the field of intrusion detection for many years. However, a lot of issues haven't been resolved successfully yet. The most important one is the loss of detection performance attribute to the difficulties in obtaining adequate attack data for the supervised classifiers to model the attack patterns, and the data acquisition task is always time-consuming which greatly relies on the domain experts. In this paper, we propose a novel network intrusion detection method based on TCM-KNN (Transductive Confidence Machines for K-Nearest Neighbors) algorithm. Experimental results on the well-known KDD Cup 1999 dataset demonstrate the proposed method is robust and more effective than the state-of-the-art intrusion detection method even provided with "small" dataset for training.

Keywords: network security, supervised intrusion detection, TCM, TCM-KNN algorithm, machine learning, data mining.

1 Introduction

With the increasing of network applications and the attacks coming with it, intrusion detection is an urgent and necessary technique for information and national security. Intrusion Detection System (IDS) are application systems which automate the process network intrusion monitoring process, analyzing and response on real time security problems. It plays vital role of detecting various kinds of attacks.

The two basic methods of intrusion detection are signature based and anomaly based [1], [2]. The signature-based method, also known as misuse detection, looks for a specific signature to match, signaling an intrusion. They can detect many or all known attack patterns, but they are of little use for as yet unknown attack methods. Most popular intrusion detection systems fall into this category. Anomaly detection focuses on detecting unusual activity patterns in the observed data and they can detect unknown attacks compared to the signature based methods while with unavoidable high false positives. Moreover, the supervised network intrusion detection is the very commonly used and effective branch in signature based methods. They usually adopt a lot of mature data mining and machine learning algorithms to construct classifier from the provided attack dataset for intrusion detection.

C.C. Yang et al. (Eds.): PAISI 2007, LNCS 4430, pp. 141–151, 2007.

In this paper, we propose a new supervised intrusion detection method based on TCM-KNN (Transductive Confidence Machines for K-Nearest Neighbors) algorithm for intrusion detection. TCM-KNN algorithm is commonly used data mining method and effective in fraud detection, pattern recognition and outlier detection. To our best knowledge, it is the first time that TCM-KNN algorithm is applied to the field of supervised intrusion detection introduced by us. Experimental results demonstrate it has good detection performance (high detection rate and low false positives) than the state-of-the-art intrusion detection techniques. Most importantly, its detection performance doesn't deteriorate obviously without adequate attack data for training, while the traditional techniques cannot as we all known. In addition, it can be further optimized for reducing the computational cost after employing feature reduction.

The rest of this paper is structured as follows. We overview the related work in Section 2 and introduce the principles of TCM-KNN (Transductive Confidence Machines for K-Nearest Neighbors) algorithm in Section 3. Section 4 details our TCM-KNN Algorithm for intrusion detection. Section 5 illustrates the relevant experiments and evaluations. We conclude our work in Section 6.

2   Related Work

In the past decades, various of machine learning methods, data mining methods, especially supervised methods have been proposed for intrusion detection and have made great success [3-7].

MADAM ID (Mining Audit Data for Automated Models for Intrusion Detection) [14] is one of the best well-known data mining projects in intrusion detection. It is an off-line IDS to produce anomaly and misuse intrusion models. Association rules and frequent episodes are applied in MADAM ID to replace hand-coded intrusion patterns and profiles with the learned rules. ADAM (Audit Data Analysis and Mining) [15] is the second most widely known and well published project in the field. It is an on-line network-based IDS. ADAM can detect known attacks as well as unknown attacks. Association rules and classification, two data mining techniques, are used in ADAM. IDDM (Intrusion Detection using Data Mining Techniques) [16] is a real-time NIDS for misuse and anomaly detection. It applied association rules, meta rules, and characteristic rules. IDDM employs data mining to produce description of network data and uses this information for deviation analysis.

Other data mining algorithms are also applied to intrusion detection. For example, decision tree and fuzzy association rules are employed in intrusion detection [17, 18]. Neural network is used to improve the performance of intrusion detection [19]. Support Vector Machine (SVM) is used for unsupervised anomaly detection [8].

However, the detection performance when employing the above traditional data mining methods is still not satisfactory. Meanwhile, for the past several years, very few effective supervised network intrusion detection methods has been proposed. The main reason is that the training dataset especially attack training data for supervised learning is very difficult to acquire in realistic network environment, it thus has great negative impact on their performances, i.e., results in not very good true positives and false positives. Hence, how to boost the detection performance of current intrusion detection techniques under the environment of lacking adequate training set for modeling is a formidable and promising job.

3 Principles of TCM-KNN

Transduction has been previously used to offer confidence measures for the decision of labeling a point as belonging to a set of pre-defined classes [9, 10]. Transductive Confidence Machines (TCM) introduced the computation of the confidence using Algorithmic Randomness Theory. The confidence measure used in TCM is based upon universal tests for randomness, or their approximation. The transductive reliability estimation process has its theoretical foundations in the algorithmic theory of randomness developed by Kolmogorov. Unlike traditional methods in machine learning, transduction can offer measures of reliability to individual points, and uses very broad assumptions except for the iid assumption, that is, the training as well as new (unlabelled) points are independently and identically distributed. It thus does not make any assumption about the data distributions.

It was proved that there exists a universal method of finding regularities in data sequences. Unfortunately, universal tests are not computable, and have to be approximated using non-universal tests called p-values [11]. In the literature of significance testing, the p-value is defined as the probability of observing a point in the sample space that can be considered more extreme than a sample of data. This p-value serves as a measure of how well the data belongs to a certain class.

The task of TCM-KNN algorithms can be described as follows: imagine we have a training set of n elements in hand, $X_i = \{x_i^1, x_i^2, ..., x_i^n\}$ is the set of feature values for point i and y_i is the classification for point i, taking values from a finite set of possible classifications. We also have a test set of s points similar to the ones in the training set, our goal is to assign to every test point one of the possible classifications. For every classification we also want to give some confidence measures. Furthermore, we denote the sorted sequence (in ascending order) of the distances of point i from the other points with the same classification y as D_i^y. Also, D_{ij}^y represents the jth shortest distance in this sequence and D_i^{-y} for the sorted sequence of distances containing points with classification different from y. We assign to every point a measure called the individual strangeness measure. This measure defines the strangeness of the point in relation to the rest of the points. In our case the strangeness measure for a point i with label y is defined as

$$\alpha_{iy} = \frac{\sum_{j=1}^{k} D_{ij}^{y}}{\sum_{j=1}^{k} D_{ij}^{-y}} \tag{1}$$

where k is the number of neighbors used. Thus, our measure for strangeness is the ratio of the sum of the k nearest distances from the same class to the sum of the k nearest distances from all other classes. This is a natural measure to use, as the strangeness of a point increases when the distance from the points of the same class becomes bigger or when the distance from the other classes becomes smaller [12].

Provided with the definition of strangeness, we will use Equation (2) to compute the p-value as follows:

$$p(\alpha_{new}) = \frac{\#\{i : \alpha_i \geq \alpha_{new}\}}{n+1} \tag{2}$$

In Equation (2), # denotes the cardinality of the set, which is computed as the number of elements in finite set. α_{new} is the strangeness value for the test point (assuming there is only one test point, or that the test points are processed one at a time), is a valid randomness test in the iid case. The proof takes advantage of the fact that since our distribution is iid, all permutations of a sequence have the same probability of occuring. If we have a sequence $\{\alpha_1, \alpha_2, ..., \alpha_m\}$ and a new element α_{new} is introduced then α_{new} can take any place in the new (sorted) sequence with the same probability, as all permutations of the new sequence are equiprobable. Thus, the probability that α_{new} is among the j largest occurs with probability of at most $\dfrac{j}{n+1}$.

4   Intrusion Detection Based on TCM-KNN Algorithm

From the earlier discussions, we can see TCM-KNN algorithm is good for detect intrusions according to the network flow because it is a classical problem of classification in essence. In TCM-KNN, we are always sure that the point we are examining belongs to one of the classes.

Figure 1 illustrates the TCM-KNN algorithm applied to intrusion detection. In the algorithm, a series of the points represent the network traffic to be determined which includes several preset features, such as the connection duration, number of packets passed in two seconds, etc. There are only two classes available for intrusion detection, "0" for normal traffic and "1" for abnormal traffic. Meanwhile, the algorithm diagnoses only one point at a time.

Therefore, according to the algorithm, to find out the strangeness α for the training dataset, we require $O(n^2)$ comparisons, where n is the number of data instances in training dataset. We observe that this step is done off-line and only once, before the detection of intrusions starts. However, if n is very large, the off-line computation may still be too costly. In addition, in the process of detection, we should recalculate the strangeness value for each test instance whenever the distance between the training instance and the new instance is less than the largest of the k distances that are used to compute the strangeness α. Moreover, the distance calculation cost also relies on the dimensions of vectors representing the points. If it is big, it might meet the "curse of dimensionality". Therefore, the computational costs greatly attribute to the scale of training dataset and the dimensions of vectors. In this case, to alleviate the complexity, we may sample the dataset, employ feature selection, and perform comparisons only with the sampled and dimension-reduced data. We perform experiments to be discussed in next section that show that this is a reasonable method to handle large datasets, with little or no significant deterioration of the results.

It is worth nothing here that just only classifying the network traffic into two classes is reasonable both in theory and practice. TCM-KNN algorithm will benefit from it for greatly reducing the computational cost based on the above analyses, and

---

Parameters: k (the nearest neighbors to be used), m (size of training dataset), c (available classes, "0" for normal and "1" for abnormal), r (instance to be determined)

for $i = 1$ to m {

        calculate D_i^y and D_i^{-y} according to definition (1) for each one in training dataset and store;

        calculate strangeness α for each one in training dataset and store;

    }

for $j = 1$ to c {

        for each instance t in class j

            if($D_{tk}^j > $ dist(t,r))

                add r in j and recalculate strangeness for t ;

        for each instance t not in class j ,

            if($D_{tk}^{-j} > $ dist(t,r))

                add r in j and recalculate strangeness for t ;

    }

calculate the strangeness of r for class j ;

calculate the p-value of r for class j ;

classify instance r as class with the corresponding largest p-value, and with confidence (1- the second largest p-value) and return;

Fig. 1. TCM-KNN algorithm

also the intrusion detection performance will not deteriorate in our experiences from a series of adequate experiments.

When applying the algorithm to the real applications, it should include two important phases: training phase and detection phase. In the first phase, three important jobs should be considered:

a) Data collection for modeling: representative data for attack and normal network behaviors should be collected for our method to modeling. However, the attack data is rare and very difficult to obtain thoroughly, we will solve the problem by adopting "small" dataset for training, it is relatively easy and reasonable. The experiments in Section 5.2 will detail the discussions.

b) Feature selection & vectorlize: the core computational cost of our TCM-KNN algorithm attributes to the distance calculation of feature vectors. Therefore, we should extracted several important features those can distinguish the ongoing attacks utmostly and form the feature vectors. For instances, the statistic information of network flow level and packet level will be considered to gather for forming the relevant features. They are mostly the same as those in KDD Cup 1999 dataset whose connections meta infos have been abstracted as 41 features, while in realistic network environment, the reduced and extended features must be emphasized.

c) Modeling by TCM-KNN algorithm: for the last step, TCM-KNN algorithm introduced in this paper then calculates the strangeness and p-value for each instance in the training dataset as discussed in Figure 1, thus to construct the intrusion detection classifiers.

For the detection phase, all the real-time data collected lively from the network also should be preprocessed to vectors according to the selected features having been acquired in training phase, then would be directed to the intrusion detection engine based on TCM-KNN, benign or malicious traffic would be determined.

5 Experiments and Discussions

In order to verify the effectiveness of our TCM-KNN algorithm for the field of intrusion detection, we take use of the well-known KDD Cup 1999 Data (KDD 99) [13] to make relevant experiments step by step. Firstly, we make contrast experiments between TCM-KNN algorithm and the most commonly used and effective supervised algorithms in intrusion detection, including SVM algorithm, Neural Networks, KNN (K-Nearest Neighbors) algorithm; Secondly, we contrast the detection performance of our method and the above classical algorithms under the circumstance of lacking adequate training dataset (provided with smaller training dataset). Finally, we make experiments in order to validate the performance of TCM-KNN algorithm when we selected a feature subset from the KDD 99 dataset in case of the "curse of dimensionality".

5.1 Experimental Dataset and Preprocess

All experiments were performed in a Windows machine having configurations Intel (R) Pentium (R) 4, 1.73 GHz, 1 GB RAM, and the operation system platform is Microsoft Windows XP Professional (SP2). We have used an open source machine learning framework – Weka [20] (the latest Windows version: Weka 3.5). Weka is a collection of machine learning algorithms for data mining tasks. The algorithms can either be applied directly to a dataset or called from your own Java code. Weka contains tools for data pre-processing, classification, regression, clustering, association rules, and visualization. It includes the machine learning algorithms (SVM, Neural Networks, KNN) to be compared with the proposed method in this paper for our next experiments. We have used the KDD 1999 Cup labeled dataset so as to evaluate our method.

As our test dataset, the KDD 99 dataset contains one type of normal data and 24 different types of attacks that are broadly categorized in four groups such as Probes, DoS (Denial of Service), U2R (User to Root) and R2L (Remote to Local). The packet information in the original TCP dump files were summarized into connections. This process is completed using the Bro IDS, resulting in 41 features for each connection. Therefore, each instance of data consists of 41 features and each instance of them can be directly mapped into the point discussed in TCM-KNN algorithm.

We sampled our experimental dataset from the KDD 99 dataset. We extracted 49402 instances as training set for our experiments. They include 9472 normal instances, 39286 DoS instances, 127 U2R instances, 112 R2L instances and 405 instances for Probe.

Before beginning our experiments, we preprocessed the dataset. First, we normalized the dataset. For the numerical data, in order to avoid one attribute will dominate another attribute, they were normalized by replacing each attribute value with its distance to the mean of all the values for that attribute in the instance space. In order to do this, the mean and standard deviation vectors must be calculated:

$$mean[j] = \frac{1}{n}\sum_{i=1}^{1} ins\tan ce_i[j] \tag{3}$$

$$s\tan dard[j] = \sqrt{\frac{1}{n-1}\sum_{i=1}^{n}(ins\tan ce_i[j] - mean[j])^2} \tag{4}$$

From this, the new instances can be calculated by dividing the difference of the instances with the mean vector by the standard deviation vector:

$$newins\tan ce[j] = \frac{ins\tan ce[j] - mean[j]}{s\tan dard[j]} \tag{5}$$

This results in rendering all numerical attributes comparable to each other in terms of their deviation from the norm. For discrete or categorical data, we represent a discrete value by its frequency. That is, discrete values of similar frequency are close to each other, but values of very different frequency are far apart. As a result, discrete attributes are transformed to continuous attributes.

Moreover, the experiments employed Euclidean distance metric to evaluate the distance between two points. The metric is defined as follows:

$$dis\tan ce(Y_1, Y_2) = \sqrt{\sum_{j=1}^{|Y_1|}(Y_{1j} - Y_{2j})^2} \tag{6}$$

where Y_1 and Y_2 are two feature vectors, Y_{ij} denotes the jth component of Y_i and $|Y_i|$ denotes the length of vector Y_i.

To evaluate our method we used two major indices of performance: the detection rate (also named true positive rate, TP) and the false positive rate (FP). TP is defined as the number of intrusion instances detected by the system divided by the total number of intrusion instances present in the test set. FP is defined as the total number of normal instances that were incorrectly classified as intrusions divided by the total number of normal instances.

5.2 Contrast Experimental Results

In the contrast experiments, we first used the extracted dataset for training and test. Moreover, since the "attack" training data is very difficult to obtain and usually scarce, we resampled a smaller dataset (4940 instances) that is ten times smaller than that discussed in section 5.1, and the distributions of instances for normal, DoS, U2R, R2L, Probe are 922, 3954, 25, 11 and 28 respectively. Hence, we use it to test whether our method is still robust and effective when provided with "small" dataset. All the experiments are employed ten-fold cross validation method, that is, pick out 90% of the dataset for training and the rest 10% for test for each time, and repeat it for ten times. We use the average detection performance measures (TP and FP) for evaluation.

The experimental parameters for SVM, Neural Networks, KNN algorithms as well as TCM-KNN algorithm were set respectively as follows. We use c-svc SVM algorithm, select radius basis function as kernel type in Weka. For KNN algorithm, k was set to 50, employ linear nearest neighbors search algorithm. As for neural networks, we take back propagation algorithm, use only one layer for all the input, output and hidden layer. Dimension for the hidden layer is set as (attribute+class)/2. We set the parameter K of our TCM-KNN algorithm 50. It is worth noting that in these experiments we repeat the experiments to adjust the parameters of each algorithm for optimization, and use their most ideal results for comparison. Therefore, it would make the contrast experimental results more persuasive.

Table 1. Experimental results on common dataset

	TP (%)	FP (%)
SVM	99.5	0.01
Neural Network	99.8	0.01
KNN	99.2	0.32
TCM-KNN	99.7	0

Table 2. Experimental results on smaller dataset

	TP (%)	FP (%)
SVM	98.7	0.73
Neural Network	98.3	1.24
KNN	97.7	4.83
TCM-KNN	99.6	0.12

Table 1 and Table 2 show the detail running results of various supervised intrusion detection methods both when provided with adequate training dataset and with "small" training dataset. It is clear that although our method demonstrates just a little higher TP and lower FP than SVM and KNN methods in common cases when provided with adequate attack data, its detection performance is amazingly good than the other methods when lacking adequate attack data for training, since the false positive rate of them sharply increased while TCM-KNN not.

5.3 Experimental Results Using Selected Features

For the next experiment, we have performed Chi-Square approach on KDD 99 to acquire the most relevant and necessary features from the 41 features. It is natural and necessary because as discussed in Section 4, the performance of TCM-KNN algorithm may deteriorate when meeting the "curse of dimensionality". By doing this, we can validate if our algorithm is robust and effective under the circumstance of adopting feature selection as well as reducing the training set to alleviate the computational cost.

The selected features and the experimental results are listed as Table 3 and Table 4 respectively. Table 4 shows the performance of our method is good both on original KDD 99 (TP=99.7%, FP=0) and on the dataset after employing feature selection (TP=99.6%, FP=0.03%). Although the FP increased a little, but it's still very manageable, thus we can argue it is possible to use a reduced-dimension dataset to detect anomalies without significant loss of performance.

Table 3. Feature selection results based on Chi-Square approach

Rank	Feature
1	dst_host_same_srv_rate
2	dst_host_diff_srv_rate
3	dst_host_same_src_port_rate
4	src_bytes
5	dst_bytes
6	count
7	hot
8	num_compromised

Table 4. Experimental results on total and selected features

	Without feature selection	After feature selection
TP	99.7%	99.6%
FP	0	0.03%

5.4 Discussions

From the above experimental results, we can clear catch that our method based on TCM-KNN algorithm prevails over the state-of-the-art intrusion detection techniques. Experimental results show it can more effectively detect intrusions with low false positives.

Intuitively, our method fulfills intrusion detection tasks using all the available points already existing in training set to measure. Therefore, it could make correct detection decision by fully exploiting the strangeness discussed in Section 3 and 4. The experimental results both on the "smaller" dataset and on the dataset being employed feature reduction evident the computational cost of our method could be effectively reduced without any obvious deterioration of detection performance, and it can remain good detection performance even training with small dataset than the state-of-the-art supervised intrusion detection methods. In this sense, we may claim our method can be optimized to a good candidate for intrusion detection in the realistic network environment.

In addition, the method does not make assumptions about the data distributions and only requires the number of nearest neighbors utilized in the distance calculation. We claim the parameter needs not careful tuning and would not affect the detection performance seriously, which is consistent with the arguments in [12]. We employed an extensive experiment to support the conclusion and the experimental results are depicted in Table 5. The TP and FP measures are little sensitive to the selection of K as

Table 5. Experimental results on various K nearest neighbors

	K=10	K=20	K=50	K=100	K=200
TP	98.8%	99.1%	99.7%	99.6%	99.3%
FP	0.01%	0.01%	0.02%	0.03%	0.03%

the results listed in Table 5. Therefore, in the real applications, we could empirically select it without much consideration of its positive or negative effect on the detection performance of our TCM-KNN algorithm.

6 Conclusions and Future Work

In this paper, we proposed a novel supervised intrusion detection method based on TCM-KNN algorithm. Experimental results demonstrate its effectiveness and advantages over the traditional intrusion detection methods.

There is a lot of future work for us. First, how to reduce the training dataset without obvious loss of detection performance is very important, random sampling is not enough and combining active learning method [21] with TCM-KNN might be a good choice; Second, the most distinguished disadvantage of supervised intrusion detection method is that it need a great deal of attack data for building a classifier, this also arises in our method proposed in this paper. Therefore, we are working on improving the current TCM-KNN algorithm towards applying it to network anomaly detection, which only needs the normal data for detect malicious network traffic. Finally, transductive machine learning methods is a promising machine learning based technique for intrusion detection, combining it with other well-known classifiers such as SVM (that would result in TSVM method) might boost the classification performance of them, thereafter the detection performance when applying them to intrusion detection greatly than the traditional single machine learning methods. We will attempt to undertake the relevant research and experiments in our future work.

Acknowledgments. The work is supported by the National Key Projects for Basic Researches of China (973-project) (No. 2004CB318109).

References

1. Bykova, M., S. Ostermann, B. Tjaden: Detecting network intrusions via a statistical analysis of network packet characteristics. In: Proc. of the 33rd Southeastern Symp. on System Theory (SSST 2001), Athens, OH. IEEE (2001)
2. Denning, D.E.: An Intrusion Detection Model, IEEE Transactions on Software Engineering. (1987) 222-232
3. Lee, W., Stolfo, S. J.: Data Mining Approaches for Intrusion Detection. Proceedings of the 1998 USENIX Security Symposium (1998)
4. Ghosh, A., Schwartzbard, A.: A Study in Using Neural Networks for Anomaly and Misuse Detection. Proceedings of the 8th USENIX Security Symposium (1999)

5. Mahoney, M., Chan, P.: Learning Nonstationary Models of Normal Network Traffic for Detecting Novel Attacks. Proceeding of the Eighth ACM SIGKDD International Conference on Knowledge Discovery and Data Mining. Edmonton, Canada (2002) 376-385
6. Barbara, D., Wu, N., Jajodia, S.: Detecting Novel Network Intrusions Using Bayes Estimators, First SIAM Conference on Data Mining. (2001)
7. Ye, N.: A Markov Chain Model of Temporal Behavior for Anomaly Detection. Proceedings of the 2000 IEEE Systems, Man, and Cybernetics Information Assurance and Security Workshop, (2000)
8. Eskin, E., Arnold, A., Prerau, M., Portnoy, L., Stolfo, S. J.: A Geometric Framework for Unsupervised Anomaly Detection: Detecting Intrusions in Unlabeled Data. In D. Barbara and S. Jajodia (editors), Applications of Data Mining in Computer Security, Kluwer (2002)
9. Gammerman, A., Vovk, V.: Prediction algorithms and confidence measure based on algorithmic randomness theory. Theoretical Computer Science. (2002) 209-217
10. Li, M., Vitanyi, P.: Introduction to Kolmogorov Complexity and its Applications. 2nd Edition, Springer Verlag. (1997)
11. Proedru, K., Nouretdinov, I., Vovk, V., Gammerman, A.: Transductive confidence machine for pattern recognition. Proc. 13th European conference on Machine Learning. (2002) 381-390
12. Daniel Barbará, Carlotta Domeniconi, James P. Rogers: Detecting outliers using transduction and statistical testing. In: Proceedings of the 12th ACM SIGKDD international conference on Knowledge discovery and data mining. USA (2006) 55-64
13. Knowledge discovery in databases DARPA archive. Task Description. http://www.kdd.ics.uci.edu/databases/kddcup99/task.html
14. Wenke Lee, Salvatore J. Stolfo: A Framework for Constructing Features and Models for Intrusion Detection Systems. ACM Transactions on Information and System Security (TISSEC), Volume 3, Issue 4 (2000)
15. Daniel Barbarra, Julia Couto, Sushil Jajodia, Leonard Popyack, Ningning Wu: ADAM: Detecting Intrusions by Data Mining. Proceedings of the 2001 IEEE, Workshop on Information Assurance and Security T1A3 1100 United States Military Academy, West Point, NY (2001)
16. Tamas Abraham: DDM: Intrusion Detection Using Data Mining Techniques. DSTO Electronics and Surveillance Research Laboratory, Salisbury, Australia (2001)
17. Sara Matzner Chris Sinclair, Lyn Pierce: An Application of Machine Learning to Network Intrusion Detection, Proceedings of the 15th Annual Computer Security Applications Conference, Phoenix, AZ, USA (1999) 371-377
18. Jianxiong Luo, Susan M. Bridges: Mining Fuzzy Association Rules and Fuzzy Frequency Episodes for Intrusion Detection. International Journal of Intelligent Systems, Vol. 15, No. 8, (2000) 687-704
19. Richard P. Lippmann, Robert K. Cunningham: Improving Intrusion Detection Performance Using Keyword Selection and Neural Networks. Computer Networks (2000) 597-603
20. WEKA software, Machine Learning, http://www.cs.waikato.ac.nz/ml/weka/, The University of Waikato, Hamilton, New Zealand.
21. Tong., S.: Active Learning: Theory and Applications. PhD thesis, Stanford University, California (2001)

Research on Hidden Markov Model for System Call Anomaly Detection

Quan Qian and Mingjun Xin

School of Computer Engeering and Science, Shanghai University, Shanghai 200072, China
qq@ustc.edu
{qqian,xinmj}@staff.shu.edu.cn

Abstract. Intrusion detection, especially anomaly detection, requires sufficient security background knowledge. It is very significant to recognize system anomaly behavior under the condition of poor domain knowledge. In this paper, the general methods for system calls anomaly detection are summarized and HMM used for anomaly detection is deeply discussed from detection theory, system framework and detection methods. Moreover, combining with experiments, the detection efficiency and real-time performance of HMM with all-states transition and part-states transition are analyzed in detail in the paper.

Keywords: Hidden Markov Model, Host System Calls, Anomaly Detection.

1 Introduction

Through pre-defining system normal parameters, for instance, CPU usage rate, memory usage rate, file checksum, etc. defined by security experts or deduced with statistical method by observing system running, Anomaly detection is comparing the system run-time values with the pre-defined parameters to recognize whether or not the system is attacked [1]. The difficulty of anomaly detection is how to define the normal parameters of the target system, which need sufficient background knowledge of system security. So it is very meaningful for real application of anomaly detection that detects abnormal behavior under the condition of poor security knowledge.

Hidden Markov Model (HMM), as a statistical method, is applied successfully in speech recognition, information extraction and other classification areas. Terran Lane, etc. use HMM for human-machine interface modeling [2], however HMM used for anomaly detection is not widely researched [3,4].

This paper is organized as follows: section 2 is related research in host system call anomaly detection. Section 3 is how to sue HMM for anomaly detection. Section 4 discusses the effectiveness of concerned methods through different experiments. Section 5 gives conclusions and discusses the future work about HMM for anomaly detection.

2 Related Research

Any computer process, essentially, is a program segment. If selection and loop sentences do not exist in program, the execution behavior of program is predictable.

C.C. Yang et al. (Eds.): PAISI 2007, LNCS 4430, pp. 152–159, 2007.

So if the process is attacked, for example, buffer overflow makes program jumping to execute "/bin/sh", the normal execution of program is destroyed, which can be used to detect abnormal behavior of system. Although if program contains selection and loop, it shows a certain kind of randomness. But there are some experiments that indicate if we partition the enough long system call sequences into small short ones, the different short sequences are relatively invariable[6]. For example, if Sendmail program generates 7,000,000 system calls, the different short sequences with size 6 is about 1000. From this, it shows that although randomness exists in system calls, but we still can use the intrinsic principles of system calls to detect the abnormal or program evidence of being attacked.

At the point of earliest host system call anomaly detection, Stephanie Forrest's research group of University of New Mexico, provided immune technology that detect anomaly depending on identifying "self". They adopted short-sequence matching method, only relying on whether a special short sequence occurrence or not, to detect anomaly but not considering the occurrence frequency and distribution of short sequence[5]. Additionally, in Stephanie method, system call database stores the lookahead pairs with length 0,1,2,...,k, while Hofmeyr extended the method, the database does not store lookahead pairs, but continuous short sequences with regular length, and the recognition accuracy is improved[6].

Frequency-based method, earlier used in text classification, Helman and Bhangoo provide frequency-based method to analyze the frequency of normal system calls and sort the frequency according to its value, which can be used to detect the system call anomaly[7]. Wenke Lee, etc. use RIPPER rule-learning method from data mining to learn rules for system normal process running patterns. They use the learned rules to monitor the running process, if the running process break the rules, then judge the process behavior is abnormal [8]. Since Stephanie Forrest's short sequence matching method is not complete and algorithm defects, Wenke Lee improve the method by proposing sliding window sequence matching method, which not only can detect abnormal counts, but also the distribution discipline of abnormity. Wenke Lee's method eliminates the incompleteness of short sequence matching algorithm and improve the recognition accuracy[8]. In paper[9], Finite state machine (FSM) is used to create the description language of system calls, but the method is not good in efficiency and practicality. Paper [10] proposes system call based online intrusion detection system.

3 Model Generation

HMM is a parameterized probability model, which describes the statistical probability feature of stochastic process, and develop on the basis of Markov chain model. Because in practical situation, the observed events are not one-by-one corresponding to states, but related with a group of probability distribution and Markov chain model cannot represent this complicated situation. HMM is a dual-stochastic process, one Markov chain describing states transition, the other describing the statistical corresponding relation between states and observed events.

As a HMM with N states, the statistical probability feature can be described by 3-tuple of parameters $\lambda = \{\pi, A, B\}$. Here, $\pi = (\pi_1, \pi_2, \cdots, \pi_N)$ is the initial probability distribution, which shows the probability at time $t = 1$ and the state S_i belongs to q_1, namely, $\pi_i = P(q_1 = S_i), 1 \le i \le N$. $A = \{a_{ij} \mid i, j = 1, 2, \cdots, N\}$ is state transition probability matrix. B is probability distribution that any observes in observed sequence O belongs to each different state.

About the HMM structure, there are 2 types: full-state-transition HMM and part-state- transition HMM. In full-state-HMM, transitions between any two states are permitted, which is a commonly used HMM in speech recognition [11]. Part-state-transition HMM has extra-limitations on transition direction and steps. Left-to-right 2-step, 3-step and multi-step are commonly used part-state-transition HMMs depicted in Fig.1. Additionally, there are two types of HMM: discrete or continuous. In discrete HMM, B is a probability matrix, while in continuous HMM, B is a observe probability density function of a state. As for anomaly detection, for instance, system calls of a privileged program, or anomaly user-command modeling, discrete HMM is mainly used. For continuous HMM, how to select observe probability density function need further study.

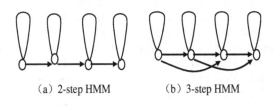

(a) 2-step HMM   (b) 3-step HMM

Fig. 1. Diagram of different HMM structure

HMM-based anomaly detection contains 2 phases: training phase and testing phase. In training phase, through using the labeled training data or system calls under normal process execution, the HMM model is trained and generated. While in testing phase, after feature extraction, the testing data is tested by the learned HMM to determine whether the system call is abnormal? In addition, in order to decrease the false recognition rate, the detection framework adds a feedback regulation module, which can update the model parameters according to recognition results. The framework of HMM-based anomaly detection is depicted in Fig2.

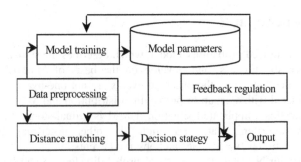

Fig. 2. Diagram of HMM-based anomaly detection

The process of HMM-based anomaly detection is as follows:

Step1: Preprocess input data and feature extraction;
Step2: Create normal or abnormal system model and learn model's parameters;
Step3: Calculate distance between testing data and system model;
Step4: Select decision strategies;
Step5: System self-adaptive regulation, updating model parameters according to recognition results.

Here, there are 2 types of decision strategies. One strategy is creating a different HMM model λ_v for each attack type of special system calls, in others words, using training data with attack labels to train HMM, then we obtain a group of estimate parameters $\lambda_v = \{\pi_v, A_v, B_v\}$ for each kind of attack. During testing phase, after feature extraction, we got the observed sequence $O = \{o_1, o_2, \cdots, o_N\}$, and use learned model to compute $P(O|\lambda_v)$, then select system call feature with highest likelihood as the recognition result, that is:

$$\mathrm{Re}\,sult = \arg\max_{1 \leq v \leq N} P(O|\lambda_v) \qquad (1)$$

The detection strategy mentioned above, need complete attacking sample data and to label the training data by hand, which is a time intensive job. The other strategy is using the normal system call sequences to train HMM, and during the testing period, after feature extraction, the observed sequence $O = \{o_1, o_2, \cdots, o_N\}$ use the normal system call HMM to calculate $P(O|\lambda_v)$. If $P(O|\lambda_v)$ is less than a given threshold, then label it as an abnormal one.

As for relatively long learning and testing sequences, we need splitting the long sequences into small short ones with sliding windows. There are 2 types of sliding window: time window and count window. Time window use a certain time interval (i.e. 2 seconds) to split sequences. In this paper, we use count window (a window with certain size) to split sequences. For example, for system call sequence $(S_1, S_2, ..., S_t, S_{t+1}, ..., S_{t+s})$, if using size t sliding window, we can get (s+1) sequence collections with length t. That is,

$$(S_1, S_2, ..., S_t) \; ; \; (S_2, S_3..., S_{t+1}) \; ; \; ......(S_{s+1}, S_{s+2}, ..., S_{t+s}) \; ;$$

3.1 Full-State-Transition HMM

Full-state-transition HMM does not exert extra limitations on state transition, which permit transition among any states. However, in real application, either system calls or user command sequences possesses a certain kind of time sequential relation, which can be represented by state transition. In this paper, we use left-to-right HMM to simulate this kind of time sequential relation. Additionally, about HMM state number selection, there are great deal of achievements in speech recognition, but in system call anomaly detection, there are less achievements and fewer efficient rules to guide the selection. Our method is to select various state number by means of experiments, so that to evaluate effects of various state number to the experimental results.

3.2 Part-State-Transition HMM

About part-state-transition HMM, it exits transition direction and transition steps constraints. Transition directions, mainly, are left-right, left-to-right or right-to-left. Transition step is the constraint of maximum transition interval among states.

For l -step left-to-right HMM, we set the corresponding value (not in the transition location) to zero (in real algorithm implementation, set the value to a very small real number) in probability transition matrix. Formally speaking, if $(j-i)>l \ or \ i>j$

($i,j=1,2,\cdots,N$) in $A=\{a_{ij} \mid i,j=1,2,\cdots,N\}$, then $a_{ij}=0$; otherwise, a_{ij} keeps unchangeably.

4   Experiments and Analysis

4.1 Experimental Data Description

In order to verify models effectiveness, we use Solaris sendmail program's system call data as the data source and train HMM models. Solaris itself has a security component BSM (Basic Security Module), which can be configured and to record security related events. BSM can record 284 kinds of security events as 284 possible states of host. Each event includes event type, user ID, group ID, process ID, etc. In our experiments, we only use event type, namely, the system call number.

Collecting the security audit data of host system call is a complicated task, which should consider the specialized program's almost all possible "normal" behavior, and then create system call database to store the program normal behavior. The system call data source can be collected from real application environment or from artificial simulating environments. New Mexico University and CERT of CMU have done lots of research, and they provided great deal of system call experimental data that can be downloaded from [12].

In experiment, we consider the sendmail privilege program's behavior (normal and abnormal). Normal group contains 7,071 system calls. The other 2 groups are abnormal behavior, in which intrusion1 (forwarding loops attack) and intrusion2 (decode attack) include 635 and 373 system calls respectively. Each row of the data contains 2 columns: process identifier (PID) and system call number. In this paper, we just use system call number to create Markov model.

In addition, we divide the testing data into 3 parts. The first part, coming from the same source of the learning data, is divided the normal system call data into 2 groups according to certain ratio, learning group accounts 2/3, and testing group 1/3. The second part (intrusion1) and third part (intrusion2) represent the abnormal system call records respectively.

4.2 Different Model Experimental Results

In experiment, we split the normal behavior sequences using sliding window algorithm, and then using Baum-welch algorithm to train HMM model. For testing, the first step is splitting the testing sequence into small segments, then using the forward algorithm of the HMM estimate problem to calculate the probability under the normal HMM model. If the probability is less than a given threshold (we use $(0.1)^a$ as the threshold and a is the size of the sliding window). The recognition results with different size of window and different state transition models are analyzed in the paper. Moreover, the detection real time ability of different HMM models are also discussed in the paper in detail.

4.2.1 Anomaly System Calls Ratio of Different Window Size

Using normal system call sequences to train HMM, select different window size to analyze the testing data. The experimental results of anomaly ratio is depicted in Tab1. (Here, the number of hidden states is 2, left-to-right 1-step transition, and the data in table is percentage).

Table 1. Anomaly system calls ratio with different windows size

Windows size	Anomaly ratio of test1	Anomaly ratio of test2	Anomaly ratio of test3	Average difference times
3	8.02	70.13	58.02	7.99
4	4.19	65.08	52.87	14.08
5	4.31	64.42	53.73	13.71
6	4.36	62.22	51.12	13.00
7	0.49	55.95	47.85	105.92
8	0.45	56.76	45.03	113.10
9	0.29	67.24	54.24	209.45
10	0.29	61.40	47.50	187.76

Table 2. Anomaly Ratio of system calls with different transition HMM models

Transition model	Anomaly ratio of test1	Anomaly ratio of test2	Anomaly ratio of test3	Average difference times
(L:0, R:1)	24.43	66.22	65.12	2.69
(L:1, R:1)	4.98	55.95	47.85	10.42
(L:0, R:2)	4.55	61.54	55.86	12.90
(L:2, R:2)	4.48	55.95	47.85	11.58

From Table.1, it shows that as the window size increases gradually, the anomaly ratio of different testing data presents certain diversity. But there exists great difference between normal and abnormal system calls. When the size of sliding window is greater than 7, the average difference is more than 100 times. Also, when size is 9, the difference is the maximum 209.45 times.

4.2.2 Anomaly Ratio of System Calls of Different Transition HMM Model

Use normal system call data to train different transition HMM models, and then use different testing data to test, and the anomaly ratio is represented in Tab.2 (Here, the window size is 7, the amount of hidden states 3, and data in table is percentage).

In Table.2, (L:a,R:b) represents transition to left a steps, and right b steps. From Tab.2, we can say that for different HMM transition models, considering the anomaly detection ratio, the left-to-right HMM model is slightly superior over the left-right model, but the difference is not obvious. So, different transition HMM models possess very little influence on detection effectiveness.

4.3 Analysis of Detection Real-Time Ability

The real time ability of Intrusion detection system affects directly the detection algorithm's utility. The program is written with Java under JDK1.4.2 and the experimental computer is PIII 800, 256M memory, and 30G hard-disk. Tab.3 indicates the real time ability for different transition HMM models (here, window size is 7, and hidden state number is 3).

Table 3. Detection real time ability with different transition HMM models

Transition models	Training time (ms)	testing1 (ms)	testing2 (ms)	testing3 (ms)
(L:0, R:1)	450	<1	<1	<1
(L:1, R:1)	460	10	<1	<1
(L:0, R:2)	260	10	10	<1
(L:2, R:2)	701	10	<1	10

From Table 3, it shows that for different HMM model, the training period is less than 0.7s and testing period is less than 10ms. Meanwhile, as some part of elements in left-to-right HMM is eliminated from transition probability matrix, the computation quantity decrease and the training phase needs relatively fewer time. So methods concerned above, possess great real-time ability, which can meet the real-time demands for IDS.

5 Conclusions

In this paper, HMM model used for system call anomaly detection is discussed from detection theory, system framework, and detection effectiveness of different HMM model with full-state transition and part-state transition. Also, combing with experiments, the detection real time ability is also analyzed in the paper.

The experimental results show that using different size of sliding window to split training and testing data, the anomaly rate present a certain variance, but there exists great difference between normal and abnormal system calls, which says the method is practicable. At the point of different transition HMM, the anomaly detection ratio with left-to-right HMM is slightly higher than that of left-right HMM, but the difference is not much. Concerning the detection real time ability, left-to-right HMM needs relatively less time. However, for each model, the training period is less than 1 second, and testing period is less than 10 milli-seconds, which can meet the real time demands for IDS.

About HMM-based anomaly detection, it covers a wide range of model parameters, such as, state number, threshold, convergence parameters, etc. In real application, we need a automatic parameter readjustment mechanisms. Moreover, the effectiveness of HMM-based detection used to other application area, for instance, other privilege program system calls or user command modeling, should do further research.

Acknowledgments. This project was supported by the Science and Technology Development Plan and Elite Young Researcher Plan of Shanghai Education Department (205649, 99-0303-06030). Biography: Qian Quan(1972-), male, Ph.D. , research direction: computer network, network security and artificial intelligence.

References

1. R. Anderson, A. Khattak. The use of information retrieval techniques for intrusion detection [EB/OL]. http://www.raid-symposium.org/raid98/index.html, 2004-10-04.
2. Terran L. Hidden markov models for human/computer interface modeling[A]. Proceedings of the IJCAI-99 Workshop on Learning about Users[C]. Stockholm, Sweden: Morgan Kaufmann Publishers,1999. 35-44.
3. Nong Y. A Markov chain model of temporal behavior for anomaly detection[A]. Proceedings of the 2000 IEEE Systems, Man, and Cybernetics Information Assurance and Security Workshop[C]. New York: IEEE Computer Society Press, 2000.171-174.
4. Sung B C, Hyuk J P. Efficient anomaly detection by modeling privilege flows using hidden Markov model[J]. Computers & Security, 2003, 22(1):45-55.
5. Stephanie F, Steven A H, Anil S, etc. A sense of self for unix processes[A]. Proceedings of the 1996 IEEE Symposium on Security and Privacy[C]. CA:IEEE Computer Society Press, 1996.120-128.
6. Steven A H, Stephanie F, Anil S. Intrusion detection using sequences of system calls[J]. Journal of Computer Security, 1998,6(3): 151-180.
7. Helman P, Bhangoo J. A statistically based system for prioritizing information exploration under uncertainty[J]. IEEE Transactions on Systems, Man and Cyberneticsm, Part A: Systems and Humans. 1997,27(4):449-466.
8. Wenke L, Salvatore J S, Chan P K. Learning patterns from UNIX process execution traces for intrusion detection[A]. AAAI Workshop on AI Approaches to Fraud Detection and Risk Management[C]. Menlo Park:AAAI press, 1997.50-56.
9. Christina W, Stephanie F, Barak P. Detecting intrusions using system calls: alternative data models[A]. Proceedings of IEEE Symposium on Security and Privacy[C]. Oakland, California: IEEE Computer Society Press, 1999.133-145.
10. D.Snyder. On-line intrusion detection using sequences of system calls[D]. Master's thesis, Department of Computer Science, Florida State University, 2001.
11. Jinhui-xie. HMM and its application in speech recognition[M] (in Chinese). Wuhan : Huazhong University of Technology Press, 1995.
12. Computer Immune Systems Data Sets. University of New Mexico[EB/OL], http://www.cs.unm.edu/~immsec/data/synth-sm.html, 2004-9-10.

Towards Identifying True Threat from Network Security Data

Zhi-tang Li, Jie Lei, Li Wang, Dong Li, and Yang-ming Ma

Computer Science Department
Huazhong University of Science and Technology
430074 Wuhan, Hubei, China
{leeying,leijie,wtwl,lidong}@hust.edu.cn, briskhorse@163.com

Abstract. Among the challenges in the field of network security management, one significant problem is the increasing difficulty in identifying the security incidents which pose true threat to the protected network system from tremendous volume of raw security alerts. This paper presents our work on integrated management of network security data for true threat identification within the SATA (Security Alert and Threat Analysis) project. An algorithm for real-time threat analysis of security alerts is presented. Early experiments performed in a branch network of CERNET (China Education and Research Network) including an attack testing sub-network have shown that the system can effectively identify true threats from various security alerts.

1 Introduction

Network security data are broadly defined as the alerts and reports generated by network security devices such as intrusion detection system, firewall, anti-virus software, vulnerability scanner and VPN etc. They provide security administrators with wealthy information as they intend to detect, analyze and initiate appropriate responses to security incidents.

However, in practice, making good use of network security data is facing a lot of challenges. As a matter of fact, as the administrating staff in Central China Network Center of CERNET (China Education and Research Network) who take charge of the network management as well as security management for the networks of over a hundred of universities, colleges and institutes in central China, we are facing with the problems brought by inefficient management of network security data everyday, which are also the challenges in the field of network security management:

- **False positives.** True threats can hardly be identified from preliminary alerts because of too many false positives and non-relevant alerts among them. It is not uncommon for an IDS to trigger thousands of alarms per day, up to 99% of which are false positives [1,2].
- **Alert flooding.** Huge network security data streams are flooding the security administrators. As indicated in [1], encountering 10-20,000 alarms per sensor per day is a common fact.

C.C. Yang et al. (Eds.): PAISI 2007, LNCS 4430, pp. 160–171, 2007.
© Springer-Verlag Berlin Heidelberg 2007

- **Lack of cooperation.** The heterogeneity and isolation of security tools have brought great difficulties in alert management, which make some distributed attacks remain undetected and cause a lot of redundancy.
- **Lack of expertise.** Interpreting the security data requires both expertise of network security technologies and in-depth understanding of protected networks, which are not widely available [3].

One promising approach to address the above problems is to develop an intelligent component to manage and analyze the network security data in an integrated way, which is also mentioned as security alert correlation system.

Related work on security alert correlation. A lot of approaches to security alert correlation have been proposed in recent years. Some researchers have proposed practical approaches to alert aggregation [4,5,3,6], which aims to fuse the alerts triggered by the same or similar attacks, for example, fusing thousands of alerts triggered by a worm attack into a single report. They either used quantitative approaches or rule-based algorithms. In addition, Siraj and Vaughn [7] proposed an alert fusing approach using fuzzy set.

Another main approach to alert correlation is multi-step attack correlation, which intends to correlate various alerts generated from a complex attack of multi attack steps by causal and temporal relationships. One main idea to perform multi-stage attack correlation is to correlate the alerts by matching the prerequisites and consequences definitions of single attack steps. The idea is first presented by Templeton and Levitt in [8] with JIGSAW: an attack modeling language based on prerequisite-consequence relation. This work has been pursued by Ning et al. [9,10]. The approach is also used by Cuppens and Miege [11] to add in the work of MIRADOR project [5]. In addition, the method of statistical causality analysis is used to perform multi-step attack correlation by W. Lee and X. Qin [12].

These two kinds of approaches generally focus on the purpose of correlating the alerts with certain relationship into synthetic security reports. But they do not directly help with identifying true threats from raw alerts, although having implicit contributions to. In fact, the alert correlation method can also be well used to identify high-threat or low-relevant alerts. For example, when the vulnerability and topology information of the victim machine (e.g. OS types, running services) is correlated with alert information, it is not difficult to identify the alerts triggered by a CodeRed II worm attack against a Linux host as false positives, because Linux is not vulnerable to CodeRed II worm attack. Marty Roesch, the developer of Snort [13] has introduced a concept called RNA [14]: Real-time Network Awareness, which aims to provide a running IDS with information about the protected network to reduce false positives. Kruegel and Robertson [15] have developed a plug-in to add an alert processing pipeline to Snort to perform alert verification with Nessus vulnerability scanner [16]. Porras, Fong, and Valdes [3] proposed M-correlator which aims to perform alert prioritization by correlating alerts with the vulnerability report and mission information. The approach of correlating IDS alerts with vulnerability information is also performed by some commercial alert management products [17,18,19]. A formal data model named M2D2 was proposed by Morin, Me, Debar, and Ducasse [20] to support correlating IDS alerts with multiple information sources.

This paper presents the work we have done on the approach of identifying true threat from network security data within the SATA (Security Alert and Threat Analysis) project, which aims to build up a platform for integrated management of security data to provide the security administrators with high-level security knowledge. The introduction to SATA system can be found in our previous work[21]. This paper focuses on the function of threat analysis of security alerts based on the last approach to alert correlation introduced above. A preliminary algorithm for threat analysis of security alerts through alert correlation named AlertRank is proposed. The algorithm provides scores of reliability, priority, asset and a final assessment to the degree of threat for each alert, to indicate how much it poses threat to the current protected network from various aspects. Although the main contributing factors concerned in the algorithm are based on conventional terminologies such as severity levels and false positives, the experiments have shown that in practice it makes good effect in true threat identification.

The remainder of this paper is organized as follows: the next section describes the AlertRank algorithm in details; After that, the experiments and discussion about the result are presented; Finally, we conclude the paper and introduce ideas for future work.

2   AlertRank Algorithm

The AlertRank algorithm is designed to compute the degrees of threat that the security alerts pose to the current protected network system through alert correlation. The incidents are then ranked by their scores of threat. Figure 1 shows the main contributors to alert ranking. Given an alert, the output of the algorithm is a set of attributes: the scores of Alert_threat, Priority, Reliability and Asset.

Given an alert,
AlertRank----calculate a tuple of attributes :

Consists of
- **Priority**:   the severity of attack classification or interest to the analyzer.
- **Reliability**: the probability of the attack to succeed.
- **Asset**: the importance of the target.
- **Alert_threat**: the overall assessment of threat.

Fig. 1. Main Contributors to Alert Ranking

2.1 Priority Score Specification

The specification of priority scores provides the administrators a means to tune the threat values of the security alerts representing the attack behaviors of their concern or the attack classes with known severity levels.

There are two ways that contribute to the priority scores in SATA system. The first way is to specify the priority scores through security policies, and the other is to set the priority scores by default setting. Given an alert, if it matches one of the priority policies, then its priority score is set according to the policy, otherwise, to the predefined priority score of its alert type.

Priority Policy. To illustrate the priority policies, Figure 2 shows a sample priority policy, which means, as to the alerts reported by sensor 211.69.xx.111 (a Snort IDS) at anytime, if it is from the external network and target at the host of 211.69.xx.103 at the port of 3306 within the signature group of Mysql attack, the priority score of this alert should be set to 4.

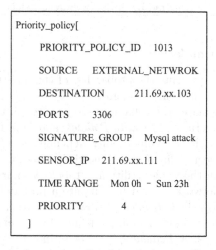

```
Priority_policy[

        PRIORITY_POLICY_ID    1013

        SOURCE    EXTERNAL_NETWROK

        DESTINATION        211.69.xx.103

        PORTS      3306

        SIGNATURE_GROUP    Mysql attack

        SENSOR_IP    211.69.xx.111

        TIME RANGE    Mon 0h – Sun 23h

        PRIORITY        4

]
```

Fig. 2. A sample policy for priority specification

Default Priority. The system has predefined default priority scores to every supported alert types. These values derive from three ways. First, some security tools already have particular fields in their report format representing the severity levels of the alerts. Second, priority specification already exists in the vulnerability specifications in CVE [22] as well as a Nessus vulnerability report. Third, the priority value is defined by administrators according to experienced knowledge. For example, consider an alert generated from Iptables firewall named *Iptables:Accept* which always carry no threat to the protected network, so the default priority score of this report type can be defined to be very low.

Table 1. VULNERABILITY DEPENDENCY DATABASE DEFINITIONS

Field Type	Description
SATA Incident ID	A unique identification to the supported incident types in this database. Not all the supported report types are associated to SATA Incident IDs.
SATA Incident Name	The name of the incident given by SATA system
Incident Classification	A broad classification scheme for attack types
Vulnerable OS	The list of the OS types and versions which are vulnerable to this incident.
Bound Ports/Services	The list of targeted ports/services.
Related alert types	The list of possible following alerts if this incident succeed in execution. It is a list of pairs of Plugin_id and Plugin_sid which represents the alert types.
Applications and Versions	The list of required applications and versions that must be enabled on the targeted host.
Description	Human readable incident description
Nessus ID	Nessus ID [16]
CVE ID	CVE ID [22]
Bugtraq ID	Bugtraq ID (http://www.securityfocus.com/bid)

2.2 Reliability Formulation

The reliability score represents the probability of the reported security incident to succeed in execution or achieve its goal.

The algorithm calculates the reliability scores through three ways: the *Reliability Correlation* function, *Reliability Policies*, and from the *default reliability levels*. Given an alert, if the vulnerability dependency information related to this attack type has been defined in the knowledge base, then the alert information is correlated with the vulnerability and topology information of the target host and Bayesian Network is used to compute a probability for its reliability scores. This process is called *Reliability Correlation*. Otherwise the reliability is set through either the reliability policies defined by administrators or the predefined reliability levels. A *Reliability_level* is an integer between 1 to R_0 with R_0 represents the max *Reliability_level* defined in the system, which is defined to be 10 in our system. A transforming function is then performed to convert the value of reliability *level* to reliability *score* which is a probability value between 0 and 1.

As the formulation of reliability policies and default reliability levels are similar to those for Priority formulation introduced before, the following subsections will focus on the function of *Reliability Correlation*.

Vulnerability Dependency Database. A vulnerability dependency database is required by the reliablity correlation function. It is maintained to provide information of the necessary vulnerability requirements for some incidents to succeed in execution. Only the incidents that have certain dependencies on specific vulnerabilities are included.

Table 1 presents the definition of entries in the vulnerability dependency database. The main content of this database generally derives from the National Vulnerability Database [23], with some augmentation and adjustments.

Reliability Correlation. Figure 3 shows the five factors that contribute to verifying a successful attack, including OS types, open ports and services, applications and versions, vulnerability report ID, and possible outcome of the incident. The facts that some of them are proved to be satisfied or unsatisfied on the target machine can reflect on corresponding adjustments of reliability score of the alert. In fact, the purpose of the reliability correlation process is to verify whether or not the vulnerability requirements (the five factors) of a given alert are satisfied in the real environment (the near real-time scanning results generated by network scanners).

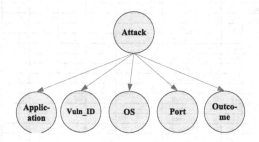

Fig. 3. Main Contributors to a Successful Attack

For each contributing factor, a special matching function is encoded. As to the *OS types* matching, one thing should note is that sometimes the vulnerable OS types are specified as Debian or Redhat in our vulnerability database, while the topology scanners may simply report as Linux with version number. The matching function should be capable of dealing with these situations. For the vulnerability ID matching, the Nessus ID suite is used. As to the matching of version numbers of OS types and applications, the latest vulnerable version numbers are defined while the version number detected below these values are recognized as *matched*.

When it comes to the verification of *outcome*, the matching function tries to search the alert pool for the alerts of the *Related Alert Types* specified in the vulnerability dependency database and with the same target or source to the given alert. For example, an incident raised by a network IDS representing a data theft is possibly followed by the reports of host IDS on the target machine representing integrity violation if it succeed in execution. When there exist the related alerts occurring in a time range T (by default, T=2s), the algorithm deems the *outcome* of the incident to be matched.

The result of the matching function is a 5-tuple:

Reliability_Correlation_Result[Application, Vuln_ID, OS, Port, Outcome]

with the value $\in$ {*yes, no, unkown*}.

The reliability score is then formulated using Bayesian Network with the result of the matching functions as inputs. Figure 3 also shows the Bayesian Network we used in reliability calculation, while Figure 4 shows part of a sample CPT that can be used in the system. In this Bayesian Network, the root node represents a successful attack. The probability of a successful attack (the root node) is related to the correlation results of the leaf nodes by means of Conditional Probability Tables (CPTs). This probability is the final reliability score of related alert. When all the attributes of the correlation result are unknown, the reliability score is set to the average reliability score, which is 0.5 by default.

						CPT (Conditional Probability Table)						
Appli-cation	Vuln_ID	OS	Port	Outc-ome	Attack	P(attack|Application, Vuln_ID, OS, Port, Outcome)	P(Application)	P(Vuln_id)	P(OS)	P(Port)	P(Outcome)	Product
Yes	Yes	Yes	Yes	Yes	Succeed	0.99	0.75	0.4	0.8	0.6	0.05	0.007128
Yes	Yes	Yes	Yes	No	Succeed	0.9	0.75	0.4	0.8	0.6	0.95	0.12312
Yes	Yes	Yes	No	Yes	Succeed	0.3	0.75	0.4	0.8	0.4	0.05	0.00144
Yes	Yes	Yes	No	No	Succeed	0.25	0.75	0.4	0.8	0.4	0.95	0.0228
Yes	Yes	No	Yes	Yes	Succeed	0.2	0.75	0.4	0.2	0.6	0.05	0.00036
Yes	Yes	No	Yes	No	Succeed	0.1	0.75	0.4	0.2	0.6	0.95	0.00342
Yes	Yes	No	No	Yes	Succeed	0.1	0.75	0.4	0.2	0.4	0.05	0.00012
Yes	Yes	No	No	No	Succeed	0.05	0.75	0.4	0.2	0.4	0.95	0.00114
Yes	No	Yes	Yes	Yes	Succeed	0.8	0.75	0.6	0.8	0.6	0.05	0.00864
Yes	No	Yes	Yes	No	Succeed	0.4	0.75	0.6	0.8	0.6	0.95	0.08208
Yes	No	Yes	No	Yes	Succeed	0.2	0.75	0.6	0.8	0.4	0.05	0.00144
Yes	No	Yes	No	No	Succeed	0.05	0.75	0.6	0.8	0.4	0.95	0.00684
Yes	No	No	Yes	Yes	Succeed	0.02	0.75	0.6	0.2	0.6	0.05	0.000054
Yes	No	No	Yes	No	Succeed	0.02	0.75	0.6	0.2	0.6	0.95	0.001026
Yes	No	No	No	Yes	Succeed	0.01	0.75	0.6	0.2	0.4	0.05	0.000018
Yes	No	No	No	No	Succeed	0.01	0.75	0.6	0.2	0.4	0.95	0.000342
Yes	Yes	Yes	Yes	Yes	Failed	0.01	0.75	0.4	0.8	0.6	0.05	0.000072
Yes	Yes	Yes	Yes	No	Failed	0.2	0.75	0.4	0.8	0.6	0.95	0.02736
Yes	Yes	Yes	No	Yes	Failed	0.7	0.75	0.4	0.8	0.4	0.05	0.00336
Yes	Yes	Yes	No	No	Failed	0.75	0.75	0.4	0.8	0.4	0.95	0.0684

Fig. 4. Part of a Sample CPT

By using Bayesian Network, the reliability scores can be computed even with very limited information input. While the CPT is tuned by expertise in initialization, it can be updated in run-time according to the results of the correlation function during a period of time.

Reliability Level Transformation. The reliability level generated from reliability policies and default reliability setting should be transformed to a decimal value between 0 and 1. This procedure is also to change the predefined reliability levels to adapt to the running state. Here is the formula used in the function of *Reliability_Level_To_Score*:

$$Reliability = \frac{Reliability\_level}{R_0} Max\_Rel(Max\_Rel - Min\_Rel) + Min\_Rel \quad (1)$$

where the *Max_Rel* and *Min_Rel* are used to define the scale of meaningful reliability scores calculated by Bayesian Network, which are set to 0.1 and 0.9 by default respectively but will be changed dynamically according to the running state. The R_0 represents the max *Reliability_level* defined in the system.

2.3 Asset Specification

The *Asset* score is specified to each asset to indicate the importance of this asset, which will contribute to the overall threat scores of the incidents targeting at this asset. The *Asset* score is set by administrators with an integer between 1 and 5. For example, the *Asset* score of the critical servers can be set to 4 or higher, while the *Asset* score of an ordinary PC is specified to 1. A default *Asset* score is given when no asset specification to the target host is given.

An *Asset* score can be specified for either a single host or a network. For instance, we can specify the asset scores of a whole staff network with the same value, as the assets share the same criticality to the protected network.

2.4 Alert_threat Formulation

The alert_threat score represents the final assessment of the threat of a given alert. It is a combination of reliability, priority and asset. The key point of this matter is to control the weight of each score to balance their impacts to the overall threat score.

$$Alert\_threat = (\delta_1 * Reliability + \delta_2 * Priority + \delta_3 * asset)/\delta_4 \qquad (2)$$

$$\delta_i > 0, i=1,2,3,4$$

The four parameters in the formula represent how much the three attributes contribute to the final threat value. By default, we use the average weight of each factors:

$$\delta_1 = 10,\ \delta_2 = 1,\ \delta_3 = 2,\ \delta_4 = 3$$

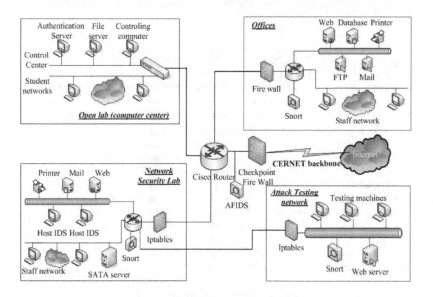

Fig. 5. Experiment Environment

The parameters can be tuned according to the running results, to make the threat assessment result to be more accurate.

3 Experiment

To validate our approach, we performed experiments in a branch network of CERNET (China Education and Research Network) including four enclaves (as shown in Figure 5), and each enclave is protected by a firewall and a Snort IDS except the open computer center. There are some critical assets within each enclave. The SATA server is deployed in the security lab and every security devices are connected to it.

We continuously ran the testing version of SATA system for two weeks and performed a set of attacks in the attack testing bed, while some background attack traffic is also detected in the experiment network.while some background attack traffic is also detected in the experiment network. The attacks we performed include:

- Several times of Brute forces attacks.
- DDoS attacks and some simple DoS attacks such as synflooding.
- A worm attack in the attack testing bed with the Windows hosts being separated from the external network by firewall.
- Attacks related to back door or trojan activities on testing machines.
- Attacks against web servers.
- Several scans, illegal logging and some abnormal behaviors.
- Miscellaneous attacks using downloaded attack tools.

Fig. 6. Alert Ranking Interface

Figure 6 demonstrates the final alert ranking result of the alerts in the whole week. The incident of the greatest threat in the ranking list is generated by a LSASS worm attack against Windows hosts which is performed by us. The asset scores of some of the infected hosts are set to be the highest values deliberately (9 or 10). The other alerts of highest threat scores include attacks against the Server-U ftp servers, DoS attacks, brute force logging attempts and so on. The numbers behind the name of the incidents in Figure 6 represent the amount of raw alerts before aggregation. We have verified all of these incidents ranked as true threat by the algorithm are against mission-critical hosts. In addition, we also noticed the alerts triggered by the LSASS attack against Linux hosts of the threat scores less than 2.5, which is a very low value.

According to the threat scores, the alerts are verified and divided into 5 levels:

1. *The alerts of the greatest threat.* Accounting for 4% (approximately). The alerts with the threat scores in a scale of 8 to 10, the majority of which targeted at critical assets and were of high priority and reliability.
2. *High-threat alerts.* Accounting for 14%. The alerts with the threat scores in a scale of 6 to 8.
3. *Mid-threat alerts.* Accounting for 25%. The alerts with the threat scores in a scale of 5 to 6, mostly ordinary IDS alerts.
4. *Low-threat alerts.* Accounting for 35%. The alerts with the threat scores in a scale of 2.5 to 5. Mostly the events logged by web servers and OS syslogs.
5. *Possible false alerts.* Accounting for 22%. The alerts with the threat scores less than 2.5, which are most likely to be false positives.

Most incidents ranked at the top of the ranking list have been verified to be of high threat in practical, and on the other hand most attacks performed by us that we considered as true threat were ranked to be high-threat alerts. So these experiments have shown that our system can effectively identify the true threat alerts. But it is also revealed that this threat assessment result largely depends on the policies and asset scores specified by security administrators, which means the human factors impact the result of our preliminary AlertRank algorithm too much, thus more technical factors should be added in the algorithm which is our future work.

4   Conclusion

This paper presents our work on true threat identification through alert correlation within SATA (Security Alert and Threat Analysis) project, which aims to build up a platform for integrated management of security data to provide high-level security knowledge. An algorithm for real-time threat analysis of security alerts called AlertRank is presented.

The AlertRank algorithm aims to provide metrics to the function of threat analysis of network security incidents. In this paper we presents the preliminary version of the algorithm, by which scores of reliability, priority, asset and a value represents the final assessment of the degree of the threat are calculated and attached to each alert. These scores are generated by correlation with security policies specified by security administrators and vulnerability and topology information of the running network system. Bayesian Network is used in the reliability calculation function which aims to estimate the probability of the attacks indicated by reported alerts to succeed in execution. Although the main contributing factors concerned in the algorithm are simply based on conventional terminologies such as severity levels and false positives, the experiments performed in a branch network of CERNET with an attack testing bed have shown that its performance in true threat identification is satisfactory.

As future directions, we intend to research on some other factors that contribute to the threat assessment of network security incidents (e.g. the probability of following attacks) through experiments on real attack data, and then seek the way to integrate those factors to improve the AlertRank algorithm.

Acknowledgment

We would like to thank Dr Li Yao for his kind support and constructive advice. We also thank the staff in Central China Regional Network Center of CERNET, as well as the anonymous reviewers for their valuable comments and suggestions.

References

1. Manganaris, S., Christensen, M., Zerkle, D., Hermit, K.: A data mining analysis of rtid alarms. Computer Networks **34**(4) (2000) 571–7
2. Julisch, K.: Mining alarm clusters to improve alarm handling efficiency. In: Proceedings 17th Annual Computer Security Applications Conference, New Orleans, LA, USA, IEEE Comput. Soc (2001) 12
3. Porras, P.A., Fong, M.W., Valdes, A.: A mission-impact-based approach to infosec alarm correlation. In: Recent Advances in Intrusion Detection. 5th International Symposium, Zurich, Switzerland, Springer-Verlag (2002) 95
4. Valdes, A., Skinner, K.: Probabilistic alert correlation. In: Proceedings of the 4th International Symposium on Recent Advances in Intrusion Detection (RAID 2001), Davis,USA (2001) 54–68
5. Cuppens, F.: Managing alerts in a multi-intrusion detection environment. In: Proceedings of the 17th Annual Computer Security Applications Conference, New Orleans, Louisiana (2001)
6. Debar, H., Wespi, A.: Aggregation and correlation of intrusion-detection alerts. In: In Recent Advances in Intrusion Detection. (2001)
7. Siraj, A., Vaughn, R.B.: Multi-level alert clustering for intrusion detection sensor data. In: 2005 Annual Meeting of the North American Fuzzy Information Processing Society, Detroit, MI, USA, IEEE (2005) 748–53
8. Templeton, S.J., Levitt, K.: A requires/provides model for computer attacks. In: Proceedings New Security Paradigm Workshop, Ballycotton, Ireland, ACM (2001) 31
9. Ning, P., Cui, Y., Reeves, D.S., Xu, D.: Techniques and tools for analyzing intrusion alerts. ACM Transactions on Information and System Security **7**(2) (2004) 274

10. Ning, P., Xu, D.: Alert correlation through triggering events and common resources. Proceedings. 20th Annual Computer Security Applications Conference, Tucson, AZ, USA, IEEE Comput. Soc (2004) 360

11. Cuppens, F., Miege, A.: Alert correlation in a cooperative intrusion detection framework. In: Proceedings 2002 IEEE Symposium on Security and Privacy, 12–15 May 2002, Berkeley, CA, USA, IEEE Comput. Soc (2002) 202

12. Lee, W., Qin, X.: Statistical causality analysis of infosec alert data. In: RAID2003, Springer-Verlag (2003) 73–94

13. Roesch, M.: Snort - lightweight intrusion detection for networks. In: Proceedings of the USENIX LISA 99 Conference. (1999)

14. Sourcefire, I.: Realtime network awareness. www.sourcefire.com (2004)

15. Kruegel, C., Robertson, W.: Alert verification: Determining the success of intrusion attempts. In: Proc. First Workshop the Detection of Intrusions and Malware and Vulnerability Assessment (DIMVA 2004). (2004)

16. Nessus: Nessus vulnerability scanner. (http://www.nessus.org/)

17. Desai, N.: Ids correlation of va data and ids alerts. http://www.securityfocus.com/infocus/1708 (June 2003)

18. Eschelbeck, G., Krieger, M.: Eliminating noise from intrusion detection systems. Information Security Technical Report 8(4) (2003) 26

19. Gula, R.: Correlating ids alerts with vulnerability information. Technical report (Dec. 2002.)

20. Morin, B., Me, L., Debar, H., Ducasse, M.: M2d2: a formal data model for ids alert correlation. In: Recent Advances in Intrusion Detection. 5th International Symposium, Zurich, Switzerland, Springer-Verlag (2002) 115

21. Wang Li, Li Zhi-tang, W.Q.h.: A novel technique of recognizing multi-stage attack behaviour. In: Proceedings. International Workshop on Networking, Architecture, and Storages, 1-3 Aug. 2006, ShenYang, China, IEEE Comput. Soc (2006) 188–193

22. CVE: Common vulnerabilities and exposures. (http://www.cve.mitre.org/.)

23. NVD: National vulnerability database. (http://nvd.nist.gov/)

Security Assessment for Application Network Services Using Fault Injection

Hyungwoo Kang[1] and Dong Hoon Lee[2]

[1] Financial Supervisory Service
27 Yoido-dong, Youngdeungpo-gu, Seoul, 150-743, Korea
kanghw@fss.or.kr
[2] Graduate School of Information Management and Security
Korea University, Seoul, 136-704, Korea
Donghlee@korea.ac.kr

Abstract. Vulnerabilities in network protocol software have been problematic since Internet infrastructure was deployed. These vulnerabilities damage the reliability of network software and create security holes in computing environment. Many critical security vulnerabilities exist in application network services of which specification or description has not been published. In this paper, we propose a security assessment methodology based on fault injection techniques to improve reliability of the application network services with no specifications published. We also implement a tool for security testing based on the proposed methodology. Windows RPC network services are chosen as an application network service considering its unknown protocol specification and are validated by the methodology. It turns out that the tool detects unknown vulnerabilities in Windows network module.

Keywords: Security assessment, Fault injection, RPC (Remote Procedure Call), Software security, Buffer overflow.

1 Introduction

A real-world system is always likely to contain faults. There have been so many efforts to remove the faults, but unknown vulnerabilities are reported without a break. As one of promising technologies for detecting and remedying the faults, fault injection has long been used, mainly in the hardware engineering communities. The philosophies are now available for software. Fault injection (or *Software* fault injection in a more specific term) is an approach whereby an auditor uses the sets of scripts designed to feed a program with various inputs, different in size and structure. It is usually possible to specify how these inputs should be constructed and maybe how the tool should change them according to the program's behavior.

There has been much research related to fault injection techniques in order to validate network protocols with published specifications and descriptions such as RFC documents. However, most of critical security vulnerabilities like Blaster [1] and Sassor [2] were found in application network services of which any specification or description has not been published yet. In case of Windows system, lots of critical

C.C. Yang et al. (Eds.): PAISI 2007, LNCS 4430, pp. 172–183, 2007.
© Springer-Verlag Berlin Heidelberg 2007

vulnerabilities have been found in RPC network services, which are application network services and have no protocol specification and description unlike TCP/IP and HTTP. Table 1 shows the statistics of security vulnerabilities found in Windows operating system from 2003 to 2005. The statistics show there are lots of security vulnerabilities in application network services with no published protocol specification and description. The vulnerabilities in application network services are serious problem because attackers can exploit victim systems remotely and can make a critical worm by making use of the vulnerabilities. It is urgent to design a security assessment methodology for application network services with no published protocol specification.

In this paper, we propose a security assessment methodology for improving reliability of network software with no published protocol specification. We observe that the size of the potential space of input is drastically reduced when only parameter field is considered as the region of fault data injection. The proposed methodology improves the efficiency of security assessment for application network services by feeding fault data to the parameter field of a target function in network packet. The methodology is tested by implementing a tool for security testing. Windows RPC network services are chosen as an application network service considering their unknown specification and are validated by the proposed methodology.

Table 1. Statistics of Windows security patches released from Microsoft during 2003~2005

Module name	Number of patches released	Percentage
Application network service	25	17%
Internet explorer	16	11%
Application server	15	10%
MS office	8	5%
Local service	8	5%
Outlook	7	5%
Windows shell	6	4%
Media player	5	3%
MS messenger	3	2%
Etc	58	38%
Total	151	100%

This paper is organized as follows. Chapter 2 reviews related researches. In Chapter 3, a new security assessment methodology for application network services is introduced. Chapter 4 describes the design and implementation of the methodology. Experimental results are presented in Chapter 5. Finally, Chapter 6 draws conclusions.

2   Related Works

Fault injection has been proposed to understand the effects of real faults, to get feedback for system correction or enhancement, and to forecast the expected system behavior. A variety of techniques have been proposed. Among them, software-implemented fault injection (SWIFI) [3] has recently risen to prominence. MAFALDA [4] uses an experimental approach based on SWIFI targeting both external and internal faults for microkernel-based systems. Fuzz [5] and Ballista [6,7] are research projects on the robustness of UNIX system software. Fuzz, a University of Wisconsin research project, studied the robustness of Unix system utilities. Ballista, a Carnegie Mellon University research project, studied the robustness of different Unix operating systems when handling exceptional conditions. Ballista performs fault injection at the API level by passing combinations of acceptable and exceptional inputs as a parameter list to the module under test via an ordinary function call, while Fuzz feeds completely random input to applications without using any model of program behavior. The Wisconsin team extends their research to the robustness of Windows NT application [8] in 2000. These researches and practices prove the effectiveness of fault oriented software robustness assessment. But their approaches are not considered to be directly applicable to examine network protocol implementations, since this test requires a solid knowledge base of protocol specification, a test engine for state transition, and a comprehensive method for message mutation.

In [9], published in 2002, Aitel describes an effective method, called Block-Based Protocol Analysis, implemented in SPIKE [10]. Protocols can be decomposed into length fields and data fields. Aitel's method can drastically reduce the size of the potential space of inputs. A good practice has been conducted by PROTOS project [11], which adopted an interface fault injection approach for security testing of protocol implementations. Surprisingly, it successfully reported various software flaws in a few protocol implementations including SNMP, HTTP and SIP [12], many of which have been in production for years. More importantly, some defects caused either DoS (Denial of Service) or total compromise of gateway services. This raised a warning for the security of future technologies. The public test suite from PROTOS has been integrated into many vendors' product test procedures to promote software robustness. We believe it introduced a pragmatic functional method for assessing protocol implementation security. Despite an effective experiment for security-oriented software robustness testing, PROTOS must need the complete description of protocols and the states of audited programs software. However surprisingly, most of critical security vulnerabilities have been found in application network services without published specification and description. Unfortunately, there has not been any systematic approach to detect security vulnerabilities in such services. Therefore, security assessment for application network services without published protocol specification is urgently needed.

3   Security Assessment Methodology for Application Service

In this chapter, we propose a novel methodology for security assessment to enhance the reliability of application network services. The methodology uses fault injection techniques in order to validate the robustness of application network services.

3.1   Methodology

The proposed methodology for security assessment is focusing on detecting system faults, such as buffer overflow and DoS, in an application network service when functions of the network service are activated. The methodology feeds fault data to the parameter field of target function in network packet in order to raise the efficiency of security assessment for an application network service.

As depicted in Figure 1, the proposed security assessment methodology consists of 3 phases: analysis, implementation, and experiment phases. Analysis phase is the first phase analyzing protocol specification of target application network service. Implementation phase is the second phase implementing security assessment module. Experiment phase is the last phase experimenting target network service by making use of security assessment implemented in implementation phase. Each phase again consists of two or three steps, making eight steps in total, where one cycle of the assessment is completed from Step 1 to Step 7. Step 8 acts as an optimization procedure to improve the efficiency of vulnerability check by modifying network packet generation code after the result analysis of fault injection. The details of each step are described below.

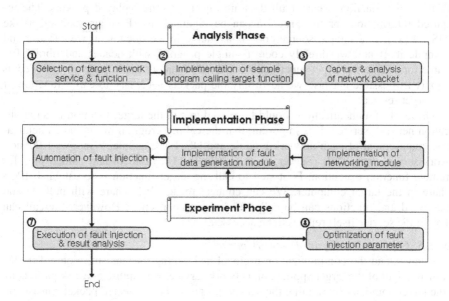

Fig. 1. The methodology for security assessment in application network service

3.1.1 Analysis Phase
In analysis phase, we analyze the protocol specifications of a target application network service.

Step 1: Selection of target network service & function
First of all, a target application network service and its functions are chosen to verify the vulnerabilities of a target system. The target network service has to be selected by considering its priority and the affect when there are defects in network services. Next, target functions, which have a string as a parameter, are selected in the network service because they have the high possibility of buffer overflow.

The selection procedure of the target application network service might be greatly reduced as follows. First, a "Start type" network service is considered as the target application network service. A network system has a lot of network services. Some of them start automatically at system booting and others are started manually by the administrator. Especially, a network services running as "Auto" in start type has big impact on users of network system throughout the world, if it contains vulnerabilities. We hence put more priority on the network service set to start as "Auto". Second, an interface function with a string argument is selected as a target function because one of the main purposes of the proposed methodology is to identify vulnerabilities of buffer overflow type.

Step 2: Implementation of sample program calling target function
A sample program, calling target functions, is coded for analysis of packets. The run of the sample program generates network packets for calling a function of the target network service in the remote computer. We capture the packets for the next calling of the same function, where fault data are injected to the replayed packets. The required information for the program can be obtained in API usage document like MSDN [13]. If a sample source code is available in the document, we can use and compile it. If not, we directly code a sample program with header and library file name for calling the target function. It is desirable that a sample program is coded as simply as possible because we need only the packets necessary to call a function of the target service.

OS level of authentication should be passed to call the target function in an application network service. It is important that the calling program meets the authentication requirement of each network module and OS. For example, Windows RPC network services run SMB (Server Message Block) [14] protocol and named pipe for remote function execution. First step to call the target function is to establish IPC$ share in the target computer. We can connect to the IPC$ share with null ID and password and functions can be called under that connection. However, the call can fails if the service itself refuses to be accessed.

Step 3: Capture & analysis of network packet
To understand the communication protocol and calling mechanism, required in the function call of the target application network service, we capture network packets to the target computer by running the sample program. The collected packet consists of network communication protocol and the function call. In this step, we analyze the protocol stack for the connection to the remote application network service and identify the configuration of fields in each protocol. In case of Windows RPC network services, all packets to the remote stub functions are carried into SMB protocol. So we only capture packets with 445 in the destination port. Unless the port information is available, network packets need to be collected, regardless of port number, and to be filtered. Figure 2 shows the analysis of the packet calling "NetrWkstaGetInfo()" function in workstation service. The number 1~14 are packets of SMB network communication protocol and the number 15~19 are packets of function call.

In Step 3, it is important to search for parameter field of function in captured packet. As noted above, the efficiency of security assessment for application network

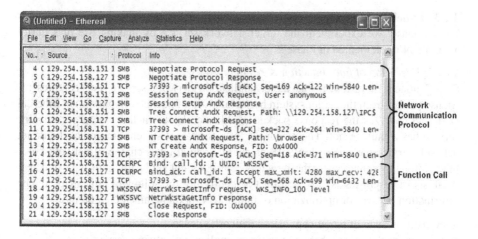

Fig. 2. Capture of packets calling NetrWkstaGetInfo() function in workstation service

services might be improved by feeding fault data to only parameter field of target function in network packet. This reduces the size of the potential space of input when only parameter field is considered as the region of fault data injection.

3.1.2 Implementation Phase
In this phase, we implement security assessment module by making use of fault injection techniques.

Step 4: Implementation of networking module
Step 4 is the first implementation stage for security assessment. In this step, we implement the common network communication part in order to send the captured packets to the target system. We find that the contents of packets, related to network communication, are similar in the different function calls except the part regarding the actual function call. It makes it easy to create a module and improve the readability and maintenance in the source code. In our tool, the networking module is implemented by making use of communication library in SPIKE [10].

Step 5: Implementation of fault data generation module
Step 5 implements the generation of packets to call the target function with fault data that is applied to the parameter of the function, passed to the remote target system. A method for fault data generation is described in Section 3.2. Depending on how to generate the fault data which will be applied to the parameter field of target function, the result of verifying the defects in target application network service can vary. To enhance the experiment, we should follow up the results of fault injection and make improvement in the generation of fault data.

Step 6: Automation of fault injection
Fault data injection should be iterated automatically in order to cause system fault on the target system. It improves the efficiency of security assessment by being able to inject various fault data as a parameter of the target function in an application network service. Number of fault data injections stands for confidence of security assessment.

3.1.3 Experiment Phase

In this phase, we experiment the target network service by making use of security assessment implemented in Phase 2.

Step 7: Execution of fault injection & result analysis
Step 7 injects fault data to the target application network service, and captures response packet from the target system by making use of packet dump tool like Ethereal [15], and analyzes the response packet in order to check whether the target network service has a fault or not. The responses from the target system are one of the target network services or one of lower layer module which takes charge of network communication. In some cases, the target system does not reply for fault data injected. Analysis of responses is very helpful for identifying the following information. The information is used for optimization of fault injection on parameters in Step 8.

- Activation state of target application network service
- Existence of abnormal behavior in target application network service
- Existence of abnormal header assemble of packet sent to target system in advance
- Existence of abnormal communication process used for establishing connection to target system.

Step 8: Optimization of fault injection parameter
If there is no fault in the target system, we might be sure that the target application network service has no security vulnerability. However, if the percentage of response from the target network service is lower than 5%, we become aware that injected packet has not reached to the target network service. In such a case, we should improve the process of packet generation so that the packet including fault data can successfully reach to the target network service. It is desirable to inject fault data to the parameter of string type in order to raise efficiency of security assessment.

3.2 Method for Fault Data Generation

Proposed methodology feeds random data in format of string generated by the methods of *TRY1* and *TRY2*. Each method is used for generation of fault data described in Step 5 of the proposed methodology. *TRY1* makes a string with SPIKE [10] global string set. There are 580 different strings in the SPIKE global string set. *TRY2* makes a string having 4 types of string formats which consists of various characters and various sizes. Details of *TRY2* method are described below.

The *TRY2* method makes random data to cause system faults, such as buffer overflow or DoS, in application network services of the target system. To do this, the *TRY2* creates a string for occurring failure with Equation 1. The function $f \circ g(x, y)$ returns a random string considering the format of string for parameter used in the function of application network services.

$$Formated\ Random\ String = f \circ g(x, y) \quad where\ f \leftarrow \{FC \mid FN \mid FU \mid FF\},$$
$$g \leftarrow \{Asc \mid Num \mid Uni\},$$
$$x \leftarrow \{Type1 \mid Type2 \mid Type3 \mid Type4\}, \quad (1)$$
$$y \leftarrow length\ of\ string$$

The function f stands for the function that returns a string which is suitable for the format of parameter used in the target function. Using random data returned from Asc, Num and Uni, f makes four types of string formats. The string is used as the value of parameter in order to perform fault injection techniques for examination of reliability in application network services of the target system. f consists of four functions such as FF, FU, FC and FN.

- Format of File name(FF): FF returns a string according to the format of file name using random data made by g
- Format of URL(FU): FU returns a string suitable for the format of URL using random data returned by g
- Format of only Character(FC): FC returns a string suitable for the format of character, so uses original random data returned by g
- Format of only Number(FN): FN returns a string suitable for the format of number

FC and FN create strings returned from Asc, Num and Uni without change. FF adds extension of file name to random data made by g according to the format of file name. FU modifies the random data according to the format of URL. The reason why the $TRY2$ method uses the format of four types in function f is that these types of strings are more reachable to inside of the target function in an application network service. That means these types of strings have high possibility causing buffer overflow in an application network service of the target system.

The function g stands for the function that returns a string which consists of random characters, selected among ASCII, number or unicode. Variable x and y are selected as the parameter of g. x is the value selected among ASCII, number or unicode and y is the length of a returned string. Function g generates a string according to type and length. Function Asc returns the string according to Equation 2.

$$RandomString = Asc\ (T, L) \leftarrow Select(T) \times L\ where Select(x) = \{x | \exists x(x \in T)\},$$
$$T = \{Type1 | Type2 | Type3 | Type4\}, \quad (2)$$
$$L = length of\ string$$

We divide acsii code into four types as shown in Table 2. Each type indicates escape character, special character, number and alphabet. In Equation 2, T means the kind of Type and L means the length of string. We confine the decimal number of ASCII code to 127.

Table 2. The value that can be inserted in Asc function

Type	Decimal number of ASCII code	Contents
Type1	0 ~ 31	Escape Character
Type2	32~47 I 58~64 I 91~96 I 123~127	Special Character
Type3	48~57	Number
Type4	65~90 I 97~122	Alphabet

Next, function Uni has only the parameter related to length of string. The Uni generates a string of unicode with random size and random character set.

Last, function *Num* generates the value that overflows boundary value of number such as int, unsigned int, long and so on. The values are used to derive an integer overflow in process of managing in parameter of the target function. The function *Num* generates the range of value according to Equation 3. *Type1* feeds only value of boundary in parameter of the target function. *Type2* adds a positive value to boundary to cause overflow and *Type3* adds a negative value to boundary to cause underflow in the function of the target application network service.

$$Num(B, F) \leftarrow B + F \ where \ B = \{PB \mid NB\},$$
$$PB = \{32767 \mid 65535 \mid 2^\wedge 31 - 1 \mid 2^\wedge 32 - 1\},$$
$$NB = \{-32767 \mid -32768 \mid 1 - 2^\wedge 31 \mid -2^\wedge 31 \mid 0\}, \tag{3}$$
$$F = \{x \mid \forall x \in I\}$$

Type1 case: Num(B, 0)
Type2 case: Num(PB, N) where N is positive number
Type3 case: Num(NB, N) where N is negative number

4   Design and Implementation of Security Assessment

In this chapter, we present the implementation of the proposed methodology. The proposed tool performs the fault injection technique by feeding random value in target in order to trigger the failure of an application network service.

The implemented tool has the following main components: TCP/UDP Sender, Packet Generator, Fault Data Generator, and Fault Data Set. In the tool, the core module is Fault Data Generator because this module creates a random data for causing system fault in an application network service. The TCP/UDP Sender and Packet Generator are implemented by making use of public library provided by SPIKE [10].

5   Experimental Result

We make experiment on the proposed methodology using the implemented tool. The operating system(OS) used for experiment is Windows XP SP2(Service Pack 2). We focus on Windows RPC network services as the target application network service for security assessment. Windows RPC is a core subsystem that implements a remote procedure call method, and used for local processes communication as well as remote procedures calls. Most of Windows network services using DEC-RPC are daemon processes, which start at system boot time. In this experiment, the target network services using DCE-RPC are workstation service, server service, and browser service. The condition of security assessment for each function of the target network service is described as follow.

- Number of fault data injection: 100,000 times
- Type of fault data injection: fault injection on parameter of target function
- Type of fault data generation: *TRY1/TRY2*

Table 3. Results of experiment on security assessment for Windows RPC network services

Module name	Target function name	Result of fault injection	
		Response type from target system	Ratio
Workstation service	NetrMessageBuffer-Send()	Response from target service	7.17%
		Response from lower protocol module	15.72%
		No response	77.11%
	NetrUseGetInfo()	Response from target service	10.92%
		Response from lower protocol module	10.85%
		No response	78.23%
	NetrUseDel()	Response from target service	10.18%
		Response from lower protocol module	11.66%
		No response	78.16%
Server service	NetprNameCompare()	Response from target service	9.15%
		Response from lower protocol module	15.63%
		No response	75.22%
	NetprPathType()	Response from target service	23.94%
		Response from lower protocol module	13.12%
		No response	62.94%
Browser service	BrowserrSetNetlogon-State()	Response from target service	17.58%
		Response from lower protocol module	0.64%
		No response	81.78%
	BrowserrServerEnum()	Response from target service	0%
		Response from lower protocol module	19.86%
		No response	80.14%

Table 3 shows the result of experiment on security assessment for Windows RPC network services. In the several functions, although we confirm that the input packets reach to the target function by making use of debugger program like WinDBG [16], the ratio of response from the target network service is zero. That means some functions do not respond to invalid input data. For the rest of target functions, the ratio of response from target function is above 5%. That means our experiment is realiable for security assessment of the target network service. We find unknown vulnerability causing DoS in SMB module when we make an experiment for "BrowserrSetNetlogonState()" function in browser service. The target system exposed under the vulnerability does not accept SMB connection using 445 port from remote system. No fault is found in the target system during experiment on the rest of the functions. Therefore, we conclude that the target functions of Windows network services have no fault, except for the SMB DoS vulnerability, based on the proposed methodology using fault injection techniques.

6   Conclusion

Fault injection has been widely used to evaluate the dependability of a system and to validate error-handling mechanisms. This technique consists of introducing faults during an execution of the system under test and then observing its behavior. We conclude by summarizing the main contributions of our work:

- A noble security assessment methodology for application network services has been proposed.
- We designed and implemented the proposed methodology as a tool for security assessment of application network services.
- An experiment on the proposed methdology was provided. Windows RPC network services are chosen as an application network service for the experiment. As we mentioned in Chapter 5, we have found unknown vulnerability causing DoS in SMB module when we perfomed an experiment for browser service. We confirmed that target functions of Windows network services have no fault, except for the SMB DoS vulnerability, based on proposed methodology using fault injection technique.

The proposed methodology has several advantages:

- It can validate the reliability of application network services without published protocol specification and description.
- It improves the efficiency of security assessment for application network services by feeding fault data to the parameter field of the target function in network packet. We can drastically reduce the size of the potential space of input when only parameter field is considered as the region of fault data injection.
- A method for fault data generation is provided. The method uses the four types of string formats which is more reachable to inside of the target function in an application network service. That means the formats of strings have high possibility causing buffer overflow in application network services of the target system.

Our immediate research results include the setting-up of methodology being able to validate the reliability of application network service. Finally natural extensions to this work will be to add results of experiment on various application network services.

References

1. Microsoft Security Bulletin MS03-026. http://www.microsoft.com/technet/security/bulletin/ MS03-026.mspx. Microsoft (2003)
2. Microsoft Security Bulletin MS04-011. http://www.microsoft.com/technet/security/bulletin/ MS04-011.mspx. Microsoft (2004)
3. J. M. Voas and G. McGraw: Software Fault Inoculating Programs Against Errors, Wiley Computer Publishing
4. J. C. Fabre, M. Rodriguez, J. Arlat, and J. M. Sizun: Building dependable COTS microkernel-based systems using MAFALDA, Pacific Rim International Symposium on Dependable Computing (PRDC'00), pp. 85-92
5. B. P. Miller, L. Fredriksen, and B. So: An Empirical Study of the Reliability of UNIX Utilities, Communications of the ACM, 33(12):32-44, 1990
6. P. Koopman, J. Sung, C. Dingman, D. Siewiorek, and T. Marz: Comparing operating systems using robustness benchmarks, 16th IEEE Symposium on Reliable Distributed Systems, pages 72-79, October 1997.

7. N. P. Kropp, P. J. Koopman, and D. P. Siewiorek: Automated Robustness Testing of Off-the-Shelf Software Components, 28th International Symposium on Fault- Tolerant Computing, pages 464-468, 1998
8. Justin E. Forrester and Barton P. Miller: An empirical study of the robustness of windows NT applications using random testing, http://www.cs.wisc.edu/_bart/fuzz/fuzz.html.
9. Dave Aitel: The advantages of block-based protocol analysis for security testing, 2002. http://www.immunitysec.com/resources-papers.shtml.
10. SPIKE Development Homepage, http://www.immunitysec/spike.html
11. PROTOS: Security Testing of Protocol Implementation, http://www.ee.oulu.fi/research/ouspg/protos
12. M. Handley, H. Schulzrinne, E. Schooler, and J. Rosenberg: SIP: Session Initiation Protocol, RFC2543
13. MSDN, http://msdn.microsoft.com/
14. Luke K. C. Leighton: DCE/RPC over SMB: Samba and Windows NT Domain Internals, ISBN 1-57870-150-3, Macmillan Technical Publishing, December 1999.
15. Ethereal, http://www.ethereal.com/
16. WinDBG. http://www.microsoft.com/whdc/devtools/debugging/default.mspx

A Secure Data Transmission Protocol
for Mobile Ad Hoc Networks

Shejie Lu, Jun Li, Zhiyuan Liu, and Guohua Cui

College of Computer Science & Technology,
Huazhong University of Science & Technology, Wuhan 430074 China
aiminglu@163.com

Abstract. Secure routing and data transmission has stimulated wide interest in Ad Hoc network research since it is more vulnerable to attacks due to its structural characteristics. Several efficient and secure schemes have been proposed to protect the network from external attacks. However, they still lack very efficient ways to detect and resist internal attacks. Here we proposed a secure data transmission protocol (SDTP) based on the Reed-Solomon error-correct coding to achieve secure data transmission in a Byzantine attack-existing environment. This protocol can distinguish malicious behaviors from transmission errors and locate the malicious node accurately. The algorithms used in this protocol also apply to secure routing protocols.

Keywords: Ad Hoc network; secure data transmission; intrusion detection; malicious behavior judgment.

1 Introduction

Ad hoc networks are self-organizing multi-hop wireless networks where all the nodes take part in the process of forwarding packets. Ad hoc networks can easily be deployed since they do not require any fixed infrastructure, such as base stations or routers. Therefore, they are highly applicable to emergency deployments, natural disasters, military battlefields, and search and rescue missions.

Communication in mobile ad hoc networks comprises two phases: route discovery and data transmission. Secure Routing Protocols (SRPs) are the basis of secure data transmission, and therefore an active area in ad hoc network research. Several SRPs and security mechanisms have been proposed [1-9]. These protocols handle external attacks quite well; however, they either only partly address the issue of an internal attack or simply assume an internal attack free environment. Despite their inadequacy to protect the network from internal attacks, some security mechanisms employed in SRPs do provide helpful insight to address the security issue for data transmission. For example, Cheung [5] shows how to use hash chains to secure routing algorithms, assuming that the routers have synchronized clocks. However, his scheme is not timely, as it can only detect attacks long after they have happened. Goodrich presented a "leap-frog" routing process in [6], which can detect a router malfunction in the flooding algorithm. In [7] and [8], a reputation mechanism is proposed, where the malicious nodes are found statistically and their activities blocked. The

C.C. Yang et al. (Eds.): PAISI 2007, LNCS 4430, pp. 184–195, 2007.

disadvantages of this approach are that the overhead it used is large, the detecting process takes a long time and the outcome is sometimes inaccurate. In [9], the author presented a secure on-demand routing protocol resilient to Byzantine failures that consists of three kinds of attacks: sniffing attacks, stop-forwarding attacks and cheating attacks. The scheme detects malicious links after log n faults occurred, where n is the length of the routing path. Again, there are several drawbacks associates with this mechanism. Firstly, it can't react to the malicious behavior in time since it only detects malicious links after a certain number of errors. Secondly, the mechanism cannot determine whether an error is caused by a malicious behavior or the transmission process itself. Thirdly, this mechanism is difficult to implement.

In this paper, we present a secure data transmission protocol (SDTP) for ad hoc networks based on Reed-Solomon codes. It exploits the redundancy of multi-path routing and remains efficient and effective even in an adverse environment suffering from Byzantine attacks. With only moderate multi-path transmission overhead and very reasonable assumptions, data transmission security is achieved without the use of intrusion detection schemes.

The rest of the paper is organized as follows: in section 2, the Reed-Solomon error correcting codes is briefly reviewed. Then the SDTP is presented in detail in section 3. The malicious node detection method is given in section 4. In section 5, simulation results of an application using SDTP on AOMDV are shown along with some analyses. Finally a summary of the paper is given in section 6.

2 The Reed-Solomon Codes

The Reed-Solomon codes are non-binary cyclic codes with code symbols from a Galois field [10,11]. Briefly, Reed-Solomon codes are defined as follows. Let α be a primitive element in the Galois Field, for any positive integer $t \leq 2^q - 1$, there exists a t-symbol-error-correcting Reed-Solomon code with symbols from $GF(2^q)$ with following parameters:

$$n = 2^q - 1, n - k = 2t ,$$

where n is the total number of code symbols in the encoded block, t is the symbol-error correcting capability of the code, and $n - k = 2t$ is the number of parity symbols.

A Reed-Solomon codeword is generated using a special polynomial. The general form of the generator polynomial is:

$$g(x) = \prod_{i=1}^{2t} \left(x - \alpha^{k_0 + i} \right).$$

Usually we assume $k_0 = 0$ or $k_0 = 1$, and $n - k \geq 2t$. When $k_0 = 0$, then:

$$g(x) = (x - \alpha)(x - \alpha^2)...(x - \alpha^{2t}) = g_0 + g_1 x + g_2 x^2 + ... + g_{2t-1} x^{2t-1} + x^{2t} ,$$

where $g_i \in GF(2^q)$ and $\alpha, \alpha^2, ..., \alpha^{2t}$ are the roots of $g(x)$.

Every element in $GF(2^q)$ can be represented uniquely by a binary q-tuple called a q-bit byte. Suppose a (n, k) Reed-Solomon code with symbols from $GF(2^q)$ is used for encoding binary data, a message of kq bits is first divided into kq -bit bytes. Each q -bit byte is regarded as a symbol in $GF(2^q)$. The k -byte message is then encoded into n -byte codeword based on the Reed-Solomon encoding rule. By doing this, we actually expand a Reed-Solomon code with symbols from $GF(2^q)$ into a binary (nq, kq) linear code, called a binary Reed-Solomon code. Binary Reed-Solomon codes are very effective in correcting bursts of bit errors as long as no more than t q -bit bytes are affected.

The details of the Encoder and Decoder Algorithms of the Reed-Solomon codes are given in [10,11].

3   Secure Data Transmission Protocol (SDTP)

Protecting the routing message from attacks is only one part of the security mechanisms of an Ad Hoc network. In certain occasions, a malicious node may behave normally in routing process, but then either drops the segment packet or modifies the content of the packet and then forwards it. It is usually difficult to determine whether an error is caused by the transmission process or by a malicious behavior, and it is even more difficult to locate the malicious node accurately. The SDTP protocol described below provides a robust and secure data transmission protocol based on the multi-path routing environment to address the issues.

3.1   Assumptions and Symbol Definitions

1. Assumptions
The SDTP is based on following assumptions:

(1) The network routing protocol can resist all external attacks. It can prevent the external nodes from taking part into the routing finding. This assumption can be easily achieved with many existing secure routing protocols.

(2) Source nodes and destination nodes are trustable, and between each pair of source node and destination node, there exists at least one route free of malicious nodes. This assumption is reasonable in reality. Even when this assumption is violated, SDTP still allows secure data transmission, but it is difficult for it to locate the malicious nodes successfully.

(3) There is no more than one malicious node in a route. This assumption is only needed to locate the malicious node and it is not required for secure data transmission.

(4) Each node is equipped with a private key while all the other nodes share a public key to it. In addition, a key pair is shared between any two nodes, which can be established by the key exchanging process such as Diffie-Hellman [12] or be initialized in the initialization of the system. The security of the key pairs must be guaranteed.

2. Symbol definitions
In order to simplify the description of the operations in SDTP, some symbols are defined in table 1:

Table 1. Symbol definition

P	The message needed to be transferred.	CP	Reed-Solomon codeword of the contents of the message P encrypted by source-destination shared key.
CP_i	The ith segment of CP	CP_i^A	Segment of CP_i received by node A
K_A^{-1}	The private key of node A	K_{XY}	The shared key of node X and node Y
$H(M)$	The hash value of the message M	$(M)_K$	Using key K to encrypt M

3.2 Process at the Source Node

To send a data message P to its destination node D, node S first encrypts P using K_{SD}. Let $EP = (P)_{K_{SD}}$, the size of EP should divide q; if not, we can take steps to fill it. Suppose the codeword can correct t faults, so the size of the codeword $n = k + 2t$, we can calculate a Reed-Solomon codeword of EP with the parameter (n,k) in $GF(2^q)$. The size of CP is nq bits and the inflation ratio is n/k. By properly choosing the value t, we can control the inflation ratio and make it reasonable.

CP is sent to node D by the following steps:

1. Divide CP into d $(2t < d \le k)$ segments as CP_0, CP_1, ..., CP_{d-1}, each segment can have a different size and the size of each CP_i must divide q. The larger the value d is, the more resilient the data transmission to resist attacks, and the higher the expense of the network communication. Therefore the number of segments should be chosen properly according to the network status of the application environment.

2. Calculate the hash value $H(CP_i)$ of each segment CP_i of CP, construct a data segment packet, the format of segment packet is:

$$[DATASEG, SOURCE, DEST, PK\_SEQ, SEG\_SEQ, CP_i, H(CP_i)],$$

where:

$DATASEG$ is the identification of data segment.

$SOURCE$ and $DEST$ are the IP addresses of the source and destination nodes.

PK_SEQ and SEG_SEQ are the sequence number of data packet and data segment packet.

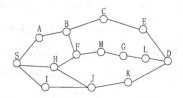

Fig. 1. The topology between source node S and destination node D

There are usually multiple routes between the source node and the destination node, e.g., in figure 1, the list of the routes from S to D includes: S-A-B-C-E-D, S-A-B-F-M-G-L-D, S-H-F-M-G-L-D, S-H-J-K-D, and S-I-J-K-D etc. Data segment packets are sent to destination node D via different routes. Different routes may contain a same node. Therefore, the number of routes between the two nodes is increased.

3.3 Process at the Intermediate Nodes

When an intermediate node receives a data segment packet, it can extract the value of $H(CP_i)$ from the packet, and see if it matches the value in its $H(CP_i)$ buffer. If yes, then the segment packet is a replaying packet and the node will drop the packet. Otherwise, the node puts this $H(CP_i)$ into its buffer and calculates the hash value of CP_i at the same time. If the two hash values match, then forward the segment packet; otherwise, an error in data transmission has occurred and an ACK packet will be sent to the source node to request the segment packet to be re-sent.

3.4 Process at the Destination Node

When the destination node receives all the segment packets of a data packet, the reconstructing process of the original data message CP starts, which includes the following three steps:

1. Calculate the syndrome symbol.
2. Calculate the error locations.
3. Calculate the error value.

If a malicious node only alters the parity code b, we can simply use the majority rule to rule out the compromised codeword. Thus, smarter attackers may want to alter the forwarded codeword m_i instead of parity code b. Since the roots of $g(x)$ are also the roots of $c(x)$, the received codeword $r(x) = c(x) + e(x)$, where $e(x) = \sum_{i=0}^{n-1} e_i x^i$ is the error polynomial, evaluated at each of the roots of $g(x)$ should yield zero only when it is a valid codeword. Any errors will result in nonzero value(s) in one or more of the computations. The computation of a syndrome symbol can be described as follows:

$$S_i = r(x)\big|_{x=\alpha^i} = r(\alpha^i) \qquad i = 1, 2, \ldots 2t$$

If there are v ($0 \le v \le t$) errors in unknown locations j_1, j_2, ..., j_v, then $e(x) = e_{j_1} x^{j_1} + e_{j_2} x^{j_2} \ldots + e_{j_v} x^{j_v}$. Define the error values to be $Y_l = e_{j_l}$, $l = 1, 2, \ldots, v$, and the error locators to be $X_l = \alpha^{j_l}$, where $l = 1, 2, \ldots, v$. We can utilize Forney's algorithm [11] to derive the Y_l. The error correcting polynomial is then:

$$e(x) = \sum_{l=1}^{v} Y_l x^{j_l},$$

and $c(x)$ can be recovered using $c(x) = r(x) - e(x)$. Consequently, the key message polynomial $m(x)$ and therefore the message EP ($EP = (P)_{K_{SD}}$) can be derived. Finally, message P that node S sent to D can be reconstructed by decrypting EP with K_{SD}.

In the above process, if no error is found in decoding process, then node D sends an ACK packet to S to confirm that the packet has been successfully received. Otherwise, if the number of error symbols is great than t so that the decoding algorithm cannot recover the codeword, node D will send an ACK packet to request the source node's resending; if the errors can be corrected, then the codeword will be recovered, and a malicious node locating process is launched.

4   Malicious Node Detection

As for sniffing attacks of Byzantine environment, a malicious node behaves like a normal node, but it will reveal all the transmitted information to attackers. Alternatively, it may also either drops (stop-forwarding attacks) or alters (cheating attacks) the packets it received. Using SDTP, the packet is encrypted by K_{SD}, and then encoded by Reed-Solomon codes' algorithm; moreover, the codeword of the packet is divided into several pieces sent through the different routes. Therefore for sniffing attacks, even if the malicious node has the key K_{SD} shared by node S and node D, it can get little meaningful information about the message. As for stop-forwarding attacks, a method to resist them is presented in [13]. So here we are mainly concerned about cheating attacks. First, we describe how to determine whether an error is occurred due to transmission error or a malicious behavior.

4.1   Distinguish Malicious Behaviors from Transmit Errors

When an intermediate node forwards a segment packet, it calculates the hash value $H(CP_i)$ of CP_i from the segment packet and then compares the result with the received $H(CP_i)$ value in the segment packet. If they don't match, then we declare the error is occurred due to a transmitting error. The node then drops the data segment packet and reports the error to its prevenient hop. Meanwhile an ACK packet is generated and sent to the source node S to request resending of the segment packet. If a node does not receive the reports within a certain period of the time, the link between the two nodes must be questionable, and the source node will no longer send a packet to it. When a destination node receives all the data segment packets of a data packet, and the calculated hash value of CP_i and $H(CP_i)$ in the packet is equal for each segment packet, but errors are found when decoding the codeword, then we can conclude that the errors are caused by malicious behaviors. The judgment is incorrect only when the transmitting errors coincidently vary $H(CP_i)$ values in the all segment packets and make them equal to the corresponding calculated values. However, the probability of this coincidence is $\dfrac{1}{2^{Hash\_Len}}$, where $Hash\_Len$ is the size of hash value and hence nearly 0.

4.2 Locating the Attacker Node

When a malicious node modifies the contents of CP_i, it may also modify its hash value $H(CP_i)$ accordingly at the same time. Thus intermediate nodes will not be able to detect the modification. In this case the modified segment packet will arrive at destination node D. During the decoding process of Reed-Solomon codes, the error can be found and a malicious node detecting process starts. Figure 2 shows the malicious node modifies the data segment from CP_i to $CP_i^{'}$.

S CP   H CP   F CP   M CP$^{'}$ G CP$^{'}$ L CP$^{'}$ D

Fig. 2. The malicious node modifies the data segment from CP_i to $CP_i^{'}$

In the decoding process, the modification can be detected and the original CP_i recovered. A detecting packet is then formed. Assume that node Y is next hop of node X, the detecting packet generated by X is

$$[\,DETECT, SEQ, (CP_i \parallel CP_i^{'})_{K_D^{-1}}, (H(CP_i^{X}))_{K_X^{-1}}, (H(CP_i^{Y}))_{K_Y^{-1}}\,],$$

where:

$DETECT$ is the identification of detecting packet.

SEQ is the sequence number of the detecting packet. This number is generated by the destination node D, increased by one for each detecting process, remains unchanged in forwarding process of the intermediate nodes.

$(CP_i \parallel CP_i^{'})_{K_D^{-1}}$ is the cipher text of the joint between the original and the modified data segment.

$(H(CP_i^{X}))_{K_X^{-1}}$ is the cipher text of the hash value of the data segment that node X received using node X's private key.

$(H(CP_i^{Y}))_{K_Y^{-1}}$ is the cipher text of the hash value of the data segment that the next node Y received using node Y's private key. X can get it from the segment packet node Y sent to it.

For example, in Figure 2, because node D is the destination node which has no next hop, the detecting packet it generates and sends to its prevenient node L is:

$$[\,DETECT, SEQ, (CP_i \parallel CP_i^{'})_{K_D^{-1}}, (H(CP_i^{'}))_{K_D^{-1}}, (H(CP_i^{'}))_{K_D^{-1}}\,],$$

The detecting packet that node L generates and sends to its prevenient node G is:$[DETECT, SEQ, (CP_i \| CP_i')_{K_D^{-1}}, (H(CP_i'))_{K_L^{-1}}, (H(CP_i'))_{K_D^{-1}}]$, and then the detecting

packet that node G generates is:$[DETECT, SEQ, (CP_i \| CP_i')_{K_D^{-1}}, (H(CP_i'))_{K_G^{-1}},$

$(H(CP_i'))_{K_L^{-1}}]$, and so on.

Fig. 3. Detecting packet delivery procedure

As shown in Figure 3, if in a route from node S to node D, the prevenient node of node W is node V, its next hop is node X, node X's next hop is node V, when node W

receives a detecting packet $[DETECT, SEQ, (CP_i \| CP_i')_{K_D^{-1}}, (H(CP_i^X))_{K_X^{-1}},$

$(H(CP_i^Y))_{K_Y^{-1}}]$, the process procedure is listed below:

(1) Decrypt $(CP_i \| CP_i')_{K_D^{-1}}$, $(H(CP_i^X))_{K_X^{-1}}$, $(H(CP_i^Y))_{K_Y^{-1}}$.

(2) Calculate the hash values $H(CP_i)$ and $H(CP_i')$ from CP_i and CP_i'

respectively. Compare with $(H(CP_i^X))_{K_X^{-1}}$, $(H(CP_i^Y))_{K_Y^{-1}}$ decrypted previously; If

they are not equal, then the detecting packet is an invalid one, and the node is removed from its neighbor table and the process return.

(3) Find $H(CP_i)$ or $H(CP_i')$ from the buffer and note it as $H(CP_i^W)$. If it equals

to $H(CP_i^X)$, then go to step (5).

(4) Generate a accusation ACK packet, send it to the source node S and the destination node D in two directions to notify them an error has been found. The accusation ACK packet may be dropped in the direction that contains the malicious node, but it is certain the packet will be successfully sent in the other direction to either node S or D.

(5) Generate a detecting packet $[DETECT, SEQ, (CP_i \| CP_i')_{K_D^{-1}}, (H(CP_i^W))_{K_W^{-1}},$

$(H(CP_i^X))_{K_X^{-1}}]$ and send it to its prevenient hop V, and the procedure returns.

From the assumptions given in section 2.1, there must be at least one secure route between source node S and destination node D, so that node D can send the value $(CP_i \| CP_i')_{K_D^{-1}}$ securely to node S via it. The format of the detecting packet in the direction of S to D is similar to that used from D to S. Because the node S is the source node which has no prevenient hop, the detecting packet it generates and sends to its next hop is: [$DETECT, SEQ, \left(CP_i \| CP_i'\right)_{K_D^{-1}}, \left(H\left(CP_i\right)\right)_{K_S^{-1}}, \left(H\left(CP_i'\right)\right)_{K_S^{-1}}$]. The detecting packet generated by node H is [$DETECT, SEQ, \left(CP_i \| CP_i'\right)_{K_D^{-1}}, \left(H\left(CP_i\right)\right)_{K_H^{-1}}$, $\left(H\left(CP_i'\right)\right)_{K_S^{-1}}$], and so on. After the bi-directional detection, accusation ACK packets received node S and node D can be combined to determine the location of the malicious node. As can be seen in Figure 2, no matter the malicious node generates the detecting packet using $\left(H\left(CP_i'\right)\right)_{K_M^{-1}}$ or $\left(H\left(CP_i\right)\right)_{K_M^{-1}}$, in reverse detecting process, node F generates and sends an accusation ACK packet to S, whereas in the other detecting process, node G generates and sends an accusation ACK packet to D. M is the only node between node F and node G. It can be seen that the two neighbor nodes of the malicious node will each generate an accusation ACK packet in the bi-directional detection process, thus if there is only one node between the two accusation nodes, the node must be a malicious node.

When the malicious node receives a detecting packet, it can process it without abiding rules described above, it can either drop the packet or does not generate a valid detecting packet and forward it. A mechanism is present below to prevent these from happening.

4.3 The Mechanism to Prevent Malicious Node Process Detecting Packet Without Abiding by the Rules

To prevent malicious node violate the rules for processing detecting packets, a detecting-receipt mechanism is presented here. In this mechanism, when a node receives a detecting packet, it should send back a receipt packet to its prevenient node for later use. The format of the receipt packet is

$$[DETECT\_RECEIPT, \left(H\left(DETECT\_PKG\right)\right)_{K_X^{-1}}],$$

where $DETECT\_RECEIPT$ is the identification of receipt packet, and $DETECT\_PKG$ stands for the detecting packet that a node received.

If within a certain interval the node can't receive the receipt packet from the next hop, we suppose that the next hop node has either moved out of the route or the node is a malicious node that is not willing to send back a receipt packet to its prevenient node. Whichever it is, the reaction of the node is to remove the questionable node from its neighbor table. The receipt packet is unforgeable by using the encryption of a node's private key, hence if the node sends back a receipt packet to its prevenient node abiding by the protocol rule but doesn't forward it, then it will not receive a receipt packet. This kind of malicious behavior can be detected easily.

If the malicious node want to modify the contents of the data segment that can't be detected by the next hop, it must generate $\left(H\left(CP_i^X\right)\right)_{K_X^{-1}}$ and $\left(CP_i \| CP_i'\right)_{K_D^{-1}}$, and make them match the relationship between them after decryption, which is theoretically impossible.

5   Simulation Results and Analysis

The simulation tool we used is ns2.28 (network simulator v2.28). The multi-path routing protocol is AOMDV [14], which is based on a prominent on-demand single path protocol known as Ad hoc On-demand Distance Vector (AODV). The parameters of the simulation environment are set in table 2.

Table 2. Simulation environment

Parameter	Value	Parameter	Value
MAC	802.11	Routing protocol	AOMDV
Number of nodes	100	Simulation area	1000m × 1000m
Bit rate	CBR	Simulation time	500s
Packet size	256 Bytes	Packet rate	4 packets/s

Figure 4(1)-(2) shows the simulation results of the system with different number of attacker nodes, where the maximum speed of each node is 10m/s, and the pause time of the waypoint is 0s. Figure 4(1) shows the function relationship between the packet delivery ratio and the number of the attacker nodes, where the packet delivery ratio is the packets that been transferred correctly over the number of total packets been transferred. It is seen that the packet delivery ratio of transmission mode via SDTP decreases slower than that of the direct transmission mode when the number of the attacker nodes increases. The main reason for that is that when a malicious behavior takes place, the malicious node can be detected and removed from the data transmission route, and then it can no longer influence the transmission process. In addition, by using the error-correcting codes of Reed-Solomon codes, even when some segments are transferred in communication process, the packet can be recovered correctly on the destination node, so a re-sending process is not needed. Because of the computation delay in encode and decode and dynamic characteristics of the Ad Hoc network, when the number of the attacker nodes is small, the significance of using SDTP is not obvious, thus makes the packet delivery ratio a little smaller than direct transmission mode. On the other hand, when the number of the attacker is very large, the malicious nodes in one route will also increase, this makes it difficult to locate the malicious node accurately while the computation overhead of encoding and decoding of the Reed-Solomon codes is not negligible. Therefore the packet delivery ratio decreases rapidly, but it is still bigger than that of direct transmission mode. Figure 4(2) shows the end-to-end delay comparisons of the data transmission between SDTP mode and the direct mode. Because of the delay of encoding and decoding process, the end-to-end delay of SDTP mode is bigger than that of direct mode. It is the cost to obtain the security of data transmission in an insecure environment.

Figure 4(3)-(4) shows the simulation results for different node moving speeds, where the number of the attacker nodes is 10, and the pause of the waypoint is 0s. Figure 4(3) shows that the packet delivery ratio of the system run on SDTP is bigger than that of the system run on direct transmission mode at all simulated speeds. Despite the delay caused by encoding and decoding processes adversely decrease packet delivery ratio in SDTP, this is overcome by the benefit of excluding the

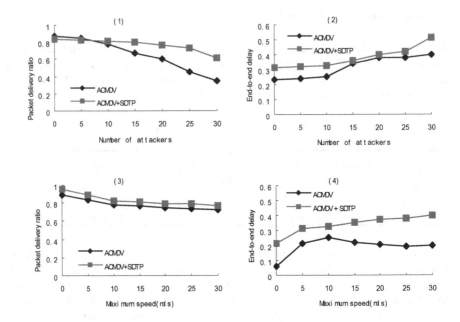

Fig. 4. Performance comparisons between direct transmitting and transmitting via SDTP

malicious node and therefore the rate that packets which correctly arrived increases. Figure 4(4) shows the end-to-end delay of these two modes, we can see that the delay of direct mode is smaller than that of the SDTP mode, however, data received by the destination node may contain error in direct mode, while SDTP can assure the received data are error free.

The proposed SDTP protocol not only can be used on disjoint route finding protocols such as AOMDV and multi-path finding DSR, it can also be used on other multi-path route finding protocols. The more paths take part in data transmitting, the more effective SDTP will be.

6   Conclusions

Based on the error-correcting Reed-Solomon codes, we present a secure data transmission protocol called SDTP for Ad Hoc networks that can resist the Byzantine attacks effectively. Data packets are all encoded by Reed-Solomon codes and cut into pieces before sending in different paths. After receiving all the pieces of a data packet, the destination node can judge whether a malicious modification has been occurred. A useful method to distinguish malicious behaviors from transmit errors is also proposed. The simulation results show that SDTP can locate the attacker nodes quickly and accurately in realistic environments and therefore may have wide applications together with a multi-path routing protocol.

References

1. Y. Hu, A. Perrig, D.B. Johnson. Ariadne: a secure on demand routing protocol for ad hoc networks. Proc. of ACM Mobicom, Atlanta, GA, Sept. 2002.
2. Y. Hu, D.B. Johnson, A. Perrig. SEAD: Secure efficient distance vector routing for mobile Ad Hoc networks. Proc. of the 4th IEEE Workshop on Mobile Computing Systems & Applications (WMCSA 2002), IEEE, Calicoon, NY, Jun. 2002.
3. B. Dahill, B. N. Levine, E. Royer, C. Shields. ARAN: A Secure Routing Protocol for Ad Hoc Networks. Umass Tech Report 02-32,2002.
4. K. Sanzgiri, B. Dahill, B. N. Levine, C. Shields, E. Belding-Royer. A Secure Routing Protocol for Ad Hoc Networks. 10th IEEE Intl. Conf. on Network Protocols (ICNP02), November 2002.
5. S. Cheung, K. Levitt. Protecting Routing Infrastructures from Denial of Service using Cooperative Intrusion Detection. Workshop on New Security Paradigms, 1997.
6. M.T. Goodrich, Efficient and Secure Network Routing Algorithms. http://www.cs.jhu.edu/goodrich/cgc/pubs/routing.pdf, Provisional patent filing, Jan. 2001.
7. S. Buchegger and J-Y.L. Boudec. Performance analysis of the CONFIDANT protocol. Proc. of the 3rd ACM international symposium on Mobile ad hoc networking & computing, Lausanne, Switzerland, Jun. 2002.
8. S. Buchegger, J-Y. Le Boudec. A robust reputation system for mobile ad-hoc networks. EPFL Technical report No. IC/2003/50, July 2003.
9. B. Awerbuch, D. Holmer, C. Nita-Rotaru, H. Rubens. An Ondemand Secure Routing Protocol Resilient to Byzantine Failures. ACM Workshop on Wireless Security (WiSe), Sept. 2002.
10. I. S. Reed and G. Solomon. Polynomial codes over certain finite fields. SIAM Journal of Applied Math, 8:300–304, 1960.
11. I. S. Reed and X. Chen. Error-Control Coding for Data Networks.Kluwer Academic PublisheReed-Solomon, 1999.
12. W. Diffie, M.E. Hellman. New directions in cryptography. IEEE Trans. Inform. Theory, IT-22:644–654, November 1976.
13. B. Yu, M. Yang, Z. Wang. Identify Abnormal Packet Loss in Selective Forwarding Attacks. Chinese Journal of Computer, 2006,29(9):1542-1552
14. K. M. Mahesh, R. D. Samir. Ad hoc on-demand multipath distance vector routing. ACM SIGMOBILE Mobile Computing and Communications Review, 2002,6(3):92-93

Defending DDoS Attacks Using Hidden Markov Models and Cooperative Reinforcement Learning*

Xin Xu[1], Yongqiang Sun[2], and Zunguo Huang[2]

[1] Institute of Automation, National University of Defense Technology,
410073, Changsha, P.R. China
[2] School of Computer, National University of Defense Technology,
410073, Changsha, P.R. China
xuxin_mail@263.net

Abstract. In recent years, distributed denial of service (DDoS) attacks have brought increasing threats to the Internet since attack traffic caused by DDoS attacks can consume lots of bandwidth or computing resources on the Internet and the availability of DDoS attack tools has become more and more easy. However, due to the similarity between DDoS attack traffic and transient bursts of normal traffic, it is very difficult to detect DDoS attacks accurately and quickly. In this paper, a novel DDoS detection approach based on Hidden Markov Models (HMMs) and cooperative reinforcement learning is proposed, where a distributed cooperation detection scheme using source IP address monitoring is employed. To realize earlier detection of DDoS attacks, the detectors are distributed in the mediate network nodes or near the sources of DDoS attacks and HMMs are used to establish a profile for normal traffic based on the frequencies of new IP addresses. A cooperative reinforcement learning algorithm is proposed to compute optimized strategies of information exchange among the distributed multiple detectors so that the detection accuracies can be improved without much load on information communications among the detectors. Simulation results on distributed detection of DDoS attacks generated by TFN2K tools illustrate the effectiveness of the proposed method.

1 Introduction

With the wide spread of the Internet, computer security has become a critical problem to our information society since large amounts of computer attacks or malicious cyber behaviors have been developed by exploiting various vulnerabilities in network protocols and operating systems and the losses caused by computer attacks increased a lot in recent years. To defend computer attacks as well as computer viruses, intrusion detection systems (IDSs) [1] have been considered to be one of most promising techniques for active defense because based on early detection of attack behaviors, corresponding response techniques can be used to stop and trace attacks. However, due to the vague distinctions between normal usages and attacks, how to detect attacks

---

* Supported by the National Natural Science Foundation of China Under Grant 60303012, National Fundamental Research Under Grant 2005CB321801.

accurately and timely is a challenging problem not only to the computer security field but also to the researchers from other communities such as machine learning, data mining [2], etc.

Until now, although there have been many research results on adaptive intrusion detection based on machine learning and data mining, much work still needs to be done in order to improve the performance of IDSs. One of the open problems remained is the accurate and early detection of denial of service (DoS) attacks. A denial of service attack is to cripple an online service by sending extremely large volumes of packets to a victim machine running the service. The attack traffic can consume the bandwidth resources of the network or the computing resources at the target machine so that legitimate requests for resources will be rejected. And it is hard to discriminate large volumes of attack traffic from transient burst of normal traffic. Although it may be easier to detect DoS attacks near the victim machine, it will be more valuable to be able to detect DoS traffic near the source [10] or in the medium network since to detect DoS traffic near the target is usually too late to take any responses to stop the attacks. The problem becomes more complicated when the attack traffic is produced by distributed attack sources, which is commonly referred to as a distributed denial of service (DDoS) attack [3-4]. A DDoS attack is launched by a master computer which can control lots of distributed "zombie" machines to send attack traffic to a particular destination machine. The distributed attack sources make it more difficult to detect DDoS attacks in the medium network or near the attack sources since the volumes of attack traffic become smaller due to distributed sources. Therefore, in recent years, there have been increasing interests on intrusion detection techniques for DDoS attacks. A popular way to establish DDoS detection model is to analyze the statistical properties of network traffic. In [5], a statistical method for detecting DDoS attacks was proposed by computing the entropy and frequency-sorted distributions of selected packet attributes. In [6] and [9], traffic models using Tcp flag rates and protocol rates were analyzed and it was shown that the two rates can be used as traffic features of flood attacks. A covariance analysis model for detecting SYN flooding attacks was proposed in [7]. In [8], an approach to reliably identifying signs of DDOS flood attacks based on LRD (long-range dependence) traffic pattern recognition has been discussed.

Despite of the above advances in DDoS detection techniques, there are still some open problems to be solved, one of which is to realize precise detection of DDoS attacks that are highly distributed. For this kind of DDoS attacks, e.g., the reflector attacks [13], it is very difficult to differentiate the statistical properties between normal traffic and DDoS traffic. Aiming at this open problem, a DDoS detection scheme based on the monitoring of new IP addresses was proposed in [11]. Since DDoS attack traffic uses randomly spoofed source IP addresses to disguise their true identities, the DDoS detection problem can be transformed to discriminate legal IP addresses from random IP addresses. Based on the above idea, a sequential non-parametric change point detection method was studied in [11] and it was shown that by using a sequential change point detection algorithm called Cusum (Cumulative sum), the temporal variations of source IP addresses can serve as important features for anomaly detection of DDoS attacks. However, the detection ability of simple Cusum algorithms may be inadequate for more distributed complex DoS attacks.

In this paper, to realize accurate anomaly detection of DDoS attacks, a sequential modeling approach based on Hidden Markov Models (HMMs) combined with source

IP monitoring is proposed. Since HMMs are a class of powerful statistical modeling tools and the variation of new IP addresses can serve as a fundamental feature of DDoS attacks, it will be very beneficial to use HMMs to differentiate normal traffic from DDoS attacks based on the monitoring of source IP addresses. Moreover, the proposed detection algorithm is integrated into a distributed detection framework so that highly distributed DoS attacks can be detected by cooperation among distributed detection agents. In the detection framework, a distributed reinforcement learning method is also presented to optimize the communication costs among detection agents. Experimental results using simulated DDoS attacks illustrate the effectiveness of the proposed methods.

This paper is organized as follows. In Section 2, a brief introduction on the distributed detection scheme for DDoS attacks is given. In Section 3, the detection algorithm based on HMMs and source IP monitoring is presented. In Section 4, a distributed cooperation algorithm based on reinforcement learning is proposed to optimize communication costs among detection agents. In Section 5, experiments of distributed detection for DDoS attacks are conducted and the results illustrate the effectiveness of the proposed method. Some conclusions and remarks on future work are given in Section 6.

2   A Distributed Detection Framework for DDoS Attacks

Earlier DDoS detection systems usually employ a centralized detection and response mechanism. Nevertheless, with the increase of network scales and traffic volumes, a centralized DDoS detection system can become a communication bottleneck due to the need to download and process all the traffic measurements at a single location. Furthermore, if there are any faults in a centralized detection system, the whole system will not be able to work until recoveries can be implemented. Therefore, decentralized detection techniques for DDoS attacks have received much attention in recent years. In a decentralized detection system, multiple DDoS detection sub-systems or agents are placed at different locations in the network, and summary statistics of these agents can be shared to improve the detection accuracy of the whole system. In [14], a multi-agent detection framework for detecting DDoS attacks was proposed and it was shown that by sharing distributed beliefs on possible attacks, the detection efficiency of DDoS attacks can be improved.

In the following, we will employ a similar distributed detection framework as in [14], which is depicted in Fig.1. In the framework, multiple detection agents are placed at the edge routers of different transit networks and there is a communication mechanism, e.g., an information broadcasting mechanism, among these detection agents. Although every single agent only observes local information, the detection accuracy can be improved by combing information or decisions among agents. Thus, a cooperation mechanism is also needed in the distributed detection system to detect any abnormal changes in the traffic. The distributed detection framework has the advantages of scalability, and robustness to a single point of failure. Based on the above framework, the main contributions of this paper will focus on a new HMM-based sequential modeling method for single detection agent using source IP monitoring and a distributed reinforcement learning strategy to optimize the communication costs among agents.

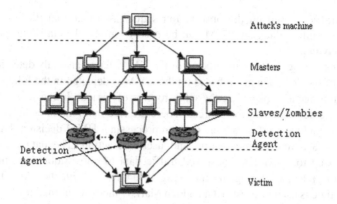

Fig. 1. A distributed detection framework for DDoS attacks

3 DDoS Detection Based on HMMs and IP Monitoring

As analyzed in previous works [11], an intrinsic feature for DDoS traffic is the increasing of new source IP addresses. It was observed in [15] that most source IP addresses are new to the victim during a DoS attack, whereas most source IP addresses in a normal flash crowd are usually not new to the victim. Thus, source IP monitoring is very promising to realize efficient DDoS detection systems.

Being a popular sequential modeling approach, HMMs have been widely studied and applied in lots of areas such as speech recognition [12], protein structure prediction, etc. In recent years, HMM-based intrusion detection models have also been studied in the literature and it has been demonstrated that HMMs are very powerful for sequential modeling of temporally related observations. However, previous results [18] mainly focused on host-based intrusion detection using sequences of system calls. In this paper, by combining the mechanism of source IP monitoring, we will present a new HMM-based DDoS detection method and it will be beneficial for the detection of more distributed and complex DDoS attacks.

In the mechanism of source IP address monitoring, an IP address database (IAD) is used to record frequently observed IP addresses and it is dynamically updated to detect new IP addresses. To update the IAD, frequently observed IP addresses can be selected and added to the IAD by two strategies. One is to select IP addresses that were observed for at least m times in a given time period. And the other is to use IP addresses that have packet numbers greater than n. In practice, the two selection strategies can be combined and only IP addresses that both satisfy the conditions of the two strategies can be selected [11]. Then, the IP addresses in the IAD can be viewed as a collection of recently appeared normal IP addresses. In real-time applications, various Hashing techniques can be employed to accelerate the querying process of the IAD.

After constructing the IAD, the incoming traffic can simply be represented by the observation features about whether a source IP address is new according to the IAD. A simple way to derive the observation features is to select two possible observation values $o_1(t)=1$ and $o_2(t)=2$, which correspond to the source IP address at time step t being a new address or an old address in the IAD, respectively. Therefore, a temporal sequence of the two-valued observation features can be used to characterize the incoming traffic. Based on the observation sequences of normal traffic, which are collected as training data, an HMM can be used to model the statistical property of normal behaviors.

Before discussing the training process of the HMM-based anomaly detection model, a structure of the detection agent based on the HMM is depicted in the following Fig.2. The detection agent is placed at the edge routers of various Intranets so that DDoS attacks can be detected near the sources. There are five main modules in the detection agent, which include model training, data preprocessing, HMM decision, IAD update, and the interface for communication and user interaction. The data preprocessing module is used to convert the observed traffic data to observation sequences $\{o(1), o(2), \ldots, o(t)\}$ by comparing the incoming IP addresses with the IAD. The model training module is used to construct a Hidden Markov model of normal traffic and based on the model, the HMM decision module computes the anomaly likelihood of an incoming observation sequence of IP addresses in real time. If the output of the decision module indicates that a DDoS attack is happening, it can send messages to the filtering module in a boundary router so that certain response actions can be taken to stop and trace the DDoS attack. The IAD update module is employed to dynamically select source IP addresses that are frequently observed by the system. Since the information of a single detection agent is usually inadequate to accurately detect highly distributed DoS attacks, information sharing among multiple agents will be essential to improve detection precision. Therefore, there is an interface for communication and user interaction in the detection agent to realize reliable communications between agents.

Using the above structure of detection agents, the DDoS detection problem can be solved by anomaly detection strategies based on the training of an HMM for normal traffic. In the following, we will present some details about the HMM and the anomaly detection strategy.

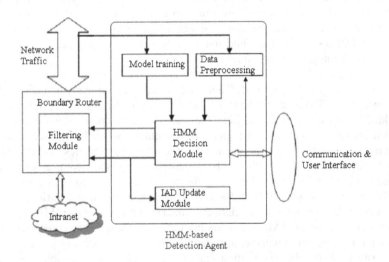

Fig. 2. An HMM-based detection agent for DDoS attacks

A discrete state, discrete time, first order hidden Markov model describes a stochastic, memory-less process. A full HMM can be specified as a tuple: $\lambda = (N, M, A, B, \pi)$, where N is the number of states, M is the number of observable symbols, π is the initial state distribution, A is the state transition probability matrix which satisfies the Markov property:

$$a_{ij} = P(q_{t+1} = j | q_t = i) = P(q_{t+1} = j | q_t = i, q_{t-1}, ..., q_0) \tag{1}$$

and B is the observation probability distribution, which can be described as:

$$b_j(k) = P(o_t = k | q_t = j), \ i \leqslant k \leqslant M \tag{2}$$

An important problem in HMMs is the model learning problem which is to estimate the model parameters when the model is unknown and only observation data can be obtained. For model learning in HMMs, the Expectation-Maximization (EM) algorithm is the most popular one which finds maximum *a posteriori* or maximum likelihood parameter estimate from incomplete data. In this paper, we make use of the Baum-Welch algorithm in the model training for normal traffic. The Baum-Welch algorithm is a particular form of EM for maximum likelihood parameter estimation in HMMs. For a detailed description of the Baum-Welch algorithm, please refer to [12].

In our implementation of the Baum-Welch algorithm, the hidden state number of the HMM is set to 2, which is equal to the number of possible observation values. When the model training of the HMM is completed, the obtained model λ can be used to compute the probability of occurrence for a particular observation sequence, $O = \{o_1, ..., o_k\}$, given the model λ, where k is the length of the observation sequence and $P(O|\lambda)$ can be computed as follows:

$$P(O \mid \lambda) = \sum_q P(O \mid q, \lambda) P(q \mid \lambda) \tag{3}$$

where q is a possible state sequence corresponding to the observation sequence O. The computation of $P(O|\lambda)$ can be implemented efficiently by using the Forward or Backward algorithm studied in the HMM literature [12].

The basic principle for anomaly detection based on HMMs is to establish an HMM-based profile for normal training data and compute the probability of occurrence for a particular observation sequence. When the probability is greater than a predefined threshold, the observation sequence can be assumed to be normal. On the other hand, an observation sequence can be detected as abnormal behaviors or DDoS attacks if the probability of occurrence is below the threshold. The threshold of the detection model can be determined using another set of training data which have both normal traffic data and abnormal data with attacks.

Then, the detection process of the HMM-based agent can be implemented by comparing the occurrence probability $P(O|\lambda)$ with a predefined threshold μ and we can use the following detection rule for DDoS attacks:

$$if \ \log P(O \mid \lambda) < -\mu, \ then \ raise \ alarms \tag{4}$$

where $\mu > 0$.

4   Cooperative RL for Performance Optimization

The HMM-based detection model and learning algorithm discussed in Section 3 provide an efficient method for sequential probabilistic modeling and anomaly detection of DDoS attacks by source IP monitoring in a single detection system. However, in real applications, it will be more practical to make use of multiple detection agents to solve the problems of data processing bottleneck and single-point failure. Thus, the distributed detection framework introduced in Section 2 needs to be employed by incorporating with the HMM-based detection method using source IP monitoring. In addition, cooperation among the detection agents is also needed since every single agent only has local information to detect possible attacks.

To share the information or detection results among agents, a simple strategy is to broadcast all the observation sequences among the detection agents and every agent can merge the observation results of the other agents to improve the detection accuracy. However, the above simple broadcast strategy will usually bring about large amounts of communication costs, which is impractical for large-scale applications with limited communication bandwidth. One solution is to make every agents learn to determine when to communicate with others or not based on the current observation and detection results. For example, when there are few evidences for possible attacks, it may be beneficial not to communicate with other agents. But too few communications may decrease the detection ability of the whole system since every agent only has local information. Hence, it is necessary to develop some optimization mechanisms for communication costs while ensuring good detection accuracies of DDoS attacks. In the following, we will present an adaptive learning method based on distributed reinforcement learning in order to find out good policies for detection agents under dynamic uncertain environments.

Reinforcement learning (RL) [16] is a class of machine learning methods that aims to solve sequential decision problems by interacting with the environment. Unlike supervised learning, RL agents do not have teacher signals for observed states during training and they only receive evaluative, usually delayed, rewards or feedbacks from the environment. So reinforcement learning is more suitable than supervised learning for many uncertain decision applications, where the expected goals or optimization objectives can only be expressed as evaluative rewards. For multi-agent problems, distributed reinforcement learning is also very promising for optimizing the cooperation policies between agents. For example, the multi-agent elevator scheduling problem introduced in [16] was successfully solved by distributed reinforcement learning (DRL) based on neural networks. Although similar DRL algorithms with delayed rewards and function approximators may be used to optimize the communication policies of DDoS detection agents, due to the demands of real-time applications, we only use a simplified DRL algorithm with immediate rewards and the state space of the learning algorithm has discrete values. The main components of the DRL include a definition of the state space, an action policy for every state, a reward function after every action and state transition, and a state-action value function to estimate the rewards obtained after a state-action pair.

In the proposed DRL algorithm, every agent has a state variable $h = P(O|\lambda)$, which is equal to the decision output defined in Section 3. As discussed above, when a threshold μ is selected, the variation of h is usually within $[-\mu, 0]$ for normal traffic since if $h < -\mu$, it is certain to raise alarms for DDoS attacks. Then, the state space can be divided into N intervals in $[-\mu, 0]$ and we can make the state variable h has N discrete values according to the intervals between $-\mu$ and 0. For every discrete value of h, a policy function can be defined to decide whether to broadcast current information to other agents. Based on the action selection and the obtained results, a reward function can be defined as follows.

(1) If a communication action was performed and after the communication, DDoS attacks were detected, a positive reward is given.
(2) If a communication action was performed and after the communication, no DDoS attacks were detected, a negative reward is given.
(3) If no communication action is performed, a zero reward is given.

For every state-action pair, a value function $Q(s, a)$ is defined to estimate the rewards to be obtained after an action taken at state s. The above definition is popularly used in the reinforcement learning literature, where Q-learning and distributed Q-learning algorithms [17] are the most famous ones. However, the simple DRL algorithm presented here only considers the estimation of immediate rewards. Following is a description of the simple DRL algorithm for the optimization of communication costs among agents.

(*Algorithm* 1: DRL for communication cost optimization)
(1) Initialize the Q values for all state-action pairs.
(2) Loop until a termination condition is satisfied:
 (2.1) For current state s, compute the probability of taking action a

$$P(a) = e^{Q(s,a)} / \sum_{a \in A} e^{Q(s,a)} \tag{5}$$

 (2.2) Select an action according to the action probability.
 (2.3) Observe the state transition from s to s', and receive an immediate reward r, which was defined above.
 (2.4) Compute new Q values

$$Q(s,a) = \alpha_t r_t + Q(S,a) \tag{6}$$

where α_t is a learning factor.
 (2.5) Let $s=s'$.   □

The termination condition for Algorithm 1 can be selected as the maximum number of iteration steps or the estimations of Q values stabilize within a given threshold.

5 Experiments

In this section, some experimental results are given to illustrate the effectiveness of the proposed method. The experiments include two stages. In the experiments of stage one, the performance of a single DDoS detection agent based on HMMs and source IP monitoring is evaluated. In the model training process, the normal data in the first week traffic of the DARPA99 data set [2] was used so that the IAD and the HMM can be constructed using the proposed method, where the Baum-Welch algorithm was employed for detection model training. After model training, the performance of the HMM-based anomaly detection model was tested on hybrid traffic combining DDoS attack data generated by the TFN2K tool with another week of normal data from the DARPA 99 data set.

As discussed in Section 3, an observation sequence $O = \{o_{t-k+1},\ldots,o_t\}$ is formed at every time step t and the occurrence probability $P(O|\lambda)$ can be computed, where k is the length of the observation sequence. Then, a threshold μ can be selected to decide whether to raise alarms based on (4). In the experiments, we used different values of observation sequence length k and the detection values $\log(P(O|\lambda))$ were depicted in Fig. 3 (a) and (b) for test sequence length $k=30$ and $k=90$, respectively.

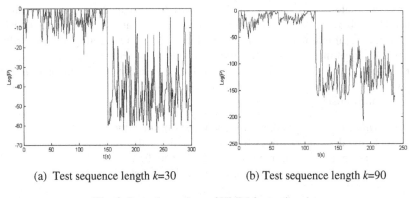

(a) Test sequence length $k=30$ (b) Test sequence length $k=90$

Fig. 3. Detection values of HMM for testing data

In Fig.3 (a), normal data from DARPA 99 data set were sent out by the tcp-replay program from $t=1$s to $t=150$s and after $t=150s$, DDoS traffic was mixed with normal data by TFN2k DDoS tools. In Fig.3 (b), the normal data from the DARPA 99 data set were sent out from $t=1$s to $t=115$s and after $t=115s$, the DDoS traffic was mixed with normal data. From Fig.3 (a) and (b), it is demonstrated that the HMM-based detection value can differentiate normal data from DDoS attacks well, especially when a relatively large observation sequence length was selected. In our experiments, it was observed that when the length of observation sequences is 90, a detection rate of 97% can be obtained with zero false alarms. And if the length of observation sequences equals 120, 100% detection rate can be obtained.

During the second stage of experiments, a prototype of the distributed detection framework for DDoS attacks was implemented with three detection agents. To simulate distributed monitoring and detection, one single agent only observes a part of the IP address space in the whole data set. The following Fig.4 shows the Detection values of a single agent without and with communication. In Fig.4 (a), it can be seen that when there are no communication and information sharing among the agents, the detection values of a single agent can not differentiate normal data from attack traffic. While in Fig.4 (b), it is shown that by making use of communication and information sharing, the detection ability of agents can be improved a lot.

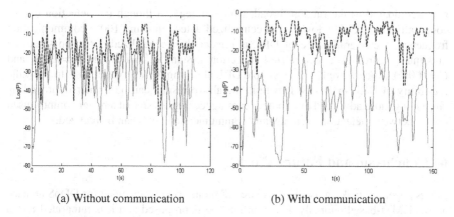

(a) Without communication   (b) With communication

Fig. 4. Detection values of a single agent without and with communication (Real line: detection values for attack traffic; dotted line: normal traffic)

Table 4.1. Performance comparison between DRL and random broadcasting

	Cooperative detection using DRL			Cooperative detection using random broadcasting		
	Detection rate (%)	Communication frequency (%)	Overall Score	Detection rate (%)	Communication Frequency(%)	Overall score
1	79.2	74.6	1.06	45.5	51.7	0.88
2	76.4	74.4	1.02	45.0	50.0	0.90
3	64.1	51.9	1.23	48.7	48.0	1.01

In addition to show the performance improvement based on information sharing among detection agents, another important objective of the experiments on distributed detection for DDoS attacks is to evaluate the performance of the proposed DRL algorithm for the optimization of communication costs among detection agents. In the experiments, a random broadcasting strategy was also implemented for comparison. The performance of the DRL approach and the random broadcasting strategy for communication and information sharing was evaluated by three criteria. One is the detection rate Dr of DDoS attacks with zero false alarms. The second criterion is the communication frequency Cr for a detection agent during the detection process. And an overall score S if computed by $S=Dr/Cr$. Thus, the overall score indicates the agent's ability to improve detection accuracy and decrease communication costs at the same time. In the experiments, three independent data sets from DARPA 99 with simulated DDoS attacks using TFN2k were used for performance evaluation. The results are shown in the above Table 4.1. From Table 4.1, it is illustrated that by making use of DRL, the performance of detection rate and communication costs can be improved when compared to the random broadcasting strategy. Although the detection rate of cooperative detection is lower than centralized detection using 100% communication frequency, the overall score of DRL is greater than centralized detection since the maximum score for a centralized detection system is $S=1$ (with $Dr=100\%$ and $Cr=100\%$). Since we only used a simple DRL algorithm in the experiments to show the feasibility of DRL in DDoS detection, the above results can be further improved by employing more advanced distributed learning techniques so that a better compromised policy between detection accuracy and communication costs can be realized.

6   Conclusion and Future Work

In this paper, by making use of the source IP monitoring mechanism for DDoS attacks, a new HMM-based anomaly detection method is proposed and it is integrated into a distributed detection framework for DDoS detection. A distributed reinforcement learning approach is presented to enable the optimization between detection accuracy and communication costs among multiple detection agents. Experimental results show that the HMM-based detection model can achieve high detection accuracy with zero false alarms. For the distributed detection scheme based on HMMs, it is illustrated that the proposed DRL is very promising to optimize the detection accuracy while reduce communication costs at the same time. However, much work still needs to be done in the near future, which include the evaluation of the HMM-based approach in real-time DDoS detection cases, and the applications of new DRL algorithms to realize better compromises between detection accuracy and communication burden.

References

1. Denning, D.: An Intrusion-Detection Model. IEEE Transactions on Software Engineering, Vol.13, No 2 (1987) 222-232
2. Lee, W.K., Stolfo, S.J.: A Data Mining Framework for Building Intrusion Detection Model. In: Gong L., Reiter M.K. (eds.): Proceedings of the IEEE Symposium on Security and Privacy. Oakland, CA: IEEE Computer Society Press (1999) 120~132
3. Mirkovic J. and Reiher P.: A Taxonomy of DDoS Attack and DDoS Defense Mechanisms. ACM SIGCOMM Computer Communications Review, 34(2), (2004) 39-54,.
4. Chang, R. K. C. Defending against flooding-based, distributed denial-of-service attacks: A tutorial, IEEE Communications Magazine 40(10), (2002) 42-51.
5. Feinstein, L., Schnackenberg, D.: Statistical Approaches to DDoS Attack Detection and Response. Proceedings of the DARPA Information Survivability Conference and Expostion(DISCEX'03), (2003) 303□314
6. Noh S., Lee C., Jung, G., Choi, K.: Using Inductive Learning for the Detection of Distributed Denial of Service Attacks, Lecture Notes in Computer Science, LNCS 2690, (2003) 286-295
7. Jin, S., Yeung, D. S.: A Covariance Analysis Model for DDoS Attack Detection. In: Proc. of the Int'l Conf. on Communications. IEEE, (2004) 1882-1886.
8. Li, M.: An Approach to Reliably Identifying Signs of DDoS Flood Attacks Based on LRD Traffic Pattern Recognition. Computer and Security, 23(7), (2004) 549-558.

9. Seo, J., Lee, C., Moon J.: Defending DDoS Attacks Using Network Traffic Analysis and Probabilistic Packet Drop. In Proc. of GCC 2004 Workshops, LNCS, Volume 3252, (2004) 390-397
10. Mirkovic, J., Prier, G. & Reiher, P.: Attacking DDoS at the Source, in Proceedings of International Conference on Network Protocols, Paris, France, (2002) 312-321.
11. Peng, T., Christopher, Kotagiri L, R.: Proactively Detecting Distributed Denial of Service Attacks Using Source IP Ad-dress Monitoring. in Proceedings of the Third International IFIP-TC6 Networking Conference, Berlin Heidelberg, Springer, (2004) 771-782
12. Rabiner, L.R.: A Tutorial on Hidden Markov Models and Selected Applications in Speech Recognition. Proceedings of the IEEE, 77(2), (1986) 257-286
13. Paxson, V,: An Analysis of Using Reflectors for Distributed Denial-of-Service Attacks. Computer Communication Review 31(3), (2001) 76-89
14. Peng, T., Leckie, C., and Kotagiri, R.: Detecting Distributed Denial of Service Attacks by Sharing Distributed Beliefs. in Proc. of 8th Australasian Conference on Information Security and Privacy, Wollongong, Australia, Lecture Notes in Computer Science, LNCS 2727, (2003) 214-225
15. Jung, J., Krishnamurthy, B. and Rabinovich, M..: Flash Crowds and Denial of Service Attacks: Characterization and Implications for CDNs and Web Sites. In Proceeding of 11th Word Wide Web conference. Honolulu, Hawaii, USA. (2002)
16. Sutton, R., and Barto, A. G.: Reinforcement Learning: An Introduction. MIT Press, Cambridge, MA, (1998).
17. Hu, J., Wellman, M. P.: Multiagent Reinforcement Learning: Theoretical Framework and an Algorithm. In *15th Intl Conference on Machine Learning*, (1998) 242-250.
18. Xu, X.: A Reinforcement Learning Approach for Host-Based Intrusion Detection Using Sequences of System Calls. *Lecture Notes in Computer Science*, LNCS 3644, (2005) 995 –1003

A Novel Relational Database Watermarking Algorithm

Yu Fu[1], Cong Jin[1,*], and Chuanxiang Ma[2]

[1] Department of Computer Science, Central China Normal University,
Wuhan 430079, P.R. China
dede91@mail.ccnu.edu.cn
[2] School of Mathematics and Computer Science, Hubei University,
Wuhan 430062, P.R. China

Abstract. We propose a new watermarking algorithm for relational database which is based on spread spectrum techniques in this paper. We assign different owners for different identification key to generate the special watermarking signal and insert it into appropriate tuples. At the watermarking detection step, we use the technique of even parity check and majority voting for the watermark accuracy. It is to establish that a false positive judgment is highly unlikely by evaluating the similarity of watermarks between the original and the one gotten from the detection step. Experimental results are also presented to support that it is robust in the present of the various attacks and positive updating such as adding, deleting and modifying.

1 Introduction

More recently, some pioneer research has been done to secure proof of rights over relational data. It is the techniques for watermarking relational database. Because of the characteristics of relational data, watermarking relational data presents a different set of challenges and associated constrains. By far, effective algorithm and watermarking software are very rare. So it is a rather practical application and research topic for solutions that deserve serious concern. Some researchers have been searching for the solutions. Among these systems proposed by R.Agrawal[1] and R.Sion[2] are the most well-known. They designed a watermarking system that protects the privacy and ownership of database. This method is a blinder algorithm. The drawback of this solution is that the algorithm is just a match method. The result of this match process can just tell us the information yes or no; it can't tell us more information about some specific meaning, such as some strings representing the name of a company. The solution proposed by R.Sion[2] starts by selecting a maximal number of unique subsets of the original data resource using a set of secret key. The subset which is collected is normalizing distributed. The distribution of these subsets is a bell shape. But this method is only suitable for the data resources which have the same distributions and have little differences between two data value because of the utilization of metrics which are defined in terms of mean squared error. The drawback of this metric is that the value which is gotten from the calculation can only be used for

---

* Corresponding author.

C.C. Yang et al. (Eds.): PAISI 2007, LNCS 4430, pp. 208–219, 2007.

a part of data items, because the span of the different attributes in the relational database is very difference. So the drawbacks of the solution will bounds on the capacity of the watermark which is inserted.

Among many watermarking algorithms, spread spectrum technique[3-4] is very important for inserting watermarking. In this paper, we propose a new watermarking algorithm especially for the relational database based on spread spectrum, and it has properties such as imperceptibility, robustness, high detection reliability, etc.

2 Relational Database Watermarking Algorithm

There are many independent tuples contained in a relational database[5-6]. Because each attribute in the tuple has a certain value, the space for redundant information is minor. It is defined that the numeric attribute is consist of integral part and that the fixed-point part, according to the definition of the relational database structure. We may define the level of the precision of the attribute higher than the need of actual application so as to take the approximate value at the operation of truncation and round-up. So based on this nature, the watermark can be inserted into the database which has increased redundant space by producing tolerate change to the minor modification of the value of the attribute.

A tolerance is the cumulative change of the data that is acceptable. On the other hand, it is the redundant space for inserting the watermark. To avoid the changes of value violating the permitted limit, we specify a relative change in value δ to constrain the violations, while protecting the normal joins between tuples. If the tolerances are too high, the intended purpose of the data cannot be preserved after watermarking. If they are too low, it may not be possible to insert a watermark in the data. So this is an important parameter since it can be used to adjust the quality of the watermark. Generally speaking, the bigger the value of the attribute, the higher of the tolerance is. Experimental results show that each value may be altered by no more than 0.0005 or 0.02 percent. Bounds on the tolerance can be specified by the domain of the attribute when tabling.

The relational database is similar to the general data sets. There is no fixed ordering among tuples of a relation. Primary key and foreign key are two kind of specific attributes in the relational data. The primary key must identify one tuple uniquely. If we simply insert the watermark into the database directly, it will result in the value of the primary key nonunique or may change the value of the foreign key which will result the join between tuples plain wrong.

The above discussion makes it clear that the critical issue of embedding the watermarks requires the new value for any attribute should be unique after the watermarking process and the change of the foreign key doesn't interfere with the normal join relationship between tuples. So tuples that will join before watermarking also can join after watermarked. Clearly, one can be permitted to modify the ordering between tuples and attribute, but can't alter the database itself directly with respect to the intended use of the data. The solution is that we can only select a portion of numeric attributes to apply a minor change.

We now propose a solution for watermarking database relations. Our technique is inserting watermark signal (w) corresponding to the text watermark (t) which represent the ownership of database into the numeric attributes that could tolerant certain error.

Spread spectrum is a means of transmission in which the signal occupies a bandwidth in excess of the minimum necessary to send the information; the band spread is accomplished by means of a code which is independent of the data, and a synchronized reception with the code at the receiver is used for dispreading and subsequently recovering the data. Under this definition, first we suppose that the percentage of the tuple which will be modified is θ in the database, avoiding massively changing the database which may results in interfering with the particular data uses and metrics of quality. The primary key attribute is the reference attribute. By using the principle of frequency hopping spread spectrum, we check the value (p), the primary key of each attribute, one by one. Another parameter is k, the private key of the watermark. The deciding function S makes the decision of into which tuple could be inserted the signal of watermark. The parameter of function S is k, θ, p, as

$$S(k,p,\theta) = \begin{cases} True......embed \\ False \ \ .....skip \end{cases}. \tag{1}$$

Then, we design the function W the watermark signal generator[7] with the parameter k which is the private key of the watermark and the information of text watermark t by using the technique of direct sequence spread spectrum. The watermark signal which is generated by $W(t, k)$ is $w=\{+1,-1\}$.

$$W(t,k) = \begin{cases} +1, & t = 1 \\ -1, & t = 0 \end{cases}. \tag{2}$$

Where t is an ASCII bits stream of the text watermark.

Suppose that the tolerance of the value of the objective attribute into which will be inserted watermark is δ. The metric of inserting the watermark signal is to change the value d of the objective attribute by positive or negative revision. The value of objective attribute which is changed is represented as

$$\hat{d} = d + \frac{\delta}{2} \times w. \tag{3}$$

After the process of making the decision which tuple could be inserted the watermark, a one-way hash function will operate on the attribute of these tuples which have been selected by the function S.

Because the modification of the ordering of the tuple and attribute don't interfere with the normal use of the data, it can insert the watermark into the data which has been processed by Hash function. The processing of Hash function is virtually a procedure of data chaotic. Therefore, it disperses the impact which caused from the distortion produced by watermark operated on the database[8], so as to enhance the ability of recovery and robustness of the watermark.

After changing the text watermark into the bit flow w, we then split this bit flow into groups, making each group contain three bits. If the last group is insufficient, we may add one or two zero to make it complete. The reason for us to do this is for the convenience of the next operation which will encode the watermark signal w by using the technique of even parity check.

For each three-bit group, correspondingly, we divide the set of attribute which have been operated by Hash function into subsets. Each subset contains three attributes and will be encoded 3 bits of one group expressed above. So each attribute will be inserted one bit watermark signal.

In the aspect of coding, we use the technique of error correction to operate on the original watermark information. New algorithm use the method of even parity check encoding, which can correct single random error, as we sets information code for 3 bits (recorded as a_0, a_1, a_2) and monitor code for 3 bits (recorded as a_3, a_4, a_5). According to the exclusive-OR operation and the majority voting principle, we present the consistent monitor relation of the even parity check as follows:

$$\begin{cases} a_0 \oplus a_1 = a_3 \\ a_0 \oplus a_2 = a_4 \\ a_1 \oplus a_2 = a_5 \end{cases} . \tag{4}$$

Transformed to

$$\begin{cases} a_0 \oplus a_1 \oplus a_3 = 0 \\ a_0 \oplus a_2 \oplus a_4 = 0 \\ a_1 \oplus a_2 \oplus a_5 = 0 \end{cases} . \tag{5}$$

So, we can inference the monitor code according to the (4) (5) after we have known the value of the information code. Then we can get the even parity check code as:

$$a = a_0 a_1 a_2 a_3 a_4 a_5 .$$

Because the grouping code supervise the information code by the additive monitor code, the two establish the relationship of supervision by establish the system of equations. Thus, when the information code has been lost, which is caused by the operation or the attack of the relational database, the mutual restriction relations correspondent to the code in the system of equations may be destroyed. So we can discover the mistakes easily during the watermark detection through parity check equations. But we can know the position of the mistakes and correct them only when the number of the mistakes is odd. In order to describe the method of the correction more concretely, we transform (5) to

$$\begin{cases} s_1 = a_0 \oplus a_1 \oplus a_3 \\ s_2 = a_0 \oplus a_2 \oplus a_4 \\ s_3 = a_1 \oplus a_2 \oplus a_5 \end{cases} . \tag{6}$$

According to the relationship of the supervision, if the information code which is gets at the watermark detection step doesn't have mistakes, in the (6) $s_1 = s_2 = s_3 = 0$. But when the information code has mistakes, at least one is not 0 in the result of s_1, s_2, s_3. Thus we can find the wrong position accurately and give the correction to the mistakes according to the different value of s_1, s_2, s_3 that is it can correct a mistake of the information code. In order to avoid the situation which there is 2 mistakes in the information code, we use the technique of majority voting to the watermark which is gotten from the watermark detection. It can not only enhance the level of the accuracy of the watermark, but also intensify the error control ability, so as to resistant attack to the large area of the watermark and increase the level of the robustness of the watermark.

As mentioned above, in order to increase the detection efficiency, we get the correct watermarking information bit by the technique of majority voting. At watermark detection time, after recovering all the watermark copies from the given data, we implored majority voting over all the recovered watermark bits in order to determine the most likely initial watermark bits.

The following is an example of majority voting over five recovered watermark copies for a 9 bits sized original watermark.

Bit	8	7	6	5	4	3	2	1	0
w_0	0	0	0	0	0	1	0	1	0
w_1	0	1	1	1	0	0	1	0	0
w_2	0	1	0	1	1	1	0	1	1
w_3	0	0	1	0	1	1	1	0	1
w_4	1	0	0	0	1	0	0	0	1
w_{result}	0	0	0	0	1	1	0	0	1

After get the result of the majority voting for the most likely initial watermarks, we will divide the result into group, each group contains 3 bits. Then each group will be subject to even parity check, the detect key is the union of the monitor code which is produced at the even parity check encoding time and the private key when inserting the watermark.

2.1 Watermark Insertion

As expressed in Section 2, we decide which tuple can be embedding the watermark by using the technique of spread spectrum, and the function $W(t,k)$ produce the watermark signal $w=\{+1, -1\}$ by the technique of direct sequence spread spectrum.

For every watermark tuple, suppose the value of the object attribute into which will be inserted the watermark is d, the tolerance for which is δ. Suppose $X=\{x_1,...,x_l\} \subset R$ is the data to be watermarked and $\overline{X}$ is the average value for the data, as the definition of the mean square error $E=\sqrt{\dfrac{\sum(\overline{X}-x_i)^2}{l}}$, so $\delta=\dfrac{E}{\overline{X}}$. The algorithm adjusts the value of d appropriately. The remainder of the d divided by δ represents the watermarking signal w. If the remainder is bigger than or equal to $\dfrac{\delta}{2}$, the watermark signal w is +1, otherwise, the watermarking signal is -1. Suppose that the value after change is $\hat{d}$, the adjustment can be represented as follows

$$
\begin{cases}
d + \dfrac{\delta}{2} & w = 1 \ and \ (d \bmod \delta) < \dfrac{\delta}{2} \\
d - \dfrac{\delta}{2} & w = -1 \ and \ (d \bmod \delta) \ge \dfrac{\delta}{2} \\
d & else
\end{cases}
\tag{7}
$$

We give the watermark insertion algorithm as follows:

Watermark (attribute, wm_key, text, db_primary_key)

t ←text_to_flow(text);   // change the text to the bit

w ←stream_W(t, wm_key)   //change the text to the bit flow

w' ←group_triple(w)   // classify the watermark into groups by 3 bits

$n \leftarrow \dfrac{length(w)}{3}$ // n is the number of the groups

C ←Even(w')   // Even parity check encoding to the w'

For each tuple $r \in R$

  if $S(w, p, \theta) = true$

    subset_bin←tuple r

    Sorted_attribute←sort_on_hash (subset_bin, db_primary_key, wm_key)

    //disarrange the order of the attribute of the tuples which will be watermarked

    V_i ←Vector_attribute (sorted_attribute, s, wm_key)

    //classify the attribute into the vectors, each vector has 3 attributes for each

attribute of V_i do

    for each 3_bit_set of w'

     index i ←index(w') mod 3

    for (k=0; $k \leq 2$; k++)

    A_K^W =Encode (A_k , w_i')   // mark the attribute

    Detect_key=($\sum_{i=1}^{n*s} C_i$) $\cup$ wm_key //generate the private key for the detection step

    Encode(A_k , w_i , wm_key)

     compute δ

    D= the value of the A_k

      $\gamma = d$ mod δ

      While (w_i' =+1 and $\gamma < \frac{\delta}{2}$) do

      $d' = d + \dfrac{\delta}{2}$

      While ($w_i' = -1$ and $\gamma \geq \frac{\delta}{2}$) do

       $d' = d - \frac{\delta}{2}$

  else

    $d' = d$

  return Detect_key

2.2 Watermark Detection

First, we assume the attackers does not change the primary key attribute or the value of primary keys since the primary key contains valuable information and changing it will make the database less useful.

At the watermark detection, we can also use the technique of spread spectrum, utilizing the function S whose parameters are the private key (wm_key), the percentage of the tuple which will be modified (θ), the value of each primary key attribute (p) to filter the tuple which is suspicious of having inserted watermark. Then we extract the watermark signal (w^*) from the value of the objective attribute d^* which is suspicious of having inserted watermark. The extraction method can be described as follows:

$$w^* = \begin{cases} +1 & if \ (d^* \bmod \delta) \geq \frac{\delta}{2} \\ -1 & if \ (d^* \bmod \delta) < \frac{\delta}{2} \end{cases}. \tag{8}$$

We give the watermark detection algorithm as follows:

Detect(attribute, wm_key, db_primary_key, Detect_key)

For each tuple $r \in R$

  if $S(w, p, \theta) = true$

    subset_bin $\leftarrow$ tuple r

    Sorted_attribute $\leftarrow$ sort_on_hash(subset_bin,db_primary_key,wm_key)

    V_i $\leftarrow$ Vector_attribute (sorted_attribute, s, wm_key)   // V_i is the vector of the attribute which will be detected whether have the watermark information

For each vector of V do

  $w_i^* \leftarrow Decode(V_i)$ // extract the watermarking bit

  $W^* \leftarrow stream\_W(w_i^*, wm\_key)$ //assemble the single bit to the bit flow

  $Rate_i \leftarrow majority\_voting(W^*, wm\_key)$ // $Rate_i$ is the rate of the voting vector for each watermarking bit

  $3\_bit\_set \leftarrow Correct^*(Rate_i, Detect\_key)$ // get the set of the watermark after even parity check and majority voting, 3 bits for each set

  text $\leftarrow$ bitflow_to_text ($\cup 3\_bit\_set$) // change the bit flow to the text return text

  $Decode(V_i, wm\_key)$ // watermarking extraction for one bit

For each attribute of V_i do

  compute δ

  d =the value of the A_k

if ($d \bmod \delta \geq \frac{\delta}{2}$)

$\quad w^* = +1$

else $w^* = -1$

return w^*

3 Analyses

Generally, we can recognize the owner of the database from the text extracted from the database. But more exactly, for the court judgment, we can use some metrics to evaluate the similarity between two watermarks to establish that a false positive judgment is highly unlikely so that an innocent party is unlikely to be wrongly accused of copying.

One method is to compute the similarity which is always used in the image watermarking. We can also apply this evaluation method to the database watermarking. We compare the extracted watermark and the original watermark to justify the existence of the watermark. We compare the watermark signal w^* which is gotten from the extraction step to the original watermark signal w. If the w^* is similar to the w, it represents that the extracted signal and the original signal are positive correlation; else, they are negative correlation. The correlation C of the two watermark signals can be described as follows:

$$C = \sum_{i=1}^{m} C_i = \sum_{i=1}^{m} w_i \cdot w_i^* .$$

(9)

where w_i and w_i^* represent the original watermark signal and the extracted watermark signal of the tuple which is been detected, m represents the total number of the detected tuples. The value of the C will be m if we choose the value of the k and θ correctly. If the two groups of signal doesn't have any relation or the value of k and θ are wrong, the value of the C will approach to 0 in theory. Then, the computing formula of the similarity can be simplified as follows:

$$Sim = \frac{\sum_{i=1}^{m} w_i \times w_i^*}{\sqrt{\sum_{i=1}^{m} w_i^* \times w_i^*}} = \frac{C}{\sqrt{m}} .$$

(10)

If the value of similarity of watermark signal produced by certain watermarking key is apparently higher than the threshold value which is set previously, we can make a decision that the database which is been detected is not illegal copyright. The threshold value is decided according to the need of the robustness of the watermark. First, we set the percentage of the tuples which can be inserted the watermark is T_θ. If the percentage of the correct watermark signal which we get from the detected tuples to the all tuples is higher than T_θ, then we can determine that the value is peak value, also we can determine that the database have been inserted the watermark signal which is produced by the private key. After setting the value of T_θ, the corresponding threshold value of similarity can be described as follows:

$$\frac{2m \times T_\theta - m}{\sqrt{m}}. \tag{11}$$

where m represents the total number of the detected tuples.

Another method is to compute the correlation coefficient which is used in the statistics. If the value of the attribute into which will be inserted the watermark is d and the value of the attribute into which has been inserted the watermark is $d + \Delta$, the modification of the value is $\Delta = \frac{\delta}{2} \times w$. At the watermarking detection time, we get the value of the objective attribute which is being detected d^*, and then the difference to the original value of the attribute is $\Delta^* = d^* - d$. We collect all the Δ of the tuples into which have been inserted the watermark and corresponding Δ^*. So they will form two sequence of number. We get the correlation coefficient by calculating the standard deviation of the two sequences of number and the result of comparing the covariance of them. The correlation coefficient can be described as follows:

$$\rho = \frac{\sum_{i=1}^{m} \Delta_i \Delta_i^* - (\sum_{i=1}^{m} \Delta_i \sum_{i=1}^{m} \Delta_i^*)/m}{\sqrt{\sum_{i=1}^{m} \Delta_i^2 - (\sum_{i=1}^{m} \Delta_i)^2/m} \cdot \sqrt{\sum_{i=1}^{m} \Delta_i^{*2} - (\sum_{i=1}^{m} \Delta_i^*)^2/m}}. \tag{12}$$

Where m is the number of the tuples which will be detected. The result of the formula for the correlation coefficient will between be 1 and -1.If the correlation coefficient is positive number, then we call that the relevance of the two sequences is positive correlation; if it is negative number, we call that the relevance of the two sequences is negative correlation; if it is equal to zero, we define that the two sequences do not have the relevance. In the statistic, we define that it is high correlation if $|\rho| \geq 0.7$ and low correlation when $0.3 \leq |\rho| < 0.7$, no correlation when $|\rho| < 0.3$. Therefore, we define the threshold ρ_θ between 0.7 and 0.3 when using this method so as to judge the existence of the watermark.

4 Experiments

For ease of deployment, we have written the system in Java to run as an Oracle 9i client application. The database used for the implementation contains 100000 tuples, where 61 attributes for each tuple. We select 10 numeric attributes for watermark inserting. The value of these numeric attributes is the arbitrary positive number between 0.0 and 9999.9. The parameter k of S and W is 7 and θ is 5% in the experiment, and there are 172736 attributes for inserting the watermark. We insert the string "ccnu" (8 bits for each character, totally 32bits) into the relational database. The totaling influence of every attribute column for the database after watermark inserting is as table bellowed, which shows that the error result is extremely minor.

Attribute	Mean	Variance	The change rate of mean	The change rate of variance
A1	2862.0	231.4	3.6E-7	902E-7
A2	138.1	103.8	0.0	0.0
A3	11.8	6.5	0.0	0.0
A4	260.6	202.8	0.0	0.0
A5	35.2	42.6	0.0	0.0
A6	3344.2	1776.8	2.5E-6	4.3E-6
A7	218.2	20.9	0.0	0.0
A8	225.5	16.7	0.0	0.0
A9	139.3	31.2	0.0	0.0
A10	3589.6	1781.4	0.0	0.0

For the experiment of the watermark robustness, the watermark is subjected to a series attacks. The results for these experiments are as follows.

Table 1. The Result of Rearrangement of Data

Rate of data rearranged	5%	10%	15%	20%	25%	30%	40%	50%
Delectability of watermark	99%	98.5%	95.2%	82%	67%	50%	24.2%	8.6%

Table 2. The Result of Data Movement for Selecting Subset

Rate of data movement	5%	10%	15%	20%	25%	30%	40%	50%
Delectability of watermark	98.4%	97.5%	94%	80%	55%	52%	20.3%	6.6%

Table 3. The Result of Random Data Replacement

Rate of data replaced	5%	10%	15%	20%	25%	30%	40%	50%
Delectability of watermark	99.6%	99%	97%	85%	72%	61.6%	28%	10%

Table 4. The Result of Linear Transformation (Add/Delete)

Rate of data transformed	5%	10%	15%	20%	25%	30%	40%	50%
Delectability of watermark	99.6%	99%	97%	85%	72%	61.6%	28%	10%

As described above, the experiment results show that new algorithm is robust against various forms of attacks.

For a deeper analysis, we random delete 3 thousand tuples and add 3 thousand incoherent tuples. At last, we attacked the database by arbitrary changing the value of the object attribute in the extent of the database can tolerant. We can also see the convex peak value obviously from the watermarking detected result of the database which has been continuously attacked (Fig.2). The result value of the similarity and correlation coefficient are all intuitively greater than the threshold. Therefore, it can testify the robustness of the inserted watermark

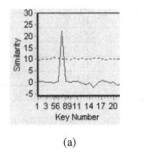 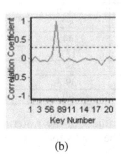

(a)   (b)

Fig. 1. The result value of the database parameter after inserting the watermark signal whose private key is 7 and parameter θ is 5% (a) we define the threshold of the similarity as 7.5 (b) the threshold of the correlation coefficient is 0.3

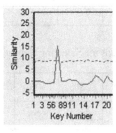 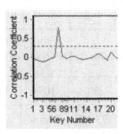

(a) Similarity is 15.145   (b) Correlation coefficient is 0.778

Fig. 2. The watermark detection result after being attacked such as deleted; added and modified

5   Conclusions

This paper propose a new relational database watermarking method based on spread spectrum techniques. Meanwhile, we use the technique of even parity check and majority voting for watermarking extraction so as to improve the accuracy of the watermark which has been extracted from the database. At last experimental results show that it is robust to the important attacks and positive updating.

Because of the particularity of the relational data, there are some difficulties to research on watermarking relational databases in depth. But the right management of the relational databases copyright with watermark should be an important topic for database research. And this research direction will be deserved serious attention more and more. In the future, we also plan to address the related problem of collaborative ownership protection for relational database.

Acknowledgments

This research was supported by the National Foundation of China under Grant No. 60603069.

References

1. Agrawal R., and Kiernan J.: Watermarking relational databases. Proceedings of the International Conference on Very Large Data Bases, Hong Kong, China (2002) 155-166
2. Sion R., Mikhail A., and Sunil P.: Rights protection for relational data. IEEE Transaction on Knowledge and Data Engineering. 16 (2004) 1509-1525
3. Cox I.J., Killian J., Leighton T. and Shamoon T.: Secure spread spectrum watermarking for multimedia. IEEE Transactions on Image Processing. 6(1997) 1673-1687
4. Pickholz R., Schilling D., and Milstein L.: Theory of spread-spectrum communications-a tutorial. IEEE Transactions on Communications. 30(1982) 855-884
5. Rakesh A., Peter J.H., and Jerry K.: Watermarking relational data: frame work, algorithms and analysis. International Journal on Very Large Data Bases. 12(2003) 157-169
6. Niu X.M., Zhao L.: Watermarking relational databases for ownership protection. Acta Electronica Sinica. 12A (2003)
7. Kunder D. and Hatzinakos D.: Digital watermarking for telltale tamper-proofing and authentication. Proceedings of the IEEE (Special Issue on Identification and Protection of Multimedia Information). 87(1999) 1167-1180
8. Wagner N.R., Fountain R.L., and Hazy R.J.: The fingerprinted database. 6th International Conference on Data Engineering. (1990) 330-336

Anticipatory Event Detection for Bursty Events

Kuiyu Chang, Qi He, Ridzwan Aminuddin, Ridzwan Suri, and Ee-Peng Lim

School of Computer Engineering,
Nanyang Technological University, Singapore 639798, Singapore
{kuiyu.chang,qihe}@pmail.ntu.edu.sg,
{muha0005,ridz0001,aseplim}@ntu.edu.sg

Abstract. Anticipatory Event Detection (AED) is a framework for monitoring and tracking important and relevant news events at a fine grain resolution. AED has been previously tested successfully on news topics like NBA basketball match scores and mergers and acquisitions, but were limited to a static event representation model. In this paper, we discuss two recent attempts of adding content burstiness to AED. A burst is intuitively a sudden surge in frequency of some quantifiable measure, in our case, the document frequency. We examine two schemes for utilizing the burstiness of individual words, one for revamping the static document representation, and the other for extracting bursty and discriminatory words from the two states of the AED Event Transition Graph.

1 Introduction

Open Source Intelligence (OSI) plays a fundamental role in Intelligence and Security Informatics (ISI), accounting for as much as 80% of the overall intelligence[1]. In fact, former US Joint Chiefs Chairman and former Secretary of State Colin Powell was noted to have said: "I preferred the Early Bird with its compendium of newspaper stories to the President's Daily Brief, the CIA's capstone daily product". Thus, the ability to constantly monitor and accurately track events from news sources all over the world is vital to ISI.

Major online portals like Google and Yahoo allows users to subscribe to news alerts by specifying list of present/absent keywords to define a particular event that he or she is interested in. Unfortunately, current alert systems are not smart enough to figure out if a news document containing all the user defined words satisfy the event or not. In fact, major portals like Yahoo rely on a human operator to approve system triggered news alerts, whereas others like Google prefer to use a completely automated approach, resulting in many false alarms [2].

The Anticipatory Event Detection (AED) system is designed to detect expected/anticipated events specified by a user. For example, it can be configured to monitor news streams for the occurence of very specific events like "Taiwan declares independence", "Coup in Thailand", "Osama bin Laden captured", etc., which we called anticipatory events (AE).

C.C. Yang et al. (Eds.): PAISI 2007, LNCS 4430, pp. 220–225, 2007.

2   Related Work

AED falls under the broader family of problems collectively known as Topic Detection and Tracking (TDT), which includes traditionally, New Event Detection (NED), Topic Tracking (TT), and Retrospective Event Detection (RED), etc. TDT defines a evaluation paradigm that addresses event-based organization of broadcast news[3], with a significant focus on NED and TT for news. AED differs from typical TDT tasks like NED/TT/RED primarily in two ways: 1) AED is concerned only with one particular user-predefined anticipatory event; 2) AED will return a hit if and only if the user-anticipated transition has consummated for that specified event genre. For example, suppose NED or RED is set up to return alerts for bombing events, then any news describing a new bombing incident or latest developments related to a known bombing could result in one or more NED/RED hits. On the other hand, AED could be configured to return a hit if and only if a bombing incident involving suicide bombers occurs in U.K.

AED systems based on classifying sentences/documents into pre/post AE states have been previously proposed [4,2]. The idea is to train a classifier using the pre/post documents of historical events with similar characteristics to the AE. For example, to create an AED system to detect the event "US invades Iran", we can train it using available documents for the pre/post states of the historical events of "US invades Afghanistan" and "US invades Iraq".

3   AED System

Given a user defined AE, the AED system attempts to first model the concept of a transition in a 2-state Event Transition Graph (ETG), e.g., the transition from the pre state (-) of "US talking about Iran invasion" to the post state (+) of "US invaded Iran". Documents or sentences can then be assigned to each of the two states and a classifier trained to differentiate between them. Figure 1 illustrates the complete AED system with the ETG shown in the lower left corner.

Numerous articles about the pre-state of an AE are typically available, e.g., articles discussing the possible invasion of Iran, rumors about a pending merger. However, for an AE that has not even happened, it is impossible for us to find

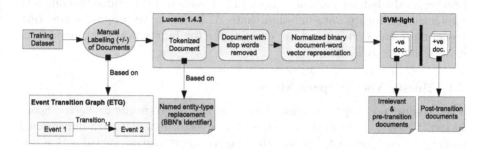

Fig. 1. Overview of the AED System

much less collect any training news articles about the post-state. How then can we train a 2-class classifier using only one class of data? There are two natural approaches to this lack-of-training-data problem:

1. One class problem (i.e., Outlier detection). Using the existing set of pre-state documents, we consider a new document that is sufficiently similar and yet far away from the single class of training set to be representative of a fired AE
2. Two class problem based on historically similar events. We can train the classifier on historically similar events that have already fired, which means we can readily collect articles for both the pre and post states easily.

One advantage of the first approach is that it can be practically automated; the AED system simply gathers a bunch of documents about the AE returned by any search engine using the keywords specified by the user. Since the event is presumed to not have occured, all returned documents would belong to the pre-state. However, the main problem is in tuning the classifier to accurately detect the desired transition instead of brand new developments of the story, which is exactly the same problem of NED and TT. In practice, it is extremely difficult to tune the outlier detector without any a priori knowledge of the desired AE.

The advantage of the second approach, which we have adopted and evaluated at both the sentence[4] and document resolutions[2], is that it can be significantly more accurate than the first. However, its main limitation is that human analysts must be involved to painstakingly find and collect the pre/post documents of historically similar events. We are now investigating ways to reduce the effort of the human analysts, by preselecting a small number of documents for him/her to label.

4   Factoring Burstiness into AED

A burst as defined by Kleinberg[5] formally corresponds to a phenomenon in which a large amount of text content about the same topic is generated in a short time period. Figure 2 plots the document frequency for the word feature "hurricane" superimposed on the topic on "Hurricane Mitch" from the TDT3[6] dataset. From the figure, we see that the feature traffic for key words does have a bearing on the hot topic of the period. In this section, we examine two different approaches to incorporate burstiness into AED. First, we propose a new text model representation. Second, we examine the top bursty words extracted from each of the two AED states.

4.1   Bursty Vector Space Model

The classical text representation, known as the bag-of-words or Vector Space Model (VSM) [7], represents a document as a vector in a very high-dimensional space; with each element denoting the weight/importance associated with a feature in the document. Popular weighting methods include binary, term frequency

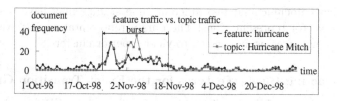

Fig. 2. Traffic overlap between a bursty topic and its feature "hurricane"

(TF), and term frequency - inverse document frequency (TFIDF). The feature space typically includes raw words, word stems, phrases, extracted named entities, etc.

The static VSM simply is not ideal in representing evolving trends in text streams, nor is it able to meaningfully model a transition from one semantic context to another. Specifically, a feature in static VSM could refer to completely different topics at various points in time, e.g., most occurrences of the word feature "war" in news collections circa 1998 refer to "the war between NATO and the Serbs", whereas the same word feature found in news collections circa 2003 mostly refers to the "war between US and Iraq" or "war on terrorism". Grouping words into phrases (e.g., n-grams) as new features and assigning part-of-speech tags to each words can improve the semantic meaning somewhat, but neither approach takes into consideration the time dimension of text streams.

An up and coming topic is usually accompanied by a sharp rise in the reporting frequency of some distinctive features, known as "bursty features". These bursty features could be used to more accurately portray the semantics of an evolving topic. Figure 3 illustrates the effectiveness of using top bursty features to represent two separate topics. Had we used the usual feature selection and weighting scheme, the word features "Gingrich" and "Newt" frequent in both related but different topics would turn up nearly important for representing documents of these two topics.

Our proposed bursty VSM representation simply boosts the weights of bursty words by an amount proportional to their burstiness value at the published time instance (document timestamp). Consequently, each document now has a dynamic bursty representation dependent on both their content and time stamp,

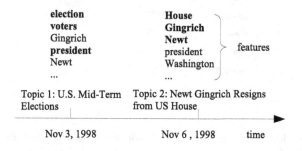

Fig. 3. Frequent features of two topics (bursty features shown in bold)

i.e., the exact document at two different time stamps may have vastly different bursty vector representations! The bursty representation was evaluated on clustering news streams and shown to yield superior clusters[8].

4.2   Extracting Bursty Features for the Event Transition Graph

As mentioned, one of the key limitations of our current AED formulation is its heavy reliance on human operators to collect a set of training documents for modelling the two states of the AED classifier. In fact, the desired AE is pretty much defined by the set of document collection *and* a set of unordered contextual keywords, e.g., "US invades bombs move into air strikes Iraq" and a collections of articles involving past invasions, e.g., invasions of Afghanistan, Iraq, Vietnam, manually labelled as negative or positive.

Since the same word may have different burstiness and importance pre and post transition, we applied Kleinberg's algorithm[5] to the word document frequencies in the pre-transition and post-transition set of documents. In other words, Kleinberg's algorithm is applied twice, independently on two streams of documents. Specifically, for each word in a stream,

1. The daily document-word frequency is fed as input to Kleinberg's algorithm.
2. Kleinberg's algorithm will calculate and output a weight and state sequence for the word. This state sequence characterizes the burstiness period of the word in time with the weight quantifying its overall burstiness.
3. If the ouput state sequence of a word has at least one transition to the bursty state, then the word will be classified as bursty.

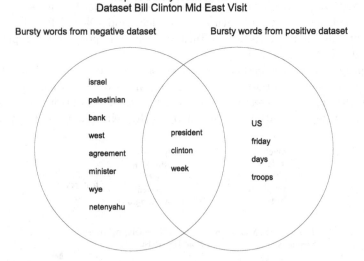

Top 15 bursty features for
Dataset Bill Clinton Mid East Visit

Bursty words from negative dataset   Bursty words from positive dataset

israel
palestinian
bank
west   president   US
agreement   clinton   friday
minister   week   days
wye   troops
netenyahu

Fig. 4. Words characterizing Clinton's Middle East visit in 1998 from the TDT3 dataset. Positive refers to post visit and negative refers to pre-visit.

The top bursty words from the negative/pre and positive/post streams form the Negative and Positive Bursty Set, respectively. In other words, for each AE transition in the ETG, we have a set of bursty words defining its post event state (positive bursty set) as well as its pre state (negative bursty set).

We computed the burstiness on 6 TDT3 news topics and plotted the overlap between the two bursty set of words for each event, one of which is shown in figure 4. Clearly, the important words before and after the visit are quite different from those prior to the visit, with 'clinton' and 'president' and 'week' as the top 3 overlapping words out of the top 20 bursty words.

It is our goal to use bursty analysis like this to help a user zero in on the precise set of keywords for defining the pre and post state of the AE, which will lead to a better returned set of documents corresponding to the two states.

5 Conclusion

We introduced AED as a viable solution to monitor and track events relevant to the ISI community. We described the various research issues associated with AED and proposed using burstiness to address them as a first step. We have yet to address the active learning strategies to select the minimal set of documents for characterizing the pre and post state of a user defined AE. There are also some practical problems associated with AED once it is deployed for mass usage, which include handling multiple users and AEs, and rare but possible multi-state and multiple-outcome AEs. All in all, we hope to continue to work on AED until it becomes a viable and practical tool for everyday use.

References

1. Wikipedia: (Open source intelligence, http://en.wikipedia.org/wiki/open_source_intelligence)
2. He, Q., Chang, K., Lim, E.P.: A model for anticipatory event detection. In Embley, D.W., Olive, A., Ram, S., eds.: 25th International Conference on Conceptual Modeling (ER 2006). LNCS 4215, Tucson, Arizona, Springer-Verlag (2006) 168–181
3. Allan, J.: Topic Detection and Tracking. Event-based Information Organization. Kluwer Academic Publishers (2002)
4. He, Q., Chang, K., Lim, E.P.: Anticipatory event detection via sentence classification. In: IEEE SMC Conf. (2006) 1143–1148
5. Kleinberg, J.: Bursty and hierarchical structure in streams. In: SIGKDD. (2002) 91–101
6. TDT03: Topic detection and tracking dataset 3, http://projects.ldc.upenn.edu/tdt3 (2003)
7. Salton, G., Buckley, C.: Term-weighting approaches in automatic text retrieval. In: Information Processing and Management. Number 24 (1988) 513–523
8. He, Q., Chang, K., Lim, E.P.: Bursty feature representation for clustering text streams. In: SIAM Datamining Conference. (2007) to appear.

Community Detection in Scale-Free Networks Based on Hypergraph Model

Rong Qian, Wei Zhang, and Bingru Yang

Scholl of Information Engineering, University of Science and Technology Beijing, Beijing
100083, China
qianrong01@yahoo.com.cn

Abstract. The investigation of community structures in networks is an important issue in many domains and disciplines. There have been considerable recent interest algorithms for finding communities in networks. In this paper we present a method of detecting community structure based on hypergraph model. The hypergraph model maps the relationship in the original data into a hypergraph. A hyperedge represents a relationship among subsets of data and the weight of the hyperedge reflects the strength of this affinity. We assign the density of a hyperedge to its weight. We present and illustrate the results of experiments on the Enron data set. These experiments demonstrate that our approach is applicable and effective.

Keywords: scale-free, hypergraph model, community structure, local density.

1 Introduction

Networks with power-law degree distributions have been the focus of a great deal of attention in the literature [1]. They are sometimes referred to as scale-free networks [2], although it is only their degree distributions that are scale-free; one can and usually does have scales present in other network properties. More recently, power-law degree distributions have been observed in a host of other networks, including notably citation networks [3], the World Wide Web [4], and the criminal or terrorist networks [5, 6]. Earlier researchers [2, 7] have demonstrated that many of these real-world interaction networks are scale-free. Most nodes in the network have low degrees while a few nodes, known as hubs, are well connected with large degrees.

Community detection in large networks is potentially very useful. Nodes belonging to a tight-knit community are more likely to have some properties in common. In law enforcement, intelligence analysts often refer to nodes and links in a criminal network as entities and relationships [8]. The entities may be criminals, organizations, vehicles, weapons, bank accounts, etc. The relationships between the entities specify how these entities are associated together. Law enforcement agencies and intelligence analysts frequently face the problems of identifying possible relationships among a specific group of entities in a criminal network. It is very important for us to discover groups of individuals and organizations that are strongly related by associations in a

C.C. Yang et al. (Eds.): PAISI 2007, LNCS 4430, pp. 226–231, 2007.

criminal network. It is also very important to understand the functions and structures of terrorist networks to win the battle against terror. However, previous studies of terrorist network structure have generated little actionable results. This is mainly due to the difficulty in collecting and accessing reliable data and the lack of advanced network analysis methodologies in the field.

2 Related Work

Many clustering algorithms of various types have been developed and used to analyze scale-free networks. However, it is very difficult for them to guarantee effective partitioning of natural groups from the core of a scale-free network.

The use of hypergraphs in data mining has been studied. For example Han et al [9] present a hypergraph model based on association rules. In their implementation, they use frequent item sets found by the association rule algorithm as hyperedges. They try to use the support of each frequent item set as the weight of the corresponding hyperedge. However, support carries much less meaning for hyperedges of size greater than two, as in general, the support of a large hyperedge will be much smaller than the support of smaller hyperedges. Furthermore, for these larger item sets, confidence of the underlying association rules can capture correlation among data items that is not captured by support.

3 Hypergraph Model Based on Local Density

The approach for community detection consists of the following two steps. During the first step, a weighted hypergraph H is constructed to represent the relations among different objects, and during the second step, a hypergraph partitioning algorithm is used to find k partitions such that the object in each partition are highly related. Here we mainly introduce our hypergraph model based on local density. We use η-dense subgraph as hyperedges.

3.1 Density of Subgraph

The natural notion of density of a graph is the following.

Definition 1. Let $G' = (V', E')$ be any undirected subgraph with n vertices and m edges. The density $\rho(G')$ of G' is the ratio defined as

$$\rho(G') = def \frac{m}{C_n^2} \tag{1}$$

The density $\rho(G')$ of a graph $G' = (V', E')$, often referred to as relative density, is defined to be the fraction of number of edges in G' relative to the maximum number of possible edges on the vertex set of G'. It is easy to see that $\rho(G') \in [0,1]$, for any subgraph G'. We are interested in subgraphs of certain densities.

Definition 2. Let $G = (V, E)$ be an undirected graph and let $0 \le \eta \le 1$ be a real number. A subgraph $G' = (V', E'), V' \subseteq V, E' \subseteq E$ is said to be an η-dense subgraph if and only if $\rho(G') \ge \eta$.

In an η-dense subgraph, the interpretation is that any two members share with probability (or frequency) at least η a relationship with each other. It is, however, immediate that even graphs of fairly high density are allowed to have isolated vertices.

3.2 Finding η-dense Subgraphs

Our algorithm of finding the η-dense subgraphs employs an iterative approach know as a level-wise search, where a subgraph with k vertices is used to explore a subgraph with $(k+1)$ vertices. First, the 2-subset of only 2 vertices which adjoin to be an edge of the graph is found. We can denote the set S_2. It is used to find the 3-subset S_3 which have 3 vertices, and so on, until no more η-dense subgraphs can be found. The finding of each S_k requires one full scan of the whole graph. To improve the efficiency of the level-wise generation of subgraphs, we use an important property to reduce the search space. This property is based on the following observation.

Property: Sort the vertices in decreasing order of their degrees. If a subset S_k does not satisfy the minimum density threshold η, that is $\rho(S_k) < \eta$. If a vertex v which has less degree than any vertex of S_i is add to the subset S_i, then resulting subset (i.e., $S_k \cup v$) cannot be a η-dense subgraph, that is $\rho(S_k \cup v) < \eta$.

Let us look at how this property is used in the algorithm. The following process consists of two steps.

1. The join step: To find S_k, a set of k-subset is generated by join S_{k-1} with itself. This set of candidates is denoted C_k. By convention, we assume that vertices within a subset (subgraph) are sorted in decreasing order of their degrees. The join, $S_{k-1} \infty S_{k-1}$ is performed, where members of are joinable if their first (k-2) vertices are in common.

2. The prune step: C_k is a superset of S_k, that is, its members may or may not be a η-dense subgraph, but all of the k-subset are included in C_k. A scan of the graph to determine the count of each candidate in C_k would result in the determination of S_k. C_k can be huge and so this could involve heavy computation. To reduce the size of C_k, we use the above property as follow. Any $(k-1)$ subset that is not a η-dense subgraph can not be a η-dense subgraph with k vertices. So, if any $(k-1)$ subset is not in S_{k-1}, then the candidate cannot be a η-dense subgraph either and so can be removed from C_k.

3.3 Hypergraph Model

A hypergraph [10] $H = (V, E)$ consists of a set of vertices (V) and a set of hyperedges (E). A hypergraph is an extension of a graph in the sense that each hyperedge can connect more than two vertices. In our model, the set of vertices V corresponds to the set of vertices being clustered, and each hyperedge $e \in E$ corresponds to a set of related vertices. A key problem in modeling of data items as hypergraph is the determination of related items that can be grouped as hyperedges and determining weights of each such hyperedge. By the above algorithm, we can get many η-dense subgraphs. And we can take each of the η-dense subgraph as a hyperedge which is weighted by its density. That is we can get the initial hypergraph. In order to detect the community structure, we must use some kind of hypergraph partitioning algorithm. HMETIS [11] is a multi-level hypergraph partitioning algorithm to minimize the weighted hyperedge cut, and thus tends to create partitions in which the connectivity among the vertices in each partition is high, resulting in good clusters. But our approach is different with the hypergraph model based on association rules. Our hypergraph model is based on local density, and the weight of a hyperedge is the density of the subset.

4 Experiments

4.1 Enron Corpus

The Enron email dataset [12] was made public by the Federal Energy Regulatory Commission during its investigation. This is the largest real email corpus, and makes an ideal target for link analysis and social network analysis. There were 150 employees from Enron with email logs recorded during a 19 month period. The corpus contains a total of about 0.5M messages. The undirected email graph is constructed as follows. First, the employees must have exchanged at least 30 emails with each other. Second, each member of the pair has sent at least 6 emails to the other. Thus we constructed an undirected graph with 758 vertices and 6727 edges. The distribution of the degree k and the number of vertices $P(k)$ is as the following

Table 1. Distribution of k and P (k) of *Enron* Email graph

k	<5	6-10	10-15	15-20	20-30	30-40	40-50	50-70	70-90	90-150	150-200	200+
$P(k)$	545	74	43	23	24	12	14	7	5	5	4	2

Table 1. There are only about 10 vertices whose degree more than 100, but there are 545 vertices with less than 5 degree. Prefuse [13] is a Java-based toolkit for building interactive information visualization applications. Figure 1 shows the Email dataset graph.

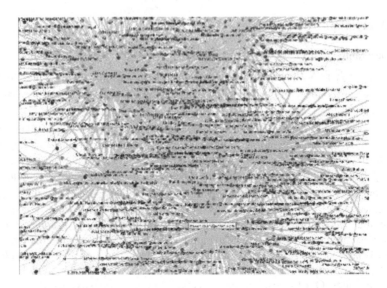

Fig. 1. Visualization of the whole *Enron* Email graph

4.2 Detecting the Community Structure

Based on our hypergraph model and the above initial graph, we identify communities in the Enron email network. We select some subsets (hyperedges) to illustrate. The following Table 2 shows some communities in the result. The number is ID of every employee. We can find 1489(named James.Steffes), 1490(named Steven.Kean), 17095(named Mary.hain), 801(named Susan.Mara), 288(named Tana.Jones), 36(named Alan.Comnes), 37(named Tim.Belden) etc. are included in different communities. As we known, Steven Kean was the Enron executive vice president and

Table 2. Some communities in the Enron corpus

181,253,801,813,817,818,1180,1463,1474,1489,1490,1547,2157,2217,3441, 3536,5416,8546
36,37,66,181,253,701,801,813,817,818,1180,1452,1474,1489,1490,1547,1786, 2222,2318,8546,9244,17095
36,37,42,55,166,181,206,253,801,813,817,1416,1474,1475,1489,1490,2222, 4001,7213,9244,17095,17252,28563,28654,48550
36,37,55,181,206,253,347,782,800,801,813,817,818,1016,1054,1180,1456, 1474,1475,1485,1489,1620,1786,2222,2238,2318,3132,3134,3152,3164,4001, 7213,8546,9244,17095,28654
181,253,347,801,817,818,1454,1489,1490,1779,2156
144,280,288,1101,2365,2390,3029,3098,3099,3101,3113,3404,5897,8379, 9117,17097,18647,20033,20382,2068,56992
33,155,280,288,318,329,401,403,437,480,551,1019,1101,1102,2186,2365, 2390,3032,3098,3100,3101,3113,3404,4854,5583,5897,7158,9094,15296, 16417,17099,18647,19980,20015,20022,20029,20030

chief of staff. Mr. James Steffes was the Vice President of Government Affairs ENRON Corporation. Mary Hain was one of Enron's in-house lawyers. Their woks were related to several different departments. So it is easy for us to understand why they are included in different hyperedges.

5 Conclusion

In this paper we present a method of detecting community structure based on hypergraph model. The hypergraph model maps the relationship in the original data into a hypergraph. A hyperedge represents a relationship among subsets of data and the weight of the hyperedge reflects the strength of this affinity. We assign the density of a hyperedge to its weight. We present and illustrate the results of experiments on the Enron data set. The experiments demonstrate that our approach is applicable and effective.

References

[1]   Albert, R. and Barabasi, A.-L., Statistical mechanics of complex networks, Rev. Mod. Phys. 74, 47–97 , 2002.

[2]   A. L. Barabasi, R. Albert, H. Jeong, and G. Bianconi. Power-law distribution of the world wide web. Science, 287, 2000.

[3]   Redner, S., How popular is your paper? An empirical study of the citation distribution. Eur. Phys. J. B 4, 131–134 , 1998.

[4]   Broder, A., Kumar, R., Maghoul, F., Raghavan, P., Rajagopalan, S., Stata, R., Tomkins, A., and Wiener, J., Graph structure in the web, Computer Networks 33, 309–320, 2000.

[5]   Jennifer J. Xu , Hsinchun Chen. Criminal network analysis and visualization. Communications of the ACM. Vol. 48, No. 6 , June 2005, Pages 100-107 .

[6]   Jennifer J. Xu , Hsinchun Chen. CrimeNet Explorer: A Framework for Criminal Network Knowledge Discovery. ACM Transactions on Information Systems, Vol. 23, No. 2, April 2005, Pages 201–226.

[7]   Girvan, M. and M. E. J. Newman (2002). "Community structure in social and biological networks." Proceedings of the National Academy of Science of the United States of America 99: 7821-7826.

[8]   Sparrow, M. The application of network analysis to criminal intelligence: An assessment of the prospects. Social Networks, 13, 251-274. 1991.

[9]   Han, E. H., Karypis, G., Kumar, V., et al. Clustering in a high-dimensional space using hypergraph models. Technical Report, TR-97-063, Minneapolis: Department of Computer Science, University of Minnesota, 1997.

[10] C. Berge. Graphs and Hypergraphs. American Elsevier, 1976.

[11] G. Karypis, R. Aggarwal, V. Kumar, and S. Shekhar. Multilevel hypergraph partitioning: Application in VLSI domain. In Proceedings ACM/IEEE Design Automation Conference, 1997.

[12] http://www.cs.cmu.edu/%7Eenron/

[13] http://prefuse.org/

The Treelike Assembly Classifier
for Pedestrian Detection

C.X. Wei[1,2], X.B. Cao[1,2], Y.W. Xu[1,2], Hong Qiao[3], and Fei-Yue Wang[3]

[1] Department of Computer Science and Technology,
University of Science and Technology of China,Hefei, 230026, P.R. China
[2] Anhui Province Key Laboratory of Software in Computing and Communication, Hefei,
230026, P.R. China
fasd@mail.ustc.edu.cn, xbcao@ustc.edu.cn, ywxu@mail.ustc.edu.cn
[3] Institute of Automation, Chinese Academy of Sciences, Beijing, 10080, P.R. China
hong.qiao@mail.ia.ac.cn, feiyue@sie.arizona.edu

Abstract. Until now, classification is a primary technology in Pedestrian Detection. However, most existing single-classifiers and cascaded classifiers can hardly satisfy practical needs (e.g. false negative rate, false positive rate and detection speed). In this paper, we proposed an assembly classifier which was specifically designed for pedestrian detection in order to get higher detection rate and lower false positive rate at high speed. The assembly classifier is trained to select out the best single-classifiers, all of which will be arranged in a proper structure; finally, a treelike classifier is obtained. The experimental results have validated that the proposed assembly classifier generates better results than most of the existing single-classifiers and cascaded classifiers.

1 Introduction

Pedestrian detection system (PDS) aims at reducing traffic accidents and saving lives. Classification technology based PDS is majority by now. Therefore, it is essential to design an effective classifier for PDS, which must satisfy the requirements of real-time car-mount detection (e.g. high detection rate and low false positive rate as well as high processing speed).

Until now, various classifiers have been proposed for PDS, most of which are single classifiers (non-cascaded classifiers) such as time-delay neural networks based classifier [2], Radial Basis Function based classifier [3], support vector machine (SVM) based classifier [4][5] and simulated annealing based classifier [6]. However, these methods usually have the disadvantages of high false positive rate and low detection speed. Until recent years, a few cascaded classifiers were designed for PDS [1][7][8]. For example, Viola and Jones adopted AdaBoost algorithm to train a serial-connected cascaded classifier [1]; we used AdaBoost and decomposed SVM algorithms to train an even more complicated cascaded classifier [8]. Although cascaded classifiers have obtained some progress in performance, some problems still exist when they are applied in urban traffic. For instance, the cascaded classifiers have

C.C. Yang et al. (Eds.): PAISI 2007, LNCS 4430, pp. 232–237, 2007.
© Springer-Verlag Berlin Heidelberg 2007

low false positive rate and high classification speed, but the false negative rate is still too high comparatively.

In this paper, we proposed a new classifier which introduced the idea of assembly learning. The assembly classifier is generated as follows: (1) To train one or two single classifier(s) basing on current assembly classifier; (2) To add the single classifiers into the assembly classifier and adjust the cascaded structure; (3) If the assembly classifier can meet the requirements of positive rate and false positive rate, then stop training and get the final cascaded classifier; else go to (1). With the proposed treelike assembly learning classifier, most effective single-classifiers can be selected and then to be organized in proper structure.

We also carried out car-mount detection to verify the performance of the assembly classifier; and the experimental results were compared with other existing single and cascaded classifiers, which showed that the assembly classifier was superior to most of the existing classifiers.

The remainder of this paper is organized as follows: Section 2 describes the method of the assembly classifier. Section 3 presents the experimental results. Section 4 concludes this paper.

2   Methods of the Assembly Classifier

The target of the assembly classifier is to select best single classifiers and then combine them with an appropriate structure. Moreover, the contribution of each single classifier strongly depends on its position in the cascaded structure. Therefore, in order to fulfill the requirements, we train single classifiers and generate the assembly classifier at the same time.

2.1   Training Procedure

The construction procedure consists of two main stages: training the first single classifier (stage 1), and generating the assembly classifier by adding two single classifiers each round (stage 2).

In stage 1, we train a single classifier which called *root-classifier* that aims at preliminary selection. And stage 2 is a loop procedure: in each round, we train two single classifiers separately and then add them into the assembly classifier.

Moreover, we will explain how to train each single classifier and how to generate the assembly classifier in detail as following.

2.1.1   Single Classifier Training
In the assembly classifier, all single classifiers are trained by applying AdaBoost algorithm [1]; however, different classifiers aim at different purposes and can get different results accordingly.

The first single classifier is for preliminary selecting, which should be fast enough with low false positive rate and low false negative rate (e.g. near to zero). Therefore, 3000 positive samples and 3000 manually-made negative samples (these samples are similar to pedestrians) were selected to form the training set, and also 200 key features were manually selected as feature set instead of random selection.

Furthermore, to satisfy the requirement of primary selection (to reject most of the non-pedestrians with a high detection rate); we need to modify the classification threshold manually in order to decrease false negative rate.

For other single classifiers, 3000 positive samples, 10,000,000 negative samples, 5000 gray-scale haar features and 5000 color haar features were adoted to train them. The huge negative samples can include various non-pedestrian objects. A classifier, which can distinguish them from the positive samples, also has a good classification precision in actual detection.

2.1.2 Construction Procedure

The construction procedure mainly includes 9 steps as shown in Fig. 1, which is similar to creating a binary tree from root to leaf. A path from root to any leaf can be a cascaded classifier; if false positive rates of all cascaded classifiers in the assembly classifier are less than threshold θ, then the construction procedure is finished.

Input : Positive Set *ps,* Huge Negative Set *ns.*

       Two feature sets fs_1, fs_2

False positive rate threshold θ .

Output: an assembly classifier *ac.*

1. Create an empty assembly classifier called *ac* and an empty list called *OPEN*.
2. Train the *root-classifier,* and then insert it into *ac* and put it on *OPEN*.
3. If *OPEN* is empty, finish the construction procedure.
4. Select the first single classifier in *OPEN*, remove it from *OPEN*. Call this classifier *c.*
5. Select training set based on the position of *c* in the assembly.
6. Train two single classifiers called c_1 and c_2 with fs_1 and fs_2 respectively. Add c_1 and c_2 to *ac* as two successors of *c*
7. Find a path from *root-classifier* to c_1 vertically, which can be seen as a cascaded classifier. If the false positive rate of the cascaded classifier is less than θ, put c_1 on *OPEN*.
8. Similarly, if the false positive rate of the cascaded classifier from *root-classifier* to c_2 is less than θ, put c_2 on *OPEN*.
9. Go to step 3

Fig. 1. Construction procedure of the assembly classifier

In the construction procedure, each single classifier (except the *root-classifier*) selects only part of negative training samples which are false-positive classified by all single classifiers in previous levels, which helps single classifiers to increase the performance of distinguishing pedestrians from similar pedestrian objects (it also means to decrease false positive rate).

2.2 Classification Procedure

The structure of the assembly classifier is a particular binary tree which called 2-tree (each node in 2-tree has 0 or 2 child classifier(s)). For example, as shown in Fig. 2, the assembly classifier has no single classifier which has only 1 child-classifier. In the classification procedure, a candidate region is regarded as containing a pedestrian only when it is classified as POSITIVE by the *root-classifier* and at least one sub assembly classifier.

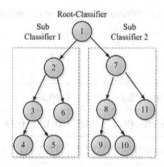

Fig. 2. Structure of the assembly classifier

A recursion algorithm is shown in Fig. 3 to describe the classification procedure in detail.

```
RESULT classificationResult (x, ac) {
/* x is the a candidate region */
/* ac is an assembly classifier */
If (ac contains only a single classifier c) {
    If c regards x as POSITIVE
                Return POSITIVE;
    Else Return NEGATIVE;
}
ELSE {
    c = root-classifier of ac;
    {subac₁, subac₂}= two sub assemblies of ac;
    If(c regards x as POSITIVE and
        (classificationResult(x,subac₁)is POSITIVE) or
        classificationResult (x,subac₂)is POSITIVE)))
            Return POSITIVE;
    Else Return NEGATIVE;
    }
}
```

Fig. 3. Pseudo-code of classification procedure

3   Experimental Results and Discussion

In order to verify that the assembly classifier can reduce false positive rate without decreasing detection rate and get better performances than single classifier and cascaded classifier, we carried out several tests on a Pentium IV 2.4G computer with 1G DDR RAM.

In our experiment, we get 10 layers (the height of the assembly classifier) assembly classifier, which contains 251 component single classifiers. We test the assembly classifier and other two cascaded classifiers with 5 types of videos. The test videos were captured in different urban traffic scenes and different brightness conditions. The two cascade classifiers were trained with Viola and Jones's method [1]. The first classifier has five serial layers, while the second one has ten layers in serial. The overall results are shown in Table I.

Table 1. Sytem performance comparing of cascaded classifiers

Test video type PDS performance		1	2	3	4	5	Average
The assembly classifier	**Detection rate (%)**	**92.1**	**90.8**	**90.3**	**89.7**	**86.1**	**89.8**
	False positive rate(‰)	**0.05**	**0.13**	**0.16**	**0.11**	**0.11**	**0.11**
	Detection speed(fps)	**12.2**	**11.2**	**12.3**	**12.8**	**12.0**	**12.1**
Cascaded classifier1 (five layers)	Detection rate (%)	91.5	90.4	85.6	84.6	81.8	86.78
	False positive rate(‰)	1.0	2.2	2.5	2.5	3.0	2.24
	Detection speed(fps)	12.5	11.8	12.7	13.1	12.4	12.5
Cascaded classifier 2 (ten layers)	Detection rate (%)	80.5	78.6	75.6	75.2	72.6	76.5
	False positive rate(‰)	0.06	0.12	0.18	0.11	0.10	0.11
	Detection speed(fps)	11.5	10.9	11.5	11.8	10.8	11.3

The experimental results in the table I indicate that:

(1) The assembly classifier gets good performance compared to the cascaded classifiers. With test videos of urban traffic, on average, the false positive is 0.11‰, and the detection rate is 89.8%; whist the detection speed is 12.1fps.

(2) Both cascaded classifiers have high detection speed. However, the detection rates and false positive rates also increase with the number of single classifiers. The cascaded classifier 1(five serial layers) has a high detection rate of 86.78% and a high false positive rate of 2.24‰; whist the cascaded classifier 2 (ten serial layers) has a low detection rate of 76.5% and a low false positive rate of 0.11‰.

Due to the tree structure, most of non-pedestrian regions were rejected by only a few of single classifiers at top layers. Therefore, the assembly classifier can get a high detection speed of 12fps on average, which can almost satisfy real-time requirement.

4   Conclusions

In this paper, we proposed an assembly classifier for pedestrian detection system. The assembly classifier can select the best single classifiers and combines them in an appropriate structure, which has lower false positive rate and higher detection rate.

The experimental results show that the proposed classifier is superior to most of existing single and also cascaded classifiers. Comparatively, the assembly classifier has following features:

(1) The organization structure is built automatically in the training procedure.

(2) Its detection rate is no more than that of any single classifier it contained.

(3) Its false positive rate can be reduced to extraordinary low (near to zero), which can make the assembly classifier suitable for real detection in urban traffic.

(4) Due to the treelike structure, its high detection speed almost satisfies the requirement of practical application.

Moreover, it is obvious that the performance of assembly classifier is affected by the independences of its component single classifiers. Therefore, classifiers trained with different methods are more suitable to form an assembly classifier. In the future, we plan to adopt different methods to train single classifiers, such as SVM, KNN and so on.

Acknowledgement

This work was supported by National Natural Science Foundation of China (60204009) and National Basic Research Program (2004CB318109).

References

1. Paul Viola, Michael Jones, and Daniel Snow, "Detecting Pedestrians Using Patterns of Motion and Appearance," International Conference on Computer Vision (ICCV), Vol. 2, pp. 734-741, 2003
2. U. Franke et al., "Autonomous driving goes downtown," IEEE Intelligent System, pp. 32-40, 1998
3. D.M. Gavrila, "Pedestrian detection from a moving vehicle," European Conference on Computer Vision, pp. 37-49, 2000
4. Grant Grubb, Alexander Zelinsky, Lars Nilsson, and Magnus Rilbe, "3D Vision Sensing for Improved Pedestrian Safety," IEEE Intelligent Vehicle Symposium, 2004
5. Qiao H, Wang FY, and Cao XB, "Application of a decomposed support vector machine algorithm in pedestrian detection from a moving vehicle," IEEE international conference on ISI 2005, pp. 662-663, 2005
6. D.M. Gavrila, and J. Geibel, "Shape-based pedestrian detection and tracking," IEEE Intelligent Vehicles Symposium, pp. 8-14, 2003
7. Fengliang Xu, Xia Liu, and Kikuo Fujimura, "Pedestrian Detection and Tracking With Night Vision," IEEE Transactions on Intelligent Transportation System, vol. 6, pp. 63-71, 2005
8. Y.W. Xu, X.B. Cao, H. Qiao, F.Y. Wang, "A cascaded classifier for pedestrian detection," IEEE Intelligent Vehicle Symposium 2006, pp. 336 – 343, June 13-15, 2006

A Proposed Data Mining Approach for Internet Auction Fraud Detection

Yungchang Ku, Yuchi Chen, and Chaochang Chiu

Department of Information Management, Yuan Ze University,
135, Far-East Rd., Chung-Li, Taoyuan, Taiwan
unicon@mail.cpu.edu.tw, s946223@mail.yzu.edu.tw,
imchiu@saturn.yzu.edu.tw

Abstract. Internet auctions are one of the few successful new business models. Owing to the nature of Internet auctions, e.g. high degree of anonymity, relaxed legal constraints, and low costs for entry and exit, etc…, fraudsters are easily to setup a scam or deception in auction activities. Undeniable fact is that information asymmetry between sellers and buyers and lacking of immediately examining authenticity of the merchandise, the buyer can't verify the seller and the characteristics of the merchandise until after the transaction is completed. This paper proposes a simple method which is detected potential fraudster by social network analysis (SNA) and decision tree to provide a feasible mechanism of playing capable guardians in buyers' auction activities. Through our simple method, buyers can easily avoid defraud in auction activities.

Keywords: Internet auction fraud, fraud detection.

1 Introduction

With the rapid development and proliferation of technologies and applications in Internet, it has not only triggered new forms of commerce but also created variously platforms to exhibit the company or personal merchandise without considering time and space. Through these platforms, people can browse, order, sell, buy, exchange, auction, or bid, and so on. In particular, the transactions between these platforms also accelerate the boom and multiformity of Internet business. Exploiting in auctions is one of the few successful new business models enabled by the Internet [1]. Through the Internet, it is no longer just for a minority to participate in auctions, but allows millions of people all over world to buy and sell almost any kind of product. At any given time, there are millions of auction listings across thousands of categories on auctions sites such as eBay and Yahoo. Nowadays, these sites also rank high in both the number of visitors and the average time spent per visit.

There is no doubt that Internet auctions have had higher potential to enlarge its economic scope. However, due to lacking of effective countercheck mechanism, Internet auctions are the leading source of top ten online frauds in recently years [2]. Many of the cases involve straightforward scams where consumers allegedly "won" the bid for merchandise through an Internet auction Web site, sent in their money, but never received the merchandise. According to the report of Federal Trade

C.C. Yang et al. (Eds.): PAISI 2007, LNCS 4430, pp. 238–243, 2007.
© Springer-Verlag Berlin Heidelberg 2007

Commission (FTC), Internet auction fraud is the single largest category of Internet related complaints in the FTC's Consumer Sentinel database, which logged 14,387 cases in 2000, 51,000 cases in 2002, and 98,653 cases in 2004 [3]. In addition, according to Internet Fraud Statistics from 2000 to 2005 of National Consumer League (NCL), the amount of lost in Internet auction fraud was $3 million in 2000, up to $15.5 million in 2002, and then increased to $25.2 million in 2004. Surprisingly, the total lost in 2005 was two times of lost in 2004 to $58.9 million [4]. It reveals that Internet auction fraud grows very rapidly and it has been a significant impact in economic and society.

Thus, this study will propose a simple method in confronting Internet auction fraud. We can easily figure out the fraudster and its relative IDs and remind the buyer to deliberate on paying the money. In the following section, it will introduce Internet auction fraud and its counteracting strategies in Section 2, and describe our method to detect the fraudster and its relative IDs in Section 3. Then, in Section 4, it gives conclusions and notes future directions.

2   Background

2.1   Confronting Internet Auction Fraud

Due to the characteristics difference between Internet auction and traditional ones, e.g. high degree of anonymity, relaxed legal constraints, and low costs for entry and exit, etc... [5], fraudsters are easily to setup a scam or deception in an Internet auction. Furthermore, the nature of Internet changes the way that a seller's information flows from the seller to the buyer. It causes a greater information asymmetry in Internet auction transactions [6], such as sellers will mask their identities, fake the reputation, shill bidding, and buyers can't verify the authenticity of the merchandise before they pay. Information asymmetry increases the incident of the Internet auction fraud and decreases chances of detection and punishment.

To combat Internet auction fraud, Chua and Wareham (2004) indicate various types of fraud in [7] and profile the fraudster of Internet auction. They figure out that most Internet auction fraudsters are professional criminals, antisocial in motives, and knowing to develop specialized fraud schemes increasing profits while minimizing risk of capture. They suggest an effective approach to fight Internet auction fraud by enforcing existing rules with combining the efforts of auction communities, governments and auction institutions. However, as they have mentioned, the approach will be costly both in monetary and managerial means.

In the meanwhile, researchers take notice of importance properties of auction activity. There are three main factors in auction activity. They are seller, buyer and merchandise to bid. Some researchers suggest auction sites to develop more explicit reputation mechanism for accelerating trust and reliability among transactions [8][9][10]. Resnick et al. (2000) define a reputation system as a system that "collects, distributes, and aggregates feedback about participants' past behavior". This system helps "people decide whom to trust, encourage trustworthy behavior, and deter participation by those who are unskilled or dishonest" [8]. Thus, a well-designed reputation system can not only decrease the cases of fraud in auction communities, but also help buyers, especially in experienced Internet auction buyers, to avoid potentially fraudulent auctions [11]. Unfortunately, not every auction site has its high quality reputation system, even if eBay or yahoo. It improves the opportunities of fraudsters to counterfeit their reputation which auction site allows the seller to remain anonymous and to easily change identities.

In "merchandise to bid", it builds the connection relationship between sellers and buyers. But, owing to the information asymmetry and lacking of immediately examining authenticity of the merchandise, the buyer can't verify the seller and the characteristics of the merchandise until after the transaction is completed. This nature of Internet auction derives the uncertain quality of merchandise to buyers and let it easily related to online fraud [12]. Fraudsters can fabricate any information about the merchandise and its quality, for example, shilling, misrepresentation, fee stacking, reproductions and counterfeits, and buy and switch, etc. Not surprisingly, only few auction sites can offer various services, e.g. feedback systems, insurance or guarantee, and escrow services, to promise the quality to buyers [13]. It still boosts the cost and complicated transactions in managerial means.

2.2 Social Network Analysis

Social network analysis (SNA) is an approach and set of technique used to study the exchange of resources among actors (i.e., individuals, groups, or organizations) [17]. SNA is used in sociology research to analyze patterns of relationships and interactions between social actors in order to discover an underlying social structure [18]. A network is usually represented as a graph which contains a number of nodes (network actors) connected by links (relationships) [19]. SNA is capable of detecting subgroups, discovering central individuals, and uncovering network organization and structure [20]. Subgroups in network can give quite important information, interaction between members and subgroups in network can be understand using an SNA approach called k-core, which is a maximal subgraph in which each point is adjacent to at least k other points: all the points within the k-core have a degree greater than or equal to k [18]. A k-core is an essential complement to the measurement of density [21]. Therefore we use the k-core approach to find any unusual links or relationships in network.

3   Our Method to Confront Internet Auction Fraud

3.1 Using SNA to Group Potential Fraudsters

In this study, it will utilize the social network analysis (SNA) technique to detect the relationship of potential fraudsters. Using SNA, it can successful distinct from the seemingly-legitimate (potential fraudsters) and legitimate users [16]. Due to the nature of Internet auction, 89.0% of all seller-buyer pairs conduct just one transaction during the time period and 98.9% no more than four [9]. It means that the repeat transaction of the same seller-buyer pair is lower than 2%. Therefore, when one seller-buyer pair transaction is normal, the k-core value is equal to 1 (it denotes 1-core). Otherwise, the k-core value will higher than 1.

For example, in Fig. 1, we employ a seller "noddrkks" which reported in "black listing" by Yahoo auction site to demonstrates abnormal transaction behavior. Seller "noddrkks" and its each buyer is 1-core, such as "noddrkks--faayensp", "noddrkks--e2000", "noddrkks--psp", etc. Seller "adssl66" and its each buyer is also 1-core. But, we calculate the k-core value in "noddrkks" and "adssl66" is 2 (it denotes 2-cores), it shows that "noddrkks" and "adssl66" have frequency and abnormal transactions. In Fig. 1, there are 2-cores and 3-cores in "noddrkks" and its relative group IDs, such as "noddrkks", "adssl66", "jank_080", and "aaa222ccc", etc. Thus, we can group "noddrkks" and its relative group IDs as a certain fraudster or fraudsters.

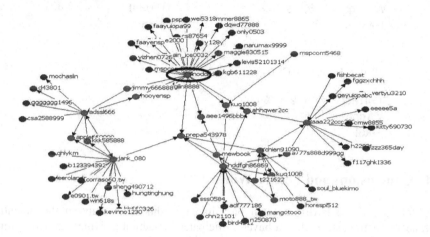

Fig. 1. The connection transaction of "noddrkks" by SNA

3.2 Using Decision Tree to Detect Potential Fraudsters

In this section, we will use SNA and decision tree to examine the accuracy of group IDs of fraudster or fraudsters. First, we random collect "black listing IDs" which reported by Yahoo auction site and also random select the legitimate IDs from the site. The sample size in each side is 50. We select several features, such as positive reputation rate, frequency of positive or negative reputation, detail information of merchandise, 2-cores or 3-cores IDs by SNA, etc. Second, we use decision tree (e.g. C5.0) as training model, then compare the accuracy of the group IDs of fraud, see Fig 2.

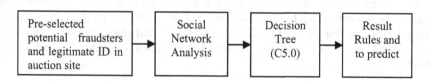

Pre-selected potential fraudsters and legitimate ID in auction site	→	Social Network Analysis	→	Decision Tree (C5.0)	→	Result Rules and to predict

Fig. 2. Processes of examining the accuracy of group IDs of fraudster

3.3 Experiment Result

In the experiment, we find that the correct rate which only calculated by SNA in simple 2-core and simple 3-core with other features are 74% and 68%. Then we join decision tree to calculate, the correct rates are higher to at least 90%, see in Table 1, Table 2, and Table. 3. We find that process SNA and decision tree can higher the correct rate to detect potential fraudster or fraudsters.

Table 1. 2-core & 3-core & C5.0

Correct	49	96.08%
Wrong	2	3.92%
Total	51	

Table 2. 2-core & C5.0

Correct	48	94.12%
Wrong	3	5.88%
Total	51	

Table 3. 3-core & C5.0

Correct	46	90.2%
Wrong	5	9.8%
Total	51	

4   Conclusions and Future Work

In this paper, we have presented our simple method and analyzed the potential fraudster or fraudsters when a buyer participates in auction activities. In confronting Internet auction fraud, we have the following contributions:

1. Although frauds will be due to either the buyer or the seller, the buyer is easily to be a victim than a seller in most cases. Thus, we can help buyers to detect potential fraudster or fraudsters by our method and remind them to deliberate on paying the money.
2. Internet auctions are high economic potential and high value-added industry, detecting fraudsters and prosecute them will keep the transaction smoothly and in order. This study will play an important role in combating fraudsters.
3. Furthermore, this study can also provide the auction sites to develop a feasible mechanism of playing capable guardians in auction activities and help them to make more effective anti-fraud strategies.

In our research, we are going to develop more accurate detecting and examining framework of confronting Internet auction fraud. We will also focus on analyzing the characteristics of fraudsters and victims. Through the real cases analysis of fraudsters and victims, we will develop more complete mechanism to combat Internet auction fraud.

References

1. van Heck, E., and Vervest, P.: How Should CIOs Deal With Web-Based Auction?, *Communication of the ACM*, Vol. 41, No. 7, (1998) 99-100.
2. National Fraud Information Center, "Internet Fraud Statistics Reports," 2005. Available from http://www.fraud.org/internet/intstat.htm.

3. Anderson K.B.: Internet Auction Fraud: What Can We Learn From Consumer Sentinel Data?, *Federal Trade Commission Report*, (2004).
4. National Consumer League Internet Fraud Watch (2000-2005), *Internet Fraud Statistics*, (2005). Available from http://www.fraud.org/internet/intstat.htm.
5. Chua C.E.H., and Wareham J.: Self-Regulation for Online Auctions: An Analysis, *Proc. 23rd Int'l Conf. Information Systems, Assoc. for Information Systems*, (2002) 115-125.
6. Kauffman R.J. and Wood C.A.: Premium Bidding in Online Auctions: An Examination of Opportunism and Seller Preference, 2006. Available from http://www.mgmt.purdue.edu/academics/mis/workshop/kw_111805.pdf.
7. Chua C.E.H. and Wareham J.: Fighting Internet Auction Fraud: An Assessment and Proposal, *IEEE Computer*, Vol. 37, No10, (2004) 31-37,.
8. Resnick P., Zeckhauser R., Friedman E., and Kuwabara K.: Reputation Systems, *Communication of the ACM*, Vol. 43, No. 12, (2000) 45-48,.
9. Resnick P. and Zeckhauser R.,: Trust among Strangers in Internet Transactions: Empirical Analysis of eBay's Reputation System, *Advances in Applied Microeconomics*, Vol 11, (2002) 127-157,.
10. Houser D. and Wooders J.: Reputation in Auctions: Theory, and Evidence from eBay, *Journal of Economics & Management Strategy*, Vol. 15, No. 2, (2006) 353-370.
11. Gregg D.G. and Scott J.E.: The Role of Reputation Systems in Reducing On-Line Auction Fraud, *International Journal of Electronic Commerce*, Vol. 10, No. 3, (2006) 95-120,.
12. Ba S., Stallaert J., Whinston A.B., and Zhang H.: Choice of Transaction Channels: The Effects of Product Characteristics on Market Evolution, *Journal of Management Information Systems*, Vol. 21, No. 4, (2005) 173-197,.
13. Ba S., Whinston A.B., and Zhang H.: Building trust in online auction markets through an economic incentive mechanism, *Decision Support Systems*, Vol. 35, No. 3, (2003) 273-286,.
14. Dolan K.M.: Internet Auction Fraud: The Silent Victims, *Journal of Economic Crime Management*, Vol. 2, No. 1, (2004) 1-22,.
15. National White Collar Crime Center, *IC3 2005 Internet Crime Report*, (2005). Available from http://www.nw3c.org/.
16. Wang J.C., Chiu C.C., and Ker H.Y.: Detecting Online Auction Fraud of Reputation Inflation through Social Network Structures Embedded in Transaction Records, *Journal of Information Management (Taiwan)*, Vol. 12, No. 4, (2004) 144-184,.
17. Haythornthwaite C.: Social Network Analysis: An Approach and Technique for the Study of Information Exchange, *Library & Information Science Research*, Vol. 18, No. 4, (1996) 323-342.
18. Scott J.: *Social Network Analysis*, SAGE Publications, London, UK, (2000)
19. XU J., Chen H,: CrimeNet Explorer: A Framework for Criminal Network Knowledge Discovery, *ACM Transactions on Information Systems*, Vol. 23, No. 2, (2005) 201–226
20. Xu J. and Chen H.: Criminal network analysis and visualization, *Communication of the ACM*, Vol. 48, Iss. 6, (2005) 100-107
21. Seidman S. B.: Network Structure and minimum degree, *Social Networks*, (1983) 267-287

Trends in Computer Crime and Cybercrime Research During the Period 1974-2006: A Bibliometric Approach

Chichao Lu[1], Wenyuan Jen[2], and Weiping Chang[3]

[1] Center for General Education, Overseas Chinese Institute of Technology, Taiwan
chichao@ocit.edu.tw
[2] Department of Information Management, Overseas Chinese Institute of Technology
denise@ocit.edu.tw
[3] Department of Student Affairs, Central Police University, Taiwan
una024@mail.cpu.edu.tw

Abstract. The aim of this study is to explore trends in computer crime and cybercrime research from 1974 to 2006. All publications for this analysis were drawn from the ISI Web of Science, the Science Citation Index (SCI), and the Social Science Citation Index (SSCI). The ISI Web of Science is considered a powerful and relatively accurate tool in bibliometric studies. About 292 papers related to computer crime and cybercrime were published during this period. The greatest number of these papers was written in English, and the annual output increased significantly after 2003. In the period under study, most papers originated in the USA. Approximately 57% of the publications were articles, and 72% of these articles had single authors. More bibliometric analyses are described in this study, which shows a high scientific production of articles on computer crime and cybercrime publications.

1 Introduction

Bell [1] defined computer crime as "an offence in which a computer network is directly and significantly instrumental in the commission of a crime." Thomas and Loader [12] defined cybercrime as "illegal computer-mediated activities that often take place in the global electronic networks." Both computer crime and cybercrime are related to illegal behavior or criminal activity. Over the last three decades, computers and computer networks have played an increasingly indispensable role in people's lives. However, both computers and computer networks have also created a new venue for criminal activity, and cybercrime and cyber terrorism have risen to the FBI's number three priority, behind counterterrorism and counterintelligence [13].

Due to an increase in Internet users and the growth of e-commerce as an important business model, the number of computer crime and cybercrime cases has risen dramatically, and the U.S. Federal Bureau of Investigation (FBI) reports that cyber criminals have attacked almost all of the Fortune 500 companies [4]. An evaluation of the distribution and scope of related scholarly papers published worldwide will be helpful in understanding the trends in computer crime and cybercrime research.

C.C. Yang et al. (Eds.): PAISI 2007, LNCS 4430, pp. 244–250, 2007.

Guzman and Kaarst-Brown [3] adopted bibliometrics and content analysis to analyze published research on skill expectations and contributions to organizational survival and strategic alignment of IT. Also employing the bibliometric method, Elmacioglu and Lee [2] analyzed the collaborative network of database researchers from the DBLP community. Mann, et al. [7] pointed out that bibliometric statistics can also provide the basis for visualizations of scientific interactions and automated historiographical analyses. Matsuura and Ebato [8] used bibliometric analysis to discuss the information security field in Japan and consider their findings the opening of a door to empirical analyses of collaboration in a particular field in a particular country. Pilkington [9] used bibliometric techniques to investigate the intellectual pillars of the technology management literature. In order to explore trends in computer crime and cybercrime, a longitudinal literature review is indispensable.

This study utilizes bibliometric technology to explore the patterns and trends in computer crime and cybercrime publications. Our goal is to study the computer crime and cybercrime publications between 1974 and 2006. The paper is organized as follows. First, methods and materials are presented. Next, employing the ISI *Web of Science*, the paper empirically investigates computer crime and cybercrime documents published in the *Science Citation Index* (SCI), the *Social Science Citation Index* (SSCI) in the 1974-2006 period. Finally, the results of the bibliometric analysis of computer crime and cybercrime publications are discussed.

2 Methods and Materials

Bibliometrics is the quantitative evaluation of scientific literature, and it is used in library and information sciences. With regard to a given topic, bibliometrics utilizes quantitative analysis and statistics to delineate patterns in publication, including the distribution of articles over journal types, document types, and distribution of publications by various fields.

Citation analysis is an important area of bibliometric studies [6]. Rao [10] pointed out that, in most bibliometric studies, the following data are collected and analyzed: 1. measures of productivity (number of publications, number of authors) 2. measures of impact (citations received, number of reviews) 3. measures of journal productivity (pages, papers). However, bibliometric findings make sense only in a macro perspective with a large number of publications [11].

The *Web of Knowledge* database of the Institute for Scientific Information (ISI) includes information from over 22,000 journals covering more than 230 scientific disciplines. ISI *Web of Science* includes SCI, SSCI, and the *Arts and Humanities Citation Index* (A&HCI). This study employed the SCI and SSCI databases included in the online version of the ISI *Web of Science*.

In this study, "computer crime" "computercrime", "cybercrime", and "cyber crime" were used as keywords to search "title," "abstract," and "keywords" fields of the SCI and SSCI databases. The downloaded information included names and addresses of authors, document types, paper titles, title of publication, keywords, year of publication, times cited, etc. In using the online ISI *Web of Science*, this study set the time span from 1965 to October 31, 2006. Both SCI and SSCI databases were used, and no language or document type limitations were set. Document types include articles, editorial material, meeting abstracts, letters, notes and reviews. The database search produced 292 documents related to computer crime and cybercrime. Examining these results, we found the first computer crime paper was published in 1974; hence, the time span of this study was defined as being from 1974 to October 31, 2006. For a longitudinal literature review, we employed bibliometric analysis to explore computer crime and cybercrime publication trends.

3 Results

Publication output
Table 1 displays computer crime and cybercrime publications by year. The first paper was published in 1974, and the average annual publications growth rate from 1974 to October 31, 2006 was 30.80%. After 2003, the number of documents regarding computer crime and cybercrime increased substantially.

Table 1. Number of publications by year

Year	NP	C.	Year	NP	C.	Year	NP	C.	Year	NP	C.	Year	NP	C.
1974	1	1	1981	5	31	1988	4	98	1995	7	135	2002	6	196
1975	2	3	1982	10	41	1989	7	105	1996	8	143	2003	21	217
1976	1	4	1983	9	50	1990	5	110	1997	6	149	2004	28	245
1977	2	6	1984	18	68	1991	7	117	1998	6	155	2005	23	268
1978	4	10	1985	10	78	1992	4	121	1999	6	161	2006	24	292
1979	11	21	1986	5	83	1993	3	124	2000	13	174			
1980	5	26	1987	11	94	1994	4	128	2001	16	190			

Average annual growth rate 30.80%

NP: Number of documents; C: Cumulative

Document type and Language of publication
From Table 2, the distribution of document types was scattered, with articles constituting a majority of all documents. The nine document types were dominated by articles (165, 56.51%), news items (52, 17.81%), and editorial material (37, 12.67%). The number of total citation times is also noted in Table 2, with articles dominating citation frequency as well. The language in which computer crime and cybercrime documents were published was dominated by English (276, 94.52%).

Table 2. Distribution of documents by type

Document type	C	P	CT	CTP	Document type	C	P	CT	CTP
Article	165	56.51%	226	91.87%	Meeting Abstract	3	1.03%	0	0.00%
Book Review	17	5.82%	0	0.00%	News Item	52	17.81%	0	0.00%
Discussion	1	0.34%	1	0.41%	Note	4	1.37%	0	0.00%
Editorial Material	37	12.67%	5	2.03%	Review	3	1.03%	14	5.69%
Letter	10	3.42%	0	0.00%	Total	292	100%	246	100%

C: Count; P: Percentage; CT: Cited Times; CTP: Cited Times Percentage

Table 3. Distribution of top 10 authors and their institutions

R	Author	NP	R	Author	NP	R	Institution	RC	R	Institution	RC
1	Schultz, E	24	5	Chou, SC	3	1	George Wash U.	5	3	U. Texas	4
2	Hancock, B	10	5	Chung, WY	3	1	U. Arizona	5	3	Natl Cent U.	3
3	Bequai, A	4	5	Dhillon, G	3	2	Cent Police U.	4	3	U. Houston	3
3	Chen, HC	4	5	Gemignani, M	3	2	Exodus Commun Inc	4	3	U. Virginia	3
5	Backhouse, J	3	5	Kalet, JE	3	2	Purdue U.	4	3	U. London	3
5	Chang, WP	3	5	Zimmerli, E	3	2	U. Calif Berkeley	4			

R: Rank; NP: Number of publications; RC: Record count; U.: University

Authorship and page count
Among the 292 papers found in the ISI *Web of Science* search, there were 27 instances (9.25%) with no author information. In the remaining 265 papers containing author data, 191 papers (72.08%) were written by a single author and 74 (27.92%) were coauthored. Totally, there were 382 authors listed on the 265 papers. Table 3 lists the top 10 of these authors, based on number of publications; Schultz, E. had 24 papers and was ranked first. There were a total of 2,066 pages in the 292 documents, with an average of 7.08 pages each.

Distribution of documents by country and institution
In the ISI *Web of Science*, there were 181 papers (38.01%) that did not contain the author's address. The 152 authors listed on the remaining 111 papers were included in this analysis. A detailed analysis of authors' countries, Table 4, reveals that most papers originated in the USA, with England, Taiwan, Germany, Canada, and The People's Republic of China following. The list of publications by institution is based on author addresses. As Table 3 shows, George Washington University and the University of Arizona led all institutions.

Table 4. Distribution of authors by country

C/T	A	P	C/T	A	P	C/T	A	P	C/T	A	P
USA	96	63.16%	Canada	5	3.29%	Australia	3	1.97%	India	1	0.66%
England	13	8.55%	P. R China	5	3.29%	Netherlands	3	1.97%	Israel	1	0.66%
Taiwan	10	6.58%	Switzerland	4	2.63%	Norway	2	1.32%	Slovakia	1	0.66%
Germany	7	4.61%				Denmark	1	0.66%			

C/T: Country/Territory; A: Author; P: Percentage

Distribution of documents by journal
There were 121 different journals represented, with an average of 2.41 papers per journal. The journals *Computers & Security* and *KRIMINALISTIK* contained the most articles by far. In the field of computer crime and cybercrime, 61 papers (20.89% of 292 papers) were published in *Computers & Security*. This is not surprising, as this journal has been devoted to this field for many years.

Distribution of documents by keyword and subject category
In computer crime and cybercrime publications, the keywords used by the authors comprised 198 different items. The top 10 keywords were "computer crime," "cybercrime," "hackers," "hacking," "Internet," "data mining," "electronic commerce,"

"information security," "profiling," and "computer fraud." However, among author designated keywords, we occasionally found misspelled or nonstandard keywords. The lack of standardization of keywords was a problem encountered in our analysis.

The most frequently cited papers
According to the record of times cited, 67 documents (22.95%) were cited, and 225 (77.05%) were not. Among the documents cited, 60 were articles, 4 were editorial materials, 2 were review papers, and 1 was a discussion paper. The ten most frequently cited documents among the computer crime and cybercrime related documents found in this study are listed in Table 5. Documents are listed in order of number of citations. The top 10 most cited documents were articles, with the exception of one review paper. All of the top 10 most cited papers were published in English. \

Table 5. Most cited among computer crime and cybercrime documents

Rank	Paper Title / Journal / Author	CT	Year
1	The effect of codes of ethics and personal denial of responsibility on computer abuse judgments and intentions / MIS Quarterly / *Harrington, SJ*	21	1996
2	The process of criminalization - the case of computer crime laws / Criminology / *Hollinger, RC; Lanzakaduce, L*	18	1988
3	Hellmann presents no shortcut solutions to the DES / IEEE Spectrum / *Tuchman, W*	16	1979
4	Transnational extradition for computer crimes: Are new treaties and laws needed? * / Harvard Journal on Legislation / *Soma, JT; Muther, TF; Brissette, HML*	12	1997
5	Lifting the "fog" of Internet surveillance: How a suppression remedy would change computer crime law / Hastings Law Journal / *Kerr, OS*	11	2003
5	Copyright protection for the electronic distribution of text documents / Proceedings of the IEEE / *Brassil, JT; Low, S; Maxemchuk, NF*	11	1999
5	A social learning theory analysis of computer crime among college students / Journal of Research in Crime and Delinquency / *Skinner, WF; Fream, AM*	11	1997
5	Legislating computer crime / Harvard Journal on Legislation / *Heymann, SP*	11	1997
9	An investigation of ethical perceptions of public sector MIS professionals / Journal of Business Ethics / *Udas, K; Fuerst, WL; Paradice, DB*	7	1996
10	Cybercrime's scope: Interpreting "access" and "authorization" in computer misuse statutes / New York University Law Review / *Kerr, OS*	6	2003
10	Consumer and business deception on the Internet: Content analysis of documentary evidence / International Journal of Electronic Commerce / *Grazioli, SF; Jarvenpaa, SL*	6	2003
10	From Katz to Kyllo: A blueprint for adapting the fourth amendment to twenty-first century technologies / Hastings Law Journal / *Simmons, R*	6	2002
10	Managing computer crime: A research outlook / Computers & Security / *Backhouse, J; Dhillon, G*	6	1995
10	DES will be totally insecure within 10 years / IEEE Spectrum / *Hellman, ME*	6	1979

* Review document; CT: Cited times

4 Conclusion

The findings indicated that there were an increasing number of papers published after 2003. As for document types, the results show that the publications were scattered among document types although around 57% of all published documents were articles. English was the major language of publication. Single authors accounted for 72% of all papers, and there were a total of 2,066 pages in 292 documents, with an average of 7.08 pages per document.

Due to the lack of complete author information in the ISI *Web of Science* database, the analysis of authorship, country, and institution name was based on incomplete records. This is one problem this study encountered. Also, due to the significance of computer crime and cybercrime, the number of documents produced annually is expected to grow.

5 Discussion

This study illustrates the development of the Internet [5] and summarizes the focus of computer crime and cybercrime literature in each decade. In the final year of the Internet implementation stage (1961-1974), the first computer crime paper was published. In the Internet institutionalization stage (1975-1993), the period from 1975 to 1980 saw the most publications focusing on the innate character of computer crime. For instance, the analysis of computer crime types and causes were major issues during that period. From 1981 to 1990, a legal focus dominated and computer crime legislation issues were explored. In 1994, the first web browser, Netscape, was made available to the general public, and Internet business applications emerged. Web browser development then led to the Internet being commercialized and computer crime entered a concomitant growth period.

From 1991 to 2000, computer crime cases increased with the number of Internet users and Internet applications. In an effort to deter computer crime and help solve cybercrime cases, the focus on legal aspects of Internet use grew. Topics of interest included the use of forensic science in computer crime and cybercrime cases and updating computer crime and cybercrime legislation. Meanwhile, viruses, hacking, sabotage, and cyberpunks increased, leading to an increased focus on security as well. From 2001 to 2005, computer crime research spread in many directions. Law enforcement, software piracy, hacker behavior, victims of computer crime, the fight against money laundering, computer crime forensics, and information security were among the topics extensively explored. Clearly, security and the legal issues were of great concern and the focus of much scholarly activity.

In the short term, more support for the study of computer crime and cybercrime is urgently needed, and such support will be crucial in the long term to meeting growing cyber-society needs. While the present integrated study of academic writing on computer crime and cybercrime serves to illustrate trends in the professional literature, continuing research will be needed if we are to realize the goal of reducing and eventually preventing this type of criminal activity.

References

1. Bell, R.E.: The Prosecution of Computer Crime. Journal Financial Crime 9, 4 (2002) 308-325.
2. Elmacioglu, E. and Lee, D.: Research articles and surveys: On six degrees of separation in DBLP-DB and more. ACM SIGMOD Record 34, 2(2005), 33-40.
3. Guzman I.R. and Kaarst-Brown, M. L.: Organizational survival and alignment: insights into conflicting perspectives on the role of the IT professional. ACM Proceedings of the 2004 SIGMIS (2004), 30-34.

4. Kshetri, N.: Pattern of global cyber war and crime: A conceptual framework. Journal of International Management 11, 4(2005), 541-562.
5. Laudon K. C. and Traver, C. G.: E-Commerce: Business, Technology, Society. Addison-Wesley, 2nd edition (2004).
6. Luukkonen, T.: Bibliometrics and evaluation of research performance. Annals of Medicine 22, 3(1990) 145-50.
7. Mann, G. S., Mimno, D., and McCallum, A.: Bibliometric impact measures leveraging topic analysis. Proceedings of the 6th ACM/IEEE-CS joint conference on Digital libraries (2006), 65-74.
8. Matsuura, K. and Ebato, K.: University-industry collaboration networks in the information security field in Japan: problems and a particular success. 2004 IEEE International Engineering Management Conference 2, 18-21 (2004), 839-844.
9. Pilkington, A.: Defining technology management: a citation/co-citation study. IEEE International Engineering Management Conference 1, 18-21 (2004), 337-341.
10. Rao, I. K. R.: Methodological and conceptual questions of bibliometric standards. Scientometrics 35, 2(1996) 265-270.
11. Skoie, H.: Bibliometrics – some warnings from the north. Scientometrics 45, 3(1999) 433-437.
12. Thomas, D. and Loader, B.D.: Cybercrime: Law Enforcement, Security and Surveillance in the Information Age. Taylor & Francis Group, New York, (2000).
13. Verton, D.: FBI chief: Lack of incident reporting slows cybercrime fight. Computerworld, October 31 2002. http://computerworld.com/securitytopics/security/cybercrime/story/0,10801,75532,00.html.

The Study of Government Website Information Disclosure in Taiwan

Yuan-Fa Chen[1], Sandy Yu-Lan Yeh[2], and Kuo-Ching Wu[1]

[1] Department of Information Management, Central Police University, Taiwan
wkc@mail.cpu.edu.tw
[2] Department of Foreign Affairs Police, Central Police University, Taiwan
sandy@mail.cpu.edu.tw

Abstract. Taiwan's Freedom of Information Act (TFOIA) aims at protecting people's right to know and making the information easily, evenly formulated and obtained by the public. The access to government information not only enhances people's understanding, trust, and supervision on public affairs, but also promotes their participation in democracy. The goal of open and transparent administration can be achieved only by sharing the information with the public. All government agencies must have everything set, especially after one-year adjustment of TFOIA that was passed in December 2005. In expectation of publicizing government's efforts and achievement, we design a score card on the basis of regulations made by TFOIA for all governmental websites. Meanwhile, we also conduct a survey of 248 governmental websites to see whether the websites offer legal and proper information to the public or not. The findings of the research confirm that the information disclosed on government websites still remains insufficient, except for data on official organizations, duties, addresses, telephone numbers, fax numbers, websites, e-mail addresses, and the like. Moreover, the information disclosed on the websites has a remarkable connection with organizational levels and functional attributes of all government offices. In general, according to the score card, TFOIA scores only 1.25 on the average, far from the regulated full score 3.0. Apparently, TFOIA still has much room for improvement.

1 Introduction

In the World Economic Forum (WEF) rating of competitiveness, Taiwan was ranked as the third in the world in 2004 when the total of internet users was approximately 10,330,000 and the population to surf the net was up to 9,050,000. With the rapid growing nature of network, much more investment on human resources, facilities, and services are urgently needed. Taiwan is presently at the third stage of planning to promote 'the advanced type' of electronic government. Retrospectively, at the first stage, the electronic government brought forth innovations in the networking of public services, expanding and promoting government information disclosure. At the second stage, the function and convenience of the electronic government helped encourage people's participation in public affairs and remold Taiwan government thoroughly, making possible progressive transition and development of a civic society.

C.C. Yang et al. (Eds.): PAISI 2007, LNCS 4430, pp. 251–256, 2007.
© Springer-Verlag Berlin Heidelberg 2007

2 Research Motive and Scope

Government information refers to governmental organizations which produce, during their operations, obtain, utilize, propagate, keep and are responsible for the information that they possess. In 2006 Taiwan claims the primary goal to promote the infrastructure construction for governmental network. Most of the government institutions and offices are equipped with wide-band facilities with 85% setup their own websites. 14,000 government institutions and more than 20,000 academic institutions are integrated altogether, capable of providing electronic delivery and exchange of document. Survey result indicates that 75% of the major offices affiliated to the Executive Yuan are available in electronic document exchange system; compared to 65% in the county or municipal government offices and agencies; 63% in local governments.

Taiwan's Freedom of Information Act (TFOIA) was passed in December 2005. People have easy access to know about the administrative information from the websites at any time since then. This research evaluates how TFOIA works so far by surveying 250 governmental websites in accordance with the Law.

3 Literature Review

Historically, US and Europe were the pioneers in the formulation of the law regarding information and the demand for the transparency of government information. But obviously there were some differences. The US Freedom of Information Act (FOIA) was passed in 1966, which decreed the government to announce its rules and orders and to ensure citizen's access to government information. The citizen had the right to claim extensive information which the government was supposed to release, except for state secrets and individual privacy materials [1]. According to the testimony of the American Bar Association, the US administrative agencies should act in accordance with the obligation to disclose and spread government information which was extended from traditional media to electronic forms, and must provide information in easy access, such as the global information network on the internet.

US made a relevant regulation to simplify the paperwork in 1995, namely Paperwork Reduction Act. It specifies the federal organizations to implement the policy of information flow, encourages the government department based on public information, and tries to combine the information resources of the government department and individual enterprises. The main idea is based on the assumption that government information is a kind of resources belonging to the people, thus any interests generated by the government's information certainly go to the entire society and should be open to the public. Hence, the United States is in conflict with people's interest to disclose federal information, offering original information to any individual enterprises so as to enable them to make decision for their best commercial interests .

To sum up, "freedom of information" and "the Paperwork Reduction" make possible to widely spread information through public network. In contrast, European countries are not active in this respect (Perritt & Rustad, 2000: 403-417).

---

[1] Perritt, Henry H., Jr., and Rustad, Zachary, Freedom of information spreads to Europe, *Government Information Quarterly*, Vol. 17, Issue 4, 4th Quarter, 2000.

4 TFOIA Measurement and Statistical Analysis

4.1 Sampling Method and Survey Design

This research starts with investigating Taiwan government organization websites. Since there are too many government's agencies in Taiwan, it is impossible to do a comprehensive study of all government agencies due to the limitation of time and resources. Hence, this research employs the purposive sampling method to get information of 250 government websites, including administrative organizations, public hospitals, judicial units, police/fire offices, county and municipal governments, congress, etc.

This research examines the total amount of 250 samples collected from central government websites, among them 248 samples are valid for analysis. The only two invalid samples indicate that these websites do not have the function to provide any service.

The research uses a 3-point scale in survey design. The questionnaire of the study, taken from Article 7 of TFOIA, corresponds to the diction and phrasing of the said law about the information that the government should disclose publicly, except for some wording commonly used in questionnaire (Table 1).

Table 1. The Content of Article 7 of TFOIA

Item no	Contents
Q1	Whether or not the website offers treaty, documents of foreign relations, law, emergency order, and order, regulation ordering and local autonomy regulation decreed in accordance with the Standard Law of Central Regulation.
Q2	Whether or not the website offers the explanatory stipulations and judgment criteria regarding the unified the explication of the law, recognition of facts, and the exercise of executive judgment, which are decreed by the government to help the government agency at a lower level or its subordinates.
Q3	Whether or not the website offers data on its organization, duty, address, telephone number, facsimile number, website, and E-mail account.
Q4	Whether the website offers administrative guidelines to documents and paper work related to the agency or not.
Q5	Whether the website offers its administrative plan, business statistics, and research paper or not.
Q6	Whether the website of the agency discloses its budget and fiscal report or not.
Q7	Whether the website offers the disposal result of petition and the decision of appealing or not.
Q8	Whether the website of discloses contracts of public projects and purchase in written form or not.
Q9	Whether or not the website discloses information of subsidy that the agency is paid or receives.

4.2 Government's Websites Profiles

By hierarchical level, 49 (19.76%) respondents (websites) are the level 1 agencies, such as: ministries and departments; 94 (37.90%) respondents from level 2 agencies; 57 (22.98%) respondents from the bureau of agency; 22 (8.87%) respondents from the local city or county council; and 26 (10.48%) respondents, the local government. By function, the majority respondents are from the general administration (111 or 44.76%), 61 criminal justice and social service (24.60%), 23 legislation/parliament (9.27%), the medicine and social welfare 16 (6.45%), and 37 state-run production (14.92%). The descriptively statistical result about measured Article 7 (Q1-Q9) of TFOIA is shown in Table 2. The average score is 1.25, which clearly indicates that the performance of Freedom of Information Act in Taiwan is still far from satisfactory. In addition, "Whether the website of the agency discloses its budget and fiscal report." (Q6) has a very high coefficient of relative variation (266%).

Table 2. Frequency Distribution of Items of Article 7, TFOIA (N = 248)

Item no	Frequency[a]	Average	CRV[b] (%)
Q1	37, 27, 63, 121	2.08	52
Q2	106, 41, 47, 54	1.20	110
Q3	0, 9, 48, 191	2.73	19
Q4	38, 70, 55, 85	1.75	62
Q5	73, 43, 58, 79	1.56	78
Q6	213, 9, 7, 19	0.32	266
Q7	160, 62, 2, 24	0.60	180
Q8	178, 17, 7, 51	0.74	164
Q9	208, 21, 4, 15	0.30	261

[a] : Correspondent to the score value of 0, 1, 2, 3, respectively.
[b] : Coefficient of relative variation.

4.3 Data Mining

Data mining refers to extracting or "mining" knowledge from large amount of data[2], which attempts to find the potential and undiscovered but available knowledge or information from any kind of information repository or data bank. Data mining is often considered as a process of discovering interesting knowledge from the specific data bank. And the purpose of data mining (or namely knowledge discovery) is to turn data into models or patterns or decision rules for decision making.

In this research, we employ a supervised data mining strategy and technique-decision tree, to find a hierarchical structure of attributes by using the SAS Enterprise Miner. Then we apply it to find the statistically significant relationships between organization level (function) and attributes (Q1-Q9). The result is shown in Table 3. Lambda is a PRE (proportionate reduction in error) measure, which means that its value reflects the percentage reduction in errors in predicting the dependent given

---

[2] Han, Jiawei, and Kamber, Micheline, *Data Mining: Concepts and Techniques*, Academic Press, 2001, p. 5.

knowledge of the independent. In Table 3, knowing organizational level and function reduces errors in guessing form of Q5 and Q4 by over 46% and 36%, respectively. Cramer's V (CV) is the most popular of the chi-square-based measures of nominal association, because it gives good norming from 0 to 1, regardless of table size. Cramer's V may be viewed as the association between two variables as a percentage of their maximum possible variation. In Table 3, all values of CV are above 0.60 (probability of chi-square < 0.0001), they indicate that there exists a strong association between organizational level (function) and Q5 (Q4).

Table 3. The Association Analysis between Organizations and Q1-Q9

Association	Controlling	Chi-square [a]	CV [b]	LA [c]	Support [d](%)
Level - Q5	Q7 <= 2 and Q4 >= 1	76.3516	0.6390	0.5000	75
	Q3 = 3 and Q2 <= 2	57.1416	0.6299	0.4634	58
Function - Q4	Q8 <= 2 and Q2 >= 2	51.3378	0.6959	0.5000	43
	Q1 >= 1 and Q7 = 0	59.4046	0.6585	0.4444	55
	Q3 = 3 and Q7 = 0	38.9289	0.6032	0.3684	43

[a]: Prob. < 0.0001, [b]: Cramer's V, [c]: Lambda asymmetric, [d]: support(P→Q) = N(P and Q)/N, where N = 248.

4.4 Implications

The TFOIA is designed to set up the kernel rule for providing access to understanding public or government affairs, especially concerning life and property of people. Both disclosure and transparency are important to stimulate the aspiration of public participation; they will reduce the defect of public policy or the risk of corruption by government officers.

The results obtained from this research indicate that the implementation of TFOIA is far from satisfactory yet. First, it has very low score of legal information, the question "Whether or not the website discloses information of subsidy that the agency is paid or receives." (Q9) only scored 0.3 averagely. Secondly, there is a very high variation at the same hierarchical level of organization, five out of total nine items are larger than 100%. It may be attributed to official inertia and laziness.

The associations between organization and items, when controlling for "Whether the website offers the disposal result of petition and the decision of appealing." (Q7) and "Whether the website offers administrative guidelines to documents and paper work related to the agency." (Q4) or "Whether ... the website offers the explanatory stipulations ... to help the government agency at a lower level or its subordinates." (Q2) and "Whether ... the website offers data on its organization, duty, address, telephone number ..." (Q3). There exits a very significant association between "Whether the website offers its administrative plan, business statistics, and research paper." (Q5) and organization level. It implies that different organization levels is related to different ways of doing or making paper work/plan. In addition, there exits a very significant association between "Whether the website offers administrative guidelines to documents and paper work related to the agency." (Q4) and organization function.

5   Conclusions

With the new legislation coming into effect, the implementation of the law does not symbolize that all government information is already disclosed to public. Taiwan is a democratic country in which the power of the government derives from the consent of the people. Except for the messages classified as secrets, the government is required to thoroughly disclose its information that has to do with public interests. Thus people are able to make arrangements of their own lives and business and to supervise governmental functions and services, according to the information that the government is in charge of. For sure, government information disclosure plays an important role in establishing a positive image of the government as well as enhancing people's trust and confidence in the government. According to the findings of this study, most government information contents are yet to be disclosed in Taiwan. It is true that valid and effective administration is the concrete foundation of a nation's sovereignty. In a modern democratic country governed by the law, the government should disclose its information as soon as possible to respond to and satisfy people's right to know.

Informed Recognition in Software Watermarking

William Zhu*

Department of Computer Science,
University of Auckland, Auckland, New Zealand
fzhu009@ec.auckland.ac.nz

Abstract. Software watermarking is a technique to protect programs from piracy through embedding secret information into the programs. As software unauthorized use and modification are ubiquitous in the world, progresses in software watermarking will certainly benefit software research and industry. In this paper, we study one of core concepts in this area – informed recognition. To recognize a watermark in a software is to judge the existence of such a watermark in the corresponding software code.

1 Introduction

Since the unauthorized use and modification of software are pervasive around the world, software security becomes an important issue [5,6,7,19,20]. Software watermarking is a method to protect copyright of programs by inserting secret messages into the programs. With the rapid development of intelligence and security informatics [8,15], we find a new potential application area of software watermarking. Combined with other techniques, software watermarking can also be used in database protection [2] and information security problems [1].

The basic definitions of software watermarking concepts appeared in the early papers by Collberg et al. [5,6]. They also defined the extraction and recognition of software watermarks, but these definitions are not very formal and detailed. Nagra et al. [12,13] and Thomborson et al. [14] classified software watermarks from a functional view. Concepts and techniques of software watermarking also abound in [6,9,11,16].

Zhu and Thomborson formally defined embedding, extraction, and recognition in papers [19] and [20]. This paper follows the above two papers to define concepts such as positive-partial informed recognitions, negative-partial informed recognitions, and informed recognitions corresponding to embedding algorithms.

This paper is organized as follows. Section 2 gives the concepts of embedding, extraction and recognition. Section 3 is the focus of this paper. We define the concepts of informed recognition such as positive-partial informed recognition, negative-partial informed recognition, and informed recognition. Section 4 concludes our paper.

---

* Research supported in part by the New Economy Research Fund of New Zealand.

C.C. Yang et al. (Eds.): PAISI 2007, LNCS 4430, pp. 257–261, 2007.
© Springer-Verlag Berlin Heidelberg 2007

2   Embedding, Extraction and Recognition

A software watermarking system must do two basic things: embed a watermark into a software object, then extract all bits of the watermark inserted by itself, or recognize whether or not there exists a watermark embedded by itself. In this section, we introduce some concepts of embedding a watermark into, extracting a watermark from, and recognizing a watermark from a software program. These issues were already addressed in our previous paper [19,20]. We need these concepts to define the concepts of informed recognition.

Informally speaking, to embed a software watermark into a program is to insert a secret message into this code. We formally define this concept as follows.

Definition 1. *(Watermark) A watermark is a message of bits of 0 and 1 with a finite length ≥ 0. We denote the set of all watermarks as* $\mathbf{W}$.

Definition 2. *(Embedding) Let* $\mathbf{P}$ *denote the set of programs and* $\mathbf{W}$ *the set of watermarks. We call a function* $A : \mathbf{P} \times \mathbf{W} \to \mathbf{P}$ *an embedder.*

If $P' = A(P, W)$ *for some* $P \in \mathbf{P}$ *and some* $W \in \mathbf{W}$, *then the* P' *is called the watermarked program and* $P \in \mathbf{P}$ *the original program.*

After a watermark is inserted in a cover message using an embedder, an important consideration is the potential for an algorithm to extract this watermark. The following definition specifies all potential watermarks an embedder can insert into a program. This set excludes messages which do not change a cover program.

Definition 3. *(Set of candidate watermarks) A* $W \in \mathbf{W}$ *is called a candidate watermark with respect to a program* P *and an embedder* A *if* $A(P, W) \neq P$. *All candidate watermarks constitute the set of candidate watermarks of the program* P *and the embedder* A. *This set is denoted as* $candidate(P, A)$.

As for the detailed concepts of extraction and recognition in software watermarking, please refer to papers [19,20].

3   Informed Recognition

For positive-partial recognizers, negative-partial recognizers, and recognizers defined in last section, we provide the original program and the suspected watermarked program as their inputs to judge whether the suspected watermarked program has a watermark. In this section, we define a new type of recognition, informed recognition, in which a recognizer is given an original program, a suspected watermarked program, and a suspect watermark as its inputs.

We divide informed recognition into three classes: positive-partial informed recognition, the negative-partial informed recognition, and informed recognition. For a positive-partial informed recognition, if a program really has a specific watermark, the recognition will detect it. But, such an informed recognition might say a program has a watermark while this program actually has no such a watermark.

Definition 4. *(Positive-partial informed recognition) Let* $A : \mathbf{P} \times \mathbf{W} \to \mathbf{P}$ *be an embedder,* $PIR : \mathbf{P} \times \mathbf{P} \times \mathbf{W} \to \{\text{TRUE}, \text{FALSE}\}$ *a function. If* PIR *satisfies that* $\forall P, P' \in \mathbf{P}$, *if there is a* $W \in candidate(A, P)$ *such that* $P' = A(P, W)$, *then* $PIR(P', P, W) = \text{TRUE}$, *we call* PIR *a* positive-partial *informed recognition function corresponding to the embedder* A, *or simply a* positive-partial *informed recognizer.*

The partial recognition concepts are very flexible. The following is an example of positive-partial informed recognition.

Example 1. (Trivial positive-partial informed recognizers) For an embedder $A :$ $\mathbf{P} \times \mathbf{W} \to \mathbf{P}$, define a function $S : \mathbf{P} \times \mathbf{P} \times \mathbf{W} \to \{\text{TRUE}, \text{FALSE}\}$, as follows:

$$\forall P', P \in \mathbf{P}, W \in \mathbf{W}, \ S(P', P) = \text{TRUE}.$$

This is a positive-partial informed recognition corresponding to A. We call such a function a trivial positive-partial informed recognizer corresponding to A and denote it as $TPIR(A)$.

For a negative-partial informed recognizer, if it says a program has a watermark, this program really has a watermark. But, such a recognizer might say a program do not have a specific watermark while this program actually has such a watermark.

Definition 5. *(Negative-partial informed recognition) Let* $A : \mathbf{P} \times \mathbf{W} \to \mathbf{P}$ *be an embedder,* $NIR : \mathbf{P} \times \mathbf{P} \times \mathbf{W} \to \{\text{TRUE}, \text{FALSE}\}$ *a function. If* NIR *satisfies that* $\forall P, P' \in \mathbf{P}$, $NIR(P', P) = \text{TRUE} \implies P' = A(P, W)$ *for some* $W \in \mathbf{W}$, *we call* NIR *a* negative-partial *informed recognition function corresponding to the embedder* A, *or simply a* negative-partial *informed recognizer.*

We present an example of negative-partial informed recognition.

Example 2. (Trivial negative-partial informed recognizers) For an embedder $A :$ $\mathbf{P} \times \mathbf{W} \to \mathbf{P}$, define a function $S : \mathbf{P} \times \mathbf{P} \times \mathbf{W} \to \{\text{TRUE}, \text{FALSE}\}$ as follows:

$$\forall P', P \in \mathbf{P}, W \in \mathbf{W}, \ S(P', P, W) = \text{FALSE}.$$

This is a negative-partial informed recognizer corresponding to A. We call such a function a trivial negative-partial informed recognizer and denote it as $TNIR(A)$.

For a complete informed recognizer, if a program has a watermark, the recognizer will say that this program has a watermark; if a program has no watermarks, the recognizer will say that this program has no watermarks.

Definition 6. *(Informed recognizer) For an embedder* $A : \mathbf{P} \times \mathbf{W} \to \mathbf{P}$, *if a function* $R : \mathbf{P} \times \mathbf{P} \to \{\text{TRUE}, \text{FALSE}\}$ *satisfies* $\forall P, P' \in \mathbf{P}, W \in \mathbf{P}$, $R(P', P, W) = \text{TRUE} \iff P' = A(P, W)$ *for some* $W \in candidate(A, P)$, *we call* R *a* complete informed recognition function *for the embedder* A, *or simply an informed recognizer. We say that* A *is informed recognizable if there exists a recognizer for* A.

Theorem 1. *For every embedder A, there exists one and only one informed recognizer corresponding to A. We denote the unique recognizer corresponding to A as IR(A).*

Proof. $\forall P, P' \in \mathbf{P}, W \in \mathbf{P}$, define $IR(P', P, W)$ as follows:
$IR(P', P, W) = \text{TRUE}$, if there is some $W \in candidate(A, P)$ such that $P' = A(P, W)$.
$IR(P', P, W) = \text{FALSE}$, otherwise.
It is easy to see IR is a recognizer corresponding to A. □

From Theorem 1 and Example 8 in [19], not all embedders are extractable, but every embedder is informed recognizable.

Theorem 1 shows there is one and only abstract informed recognizer, but there might be several concrete recognition algorithms to realize such an informed recognizer.

Property 1. For every embedder A, $IR(A)$ is both the positive-partial and the negative-partial informed recognizers corresponding to A.

An extreme positive partial informed recognizer will always say a program has a watermark while an extreme negative partial informed recognizer will always say a program has no watermarks. These two informed recognizers are not useful in practice. Now we consider the relative strength of two informed recognizers.

Definition 7. *(Strength of partial informed recognizers) Let PIR1 and PIR2 be two positive-partial informed recognizers corresponding to an embedder A. If $\forall P, P' \in \mathbf{P}, W \in \mathbf{W}$, $PIR_2(P', P, W) = \text{TRUE} \implies PIR_1(P', P, W) = \text{TRUE}$, we say PIR_2 is at least as strong as PIR_1.*

Let NIR_1 and NIR_2 be two negative-partial informed recognizers corresponding to an embedder A. If $\forall P, P' \in \mathbf{P}, W \in \mathbf{W}$, $NIR_1(P', P, W) = \text{TRUE} \implies NIR_2(P', P, W) = \text{TRUE}$, we say NIR_2 is at least as strong as NIR_1.

Property 2. For an embedder A, $TPIR(A)$ is the weakest positive-partial informed recognizer and $IR(A))$ is the strongest positive-partial informed recognizer corresponding to A.

$TNIR(A)$ is the weakest negative-partial informed recognizer and $IR(A)$ is the strongest negative-partial informed recognizer corresponding to A.

4 Conclusions

Recognition is a very complicated concept in software watermarking. In this paper we define the concepts involved in informed recognition. We have not considered the attack issue in this paper. How to recognize watermarks from attacked programs is challenging research topic in software watermarking. We will also study how to combine software obfuscation [3,4,17,18] and software watermarking to develop more secure software watermarks.

References

1. Aleman-Meza, B., Burns, P., Eavenson, M., Palaniswami, D., Sheth, A.: On onto-logical approach to the document access problem of insider threat. In: ISI 2005. Volume 3495 of LNCS. (2005) 486–491
2. Chen, Y., Chu, W.W.: Databases security protection via inference detection. In: IEEE ISI 2006. Volume 3975 of LNCS. (2006) 452–458
3. Collberg, C., Thomborson, C., Low, D.: A taxonomy of obfuscating transformations. In: Tech. Report, No.148, Dept. of Computer Sciences, Univ. of Auckland. (1997)
4. Collberg, C., Thomborson, C., Low, D.: Manufacturing cheap, resilient, and stealthy opaque constructs. In: POPL'98. (1998) 184–196
5. Collberg, C., Thomborson, C., Low, D.: On the limits of software watermarking. In: Technical Report #164, Department of Computer Science, The University of Auckland. (1998)
6. Collberg, C., Thomborson, C.: Software watermarking: Models and dynamic embeddings. In: Proceedings of Symposium on Principles of Programming Languages, POPL'99. (1999) 311–324
7. Collberg, C., Thomborson, C.: Watermarking, tamper-proofing, and obfuscation - tools for software protection. IEEE Transactions on Software Engineering **28** (2002) 735–746
8. Mehrotra, S., Zeng, D.D., Chen, H., Thuraisingham, B.M., Wang, F.Y.: Intelligence and security informatics. In: ISI 2006. Volume 3975 of LNCS. (2006)
9. Monden, A., Iida, H., ichi Matsumoto, K., Inoue, K., Torii, K.: Watermarking java programs. In: International Symposium on Future Software Technology '99. (1999) 119–124
10. Moulin, P., O'Sullivan, J.: Information–theoretic analysis of information hiding. IEEE Transactions on Information Theory **49** (2003) 563–593
11. Myles, G., Collberg, C.: Software watermarking through register allocation: Implementation, analysis, and attacks. In: LNCS 2971. (2004) 274–293
12. Nagra, J., Thomborson, C., Collberg, C.: A functional taxonomy for software watermarking. In Oudshoorn, M.J., ed.: Twenty-Fifth Australasian Computer Science Conference (ACSC2002), Melbourne, Australia, ACS (2002)
13. Nagra, J., Thomborson, C.: Threading software watermarks. In: IH'04. (2004)
14. Thomborson, C., Nagra, J., Somaraju, He, Y.: Tamper-proofing software watermarks. In: Proc. Second Australasian Information Security Workshop(AISW2004). (2004) 27–36
15. Xia, Z., Jiang, Y., Zhong, Y., , Zhang, S.: A novel policy and information flow security model for active network. In: ISI 2004, LNCS. Volume 3073. (2004) 42–55
16. Zhu, W., Thomborson, C., Wang, F.Y.: A survey of software watermarking. In: IEEE ISI 2005. Volume 3495 of LNCS. (2005) 454–458
17. Zhu, W., Thomborson, C.: A provable scheme for homomorphic obfuscationin in software security. In: The IASTED International Conference on Communication, Network and Information Security, CNIS'05, Phoenix, USA (2005) 208–212
18. Zhu, W., Thomborson, C., Wang, F.Y.: Application of homomorphic function to software obfuscation. In: WISI 2006. Volume 3917 of LNCS. (2006) 152–153
19. Zhu, W., Thomborson, C.: Extraction in software watermarking. In: ACM MM&Sec'06, Geneva, Switzerland. (2006) 175–181
20. Zhu, W., Thomborson, C.: Recognition in software watermarking. In: 1st ACM Workshop on Content Protection and Security, in conjuction with ACM Multimedia 2006, October 27th, 2006, Santa Barbara, CA, USA. (2006) 29–36

An Inference Control Algorithm for RDF(S) Repository*

Jianjiang Lu[1], Jinpeng Wang[1], Yafei Zhang[1], Bo Zhou[1],
Yanhui Li[2], and Zhuang Miao[1]

[1] Institute of Command Automation, PLA University of Science and Technology,
Nanjing 210007, China
[2] School of Computer Science and Engineering, Southeast University,
Nanjing 210096, China
jjlu@seu.edu.cn

Abstract. Protecting RDF(S) repository is a topic in many Web applications. In RDF(S) repository, sensitive information can be inferred from non-sensitive data by iteratively applying the inference rules. Therefore, the problem of inference control is a crucial need for protecting RDF(S) repository. This paper presents an inference control algorithm that can prevent illegal inference effectively. In the algorithm, the inference dependence graph is defined to compute the logic expression of sensitive RDF(S) triples set, which is translated into the disjunctive normal form for obtaining the answers of the inference control problem.

1 Introduction

RDF(S) is a language for representing information on the Web [1,2]. Protecting RDF(S) repository is a topic in many Web applications. Thuraisingham B first described the developments in standards for the Semantic Web and then describes standards for secure Semantic Web. In particular XML security, RDF security, and secure information integration and trust on the Semantic Web are discussed [3]. Reddivari P described the motivation for an RDF store with complete maintenance capabilities and access control. He proposed a policy based access control model providing control over the various actions possible on an RDF store [4]. Dietzold S presented a lightweight access control framework based on rule-controlled query filters [5]. Jain A proposed an access control model for RDF. The model is based on RDF data semantics and incorporates RDF and RDFS entailments [6].

Access control models protect sensitive data from unauthorized disclosure via direct accesses; however, they fail to present indirect accesses. This paper presents an inference control algorithm that can prevent illegal inference effectively. In the algorithm, the inference dependence graph is defined to compute the logic expression of sensitive RDF(S) triples set, which is translated into the disjunctive normal form for obtaining the answers of the inference control problem. This paper is organized as

---

* This work was supported in part by the NSFC (60403016).

C.C. Yang et al. (Eds.): PAISI 2007, LNCS 4430, pp. 262–268, 2007.

follows: Section 2 presents the definition of RDF(S) inference dependence graph. Section 3 presents the inference control algorithm. Section 4 presents an example. Finally, conclusions are given in section 5.

2 Inference Dependence Graph

RDF(S) repository S consists of triples, these triples are explicitly contained in S. Given a fixed set of inference rules, the implied triples can be inferred from the triples explicitly contained in S. RDF(S) has thirteen inference rules, table 1 only shows some inference rules [7]. The closure of RDF(S) repository S is the set of all explicit and implicit triples. We denote the closure of a repository S as S^*.

Table 1. Some inference rules

Rule	If contains	Then add
rdfs4	uuu aaa xxx.	uuu rdf:type rdfs:Resource. xxx rdf:type rdfs:Resource.
rdfs5	uuu rdfs:subPropertyOf vvv. vvv rdfs:subPropertyOf xxx.	uuu rdfs:subPropertyOf xxx.
rdfs7	aaa rdfs:subPropertyOf bbb. uuu aaa yyy.	uuu bbb yyy.
rdfs9	uuu rdfs:subClassOf xxx. vvv rdf:type uuu.	vvv rdf:type xxx.
rdfs11	uuu rdfs:subClassOf vvv. vvv rdfs:subClassOf xxx.	uuu rdfs:subClassOf xxx.

For example, tap-cmu.rdf and tap-cmu-schema.rdf are RDF(S) repositories (http://tap.stanford.edu) which describe the information of Wilson Harvey. Fig.1 shows the implied triples inferred from the following triples of the RDF(S) repositories.

```
<tap:CMU_RAD df:ID="http://tap.stanford.edu/data/CMUSpecialFacultyHarvey,_Wilson">
    <tap:homePage> http://people.cs.cmu.edu/person/7018.html</tap:homePage>
    <rdfs:label xml:lang="en">Harvey, Wilson</rdfs:label>
    <tap:hasEmailAddress> wah@cs.cmu.edu</tap:hasEmailAddress>
    <tap:worksFor
    rdf:resource="http://tap.stanford.edu/data/CMU_ComputerScienceDepartment"/>
    <tap:hasPosition>ProjectScientist</tap:hasPosition>
</tap:CMU_RAD>
```

To construct an effective inference control algorithm, the concept of inference dependence graph is defined to describe the inference relations between RDF(S) *triples*. RDF(S) inference dependence graph is a directed label graph. Each node in graph represents one triple, each directed edge from condition to result represents inferred relation between triples, each directed edge is corresponding to one condition. Table 1 shows that most rules have two conditions, other rules such as

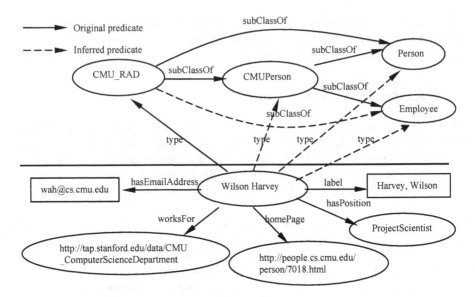

Fig. 1. RDF(S) triples

rdfs4 have only one condition. To distinguish two cases, for the rules with one condition, a directed edge is labeled by the condition itself; for the rules with two conditions, a directed edge is labeled by another condition.

3   Inference Control Algorithm

Let S be a set of triples of a RDF(S) repository, let S^* be a closure of S, let $S_n=\{s_1,s_2,\ldots,s_k\}\subset S^*$ be a set of unauthorized triples. A subset S' of S is called a candidate result, if $(S')^*\cap S_n=\phi$.

Let s be a triple, a direct condition R of s is the form $<s, r_1, r_2>$, where r_1 and r_2 satisfy one of the following conditions: (1) s can be inferred from r_1 and r_2, or (2) s can be inferred from r_1 alone, and $r_2=\phi$, or (3) $s\in S$, and $r_1=r_2=\phi$. $R(s)$ represents the set of direct conditions of triple s.

An inference condition C of s is a set of triples, satisfying the following conditions: (1) $C\subseteq S$, and (2) s can be inferred from C, and (3) s cannot be inferred from any proper subset of C. $C(s)$ represents the set of inference conditions of triple s. Apparently, each inference condition is corresponding to an inference channel. Given a sensitive triple s, if all the inference conditions in $C(s)$ are false, we say s cannot be inferred from other triples.

Logic expressions for triples are defined to compute the set of inference conditions of sensitive triples. Logic expressions can embody the inference relations between triples, and the problem of computing the set of inference conditions can be converted to a series of operations on logic expressions.

Definition 1. Let $R(s)=\{R_1,R_2,...,R_n\}$ be the set of direct conditions of triple s, the logic expression $E(s)$ of s is defined as following:

$$E(s)=E(R_1)\vee E(R_2)\vee...\vee E(R_n).$$

Each $E(R_i)$ is the logic expression of direct condition R_i (see definition 2), where $i = 1,2,...,n$. A logic expression $E(s)$ is true, if at least one element $E(R_i)$ in $\{E(R_1), E(R_2),...,E(R_n)\}$ is true, which means s can be inferred by corresponding R_i.

Definition 2. Let $R=<s, r_1, r_2>$ be a direct condition of triple s, the logic expression of R is defined as following:

$$E(R) = \begin{cases} E(r_1)\wedge E(r_2) & r_1\neq\phi,r_2\neq\phi \\ E(r_1) & r_1\neq\phi,r_2=\phi \\ s & r_1=r_2=\phi \end{cases}$$

$E(R)$ is true means s can be inferred from R, otherwise $E(R)$ is false. As for the last case, $E(R)$ is true if $s\in S$.

Let $S_n=\{s_1,s_2,...,s_k\}$ be a set of sensitive triples, the aim of inference control is to make sure each triple in S_n cannot be inferred from other triples, namely, $E(s_i)=0$, $\forall i\in\{1,2,...,k\}$, $\overline{E(s_1)}\wedge\overline{E(s_2)}\wedge...\wedge\overline{E(s_k)}=1$. Translate this expression into the disjunctive normal form $E_1\vee E_2\vee...\vee E_n$, if any E_j is true where $j=1,2,...,n$, the whole expression is true. So each E_j stands for a candidate result. According to De Morgan' low, each E_j is the form $\overline{t_1}\wedge\overline{t_2}\wedge...\wedge\overline{t_m}$, to make E_j true, $\{t_1,t_2,...,t_m\}$ should be removed from S, and $\{t_1,t_2,...,t_m\}$ is a candidate result. The RDF(S) inference control algorithm is shown as following:

RDF(S) inference control algorithm:

Input: RDF(S) repository S, sensitive triples set S_n.

Output: a subset S' of S, that $(S')^*\cap S_n=\phi$

Step 1: Use an iterative, pruning forward chaining algorithm [7] to compute the closure S^* of S, during the computing process, record all inference relations between triples for inference dependence graph.

Step 2: For each s_i in S_n, compute it's logic expression $E(s_i)$ with the direct conditions computed in step 1.

Step 3: According to the result of step2, computing the logic expression $\overline{E(s_1)}\wedge\overline{E(s_2)}\wedge...\wedge\overline{E(s_k)}$.

Step 4: Translate $\overline{E(s_1)}\wedge\overline{E(s_2)}\wedge...\wedge\overline{E(s_k)}$ to the disjunctive normal form $E_1\vee E_2\vee...\vee E_n$.

Step 5: Select the best result E_i among $E_1, E_2,...,E_n$, remove all triples in it from S then get S'. The quality of a candidate results is estimated by the difference in size between S^* and $(S')^*$. It assumes that the less different they are, the better the result is.

Step 6: Assign a label for each triple in S^*, every triple appear in $(S')^*$ should be labeled as authorized.

4 Experiment

Let tap-cmu.rdf and tap-cum-schema.rdf be RDF(S) repositories. In the experiment, we use J2RE1.4.2 as the development platform, Jena 2.1 as the RDF API

Table 2. RDF(S) triples

Triples			No.
Subject	Predicate	Object	
http://tap.stanford.edu/data/CMU SpecialFacultyHarvey,_Wilson	tap:hasEma ilAddress	wah@cs.cmu.edu	1
http://tap.stanford.edu/data/CMU SpecialFacultyHarvey,_Wilson	tap:hasPosi tion	ProjectScientist	2
http://tap.stanford.edu/data/CMU SpecialFacultyHarvey,_Wilson	tap:homePa ge	http://people.cs.cmu.edu/perso n/7018.html	3
http://tap.stanford.edu/data/CMU SpecialFacultyHarvey,_Wilson	tap:worksF or	http://tap.stanford.edu/data/C MU_ComputerScienceDepart ment	4
http://tap.stanford.edu/data/CMU SpecialFacultyHarvey,_Wilson	rdf:type	http://tap.stanford.edu/data/C MU_RAD	5
http://tap.stanford.edu/data/CMU SpecialFacultyHarvey,_Wilson	rdfs:label	Harvey, Wilson	6
http://tap.stanford.edu/data/CMU SpecialFacultyHarvey,_Wilson	rdf:type	http://tap.stanford.edu/data/C MUPerson	7
http://tap.stanford.edu/data/CMU SpecialFacultyHarvey,_Wilson	rdf:type	http://tap.stanford.edu/data/Per son	8
http://tap.stanford.edu/data/CMU SpecialFacultyHarvey,_Wilson	rdf:type	http://tap.stanford.edu/data/Em ployee	9
http://tap.stanford.edu/data/CMU _RAD	rdfs:subCla ssOf	http://tap.stanford.edu/data/C MUPerson	10
http://tap.stanford.edu/data/CMU _RAD	rdfs:subCla ssOf	http://tap.stanford.edu/data/Per son	11
http://tap.stanford.edu/data/CMU _RAD	rdfs:subCla ssOf	http://tap.stanford.edu/data/Em ployee	12
http://tap.stanford.edu/data/CMU Person	rdfs:subCla ssOf	http://tap.stanford.edu/data/Per son	13
http://tap.stanford.edu/data/CMU Person	rdfs:subCla ssOf	http://tap.stanford.edu/data/Em ployee	14
http://tap.stanford.edu/data/CMU SpecialFacultyHarvey,_Wilson	rdf:type	rdfs:Resource	15

Table 3. Experiment results

S_n	{1,2,3,4,7}	{1,2,3,4,5}	{1,2,3,4,7,9}	{1,2,3,4,5,7,9}
Candidate result /difference in size between S^* and $(S')^*$	{1,2,3,4,10} /304 {1,2,3,4,5}/9	{1,2,3,4,5} /9	{1,2,3,4,10} /304 {1,2,3,4,5}/9	{1,2,3,4,5}/9
The best result	{1,2,3,4,5}	{1,2,3,4,5}	{1,2,3,4,5}	{1,2,3,4,5}
Computing cost	28.511s	1.000s	27.313s	1.000s

(http://jena.sourceforge.net), and MySQL4.1. To show simply, number is used to label RDF(S) triple, table 2 shows the RDF(S) triples. Supposing that Wilson Harvey doesn't want anyone to know his personal information (such as homepage, e-mail address, workplace and position) and the fact that he is a CMUPerson. Then the sensitive triple set S_n is {1,2,3,4,7}, after computing, get two candidate results: {1,2,3,4,10} and {1,2,3,4,5}. Comparing the two candidate results, we find that the first result make S^* lose 304 triples, while the number of the second one is only nine. The reason why the two results are so different is that they contain different triples. The first one contains triple 10(<CMU_RAD, subClassOf, CMUPerson>), which describes the subclass relation between CMU_RAS and CMUPerson, and many instances of CMU_RAD concern it. However, the second result contains triple 5 (<Wilson Harvey, type, CMU_RAD>) instead, which involves only one instance: Wilson Harvey. Apparently, the second one loses lesser information than the first one, so we choose it as the best result. Table 3 also shows other inputs S_n and results.

5 Conclusions

To prevent the indirect access of sensitive information via inference using RDF(S) entailment rules, an inference control algorithm for RDF(S) repository is proposed in this paper. The algorithm can prevent illegal inference. In the future work, we will provide query engine with inference control for RDF and distributed RDF repositories.

References

1. Lassila, O., Swick, R.: Resource description framework (RDF) model and syntax specification. Working draft, W3C. http://www.w3.org/TR/1999/REC-rdf-syntax-19990222 (1999)
2. Hayes, P.: RDF semantics. Working draft, W3C. http://www.w3.org/TR/2004/REC-rdf-mt-20040210/ (2004)
3. Thuraisingham B: Security standards for the semantic web. Computer Standards & Interfaces 27 (2005) 257-268
4. Reddivari, P., Finin, T., Joshi, A.: Policy based access control for a RDF store. In: Proceedings of Policy Management for the Web workshop. Chiba, Japan (2005) 78-83

5. Dietzold, S., Auer, S.: Access control on RDF triple stores from a Semantik Wiki perspective. In: Proceedings of the 2nd International Workshop on Scripting for the Semantic Web. Budva, Montenegro (2006)
6. Jain, A., Farkas, C.: Secure resource description framework: an access control model. In: Proceedings of ACM Symposium on Access Control Models and Technologies. California, USA, (2006)121-129
7. Broekstra, J.: Storage, querying and inferencing for semantic web languages. Amsterdam: Department of Mathematics and Computer Science, Vrije Universiteit Amsterdam (2005)

PPIDS: Privacy Preserving Intrusion Detection System*

Hyun-A Park, Dong Hoon Lee, Jongin Lim, and Sang Hyun Cho

Center for Information Security Technologies (CIST),
Korea University, Anam Dong, Sungbuk Gu, Seoul, Korea
{kokokzi, donghlee, jilim, bungae}@korea.ac.kr

Abstract. The goal of intrusion detection systems(IDS) is to protect from the signs of security problems. However, since an IDS usually depends on the monitored data and has to identify an intruder, the running of IDS comes to threaten users' privacy. In this paper, we propose a new privacy preserving method in intrusion detection system by applying cryptographic methods to log files. It can meet the enhanced privacy of users as well as the security of network providers without TTP.

Keywords: Privacy, Intrusion Detection System, Host-based IDS, Privacy Homomorphism, Audit log.

1 Introduction

Recently, intrusion detection systems (IDS) have been introduced as a solution of side effects such as hacking attacks in complicated networks. However, since an IDS usually depends on the monitored data and has to identify an intruder, its running leads to threaten users' privacy. For example, the service provider of obscene moving pictures runs an IDS to prevent hacking attacks. Intrusions are detected by monitoring audit logs but users may not want their log information to be monitored. It's not so easy to figure out this conflict.

After the first systematic approach by D.E.Denning [6], there are representative papers of [1] and [10] among the works on protection of privacy in IDS. Since both of [1] and [10] are based on the pseudonyms generated in cooperation with a trusted third party (TTP), they need the intervention of TTP such as IP(identity protector).

In this paper, we propose a new privacy preserving intrusion detection system (PPIDS), using cryptographic methods to log files without TTP. PPIDS encrypts the audit log file and can detect intrusions using the secure computation methods over encrypted data. It can be accomplished through privacy homomorphism, partitioning method, and so on. Therefore, PPIDS can meet the more enhanced privacy of users than the previous solutions without TTP and the more security of network providers at the same time.

---

* This research was supported by the MIC(Ministry of Information and Communication), Korea, under the ITRC(Information Technology Research Center) support program supervised by the IITA(Institute of Information Technology Assessment).

C.C. Yang et al. (Eds.): PAISI 2007, LNCS 4430, pp. 269–274, 2007.

2   Privacy

Privacy can be defined as fair information practices(FIPs) meaning the right of individuals to determine the disclosure and use of their personal data. Hence, privacy requirements should cover the followings; 1 Anonymity-a user may use a resource or service without disclosing the user's identity. 2 Pseudonymity-it protects the user's identity in cases where anonymity cannot be provided, e.g. if the user has to be held accountable for his activities. 3 Unobservability-a user may use a resource or service without others being able to observe that the resource or service is being used. 4 Unlinkability-a user may make use of resources and services without others being able to link these being used together[5].

Privacy Homomorphism. The arithemetic operations over encrypted data is accomplished through privacy homomorphism.

Definition. $\forall a \in A$, $D_k(E_k(a)) = a$. Let $\tilde{\alpha} = \alpha_1, \alpha_2, ..., \alpha_n$ and $\tilde{\beta} = \beta_1, \beta_2, ..., \beta_n$ be two (related) function families. The functions in $\tilde{\alpha}$ are defined on the domain A and the functions on $\tilde{\beta}$ are defined on the domain of encrypted values of A. $(E_k, D_k, \tilde{\alpha}, \tilde{\beta})$ is defined as a privacy homomorphism if $D_k(\beta_i(E_k(a_1), E_k(a_2), ..., E_k(a_m))) = \alpha_i(a_1, a_2, ..., a_m) : 1 \le i \le n$ [7].

3   The Construction of PPIDS

The setting of our system.   Our scheme is a rule- based pattern matching system which is based on host-based intrusion detection system. This system consists of a host server administrator and several agent managers. Among those several agent managers, there is an AM(agent manager) for detecting intrusion in log directories. From now on, we call it AM in brief.

AM plays a role of the director who detects intruders by monitoring all the log directories. For this purpose, he uses the secure computation method over encrypted data. However, he has limited computation power and storage. AM does not encrypt and compute the log information. Furthermore, AM can not even access all the log directories. If AM needs to access to log directories for some reasons, he should obtain an authorization from the host server administrator. AM just can command each directory to implement the operation(computation) for intrusion detection.[1] AM is the only owner of decryption key and decrypts the results which are reported by log directories. By this process, AM analyze the results so that he can detect attacks and take proper actions. Through these periodically repeated processes, he can determine the most optimal policies and audit reduction.

Each log directory stores all the records encrypted automatically by IDS program in the SQL table.[2] Thus every directory just implements the orders from AM without decrypting any records and then reports the results to AM. Namely,

---

[1] This is similar to the function of access permission of '$rwxrwxrwx'$ in Unix system.

[2] Generally, log directory is a file system. However, the log directory of our system uses the SQL table transformed by the method such as [2].

each directory functions as a kind of automated software program for detection of intrusion.

Our scheme is composed of encryption process, detection process, and policy-decision process.

3.1 Encryption Process

In this process, log information of users is encrypted and stored in a SQL table of each directory. We classify audit log's data into two types of information; quantity-type information and text-type information.

3.1.1 Quantity-Type Information

1. **Equality queries.** The PH(privacy homoomrphism) used in this paper is the same as [3] and [4].
   - public parameters : $\{d(> 2), m(\gtrsim 10^{200})\}$, • secret parameters : (r, m').
   - $r \in Z_m$ such that r^{-1} (mod m) exists and a small divisor $m' > 1$ of m.

   Encryption. Randomly split $a \in Z_{m'}$ into secret $a_1, ..., a_d$ such that $a = \sum_{j=1}^{d} a_j$ mod m' and $a_j \in Z_m$. Compute;
   $$E_k(a) = (a_1 r \ mod \ m, \ a_2 r^2 \ mod \ m, ..., a_d r^d \ mod \ m)$$

   Decryption. Compute the scalar product of the j-th coordinate by r^{-j} mod m to retrieve a_j mod m. Compute $a = \sum_{j=1}^{d} a_j \ mod \ m'$ to get a;
   $$D_k(E_k(a)) = (a_1 r^{-1} + a_2 r^{-2} +, ..., a_d r^{-d} \ mod \ m') = a$$

   The set F' of ciphertext operations consists of Addition and subtraction, Multiplication, and Division.

2. **Inequality queries**

   For inequality comparisons, we utilize the partitioning method. Firstly, we partition the field's domain into a set of partitions and assign an identifier chosen by AM at random for each partition [7]. Then, AM has to store the partition table generated by himself.

3.1.2 Text-Type Information

Text information includes both of quantified data such as IP address and non-quantified data such as ID. Although Quantified data such as IP address is expressed in numeral letters, it is inappropriate for applying to the encryption method of quantity information. We encrypt these information using a deterministic encryption such as AES.

3.2 Detection Process

Order $\mathcal{O}$ means the commands which are transferred to each directory by AM. To solve the authentication problem of orders and results, we use the message authentication code(MAC). More details are as follows.

1. **Conveying Orders**
   $$\{\mathcal{O} = (T, \ P_1, \ P_2, ..., \ P_q), \ MAC(K_A, \mathcal{O})\} \qquad (where, P_i =$$
   $\{j - th \ field, \ S|V_i \ or \ C|C_i\}, \quad i \in [1, t], \quad q \ is \ the \ number \ of \ policies$
   $and \ K_A \ is \ the \ MAC \ key \ shared \ between \ AM \ and \ a \ log \ directory \ A.)$

The AM sends the distinctive order $\mathcal{O}$ and its MAC to each directory. The message for every directory is different from each other. T is the time that a directory implements orders periodically or in real time. P_i means a policy set by the AM and consists of specific operations to be conducted in the directory. $S|V_i$ means 'scanning a value V_i' and $C|C_i$ is 'computing a operation C_i' in j-th field.

2. **Implementing Orders**
   After verifying the MAC, according to the order $\mathcal{O}$, each directory implements the operations at time T.

3. **Reporting**
   $$\{R = (t, (P_1, r_1, r_{100}, ...), (P_2, r_7, r_{57}, ...), ..., (P_k, r_{100}, r_{164}, ...)), MAC(K_A, R)\}$$
   Each directory reports the result R of implementations as above. t is the implemented time. $(P_i, r_1, r_{100}, ...)$ is the result to i-th policy. r_j is the row satisfying the policy P_i and it is reported with the encrypted form without being decrypted.

4. **Decrypting**
   Receiving the reportings, AM verifies the MAC and decrypts the reported rows partially or totally. Then, AM can determine the intruders through careful analysis.

5. **Taking action**
   By rules of the policy, AM takes proper actions on the detected intruders.

3.3 Policy Decision Process

In a host-based IDS, policy decision is one of the most important things to be correct and efficient. Hence, audit reduction is required necessarily as its solution so that AM should update the policy periodically. This process is done through repeating the analysis of Detection Process.

4 Application Scenario

We assume that a host server is the service provider of obscene moving pictures for only adults and the information of login-log file is composed of a user's ID, password, IP address, a date, access time, success/failure of access, time duration. The policies for intrusion detection of this server are; 1)Access failures are more than three times, 2)Access time is from 07:00 to 09:59. Then, AM of the IDS keeps the partition table like the Table 1. The encrypted recordings of login information are presented at the SQL table in a login-log directory such as Table 2. In Table 2, a random number is assigned to each field name. Namely, in the first row of Table 2, 11 means the field name of ID, 54 - password, 868 - IP address, and so on.

Then, in the 1st and 3rd fields, each user's ID and user's IP address are encrypted by deterministic function f with AM's secret key k_m. In the 2nd field, password is encrypted by one way hash function h. In the 6,7,9-th fields, identifiers of access time, success/failure, and time duration are mapped respectively according to AM' partition table.

Table 1. Partition table of AC

Time Partitions	Identifier	Sucess/Failure	Identifier	Time Duration	Identifier
00:00 - 03:59	48	success	3	00:00-00:00	38
04:00 - 06:59	29	failure	5	01:00-02:00	24
07:00 - 09:59	91			02:00-03:00	55
10:00 - 15:59	33			03:00-04:00	17
16:00 - 19:59	54			04:00-05:00	99
20:00 - 23:59	78			05:00-24:00	43

Table 2. Encrypted login recordings in AM's SQL Table

11	54	868	56	232	444	89	21	68
$f_{k_m}(Alice)$	$h(pw_1)$	$f_{k_m}(123\|234\|45\|1)$	$E(12)/E(15)$	$E(21):E(08)$	78	3	$E(02):E(15)$	55
$f_{k_m}(Carol)$	$h(pw_2)$	$f_{k_m}(123\|234\|45\|2)$	$E(12)/E(15)$	$E(23):E(18)$	78	5	$E(00):E(00)$	38
$f_{k_m}(Bob)$	$h(pw_3)$	$f_{k_m}(123\|234\|45\|3)$	$E(12)/E(15)$	$E(23):E(30)$	78	3	$E(01):E(30)$	24
$f_{k_m}(Carol)$	$h(pw_2)$	$f_{k_m}(123\|234\|45\|5)$	$E(12)/E(15)$	$E(02):E(04)$	48	5	$E(00):E(00)$	38
$f_{k_m}(Carol)$	$h(pw_2)$	$f_{k_m}(123\|234\|45\|1)$	$E(12)/E(15)$	$E(07):E(10)$	91	5	$E(00):E(00)$	38

In the 4,5,8-th fields, the information about date, access time, and time duration is encrypted by privacy homomorphism as it is mentioned in 3.1.1. For simple computation, suppose $d = 2, r = 2, m' = 23, m = 69$, then $r^{-1} = 35$. Well, date information 12/15 is encrypted like this; $E(12) \mid E(15) = E(6,6) \mid E(7,8) = (12,24) \mid (14,32)$. Also access time and time duration are encrypted by the same method.

For detection, AM conveys the order $\mathcal{O} = \{T, P_1, P_2\} = \{(10 : 00/day), (89, C\|COUNT(5) \geq 3), (444, S\|91)\}$ and its MAC to a login log directory. Then, after verifying the MAC, it implements the received order and reports the result $R = \{(10 : 00, 12/15), (P_2, r_2, r_4, r_5), (P_1, r_5)\}$ with its MAC. These processes say that at ten a.m. on the 15-th of December, the cases that the number of access failures is more than three times are checked in rows r_2, r_4, r_5, and the case that access time is from 07:00 to 09:59 is checked in row r_5. Thus, AM decrypts the rows r_2, r_4, r_5. For r_2, $(f_{k_m}^{-1}(f_{k_m}(Carol)) = Carol, f_{k_m}^{-1}(f_{k_m}(123\|234\|45\|2)) = 123\|234\|45\|2$, $(12,24) \mid (14,32) = (12 \times 35 + 24 \times 35^2 \bmod 23) \mid (14 \times 35 + 32 \times 35^2 \bmod 23) = 12 \mid 15$, $(6,11) \mid (24,24) = (6 \times 35 + 11 \times 35^2 \bmod 23) \mid (24 \times 35 + 24 \times 35^2 \bmod 23) = 23 : 18$, $(4,15) \mid (6,11) = 00 : 00$. r_4, r_5 are decrypted in the same ways. Then, AM gets to know that Carol is against the policy and takes proper action on Carol according to the rules of the policy.

5 Discussion and Conclusion

The main focus of our scheme is to preserve users' privacy in IDS of network providers, whereas it's not to improve the performance or correctness of IDS itself.

By using cryptographic methods, PPIDS can provide anonymity(encryption of ID), pseudonymity (encryption of quasi-identifier such as IP address), confidentiality of data, and unobservability. Unfortunately, it can not provide perfect unlinkability. Because we use the deterministic symmetric encryption function for detection, the cyphertexts corresponding to the same plaintexts are equal. Hence, it allows others to link the same ciphertexts to some resources even if they don't know the meaning of the ciphertexts. Anyway, using cryptographic methods, PPIDS prevents users' log information from being monitored and misused. It means fair information practices(FIPs). In addition, PPIDS is much superior to the previous solutions using pseudonym in privacy preserving aspects. This is largely because the previous pseudonymous solutions can meet pseudonymity but can not meet other properties of privacy perfectly. Furthermore, applying the arithmetic operative methods into encrypted data, PPIDS enables intrusion detection as well as preserving privacy of users without a TTP.

In efficiency, PPIDS raises the problem of a lowering of performance due to encryptions. In each directory, it requires additional cost only when log information is stored in SQL table and AM decrypts the reported results. However, PPIDS does not need the intervention of TTP such as IP(identity protector) to use pseudonym.

In conclusion, we say that our new approach, PPIDS can provide users with more secure privacy without intervention of IP as well as intrusion detection.

References

1. R. Büschkes, Privacy enhanced intrusion detection, Aachen University of Technology, 1999
2. http://www.oracleadvice.com/Tips/external.htm
3. J. Domingo-Ferrer, A new privacy homomorphism and applications, Information Processing Letters, 1996
4. J. Domingo-Ferrer, A Provably Secure Additive and Multiplicative Privacy Homomorphism, ISC, LNCS 2433, pp. 471-483, 2002.
5. S. Fischer-Hubner, Privacy-Enhancing Technologies, Proceedings of IFIP/SEC 97, LNCS 1958, pp. 107-165, 2001.
6. Dorothy E. Denning: An Intrusion-Detection Model. IEEE Trans. Software Eng, 1987
7. H. Hacigumus, B. Iyer, and S. Mehrotra, Efficient Execution of Aggregation Queries over Encrypted Relational Databases, DASFAA, LNCS 2793, pp.125-136, 2004
8. U. Lindqvist and Phillip A. Porras, eXpert-BSM: A Host-based Intrusion Detection Solution for Sun Solaris, 17th Annual Computer Security Applications Conference, 2001
9. B. Mukherjee, L.T. Heberlein, and K.N. Levitt, Network Intrusion Detection, IEEE Network, 8:26-41, 1994
10. M. Sobirey, S. Fischer-Hubner, and K. Rannenberg, Pseudonymous Audit for Privacy Enhanced Intrusion Detection, IFIP/SEC, 1997
11. Tripwire Evaluation Guide for Unix
12. J. Biskup and U. Flegel, Transaction based Psedonyms in Audit Data for Privacy Respecting Intrusion Detection, RAID 2000, LNCS 1907, p.p. 28-48, 2000

Evaluating the Disaster Defense Ability of Information Systems

Baowen Zhang[1], Jing Zhang[1], Ning Zhou[1], and Mingang Chen[2]

[1] School of Information Security Engineering,
Shanghai Jiaotong University, Shanghai, China
{zhangbw,zjing,zning}@sjtu.edu.cn
[2] Shanghai Science and Technology Information Center

Abstract. Disaster prevention and recovery is an important branch of security informatics. People need to investigate the disaster prevention and recovery capacity of information systems in order to make them more robust. In this paper we propose a framework to evaluate the disaster defense ability of information systems. In the research a hierarchy of criterions is built up which covers both the disaster prevention ability and the disaster recovery ability. And a fuzzy assessment method is designed to fit the evaluating process. We also develop a software tool based on the framework to assist the information security evaluators.

1 Introduction

With growing concern of threat of terrorist attacks, intelligence and security informatics becomes an important research topic [16] [13] [9]. A disaster strike, such as an earthquake or a terrorist attack, can cause disruption to IT functions and thus bring a breakdown of business. Sometimes it may even threaten the survival of a business. Thus, the problem of how to strengthen IT capabilities to defend from the disasters becomes a serious concern for researchers in security informatics.

Several kinds of plans of disaster-related topics, such as Business Continuity Plan and Disaster Recovery Planare proposed by security organizations and institutes [4] [5] [6] [12]. The objectives of these plans are to ensure an organizations IT systems operate uninterruptedly during and after the occurrence of a disaster. Researches on how to implement a disaster prevention and recovery process are also presented in [1] [10] [11]. However a new issue arises: How to evaluate the disaster prevention and recovery ability of an IT systems before we ensure them more robust?

In this paper we propose a framework to evaluate the disaster defense ability for information systems. In the research a hierarchy of criterions is built up which covers both the disaster prevention ability and the disaster recovery ability. And a fuzzy assessment method is designed to fit the evaluating process. We also develop a software tool based on the framework to assist the information security evaluators.

C.C. Yang et al. (Eds.): PAISI 2007, LNCS 4430, pp. 275–281, 2007.

The rest of the paper is organized as follows: Section 2 discusses the backgrounds of disaster prevention and recovery process. The generation of criterion set is presented in Section 3. Design of fuzzy synthetic judgement method for the evaluation process is proposed in Section 4. The system architecture of the tool and its application are described in Section 5. Finally the conclusion is given and topics are suggested for future research in Section 6.

2 Backgrounds

To evaluate the disaster prevention and recovery capacities is a hard work because of the complexity of the disaster prevention process. Generally the disaster prevention process can be described as follows:

First IT security management needs to perform a Business Impact Analysis (BIA) to correlate specific system components with the critical services that they provide, and thus to characterize the consequences of a disruption to the system components. Later, preventive controls such as fire suppression systems need to be identified depending on system type and configuration. Next recovery strategies are developed, which include the backup and recovery solution, roles and their responsibilities, costs and etc. Then the staff need to be trained and the related plan such as Disaster Recovery Plan (DRP) has to be tested ,exercised and maintained.

The way used in our work here is depicted in Fig.1. We build up a hierarchy of criterions cover both disaster prevention phases and recovery phases. And we conduct the BIA in the objects IT systems to generate the objects to be evaluated. Thus we implement a fuzzy synthetic evaluation method to create the assessment reports as the results. Different with traditional IT risk analysis process the criterions set is totally "disaster-defense" oriented and we lay more emphasis on BIAs to conduct the assessment process.

3 Generation of Criterion Set

The criterion set is essential for conducting a meaningful and valid assessment process. Unfortunately we have found no such existing criterion set in similar works. Thus we need to build a criterion set before evaluating the systems. To consider a criterion set to for disaster prevention and recovery processes is an exaggerative work, which involves many factors such as human, facilities, IT systems and physical environments. Different from risk assessment we focus more attention on critical business and assets when designing the criterion set. In our work we split the criterion set into disaster prevention part and disaster recovery part and deal with each part separately.

We used several security standards such as BS7799 and ISO13335 for reference to build the criterion set of disaster prevention part[2][3][14]. The criterion set comprises of five parts: management, physical environments, communication, access control, and system development and maintenance. The design of criterion set of disaster recovery part is rather complex. The distance between original

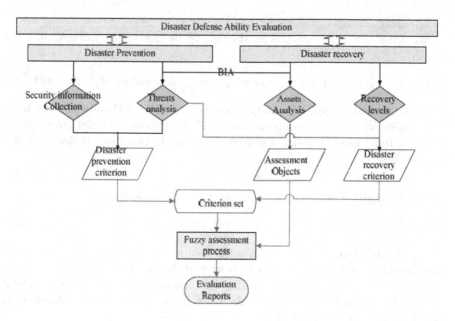

Fig. 1. Evaluation process of the disaster defense ability

sites and backup sites is a critical factor for the selection of backup and recovery solution. We create the criterions respectively for local backup mechanism and remote backup mechanism. These criterions are also graded. In detail criterions for local mechanism are classified into the following levels according to its implementation layer : 1),0 level, no local backup data; 2),1 level, data backup; 3) 2 level, system backup; and 4), application backup. We use the disaster recovery levels in the standards of the Share 78 seminar in Anaheim for reference to grade the criterions for remote mechanism.

4   Design of the Fuzzy Synthetic Assessment Method

Generally assessment methods can be classified into two types: quantitative methods and qualitative methods. There are both categorical factors and numerial factors involved in our assessment process. Thus we adopt a fuzzy synthetic assessment method to evaluate the disaster defense ability for information systems. Though the fuzzy method is a quantitative one it can also deal with categorical (crisp) factors well. The method is designed as follows:

1), Indexes set: Most criterions are fuzzy in disaster prevention systems. But some criterions are crisp such as "Yes/No" ones. However we take the crisp ones as the special type of the fuzzy. Thus we map all the criterions in the criterion set to the indexes used as the fuzzy assessment objects in a 1:1 way. We use

$$U = (u_1, u_2, ...u_n) \tag{1}$$

to denote the index set, in which the element u_i(i=1,2...n) denotes the index.

2), Fuzzy concepts of assessment:
We define the fuzzy concepts for the disaster defense ability assessment as the set V,

$$V = (v_1, v_2, v_3, v_4, v_5) = \{verystrong, strong, general, weak, veryweak\} \quad (2)$$

3),Weights set: We combine Delphi method and AHP method together to build the weights set in a bottom-up manner[8][17]. We choose the Delphi to build the Relative Importance Matrix of indexes.The consultation table is designed as a matrix A:

$$A = \{a_{ij}\}_{m*m} \quad (3)$$

in which a_{ij} either is an integer w or the inverse of w and

$$w \in [1, 9] \quad (4)$$

4), Membership function: We use the k-order parabolic distribution as the membership function. After many tests we find the membership function is more unitary when k =1.2. Different membership functions are adopted for different fuzzy concepts in V. For example, the following is the membership function of the fuzzy concepts "very strong":

$$A_1(x) = \begin{cases} 0, & x < 70, & (5) \\ (\dfrac{x-70}{20})^{1.2}, & 70 \le x \le 90. & (5') \\ 1, & x > 90. & (5'') \end{cases}$$

5), Multiple-layer fuzzy synthetic assessment: Let the fuzzy relationship matrix between U,the object set, and V,the fuzzy assessment concepts set be R,

$$R = (r_{ij})_{n*m} \quad (6)$$

and the weight set A,

$$A = \{a_1, a_2, ...a_n\} \quad (7)$$

then we can get B,

$$B = \{b_1, b_2, ...a_m\} = \{a_1, a_2, ...a_n\} \circ (r_{ij})_{n*m} \quad (8)$$

in which b_j denotes the significance of the j-th factor on V.

Because the criterion hierarchy has multiple layers, we use the above equation recursively by the layers to get the evaluation results.

5   Application

We implement our framework into a tool named as DDAET(Diaster Defense Ability Evaluation Tool). The software DDAET, which is based on B/S computing model, is developed on Microsoft .Net platform. The system architecture

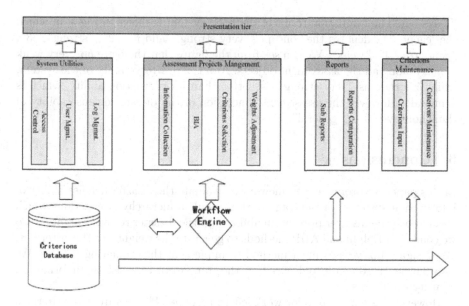

Fig. 2. DDAET system architecture

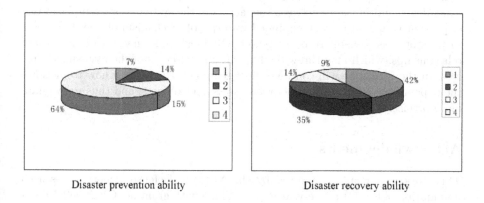

Disaster prevention ability   Disaster recovery ability

Fig. 3. A sample assessment result

of DDAET is illustrated in Fig.2. The business tier of DDAET consists of four modules: assessment project managents, reports, criterions maintenance and system utilities. Assessment project managents module contains the core procedures such as information collection, BIA, criterions selection and weights adjustment. Reports module is used to generate reports as the system output. Criterions maintenance module and system utilities module enable users to database I/Os and modifications, logs managements, users managenments and etc. A typical application of our evaluation methods is an ERP system of a famous tobacco logistics company in Shanghai, China, which greatly concerns its IT system security. Assisted by the tool DDAET we have conducted a full assessment on its

IT system. The evaluation result of the ERP system is shown in Fig.3, in which the legend "1" denotes the concept " very strong", and for "2", "strong", "3", "general", "4", "weak". We can see from the figure that there are no "very weak " ones among all the assessment objects. And the recovery ability of the system, which is grade as "very strong", is better than its prevention ability, which is "general". However the assessment conclusion of the disaster defense ability of the whole system is "general".

6   Conclusions

In this paper we proposed a framework to evaluate the disaster defense ability of information systems. In the framework we built a hierarchy of criterions which covers both the disaster prevention ability and the disaster recovery ability. Also we combined Delphi and AHP methods to generate the weights for the criterions. We design a fuzzy assessment method to implement the evaluating process. We also develop a software tool based on the framework to assist the information security evaluators.

However there are still a lot work left to be done. The hierarchy of criterions built in our research now only reflects the static features in the disaster prevention and recovery process, which is actually dynamic. In fact there are logical dependence and causality between the factors in the system. For example, as one of preventive measures, well-equipped waterproof mechanism of a system helps to promote it's disaster recovery power. Obviously it's unwise to ignore these relationships, which may throw doubt on the preciseness of the assessment process. In the future we will continue the research on the issue of how to measure the dependence and causality between assessment objects, and thus to evaluate more precisely.

Acknowledgements

This work is partially supported by the National Defense Scientific Research Foundation of the 11th Five-year Plan of China with grant no. C1120060497 and by the Scientific and Technology Committe Foundation with grant 045115035.

References

1. Adachi, Y., Obata, H. Disaster prevention measures of NTT for telecommunications network systems, IEEE Communications Magazine, Volume 28, Issue 6, June 1990 Page(s):18 - 24
2. British Standard Institute. Information Security Management - Part 1:Code of Practice for Information Security Management (BS7799-1:1999). British Standard Institute, 1999.05
3. British Standard Institute. Information Security Management Systems-Specification with guidance for use. British Standard Institute(BS 7799-2:2002), 2002.09

4. Contigency Planning Management Group. BCP Handbook. http://www.contingencyplanning.com/tools/bcphandbook/2004 A.
5. David J. Smith. Business Continuity Management: Good Practice Guidelines. The Business Continuity Institute, 2002.01
6. DRI International . Professional Practices for Business Continuity Planners. http://www.chinacissp.com/download/ProfessionalPractices.pdf2002
7. Floyd PiedadMichael Hawkins. High availability. Printice-Hall, Inc.2001.06
8. Harold A. Linstone and Murray Turoff: The Delphi Method: Techniques and Applications. Massachusetts: Addison-Wesley (1975)
9. HyangChang Choi, SeungYong Lee, and HyungHyo Lee. Design and Implementation of a Policy-Based Privacy Authorization System.ISI 2006, LNCS 3975, pp. 129 C 140, 2006.
10. Iyer, R.K., Sarkis, J. Disaster recovery planning in an automated manufacturing environment ,IEEE Transactions on Engineering Management, Volume 45, Issue 2, May 1998 Page(s):163 - 175
11. Kun Wang, Lihua Zhou, Zhen Cai, Zengxin Li. A Disaster Recovery System Model in an E-government System , Sixth International Conference on Parallel and Distributed Computing, Applications and Technologies, 2005. PDCAT 2005.
12. Marianne Swanson, Tim Grance, Joan Hash, etc. Contigency Planning Guide for Information Technoloty SystemsNIST Special Publication 800-34.National Institute of Standards and Technoloty, http://csrc.nist.gov/publications/nistpubs/800-34/sp800-34.pdf2001.12
13. Paul J.H Hu, Daniel Zeng, Hsinchun Chen, Catherine Larson, Wei Chang, and Chunju Tseng. Evaluating an Infectious Disease Information Sharing and Analysis System. ISI 2005, LNCS 3495, pp. 412 C 417, 2005
14. Sturgeon. Concepts and models for IT Security (ISO/IEC TR 13335-1). ISO/IEC, 1996.12
15. Toigo.J.W. Disaster Recovery PlanningPreparing for the Unthinkable. Pearson EducationInc., 2004.5
16. William Zhu, Fei-Yue Wang: Covering Based Granular Computing for Conflict Analysis. ISI 2006: 566-571, 2006
17. Xu Shubo: Practical decision-making method: the theory of analytic hierarchy process. Tianjin University press (1988)

Airline Safety Evaluation Based on Fuzzy TOPSIS

Yong Deng[1,2,*], Jia Xiong[2], and Ping Fu[1]

[1] Zhejiang Police Vocational Academy, 310018, Hangzhou, P.R. China
[2] School of Electronics and Information Technology, Shanghai Jiao Tong University, 200240, Shanghai, P.R. China
dengyong@sjtu.edu.cn, doctordengyong@yahoo.com.cn

Abstract. Safety is a critical element to the business success of the passenger airline industry. It is because of the imprecision or vagueness inherent in the subjective assessment of the experts that we use fuzzy set theory to deal with safety evaluation problems. In this paper, A novel airline safety evaluation method based on fuzzy TOPSIS is proposed. The merit of the method is that it can deal with both quantitative and qualitative assessment in the process evaluation. In addition, the method can be easily applied to safety evaluation with little computation load. A numerical example is used to illustrate the efficiency of the proposed method.

1 Introduction

Evaluating the overall airlines safety level plays a very important role in air safety management systems. To examine comparative safety levels among airlines for safety management and improvement purposes, an evaluation mechanism for measuring the overall safety of airlines is needed. Extensive works have been done to deal with airlines safety evaluation [1,2,3].

It is obvious that the an airline safety is relative to some attributes, such as the management level and the maintenance of the companies. These attributes are independent and compensatory of each other in terms of their contribution to the overall level of airline safety. Some of these attributes are qualitative measures, which require subjective assessments by human experts. From this point, evaluating airlines safety can be seen as a multiattribute decision making (MADM) problem.

MADM has proven to be an effective approach for ranking a finite number of alternatives characterized by multiple conflicting criteria . The technique for order preference by similarity to an ideal solution (TOPSIS), one of the known classical MADM methods, was initiated by Hwang and Yoon [4]. This technique is based on the concept that the ideal alternative has the best level for all attributes considered, whereas the negative-ideal is the one with all the worst attribute values. TOPSIS defines solutions as the points which are simultaneously farthest from the negative-ideal point and closest to the ideal point and is successfully applied to selecting the location of a manufacturing plant. In the process of TOPSIS, the performance ratings and the weights of the criteria are given as crisp values. Thus, the measurement of weights and qualitative attributes did not consider the uncertainty associated with the mapping of human perception to a

---

* Corresponding author.

C.C. Yang et al. (Eds.): PAISI 2007, LNCS 4430, pp. 282–287, 2007.

number. However, crisp data are inadequate to model real-life situations since the evaluation data of the facility location under different subjective attributes and the weights of the attributes are often expressed linguistically. Thus, a more realistic approach may be to use linguistic assessments instead of numerical values .

Fuzzy set theory has proven to be a powerful modelling tool for coping with the subjectiveness and imprecision of human judgments. Many fuzzy TOPSIS method has been proposed to handle linguistic decision making[5,6,7,8,9]. However, all existing approaches is not efficient due to two main reasons. First, in the decision making process of existing fuzzy TOPSIS, it is inevitable to determine the ideal point and the negative-ideal point by the means of ranking fuzzy number. While, it is very known that ranking fuzzy number is an open issue that cannot efficiently be solved [10]. The other reason is that it is not correct to determine the distance between fuzzy numbers due to the distance function used in existing works is not a reasonable distance function [11]. In this paper, a new and simple fuzzy TOPSIS with little computation load is presented to evaluate airlines safety. we formulate the evaluation of airline safety as a fuzzy MADM problem. The papers is organized as follows. In section 2, some basic preliminaries are introduced. In section 3, a simple fuzzy TOPSIS method is proposed to deal with fuzzy MADM. A numerical example is illustrated to show the use of the proposed method in airlines safety evaluation. Some Conclusions are made in section 5.

2 Definition and Formulation

In this section, for the purpose of reference, we will cover some basic definitions and formulas that are used in our paper.

2.1 Fuzzy Numbers

Definition 2.1. *"Fuzzy set": Let X be a universe of discourse. Where $\tilde{A}$ is a fuzzy subset of X; and for all $x \in X$, there is a number $\mu_{\tilde{A}}(x) \in [0,1]$ which is assigned to represent the membership degree of x in $\tilde{A}$, and is called the membership function of $\tilde{A}$ [12,13].*

Definition 2.2. *"Fuzzy number": A fuzzy number $\tilde{A}$ is a normal and convex fuzzy subset of X [13].*

Here, "normality" implies that:

$$\exists x \in \mathbb{R}, \ \bigvee_x \mu_{\tilde{A}}(x) = 1 \tag{1}$$

and "convex" means that:

$$\forall x_1 \in X, \ x_2 \in X, \ \forall \alpha \in [0,1], \ \mu_{\tilde{A}}(\alpha x_1 + (1-\alpha)x_2) \geqslant \min(\mu_{\tilde{A}}(x_1), \mu_{\tilde{A}}(x_2)) \tag{2}$$

Definition 2.3. *A triangular fuzzy number $\tilde{A}$ can be defined by a triplet (a, b, c) , where the membership can be determined as follows*

$$\mu_{\tilde{A}}(x) = \begin{cases} 0, x < a \\ \frac{x-a}{b-a}, a \leqslant x \leqslant b \\ \frac{c-x}{c-b}, b \leqslant x \leqslant c \\ 0, x > c \end{cases} \tag{3}$$

2.2   Canonical Representation Operation on Fuzzy Numbers

In this paper, the canonical representation of operation on triangular fuzzy numbers which are based on the graded mean integration representation method [14], is used to obtain a simple fuzzy TOPSIS method.

Definition 2.4. *Given a triangular fuzzy number $\tilde{A} = (a_1, a_2, a_3)$, the graded mean integration representation of triangular fuzzy number $\tilde{A}$ is defined as:*

$$P(\tilde{A}) = \frac{1}{6}(a_1 + 4 \times a_2 + a_3) \tag{4}$$

Then by applying Eq.(4), the importance weights of various criteria and the ratings of qualitative criteria, considered as linguistic variables which can be expressed in positive triangular fuzzy numbers.

Let $\tilde{A} = (a_1, a_2, a_3)$ and $\tilde{B} = (b_1, b_2, b_3)$ be two triangular fuzzy numbers. The representation of the addition operation $\oplus$ on triangular fuzzy numbers $\tilde{A}$ and $\tilde{B}$ can be defined as :

$$P(\tilde{A} \oplus \tilde{B}) = P(\tilde{A}) + P(\tilde{B}) = \frac{1}{6}(a_1 + 4 \times a_2 + a_3) + \frac{1}{6}(b_1 + 4 \times b_2 + b_3) \tag{5}$$

The canonical representation of the multiplication operation on triangular fuzzy numbers $\tilde{A}$ and $\tilde{B}$ is defined as :

$$P(\tilde{A} \otimes \tilde{B}) = P(\tilde{A}) \times P(\tilde{B}) = \frac{1}{6}(a_1 + 4 \times a_2 + a_3) \times \frac{1}{6}(b_1 + 4 \times b_2 + b_3) \tag{6}$$

3   Fuzzy TOPSIS Approach

Suppose a MCDM problem has m alternatives, $A_1, \ldots, A_m$, and n decision criteria, $C_1, \ldots, C_n$. Each alternative is evaluated with respect to the n criteria. All the ratings assigned to the alternatives with respect to each criterion form a decision matrix denoted as follow:

$$D = \begin{array}{c} \\ A_1 \\ A_2 \\ \vdots \\ A_m \end{array} \begin{array}{c} C_1\ C_2\ \cdots\ C_n \\ \left[\begin{array}{cccc} r_{11} & r_{12} & \cdots & r_{1n} \\ r_{21} & r_{22} & \cdots & r_{2n} \\ \vdots & \vdots & \ddots & \vdots \\ r_{m1} & r_{m2} & \cdots & r_{mn} \end{array} \right] \end{array}$$

where r_{ij} is the rating of alternative A_i with respect to criteria C_j. Let $W = (\omega_1, \ldots, \omega_n)$ be the relative weight vector about the criteria. In this paper, the rating r_{ij} of alternative A_i and the weights ω_j of criteria are assessed in linguistic terms represented as triangular fuzzy numbers as shown in Table 1 and 2.

Then the TOPSIS method can be summarized as follows:

1. Calculate the weighted decision matrix $X = (x_{ij})_{m \times n}$

$$x_{ij} = \omega_j r_{ij}, \ i = 1, 2, \ldots, m; \ j = 1, 2, \ldots, n \tag{7}$$

where ω_j is the relative weight of the jth criterion or attribute. It should be noted that the results are crisp numbers whether the weight and rating is fuzzy number of crisp number.

2. Normalize the decision matrix $X = (x_{ij})_{m \times n}$ using the equation below:

$$v_{ij} = \frac{x_{ij}}{\sqrt{\sum_{k=1}^{m} x_{kj}^2}}, \; i = 1, 2, \ldots, m; \; j = 1, 2, \ldots, n \tag{8}$$

we get the weighted normalized decision matrix $V = (v_{ij})_{m \times n}$.

3. Determine the ideal and negative-ideal solutions:

$$A^* = (v_1^*, v_2^*, \ldots, v_n^*) \tag{9}$$

where $v_j^* = \{(\max_{i=1,2,\ldots,m} v_{ij} \,|\, j \in \Omega_b), (\min_{i=1,2,\ldots,m} v_{ij} \,|\, j \in \Omega_c)\}$

$$A^- = (v_1^-, v_2^-, \ldots, v_n^-) \tag{10}$$

where $v_j^- = \{(\min_{i=1,2,\ldots,m} v_{ij} \,|\, j \in \Omega_b), (\max_{i=1,2,\ldots,m} v_{ij} \,|\, j \in \Omega_c)\}$
and Ω_b and Ω_c are the sets of benefit criteria/attributes and cost criteria/attributes, respectively.

4. Calculate the Euclidean distances of each alternative from A^* and A^-, as follows:

$$d_i^* = \sqrt{\sum_{j=1}^{n} (v_{ij} - v_j^*)^2}, \; i = 1, 2, \ldots, m \tag{11}$$

$$d_i^- = \sqrt{\sum_{j=1}^{n} (v_{ij} - v_j^-)^2}, \; i = 1, 2, \ldots, m \tag{12}$$

5. Calculate the relative closeness of each alternative to the ideal solution. The relative closeness of the alternative $A_i(\, i = 1, 2, \ldots, m)$ with respect to A^* is defined as:

$$CC_i = \frac{d^-}{d^* + d^-}, \; i = 1, 2, \ldots, m \tag{13}$$

6. Rank the alternatives according to the relative closeness to the ideal solution. A large value of index CC_i indicates a good performance of the alternative A_i. The best alternative is the one with the greatest relative closeness to the ideal solution .

Table 1. Dimensions and measures used for evaluating safety levels of airlines

Dimension	Safety measure
C_1 Management	C_{11} Safety policy and strategy (fuzzy assessment via surveys)
	C_{12} Management attitude/commitment (fuzzy assessment via surveys)
	C_{13} Employee attitude/commitment (fuzzy assessment via surveys)
	C_{14} Safety personnel rate (total number of flights/total number of safety personnel)
C_2 Operations	C_{21} Competence status of flight crew (fuzzy assessment via surveys)
	C_{22} Compliance with aviation task procedures (fuzzy assessment via surveys)
	C_{23} Training status of pilots (average training activities per pilot)
	C_{24} Incident and accident rate (number of accidents per 100,000 departures)
C_3 Maintenance	C_{31} Compliance with maintenance task procedures (fuzzy assessment via surveys)
	C_{32} Training status of personnel (average training activities per worker)
	C_{33} Crew competence rate (number of certificated technicians/number of maintenance crew)
C_4 Planning	C_{41} Average age of fleet (years)
	C_{42} Aircraft types (number)

Table 2. The final ranking order

	A1	A2	A3	A4
$d+$	0.0521	0.0441	0.0355	0.0701
$d-$	0.0621	0.0569	0.0599	0.0446
CC	0.5437	0.5634	0.6275	0.3888

4   Evaluating Airlines Safety

In the passenger airline industry, there is no universal agreement among researchers and practitioners about what exactly constitutes safety indicators [15]. This suggests that airlines safety measures are context-dependent and should be selected to reflect the operational environment investigated. For safety management and improvement purposes, safety measures to be identified for airlines are classified into four safety dimensions. These dimensions correspond to organizational divisions of airlines, involved directly in contributing to airline safety, including (a) management, (b) flight operations, (c) engineering and maintenance, and (d) fleet planning (finance and property).

The weighting vectors W and W_j represent the relative importance of n safety dimensions $C_j (j = 1, 2, ..., n)$ and p_j safety measures $C_{jk} (k = 1, 2, ..., p_j)$ for the problem and their corresponding dimension respectively. The weighting vectors $C_{jk} (k = 1, 2, ..., p_j)$ are obtained by using the pairwise comparison of the analytic hierarchy process [16] assessed by safety experts via surveys. Due to the limited space, the detailed datum are not shown in this paper, please refer [15] for more information. We just listed the final result of our proposed fuzzy TOPSIS method in the following table 2. It can be easily seen that the final safety ranking of the four airlines is a_3, a_2, a_1, a_4.

5   Conclusions

In this paper, a new method to evaluate airline safety based on fuzzy TOPSIS is proposed. The new method can deal with both quantitative and qualitative assessment of multiple safety measures. The numerical example shows that our approach can be easily applied to airline safety evaluation.

Acknowledgement

This work was supported by National Defence Key Laboratory grant no. 51476040105JW0301, Aerospace Basic Support Foundation grant no. 2004-JD-4, Science and Technology of Zhejiang province grant no. 20060028.

References

1. Foreman S. E.,: An application of Box-Jenkins ARIMA techniques to airline safety data. Logistics and Transportation Review . **29** (1993) 221-240.
2. McFadden, K. L., : Comparing pilot-error accident rates of male and female airline pilots. Omega. **24** (1996) 443-450
3. Chang Y. H., Yeh C. H.,: A survey analysis of service quality for domestic airlines. European Journal of Operational Research. **139** (2002) 166-177
4. Yoon. K., Hwang. C. L,: Manufacturing plant location analysis by multiple attribute decision making: single-plant strategy. International Journal of Production Research. **23** (1985) 345-359
5. Chen. C. T., Extension of the TOPSIS for group decision making under fuzzy environment. Fuzzy Sets And Systems. **114** (2000) 1-9
6. Chu. T. C., Selecting plant location via a fuzzy TOPSIS approach. Int J Adv Manuf Technol, **20** (2002) 859C864
7. Braglia. M., Frosolini. M., Montanari. R., Fuzzy TOPSIS approach for failure mode, effects and criticality analysis. Quality and Reliability Engineering International, **19**, (2003) 425-443
8. Deng Y., Liu Q.,: A TOPSIS-based centroid-index ranking method of fuzzy numbers and its application in decision-making. Cyber. Sys. **36** (2005) 581-595
9. Deng. Y.,: Selecting plant location via a fuzzy TOPSIS approach. Int J Adv Manuf Technol, **28** (2006) 839-844
10. Deng. Y., Zhu .Z. F., Liu Q.,: Ranking fuzzy numbers with an area method using radius of gyration. Computers and Mathematics With Applications. **51** (2006) 1127-1136
11. Tran. L., Duckstein. L.,: Comparison of fuzzy numbers using a fuzzy distance measure. Fuzzy Sets and Systems, **130** (2002) 331-341
12. Zadeh. L. A.,: Fuzzy sets. Inform. and Control, **8**, (1965) 338-353
13. Kauffman. A., Gupta. M. M., Introduction to fuzzy arithmetic: Theory and applications. VanNostrand-Reinhold, (1985)
14. Chou. C. C.,: The canonical representation of multiplication operation on triangular fuzzy numbers. Computers and Mathematics with Applications, Vol.45, No.10-11, (2003)1601-1610
15. Chang Y. H., Yeh C. H.,: A new airline safety index. Transportation Research Part B: Methodological. **38** (2004) 369-383
16. Satty. T,: The Analytic Hierarchy Process. McGraw-Hill, New York. 1980

A Framework for Proving the Security of Data Transmission Protocols in Sensor Network*

Mi Wen, Ling Dong, Yanfei Zheng, and Kefei Chen

Department of Computer Science and Engineering Shanghai Jiao Tong University
200240, Shanghai, China P.R.C.
{superwm,ldong,zheng-yf,kfchen}@sjtu.edu.cn

Abstract. This paper presents an framework to analyze the security of data transmission protocols in wireless sensor network (WSN). The proposed framework is based on the simulation paradigm and it defines three attack models in terms of the adversary's attacking ability. Furthermore, it provides a ideal model to verify whether a given protocol is secure or not under these three different attack models. The framework is proved to be effective by analyzing a "secure" data transmission protocol SDD. This is the first time that the notion of provable security is applied in wireless sensor networks.

Keywords: Provable Security, Sensor Network, Data Transmission Protocol.

1 Introduction

A basic task in WSN systems is to interactively distribute commands to or gather data from a subset of the sensor nodes. Therefore, one of the primary challenges in the designing of these systems is how to guarantee the data transmission protocols, which may run in hostile or unattended environments, robust and secure. Some secure data transmission protocols for sensor networks have been proposed, e.g.[6] [7], and their security have been discussed informally and incompletely. When these protocols are put into practice, they are likely to result in unexpected damages. Here a fundamental challenge exists: is there any approach to prove the security of data transmission protocols in WSNs?

To answer this challenge, we present a simulation-based formal framework to prove the security of the data transmission protocols in WSNs (following the idea of [1][8]). This framework defines three attack models in terms of the adversaries' attacking abilities, and constructs an ideal model to simulate a protocol's operation and analyze its security. The verification of the protocol's security in ideal model relies on checking errors reachable under the given attack model. Once an error is identified in the attack model, a flaw is founded and the protocol is proved to be insecure in that attack model. Reversely, if no error is found, the protocol is proved to be statistically secure in that attack model. This idea

---

* This work is supported by SRFDP of China under grant 20050248043.

C.C. Yang et al. (Eds.): PAISI 2007, LNCS 4430, pp. 288–294, 2007.

is similar to the fault-oriented test [3] method and it helps to mitigate the state space explosion problems in other techniques such as model checking [2] etc. Moreover, we give out security definitions under different attack models. At last, SDD [6] is analyzed to prove if it satisfies those security definitions.

The remainder of this paper is organized as follows. Section 2 presents the framework of our approach. Security definition and checking process are given in section 3. Section 4 analyzes the security of SDD. Section 5 concludes the paper.

2   The Framework of Our Approach

2.1   Network Model

Define the wireless sensor network as an undirected labeled graph $struc = (V, E, C_v, C_e)$. Where V is the set of vertices, which represents the identities of the participating senors. E is the set of edges, which represents the radio links between each pair of sensors. C_v is the cost value of sensors, C_e is the cost value of the edges.

2.2   Attack Model

The attack models are classified according to the adversaries' abilities [9].

(1) The first attack model: Outsider attack. In this level the attacker can illegally join the WSN or read and alter messages transmitted by legitimate nodes. The known attacks include eavesdropping, altering, replaying attacks etc.

(2) The second attack model: Insider attack. A malicious insider can perform all the attacks that an outsider can. The malicious insiders can spoof or inject bogus information, send fake messages to any protocol participant or send observations about the monitored area to a malicious user. The known attacks include selective forwarding, acknowledgement spoofing, Sybil , sinkhole etc.

(3) The third attack model: Laptop-class attack. A laptop-class adversary with a powerful transmitter can cause a large number of nodes to attempt to send their packets to it, but those nodes sufficiently far away from the adversary would be sending packets into oblivion. The known attacks include sinkhole attacks, wormhole attack, HELLO flood attack and denial of service attack etc.

2.3   Communication Model

The main idea of the simulation paradigm we used is to construct two models: a real model that describes an instance of the protocol in real environment, and an ideal model that captures the defined specification of the protocol under different attack models.

The Real Model. A real model is corresponding to the configuration of $conf_{real} = (stru = (V, E, C_v, C_e), A)$, and the system $Sys_{real,A}$ is described as a real system running in it. A represents the adversary in the network.

We define the whole network communication model for data transmission as Fig 1. $\{D,v_1,\cdots,v_l, S\}$ is a set of interactively communicating probabilistic state machines, connected via buffered channels. Each machine can be initialized with some initial states. The machines operate in a reactive manner. Each channel is considered as an output channel for the machine before it and an input channel for another machine behind it, and it is also able to determine the target of the message and to which channel it belongs. Machine D represents the sink. Machine $v_1,\cdots,v_l$, are the intermediate nodes and machine S is the source nodes. In_i is the input channel of the machine i. rep_i is a response to the request In_i. Each machine has more than one input and output buffered channels, which means our model allows several parallel runs of the protocol.

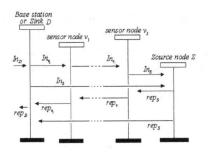

Fig. 1. The communication model of the system

There are four types of delivery pairs in Fig1: sink $\leftrightarrow$ sensor node, sensor node $\leftrightarrow$ sensor node, sensor node $\leftrightarrow$ source node, sink $\leftrightarrow$ source node. We define the two entities of each pair as Sender and Receiver in Fig 2. The machine T is triggered by the information in In_T from the previous node. Machine R communicates with machine T through its channel In_R and rep_R. The adversary A may try to tamper the messages in In_R or rep_R. The whole communication ends when reaches one of its final states. We denote the output of the $Sys_{real,A}$ as $Out_{real,A}(x)$. Where x is the initiated *interest*.

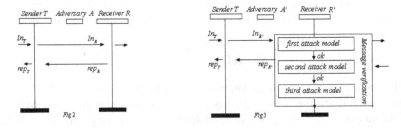

Fig. 2. The pair of Sender and Receiver in real model

Fig. 3. The pair of Sender and Receiver in ideal model

The Ideal Model. The ideal model is corresponding to the configuration $con f_{ideal} = (stru = (V, E, C_v, C_e), A')$, and the system $Sys_{ideal,A'}$ is described as an ideal system running in this model. The whole network communication model for data transmission is same to Fig1. The main difference in each pair of Sender and Receiver is that machine R is replaced by a new machine R' as Fig3. The other operation is similar to that in the real model. Machine R' is initiated with the verification rules. When the messages arrive at its input channel $In_{R'}$ it can do the message verification while processing the contents. Thus, it can detect the system errors. Once an error is found, R' records it in its error-recording tables and the communication continues as if nothing wrong had happened. We denote the output of the $Sys_{ideal,A'}$ as $Out_{ideal,A'}(x)$. The whole communication also ends when it reaches one of its final states.

2.4   Unification of the Real Model and the Ideal Model

The goal of this section is to prove that the real model can be completely simulated by the ideal model in the statistical sense.

Theorem 1. *(statistically security) Let $Sys_{real,A}$ and $Sys_{ideal,A'}$ be systems running in the real model and the ideal model for the same protocol. We say that $Sys_{ideal,A'}$ is statistically as secure as $Sys_{real,A}$ for the honest users with the same initial interest x, if two systems get the same outputs, with the statistical difference of at most ϵ, written as:*

$$\epsilon = \triangle_{sta}(Out_{real,A}(x), Out_{ideal,A'}(x))$$

ϵ is the negligible probability.

Proof: From the construction of our models and systems, we can see that the steps of the $Sys_{real,A}$ and the $Sys_{ideal,A'}$ are exactly the same. If no errors are found in the error-recording tables of the ideal system $Sys_{ideal,A'}$, not only the steps, but also the output of the two systems will be the same, namely, $Out_{real,A}(x) = Out_{ideal,A'}(x)$. On the other hand, if there an error $Malice$ is found in the ideal system $Sys_{ideal,A'}$, search backward in the simulation paradigm, there must exist an adversary A', which leads $Malice \in Ertab$ appear. Apparently, by using this adversary A' to construct $A = A'$, the adversary A can do the same attack to $Sys_{real,A}$. And thus $Out_{real,A}(x) = Out_{ideal,A'}(x)$. Whereas, if adversary A in real system can lead $Malice' \in Ertab$ appear in $Sys_{real,A}$. There may be two possible cases in the ideal system. One is the $Malice' \in Ertab$ will also be arrived in the ideal system, then $Out_{real,A}(x) = Out_{ideal,A'}(x)$. The other one is $Out_{real,A}(x) \neq Out_{ideal,A'}(x)$. This case is possible only when some of the messages during the communication are lost due to the wireless nature of WSN, which occurs only with negligible probability.

Lemma 2. *If the statistical difference between the outputs of the ideal system and the real system is a (small) error ϵ. We say the ideal model can completely simulate the real model in the statistical sense.*

Proof: This lemma can be deduced from Theorem 1.

3   Correctness and Security Definition

The correctness and security definition here are aiming at the data transmission protocols. This paper just focuses on the directed diffusion protocol [5], which is the most important representative of the data transmission protocols.

3.1   Correctness

We assume the correctness definition of a protocol is given by its applications. Generally, a perfect data transmission protocol should be able to securely transmit data in the presence of any number of attackers. There are four criteria that define the secure data delivery through the network expressed as: *data confidentiality, data authentication, data integrity and data freshness.*

Usually, errors are defined in conjunction with the correctness criteria. In our case, the corresponding errors we address are message leakage, message loss, message modification, and message duplication. These errors may manifest themselves in the ways as described in section 2.2.

3.2   Security Definition

Now, we are ready to introduce the definition of secure data delivery according to our attack models and correctness criteria.

Definition 3 (First Attack Model Security, FAMS). *A data transmission protocol is said to be (statistically) secure in the first attack model if, for configuration $conf_{ideal}$ and any outside node-class adversary A', the protocol still satisfies the correctness criteria of its application.*

Definition 4 (Second Attack Model Security, SAMS). *A data transmission protocol is said to be (statistically) secure in the second attack model if, for configuration $conf_{ideal}$ and any inside node-class adversary A', the protocol still satisfies the correctness criteria of its application.*

Definition 5 (Third Attack Model Security, TAMS). *A data transmission protocol is said to be (statistically) secure in the third attack model if, for configuration $conf_{ideal}$ and any Laptop-class adversary A', the protocol still satisfies the correctness criteria of its application.*

3.3   Security Checking in the Ideal Model

The security checking in ideal model includes two steps. Firstly, during the data delivery process, the message verification is done at each machine R' in Fig3. This process is beginning from the first attack model to the third attack model, and errors will be recorded in the error-recording tables *ExerI*, *ExerII* and *ExerIII*. Secondly, when the communication ends, back searches the three error-recording tables to see if there are some errors and determine the security level of the protocols. The Algorithm 1 in Fig4 describes the whole process.

Algorithm 1 Security checking

Ertab: A table contains the possible error states in data transmission protocol.
AtabI, AtabII, AtabIII: Tables contain possible attacks in three attack models.
ExerI, ExerII, ExerIII: Tables contain the errors found in three attack models.
Adv: is an attack.
Mal: is an error.
Security checking // the procedure end when reach one of its terminal state.
{For each (pair of delivery)
    {Message sending;
    Message verification: // verification for each pair
      If $\exists Adv \in AtabI$ leads a $Mal \in Ertab$ then
        Record the error $Mal \longrightarrow ExerI$;
      Else if $\exists Adv \in AtabII$ leads a $Mal \in Ertab$ then
        Record the error $Mal \longrightarrow ExerII$;
      Else if $\exists Adv \in AtabIII$ leads a $Mal \in Ertab$ then
        Record the error $Mal \longrightarrow ExerIII$;}
    Determine the security level
      {IF $\exists Mal \in ExerI$
      Output that" The protocol is insecure!";
      Else if $\exists Mal \in ExerII$
      Output that" The protocol satisfies FAMS !";
      Else if $\exists Mal \in ExerIII$
      Output that" The protocol satisfies SAMS !";
      Else Output that" The protocol satisfies TAMS !" ;}}

Fig. 4. The security checking process in the ideal model

4 Security Level of SDD

In this section, SDD is simulated in the ideal model to demonstrate the usefulness of our framework. According to the security checking process in section 3.3, SDD is simulated and proved to be insecure in the confidential applications, but it satisfies FAMS in non-confidential applications. The detailed analysis is omitted due to the paper length limit, and one can contact the author for further discussion.

5 Conclusion

The main contributions of this paper is that it provides a simulation based ideal model to prove the security of a protocol. In which the protocol is analyzed according to the defined three attack models and its efficiency is demonstrated by analyzing the "secure" directed diffusion protocol SDD [6]. To the best of our knowledge, we are the first one who applied the notions of provable security and the simulation paradigm to the protocols in sensor networks.

References

1. W. Mao.Modern Cryptography:Theory and Practice. Prentice Hall PTR,2004.
2. E. Clarke, O. Grumberg and D. Long. Verification tools for finite-state concurrent systems. In: A Decade of Concurrency - Reflections and Perspectives. Lecture Notes in Computer Science, 803, 1994.
3. A.Helmy, D. Estrin, S. Gupta. Fault-oriented test generation for multicast routing protocol design. In FORTE, pages 93-109, Vol. 135, 1998.

4. I. Cervesato, N. Durgin, P.D. Lincoln, J.C. Mitchell, A. Scedrov, A meta-notation for protocol analysis, in: 12th Computer Security Foundations Workshop C CSFW 1999, IEEE Computer Society Press, 1999, pp. 55-71.
5. C. Intanagonwiwat, R. Govindan, D. Estrin,et al. Directed diffusion for wireless sensor networking, IEEE Trans. Networking, vol. 11, no. 1, pp. 2-16, 2003.
6. X.Wang, L. Yang, K Chen. SDD: Secure Distributed Diffusion Protocol for Sensor Networks, ESAS 2004, LNCS 3313, Springer-Verlag, 2005.
7. A.Perrig, R. Canetti, D. Song, and J. D. Tygar. Efficient and secure source authentication for multicast. In Proceedings of the IEEE Symposium on Network and Distributed System Security (NDSS 2001), pages 35-46, 2001.
8. G.Ács, L. Buttyán, and I. Vajda. Provable Security of On-Demand Distance Vector Routing in Wireless Ad Hoc Networks,ESAS 2005, LNCS 3813, pp. 113-127, 2005.
9. C.Karlof,D.Wagner. Secure routing in wireless sensor networks: attacks and countermeasures,Ad Hoc Network Journal, pages 293-315, and Sep.2003.

Port and Address Hopping for Active Cyber-Defense

Leyi Shi [1,3], Chunfu Jia[1], Shuwang Lü[2], and Zhenhua Liu[2]

[1] College of Information Technical Science, Nankai University, Tianjin, 300071, China
[2] State Key Laboratory of Information Security, Graduate School of Chinese Academy of
Sciences, Beijing, 100049, China
[3] College of Computer and Communication Engineering, China University of Petroleum,
Dongying, 257061, China
shileyi@mail.nankai.edu.cn, cfjia@nankai.edu.cn

Abstract. Motivated by frequency hopping, port and address hopping technique
is thought to be essential and efficient for active cyber-defense and intelligence
security. A novel scheme of timestamp-based synchronization is proposed and a
prototype using port and address hopping tactic is carried out. Then a test-bed is
implemented for the fragment transmission of plaintext over different LANs. In
order to evaluate the performance of the hopping tactic, experiments on DoS
and eavesdropping attacks are performed which demonstrate that port and
address hopping mechanism has better performance than no hopping tactic and
simple port hopping service.

Keywords: Port and address hopping, Active cyber-defense, Denial of Service,
Eavesdropping.

1 Introduction

With the pervasiveness of the Internet, we have acquired enormous benefits and
conveniences; meanwhile suffered more attacks and threats. Internet has become a
double-edge sword. Various Trojan-horses, virus, worms, and malicious codes puzzle
the whole world. Computer networks are playing an increasingly important role in
military, government, and intelligence environments.

Several security mechanisms, such as firewall and intrusion detection/prevention
systems (IDS/IPS), have been proposed to address these problems. But most of these
countermeasures against threats are passive in nature because the attackers exist in the
dark side while the server in the bright. The potential intruders from any place could
attack the conspicuous server at any time. This makes the traditional security tactics
in a devil of hole for those attacks such as Denial of Service or eavesdropping.

In military communication systems, frequency hopping is an efficient tactic which
can keep the enemies in the dark by changing the radio frequency pseudo-randomly.
Inspired by frequency hopping, port and address hopping paradigm is introduced to
puzzle the adversaries by hopping the port and address information pseudo-randomly
during data transmission. Thus we can perform active cyber-defense.

The paper proceeds as follows. Section 2 describes the related works. Section 3
details the design and implementation of a prototype system using port and address

C.C. Yang et al. (Eds.): PAISI 2007, LNCS 4430, pp. 295–300, 2007.
© Springer-Verlag Berlin Heidelberg 2007

hopping tactic. Section 4 evaluates the performance for cyber-defense though experiments upon DoS and eavesdropping attacks. Section 5 concludes the paper.

2 Related Works

In the TCP/IP protocol suite, Internet applications use the socket interface to establish a communication channel for exchanging data. Well-known ports (0 through 1023) are used by servers to provide standard services. However, the well-known port design is vulnerable to port scanning and eavesdropping because of the fixed service port. When the vulnerability is discovered, Eavesdropping or DoS attacks can be launched against the target immediately. This makes it very difficult to detect and thwart these attacks reliably.

Port and address hopping is a dynamic tactic that changes the service's IP address and port number pseudo-randomly during data transmission. In the recent years, different hopping tactics were proposed for various security applications. Port hopping was introduced to detect and mitigate the effect of DoS attacks for public service [1, 2]; while port and address hopping method was mentioned to evade port attacks [3, 4] in the DARPA APOD [5] project. Generally speaking, the crucial issue of these hopping tactics is the synchronization problem that the communication pairs need to be coordinated so that the clients can acquire the right service.

In [1] the authors proposed a time synchronization scheme in which time is divided into discrete slots S_i $(i=0, 1, 2...)$ with duration τ. The service port changes dynamically as a function of the slot number i and the cryptographic key k shared between the server and the client. When a client needs to communicate with the server, it will determine the current service port using k and i. Authorized clients who have the key will be able to determine the current service port whereas the attackers will not. In this scheme, TCP service's port can not be changed once a TCP connection is established, making the TCP service vulnerable to attack. Moreover, the time synchronization scheme is simple but requires too much for clients over WAN or multiple LANs because of transmission delay and traffic jam. In [2] an ACK-based synchronization scheme was introduced for two parties' communication merely. A cryptographic key is shared between the communication pair also and a time-based proactive re-initialization of the ports for ACK-based protocol was proposed to puzzle the attacker. This scheme is realistic but not competent for multiparty communication because other members will not be able to know the current port while two parties are hopping. ACK-based scheme requires no precise clock, but the adversaries can acquire the hopping information easily by sniffing and analyzing the ACK frames. Port hopping tactics in [1, 2] show no benefits for thwarting eavesdropper. The inside attackers can obtain port information easily and launch improved DoS attacks immediately via sniffing the communication after it has been decrypted.

Closely related work was presented in [3, 4] which proposed a port and address hopping tactic relying on time synchronization and random number generators. The paradigm performs a mapping between the fake address-port pair and real pair which is implemented by a hopping delegate and NAT (network address translation) gateway. The hopping delegate is directly located on the client machine, intercepts

RPC calls to the real server, and replaces all header information with fake address-port pair. The NAT gateway is located on the server side, performs the reverse mapping from the fake address-port pair to the real pair. Two designs are implemented for different cases according to the clients and the server. Tunnels is used for port hopping within the same LAN while NAT gateway for port and address hopping on different LANs. It is interesting that this hopping tactic is carried out just through generating various fake address-port pair according to the time and pseudo-random number synchronization, while the real service's pair is fixed yet. The outside adversary can only see traffics between random addresses and ports. However, the inside attacker will be able to acquire and attack the service through eavesdropping.

The main contribution of our work is in presenting a novel scheme of timestamp-based synchronization which can be competent for the hopping service over MAN, carrying out a port and address hopping prototype, and validating the confidentiality and availability performance through experiments.

3 Prototype Skeleton and Implementation

We performed a design and implementation of prototype using port and address hopping tactic. Firstly, consider a scenario as follows: an intelligence department needs to receive secret information from distributed sub-agencies every day. The department should acquire intelligence data correctly and securely even under the attacks of DoS/DDoS or eavesdropping. Obviously, confidentiality and availability are the two most important factors for this deployment. A simplified cyber-defense prototype is established and implemented to reveal this scenario. Figure 1 shows the skeleton of the prototype.

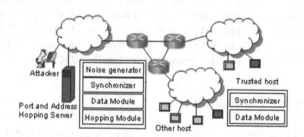

Fig. 1. Skeleton of the prototype based on port and address hopping

The prototype uses port and address hopping tactic, including server and client part. The server consists of 4 modules, i.e. noise generator, synchronizer, data module and hopping module, which are coordinated to provide hopping service. The client part performs data transfer through the synchronizer and data module. A trusted hosts table is preserved by the server while a hopping addresses list is shared between the server and the clients.

Data module provides hopping service, exchanging data with the clients. Before transmission, message is divided into lots of small fragments first, and then these fragments are to be transmitted in burst mode at different service slots to puzzle the eavesdropper. Noise generator also puzzles the eavesdropper or even breaks them down by yielding enormous noise packets which contain lots of fake addresses and ports. Hopping module can generate (address, port) pair for current service according to the hopping algorithm shared between the server and trusted hosts. Synchronizer carries out synchronization so that the clients could acquire the right service.

Synchronization is very essential for hopping service. There exist several schemes such as time-synchronization and ACK-based synchronization. Time-synchronization requires precise clock for both the server and the client. Hopping information is determined by the communication pairs according to the current clock. This scheme is simple but requires too much for exploits over MAN or multiple LANs because of transmission delay and traffic jam. ACK-based synchronization is an asynchronous scheme in fact. The hopping information is transferred through an ACK frame. ACK-based scheme requires no precise clock, but the adversaries can acquire the hopping information easily by analyzing the ACK frames.

This paper proposed a compromised scheme of timestamp-based synchronization which is described as follows. A hopping algorithm is shared between the hopping server and the trusted clients. When a hopping service is to be launched, the (address, port) pair is determined by the hopping algorithm with the server's current timestamp. The timestamp is then transferred to the trusted client. Once receiving the timestamp, the trusted host will be able to determine the current service by the hopping algorithm with the timestamp. Neither precise clock nor hopping information is needed for this scheme, but a timestamp instead. Adversaries can not determine current service because they know nothing about the hopping algorithm. Thus the timestamp-based scheme is efficient and competent for hopping service over MAN or multiple LANs which have transmission delay or traffic jam frequently.

The prototype has been carried out on Linux (Kernel 2.4) based computers. The hopping server has 3 Ethernet cards with data rate up to 100Mbps. Each NIC can be configured multiple IP addresses for hopping service. The port number of hopping service varies from 10000 to 65535 in order to avoid collisions with the well known ports (0 through 1023) and the temporary ports (usually 1024 through 5000).

4   Performance Evaluations

DoS and eavesdropping attack experiments have been carried out to evaluate the performance of port and address hopping tactic. The DoS experiment is performed to evaluate the availability of the prototype. Table 1 details the configuration information of the DoS attack experiment.

Table 1. Configuration of the DoS attack experiment

	Hopping server	Client	DoS attacker
CPU/Memory	P4 2.8GHz/256M	PM 1.5GHz/128M	P4 2.8GHz/256M
Bandwidth	100Mbps (3 NICs)	10Mbps	1Gbps
OS	Red hat Linux 9	VMWare Linux	Red hat Linux 9

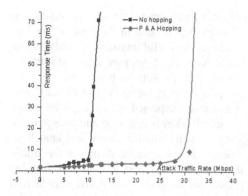

Fig. 2. Fitting curves of DoS experimental data

Table 2. DoS attack experimental data

ATR (Mbps)	Average Response Time (ms)	
	No hopping	P&A hopping
0	1.4258	1.4675
5	2.2436	1.5884
10	4.8988	2.5003
10.5	12.1402	2.6182
12	71.2185	2.9593
13	-	3.1387
20	-	3.2694
25	-	3.6639
31	-	9.0805
32	-	-

A worst scenario is considered: the DoS attackers know the hopping tactic and hopping addresses used by the server, and launch directed attacks to the hopping service through SYN-flooding. Response time is introduced to intuitively reveal the availability of service under attacks. Table 2 demonstrates the main results of DoS attack experiment, and figure 2 shows the fitting curves corresponding to no hopping service versus port and address hopping tactic.

As can be seen, the two services have approximately equal response time under no attacks. No hopping service becomes worse sharply when the attack rate up to 10.5Mbps, and then collapses at 13Mbps, whereas the hopping server provides good service as well as before. Hopping service falls down when the attack rate up to 32Mbps. This experiment shows that the port and address hopping mechanism can greatly improve the availability under the DoS attacks.

Another experiment is performed to evaluate the confidentiality of the hopping service. Also we consider a worst scenario: the server, the client and the eavesdropper are located on the same LAN whose heart is a HUB. No other hosts are alive on the LAN except a virtual machine with multiple virtual IP addresses which are used to confuse the eavesdropper. The hopping server occupies 24 IP addresses for hopping service. The attacker uses Windows XP based computer with a professional sniffing tool of Sniffer pro 4.70 to eavesdrop all the packets on the LAN. A short plaintext of intelligence is transferred. Figure 3 gives the traffic dispersion results which are analyzed by Sniffer pro 4.70 for different cases.

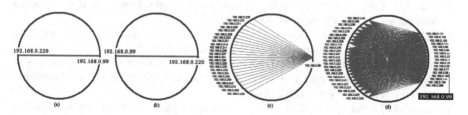

Fig. 3. Traffic dispersion results by sniffing attack, (a) no hopping (b) port hopping (c) port and address hopping (d) port and address hopping with virtual clients

In the case of no hopping service, the eavesdropper can acquire the entire plaintext easily, but can capture large amounts of fragments instead in the case of hopping service. Thus the attackers are obliged to pick out the useful fragment by analyzing all the packets with various addresses and ports. As a result, hopping tactics disturb the attackers or even lead them to disaster if lots of noise packets are generated.

Further research is performed on simple port hopping tactic. As can be seen from figure 3(b) which is identical to (a), no traffic is dispersed although packets with various port numbers are captured. The service IP address is unique and conspicuous. Thus the attackers can acquire the hopping port information easily and launch an improved DoS attack. While port and address hopping tactic disperses the traffic successfully as shown in (c) and (d). It is obvious that port and address hopping mechanism shows better confidentiality than no hopping service and simple port hopping tactic. Furthermore, the traditional cryptography techniques can be used for the hopping mechanism, and will improve the confidentiality greatly.

5 Conclusions

Our work has focused on active cyber-defense using port and address hopping tactic. We have proposed a practical scheme of timestamp-based synchronization which is competent for the hopping service over MAN or multiple LANs. Considering a scenario of intelligence transmission, we have designed and carried out a prototype system based on port and address hopping technique. Thereafter a test-bed has been implemented for the fragment transmission of plaintext over different LANs.

In order to evaluate the availability and confidentiality of the hopping service for active cyber-defense, we have carried out experiments on DoS and eavesdropping. The experiments demonstrate that port and address hopping mechanism has better performance than no hopping tactic and simple port hopping service under the attacks of DoS and eavesdropping.

Acknowledgments. This paper is supported by the National Natural Science Foundation of China (NSFC) under grant No. 60577039, Science and Technology Development Project of Tianjin under grant No. 05YFGZGX24200.

References

1. Lee HCJ, Thing VLL. Port Hopping for Resilient Networks. Conf. 60th IEEE Vehicular Technology, IEEE CS Press, 2004. 3291-3295.
2. Badishiy G, Herzberg A, Keidar I. Keeping Denial-of-Service Attackers in the Dark. Int"l Symp. Distributed Computing (DISC), Springer-Verlag, 2005. 18-31.
3. Atighetchi M, Pal P, Webber F et al. Adaptive Use of Network-Centric Mechanisms in Cyber-Defense. Proc. 6th IEEE Int"l Symp. Object-Oriented Real-Time Distributed Computing, IEEE CS Press, 2003. 183-192.
4. Atighetchi M, Pal P, Jones C et al. Building Auto-Adaptive Distributed Applications: The QuO-APOD Experience. Proc. 3rd Int"l Workshop Distributed Auto-adaptive and Reconfigurable Systems (DARES), IEEE CS Press, 2003. 104-109.
5. BBN Technologies. Applications that Participate in their Own Defense. http://apod.bbn.com

A Hybrid Model for Worm Simulations in a Large Network

Eul Gyu Im, Jung Sik Kim, In Woo Noh, and Hyun Jun Jang

College of Information and Communications
Hanyang University, Seoul, 133-791
Republic of Korea
imeg@hanyang.ac.kr

Abstract. Internet becomes more and more popular, and most companies and institutes use web services for e-business and many other purposes. As results, Internet and web services become core infrastructure for a company or an institute and become more and more important. With the explosion of Internet, the occurrence of cyber terrorism has grown very rapidly. It is difficult to find and close all security flaws in a computer system that is connected to a network. Internet worms take advantages of these security flaws, and attack a large number of hosts with self-propagating techniques.

It is quite challenging to simulate very large-scale worm attacks. This paper propose a hybrid model for large-scale simulations, and the proposed model will be both detailed enough to generate realistic packet traffic, and efficient enough to model a worm spreading through the Internet.

Keywords: Network modeling, Internet incidents, Internet worms, simulation.

1 Introduction

As Internet popularity grows explosively, so does the number of cyber incidents. Since most of computer systems have vulnerabilities and it is difficult to close all security holes in a computer system, some attackers may be able to find a way to penetrate the system [1]. In these days, instead of targeting specific hosts, attackers develop Internet worms that can spread to computers in all over the world. Examples of worms include CodeRed, Nimda, Slammer, and Blaster [2]. Since some worms can attack a large number of systems, it is difficult to evaluate and study damages caused by these kinds of worms through experiments.

One of the best feasible ways to study effects of worms is to use simulations. However, simulating the effects of large-scale worm infections on infrastructure is quite challenging because of the following: 1) a worm that infects tens or hundreds of thousands of hosts on the Internet gives rise to an inherently large-scale phenomenon, and requires the model to be of appropriate scale to correctly model the propagation dynamics; 2) with few exceptions, most worms have propagated

C.C. Yang et al. (Eds.): PAISI 2007, LNCS 4430, pp. 301–306, 2007.

over time scales of hours to days, thus it may result in a large span of timescales where network events at timescales down to microseconds are simulated over days [3].

The model we proposed here combines modeling at multiple levels of abstraction in order to be both detailed enough to generate realistic packet traffic, and efficient enough to model a worm spreading through the Internet.

The rest of paper is organized as follows: Section 3 addressed related work after short problem definition in Section 2. Our proposed model is explained in Section 4, and the Slammer worm example is explained in Section 5, followed by conclusions and future directions in Section 6.

2   Problem Definition

Abstract models such as epidemic models have so far been the general means of choice for modeling worm propagation. However, such models possess limitations due to their simplifying assumptions [4].

An effective alternative is packet-level modeling, which is capable of capturing many fine details. But, packet-level simulations have been considered computationally expensive.

Lately, with the advent of effective parallel/distributed processing techniques, packet-level network simulations are enabling the execution of very large-scale network models at packet-level.

The accuracy and/or performance of fluid-based techniques for network simulation have been examined in [5]. Reasonable accuracy has been achieved along with considerable performance improvement under certain circumstances. Compared to packet-level simulation, the largest performance gains are achieved with small networks and cases where the number of packets represented is much larger than the number of rate changes [6].

3   Related Work

Network security simulation is widely used to understand cyber attacks and defense mechanisms, their impact analysis, and traffic patterns because it is difficult to study them by experimenting such dangerous and large-scale attacks in the real environments. Network security simulation is begun from IAS (Internet Attack Simulator) proposed by Mostow, et al. [7]. Several scenarios are simulated using IAS. The simulations on password sniffing attacks and effects of firewall systems are reported in [8]. Simulation is also used to estimate traffics by changing the network topology [9,10]. However, these simulators have limitations to represent the real-world network environments and configuration, and realistic security scenarios [11]. For example, as we mentioned above, the existing simulators are not scalable enough to simulate Internet attacks and defense mechanisms in a large-scale network.

An object-oriented network security simulation model was proposed by Donald Welch et al. [8]. The object-oriented simulation model has several benefits such as easy-to-model, inheritance, information hiding, and reusability. For example, the object classes used to design the scenario can be inherited to driven classes or reused for other scenarios.

Michael Liljenstam et al. [3] simulated CodeRed v2 and the Slammer worm using SSFnet, and compared the simulated results with real traffic data collected by the Chemical Abstract Service (CAS). They adopted the epidemic model that is originally used in biology to express virus infections. One of the problems with this approach is that data exchanges between macroscopic networks and microscopic networks are quite limited.

Fluid models have been shown to be effective in modeling large-scale IP networks. Yu Gu et al. [12] presented a hybrid simulation method that maintains the performance advantage of fluid models while providing detailed packet level information for selected packet traffic flows. A problem with this approach is that traffics caused by selected packet traffic flows are not updated in the fluid model. For example, the slammer worm caused traffics of backbone networks to be increased a lot instead of increasing only selected packet traffic flows.

The hybrid technique in which packet flows and fluid flows are integrated is a recent development. The Global Mobile Information System Simulator (GloMoSim) [13] is divided into components that model at the packet level and components that use analytical fluid-based models. The fluid-based components calculate delays and loss of traversing packet flows and pass this information to the destination packet modeling components. The Hybrid Discrete-Continuous Flow Network Simulator (HDCF-NS) [14] and the hybrid model proposed in [6] also enable packet flows and fluid flows to coexist.

Kalyan S. Perumalla *et al.* [4] proposed high-fidelity modeling mechanism for computer network worm simulation. In their proposed *constructive* emulation architecture, real honeypot systems are worked together with virtual models implemented with PDNS.

4   Our Proposed Model

The fluid model is one of efficient ways to simulate worm propagation in the Internet by dividing networks into two kinds: foreground networks and background networks. But in this approach, since background traffics are generated uniformly, network traffics caused by worm infections are not included in the background traffic modeling even though increases of background traffics can directly affect propagations of worms. Therefore, to model worm propagations more precisely, interactions between worm traffics and background traffics must be represented in the model.

The epidemic model is used to model worm propagation in leaf nodes, i.e. hosts. But, worm propagation in the epidemic model follows fixed behavioral patterns, and interactions between epidemic networks and backbone networks are limited.

To solve the above problems and to model worm propagations more precisely, we propose a hybrid network model for worm simulations. As shown in Figure 1,

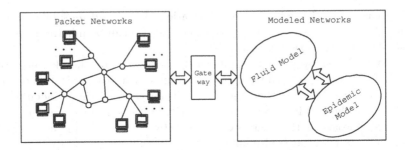

Fig. 1. The Architectural View of Our Hybrid Model

our proposed model consists of three main parts: packet network, modeled network, and gateway.

Modeled network: Fluid network and epidemic network merged into a single network, i.e. fluid network to represent backbone network and epidemic network to represent individual hosts.

A fluid model node encompasses a set of actual network nodes and each set is disjoint with the other sets. Characteristics of a fluid model node will be determined mostly by one or two bottlenecked nodes, and these characteristics are updated with traffics generated from the packet network as well as epidemic network.

Sets of epidemic nodes are inter-connected through fluid nodes.

Packet network: In the packet network, actual detailed simulations are performed, and the simulation results are used to update models in the other network.

The packet networks are used to simulate a relatively small size of networks, e.g. up to 1,000 nodes of networks. Event-driven simulations are performed in the packet networks, and simulated results are sent to other models to update their models.

Gateway: Parameters are passed between the modeled network and the packet network. The gateway is responsible for converting parameters in accordance with modeling parameter requirements.

The gateway gathers data from packet network to update models in the fluid network and the epidemic network. The data collector module of the gateway can be easily configurable so that it can cope with various kinds of worms.

One of the key advantages of our model is that it enables various new worms to be modeled and simulated easily. Previous approaches represent models for well-known worms, such as CodeRed worm and Slammer worm, and they lack flexibility to simulate new kinds of worms since interactions between worm traffics and backbone traffics are limited. The model proposed in this paper provides feedback mechanisms from packet-level worm simulation network to modeled network.

5   Example: Slammer Worm Simulation

An accurate representation of a certain worm or virus attack helps to understand their behavior, propagation rate, and impacts on the Internet society. There are several approaches to represent Internet worm models. In epidemiology research area, stochastic models and deterministic models are used to model the spread of infectious diseases. Stochastic models are well suited in small systems with simple dynamics of viruses. Our proposed hybrid model is suitable for simulations of the slammer worm because of large-scale worm activities and backbone traffic increases.

Our simulation results are shown in Figure 2. The graphs show similar propagation results as other previously published data, such as those in [15].

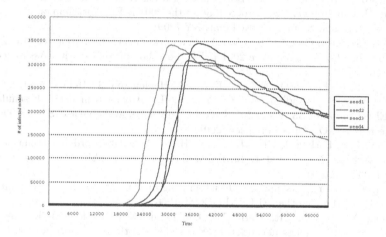

Fig. 2. Experimental results of CodeRed v2 simulation

6   Conclusions and Future Directions

With the explosion of Internet, the occurrence of cyber terrorism has grown very rapidly. Internet worms take advantages of security flaws in a system, and attack a large number of hosts with self-propagating techniques.

This paper proposed a hybrid model that is scalable enough to simulate large-scale worms while dynamically reflecting increases of network traffics caused by worms through interactions between the packet network and the modeled network. As future directions, we will simulate various worms with our proposed model to show the correctness of the model.

References

1. Lala, C., Panda, B.: Evaluating damage from cyber attacks: A model and analysis. IEEE Transactions on Systems, Man and Cybernetics **31** (2001) 300–310
2. Center, C.C.: CERT advisories, http://www.cert.org/advisories/. (2004)

3. Liljenstam, M., Nicol, D.M., Berk, V.H., Gray, R.S.: Simulating realistic network worm traffic for worm warning system design and testing. In: Proceedings of the 2003 ACM workshop on Rapid Malcode, ACM Press (2003) 24–33

4. Perumalla, K.S., Sundaragopalan, S.: High-fidelity modeling of computer netowrk worms. In: Proceedings of the 20th Annual Computer Security Applications Conference. (2004)

5. Liu, B., Figueiredo, D., Guo, Y., Kurose, J., Towsley, D.: A study of networks simulation efficiency: Fluid simulation vs. packet-level simulation. In: Proceedings of the Twentieth Annual Joint Conference of the IEEE Computer and Comunications Societies (INFOCOM). (2001) 1244–1253

6. Kiddle, C., Simmonds, R., Williamson, C., Unger, B.: Hybrid packet/fluid flow network simulation. In: Proceedings of the Seventeenth Workshop on Parallel and Distributed Simulation (PADS'03). (2003)

7. Mostow, J.R., Roberts, J.D., Bott, J.: Integration of an internet attack simulator in an HLA environment. In: Proceedings of the 2001 IEEE Workshop on Information Assurance and Security, West Point, NY (2001)

8. Donald Welch, Greg Conti, J.M.: A framework for an information warfare simulation. In: Proceedings of the 2001 IEEE Workshop on Information Assurance and Security, West Point, NY (2001)

9. Breslau, L., Estrin, D., Fall, K., Floyd, S., Heidemann, J., Helmy, A., Huang, P., McCanne, S., Varadhan, K., Xu, Y., Yu, H.: Advances in network simulation. IEEE Computer **33** (2000) 59–67 Expanded version available as USC TR 99-702b.

10. Technology, O.: Opnet modeler (2001)

11. Yun, J.B., Park, E.K., Im, E.G., In., H.P.: A scalable, ordered scenario-based network security simulator. In: Proceedings of the AsianSim 2004. Also in LNAI vol. 3398. (2004)

12. Gu, Y., Liu, Y., Towsley, D.: On integrating fluid models with packet simulation. In: Proceedings of the IEEE INFOCOM. (2004)

13. Zeng, X., Bagrodia, R., Gerla, M.: GloMoSim: A library for parellel simulation of large-scale wireless networks. In: Proceedings of the 12th Workshop on Parallel and Distributed Simulation. (1998) 154–161

14. Melamed, B., Pan, S., Wardi, Y.: Hybrid discrete-continuous fluid-flow simulation. In: Proceedings of ITCOM 2001, Scalability and Traffic Control in IP Networks. (2001)

15. Moore, D., Paxson, V., Savage, S., Shannon, C., Staniford, S., Weaver, N.: Inside the slammer worm. IEEE Security & Privacy **1** (2003) 33–39

A Web Portal for Terrorism Activities in China

Daniel Zeng[1,2], Li Zhang[1], Donghua Wei[1], and Fei-Yue Wang[1]

[1] Institute of Automation, Chinese Academy of Sciences, Beijing, China
[2] University of Arizona, Tucson, Arizona, USA
zeng@email.arizona.edu
{li.zhang, donghua.wei, feiyue.wang}@ia.ac.cn

Web-based open source information collection and analysis are playing a significant role in terrorism informatics studies [1, 2]. In this paper, we present a research effort in this area with a particular focus on China-related terrorism activities.

China has been facing significant terrorism threats in the past several decades. In the recent decade or so, a number of small-scale attacks have been carried out. According to the official records published by the Ministry of Public Security, since 1990s, there have been about 260 terrorism attacks, mainly in the Sinkiang (Xingjiang) region. These attacks mainly took the form of bombing, poisoning, and assassination, and have resulted in hundreds of deaths and enormous economic losses. Counter-terrorism and more broadly, emergency response, are being approached as a national priority by the Chinese government.

Our research project is aimed at developing an integrated, Web-based information collection and analysis system, called the China Dark Net (CDN), for China-related terrorism activities. CDN collects information from a wide range of open sources, including terrorist groups' websites, government information sources, media reports on terrorism events, and terrorism incident databases. It also makes available a number of analytical tools such as social network analysis and various statistical methods. Below we summarize the architectural design and major components of CDN and discuss several specific research topics investigated in the context of this system.

As many similar online portal systems, CDN is designed as a three-layer system. The first layer manages the set of related information resources. The second layer implements backend information query and analysis functions. The third layer implements front-end user functions and interface through the Web. We now discuss these three layers in turn. Depending on the type of information to be collected, the resource layer of CDN implements or makes use of a range of data collection programs, including Web crawlers, parsers for dynamic Web contents served through databases, and parsers for online-forum contents. CDN now makes available the following terrorism-related information: (a) a collection of China-related terrorist groups' websites covering all the officially-designated terrorist groups by the Chinese government and groups that were referred to in past official news reports as being directly involved in China-related terrorism activities; (b) a terrorist activity database providing a structured, queriable repository of detailed case data concerning terrorist attacks that occurred in China in the past 20 years; (c) a terrorist and terrorist group database offering detailed information on individual terrorists and terrorist groups based on manually-collected information from a range of open sources including the online news, government websites, and printed materials; and (d) a large collection of

C.C. Yang et al. (Eds.): PAISI 2007, LNCS 4430, pp. 307–308, 2007.
© Springer-Verlag Berlin Heidelberg 2007

news articles, online forums, and government reports on China-related terrorism activities. The second layer of CDN implements backend support for structured and semi-structured information query and processing. It provides various Web information retrieval functions including the methods to process Chinese text. This layer also implements data analysis functions and provides interface to several underlying open-source social network analysis engines. Selected research issues are discussed below. The third layer of CDN serves the end user through an AJAX-based Web presentation framework and implements application-specific Web features. It also provides various visualization environments to facilitate data exploration.

Our ongoing CDN research efforts aim to meet the following specific challenges. First, a significant portion of information collected by CDN is in Chinese. Our domain-specific Chinese information processing has focused on Chinese word segmentation and Chinese information extraction. For segmentation research, we have investigated a new technique integrating statistical models with a thesaurus-based method. This method can achieve better performance as measured by precision than existing general-purpose word segmentation methods in the domain of terrorism informatics. Our Chinese information extraction approach is based on event frames, which was shown to be able to effectively extract useful information from catastrophic event reports [3]. In our research, we have developed a comprehensive set of terrorism-specific templates and patterns with encouraging initial experimental results.

Second, we are conducting research in cross-language terrorism information retrieval [4]. A majority of China-related terrorist groups' websites are offered in either English or Chinese. However, the remaining contents are in Uigur, Turkish, and others. Developing cross-language information retrieval capabilities will greatly facilitate information accessing. Our approach uses both a thesaurus-based method and parallel corpora.

CDN represents a regional terrorism informatics project with a rich information repository and interesting multi-lingual research challenges. We are currently conducting additional experimental studies to further evaluate our technical research. Overall evaluation of CDN as a system is also planned for the near future.

Acknowledgments. This work was supported in part by the Chinese Academy of Sciences Innovative Research International Partnership Project (2F05NO1).

References

1. Chen, H., Qin, J., Reid, E., Chung, W., Zhou, Y., Xi W., Lai, G., Bonillas, A., and Sageman, M.: The Dark Web Portal: Collecting and Analyzing the Presence of Domestic and International Terrorist Groups on the Web, in the Proceedings of the 7th International Conference on Intelligent Transportation Systems (ITSC), Washington, D.C. (2004)
2. Chen, H., Wang, F.-Y., and Zeng, D.: Intelligence and Security Informatics for Homeland Security: Information, Communication, and Transportation, the *IEEE Transactions on Intelligent Transportation Systems*, Vol. 5, No. 4, pp. 329—341. (2004).
3. Liang, H., Chen, X., Wu, P.: Information Extraction System Based on Event Frame, in *Journal of Chinese Information Processing*, Vol. 20, No. 2. (2006).
4. Li, K.W. and Yang, C.: Automatic Cross-Lingual Thesaurus Generated from Kong Kong SAR Police Department Web Corpus for Crime Analysis, J. of American Soc. Of Information Sciences and Technology, Vol. 56, No. 3. (2005).

An Overview of Telemarketing Fraud Problems and Countermeasures in Taiwan

Jau-Hwang Wang[1], Jiing-Long Jow[1], You-Lu Liao[1], Tyan-muh Tsai[1],
and Garfield Hung[2]

[1] Central Police University
jwang@mail.cpu.edu.tw, im943088@mail.cpu.edu.tw,
ylliaw@mail.cpu.edu.tw, una101@mail.cpu.edu.tw
[2] Institute for Information Industry
garhung@iii.org.tw

Telemarketing Fraud Problems. Nowadays, computers and computer networks are ubiquitous and used in every facet of modern society. Although information technology has enabled global businesses to flourish, it also becomes one of the major enablers for sophisticated fraud schemes. The computer and network reliant world allows fraudsters to make the acquaintance of victims, acquiring them and eventually committing crimes without any face-to-face contact. Theft of identification, a traditional problem in our society also deteriorated, since it becomes much easier to collect personal data in the information era. Together with the conveniences introduced by financial technology, such as automatic teller machines (ATM), criminals are able to cheat and take away their victims' money without being identified. According to the statistics released by the National Police Agency, the number of financial frauds in Taiwan increased dramatically and the annual financial losses due to fraud crimes amounted to millions of dollars in recent years [1]. Although the high benefit/investment ratio is one of the major factors contributing to the rapid increase of financial frauds, the convenient and efficient environment enabled by communication and information technologies should

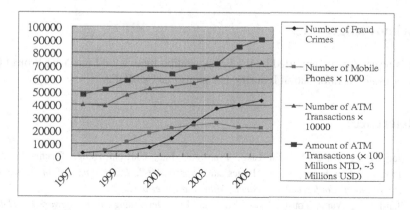

Fig. 1. The Relationship between Fraud Crimes and the Usages of Mobile Phones and ATMs

C.C. Yang et al. (Eds.): PAISI 2007, LNCS 4430, pp. 309–310, 2007.
© Springer-Verlag Berlin Heidelberg 2007

also bear a substantial part of the blame. The statistics released by the National Communication Commission, the National Police Agency, and the Financial Supervisory Commission, Executive Yuan, show that there is a close relationship between fraud crimes and the prevalence of communication technology and the application of automatic financial systems [2], as shown in Figure 1.

Countermeasures. Since fraudsters are heavily reliant upon modern communication facilities and automatic financial systems, the law enforcement agencies in Taiwan have built many collaborative mechanisms among several government agencies and related industries. The collaborative mechanisms can be divided into three categories: strengthen regulation and law enforcement in the communication industry, establish fraud account reporting and information sharing mechanisms among financial institutions, and provide timely consulting services to citizens. Firstly, the Criminal Investigation Bureau, the National Communication Commission, the Telecommunication Police Corps, and local communication industries have built a collaborative task force to strengthen the regulation and law enforcement on communication services. For examples, two photo identifications are required to apply for a telecommunication service account, text messages related to fraud crimes are filtered and removed, strengthen detection and crack down illegal communication services, and limit the communication services around the Kinmen area. Secondly, the National Police Agency, the Financial Supervisory Commission, the Joint Credit Information Center, and the Bankers Association of the Republic of China have established a mechanism to report and share bad and derived bad accounts among bank members. Financial transfers to bad or derived bad accounts are automatically stopped, and financial transfers and all subsequence transfers will be frozen as soon as possible if they are reported to be fraud related. ATM transfers to non-designated accounts will be suspended if the amount of each transfer is more than US$900. Furthermore, all financial institutions are also required to deploy surveillance systems to detect anomalous financial transactions. Thirdly, armed with the information gathered from local communication industries and financial institutions, the Crime Investigation Bureau has also set up an "165" hot line to provide timely consulting services and necessary helps for reporting suspicious fraud activities, and to initiate the investigation process as soon as possible.

Acknowledgements

This research was supported by the E-Application Innovation Four-Year Project (2/4) of Institute for Information Industry and sponsored by MOEA.

References

1. Jau-Hwang Wang, You-Lu Liao, Tyan-muh Tsai, Garfield Hung, "Technology-based Financial Frauds in Taiwan: Issues and Approaches", *Proceedings of the 2006 IEEE International Conference on Systems, Man, and Cybernetics*, 2006.
2. Jau-Hwang Wang, You-Lu Liao, Tyan-muh Tsai, *Developing the Framework for IT-based Countermeasures for Financial Frauds*, Final report to Institute for Information Industry, 2006.

Mining the Core Member of Terrorist Crime Group Based on Social Network Analysis

Qihong Liu[1,2], Changjie Tang[1], Shaojie Qiao[1], Qiwei Liu[3], and Fenlian Wen[1]

[1] DB&KE Institute, School of Computer, Sichuan University, Chengdu, 610065, China
[2] School of Electric Information, Sichuan University, Chengdu, 610065, China
[3] School of Commonality Administer, Sichuan University, Chengdu, 610065, China
{liuqihong, tangchangjie}@cs.scu.edu.cn

Since the incident about 9.11, the Security Sectors of many countries have put great attentions on gathering and mining of crime data and establishing anti-terrorist databases. With the emergence of anti-terrorist application, data mining for anti-terrorist has attracted great attention from both researchers and officers as well as in China. The purpose of analyzing and mining related terrorist or crimes data is that analyzing of psychology, behavior and related laws about crime, and providing hidden clues to prevent a criminal case, and forecasting terror happening to keeping with crime limits.

A terrorist criminal group is composed by many terrorist criminals who mutually cooperate and participate on task together in a crime groups. And a terrorist criminal network is composed by a lot of sub-network that connects with the many terrorist cahoot. Except for some common characters of social network, the terrorist crime network has other special characters as follows:

(1) A node in the network represents a terrorist or criminal, the edge between nodes represents connections between terrorist or criminals such as passing message, joining in a crime together.

(2) The position or role of each node in the network is basically different with each other. As the core terrorist members usually grasp the important information of terrorist group, they are minority in crime network of the terrorist group.

(3) Large terrorist crime groups are always composed by several sub-groups. Every sub-group will take charge of different responsibilities and tasks.

(4) Terrorist criminal groups do not exist in isolation and there are many relation and interaction between these groups.

The social network SN which is described formally above is a very similar to the mathematical model of the terrorist or crime group networks which we study.

In recent years, an increasing number of SNA has been used in analysis of criminal group network and enterprise structure [1]. Social Network Analysis (SNA) is to describe the social entities and their inter-relationship mode[2]. Their inter-relationship includes social relationship such as friends, relatives, and the cooperation between the groups.The transaction relationship can also be included, such as trade relations between the enterprise or countries [3].

C.C. Yang et al. (Eds.): PAISI 2007, LNCS 4430, pp. 311–313, 2007.

For exploration of mining terrorism or crime data, this paper first puts forward a enhanced shortest path algorithm ESPLW(Shortest Path algorithm based on Link-Weight) based on *Watts-Strogatz models*. The study (1)labels a node with a mobster's name and marks the link-weight with the frequency of sending and receiving emails between two mobsters at will. (2) finds the shortest path between any two random nodes through Dijistra algorithm. (3)sets a threshold to represent the number of nodes that pass through from one node to another, and reserves the shortest paths which threshold is less than 6 and then integrates the mining results. On the basis of ESPLW algorithm, we design an algorithm that mine the core member of a terrorist group (CMM). This paper's contribution includes:

(1) Establish a criminal network according to communications of E-mail between the terrorist and criminal group.
(2) Mine sub-group of terrorist by using hierarchical clustering methods.
(3) Scoop out the core-member of terrorist group based on ESPLW algorithm in the network.
(4) The experimental results show the validity of the new algorithm. Forecast accuracy of the core-members of terrorist group reach 92.3%.

We report our experiments by CMM mining algorithm and analyze the experimental results in comparison with other algorithms. All of experiments are done on 1.8 GHZ processor, 1 GB memory and Microsoft Windows XP. And we implemented the programs in Java SDK1.5. To verify the validity of CMM algorithm, we can use the data in literature [4] as the experimental data to establish terrorist group network and mine the core-member in network.

In this paper, we can establish a terrorist criminal group network by use of the data from the emulational mail system. We propose an enhanced shortest path algorithm ESPLW which based on the *Watts-Strogatz models*[5] of the social network, and we can mine the core-member of terrorist criminal group by improved CMM algorithm on this basis. It was shown the validity and efficiency of the new algorithm by extensive experiments. Experiments indicate that the new algorithm can successfully mine the core-member of the terrorist criminal group, which accuracy reach 92.3%.Its average efficiency improve remarkably than the traditional algorithm.

A large terrorist criminal group often is composed of several smaller groups. It is our next research direction how we mine more accurate the information about these small groups interacting with large groups each other. Although the criminal group mining algorithm can accurate scoop out the core-member of the terrorist criminal group, there is still a problem that the run time of the whole mining algorithm is a still quite long. We will make efforts to further improve the efficiency of the whole mining algorithm in future work.

Acknowledgments. This work was supported in part by Grant of National Natural Science Foundation of China(60473071) and the Science. Tackle Key Problem Fund of Sichuan Province(2006Z01-027).

References

1. MCANDREW, D. The structural analysis of criminal networks. In The Social Psychology of Crime: Groups, Teams, and Networks. D. Canter and L. Alison, Eds. Dartmouth Publishing, Aldershot, UK, 1999. 53–94.
2. Duncan Watts An Experimental Study of Search in Global Social Networks, In Proc. Journal of SCIENCE VOL 301 No.8 August 2003.
3. Hsinchun Chen. Crime Data Mining: A General Framework and Some Examples. ComputerPublished by the IEEE Computer Society April 2004.
4. BREIGER, R. L. The analysis of social networks. In Handbook of Data Analysis, M. A. Hardy and A. Bryman, Eds. Sage Publications, London, U.K. Spring 2004.505–526.
5. D.J.Watts and S.H.Strogatz,Nature (London), 393(1998), 440.

Providing Personalized Services for HWME System by Item-Based Collaborative Filtering

Qiudan Li, Yaodong Li, Huiguang He, Guanggang Geng,
Yuanping Zhu, and Chunheng Wang

Key Laboratory of Complex Systems and Intelligence Science,
Institute of Automation, Chinese Academy of Sciences, Beijing
{qiudan.li, yaodong.li, huiguang.he, guanggang.geng,
yuanping.zhu, chunheng.wang}@ia.ac.cn

1 Background

The Hall for Workshop of Metasynthetic Engineering (HWME) is a methodology that can be used to deal with problems in open complex giant systems, such as strategic decisions of national emergency actions. The discussion process is the key component of the HWME system, in which the generalized experts provide a valuable knowledge to human experts. In this paper, a novel framework is proposed, which can explore the personalized information of generalized experts. An item-based collaborative filtering approach is adopted to recommendation for HWME system. Under this framework, human experts can make the best use of information provided by the generalized experts and then give a more effective judgment.

2 Overview of Recommendation Framework for a HWME System

The Hall for Workshop of Metasynthetic Engineering (HWME) is a methodology that can be used to deal with problems in open complex giant systems [1]. During the discussion process for a specified complex problem, i.e. a strategic decision of national emergency actions, discussion master is a manager and announces the discussion topic, generalized experts, regarded as relevant web pages to the current discussion topic, embody knowledge of people in the web, they provide evidences or valuable knowledge for human experts. Therefore, how to make the best use of information provided by the generalized experts is very important to the HWME system.

The proposed recommendation framework aims to recommend N generalized experts that will be of interest to human expert, basing on the similar human experts' rating information for generalized experts. It consists of information retrieval model and generalized experts recommendation model. Firstly, cooperative information retrieval model searches some web pages from WWW based on the discussion topic, generates and updates the generalized experts, and stores them in the database of HWME system [2]-[3]. Discussion logs record the browsing patterns of human experts for generalized experts. The recommendation data is extracted from the logs. Secondly, generalized experts recommendation model adopts item-based

C.C. Yang et al. (Eds.): PAISI 2007, LNCS 4430, pp. 314–315, 2007.

collaborative filtering to mine the similarity relationships among generalized experts to generate recommendations, it includes the following three parts:

Representation
The recommendation space is a matrix, whose rows are indexed by human experts, and columns are indexed by generalized experts. The (i,j) th entry gives the rating information of human expert i for generalized expert j, 1 means the jth generalized expert has been read by human expert i, and 0, vice versa.

Similarity computation of generalized experts
Following the algorithms in [4], we model the generalized experts as vectors in the human experts space, and use the cosine function to measure the similarity. Namely, this process aims to build a similarity matrix where we store the similarity values among generalized experts. For example, an $m \times m$ matrix S is the similarity matrix, the jth column stores the k most similar generalized experts to generalized expert j, the value of $S_{i,j}$ indicates the similarity degree between generalized expert j and i. The construction of S is as follows: for each generalized expert j, computes the similarity between j and other generalized experts, and stores the results in jth column of S. Then we only keep k largest values for each column.

Recommendation generation
An active human expert is represented as an $m \times 1$ vector H , it contains some rated generalized experts information. The recommendation generation process can be performed as follows [4]: firstly, multiply S with H; secondly, the entries correspond to generalized experts that have already been read by the active human expert are set to zero; finally, the generalized experts with N largest values will be recommended to the active human expert.

From the above processes, we can see that the similar relationships among different generalized experts can be identified offline, which makes the whole recommendation mechanism more feasible in the real-time discussion environment for the HWME system.

Acknowledgments. This work is supported in part by NSFC (Grant 60602032, 60573078, 60334020, 79990580).

References

1. Tsein, T., Dai, R., Yu, J.:A New Scientific Field: Open Complex Giant Systems and Its Methodology, Ziran Zazhi, vol. 13, (1990) 3-10
2. Li, Y., Dai, R.: Framework for a Man-Computer Cooperative Information Retrieval System for Online Discussion Systems, International Journal of Computer Processing of Oriental Languages, vol. 17, (2004) 273-285
3. Li, Y., Study on the Design and Implementation of Hall for Workshop of Metasynthetic Engineering. Ph.D dissertation, Institute of Automation, Chinese Academic of Sciences. 2003.
4. Deshpande, M., Karypis G.: Item-based Top-N Recommendation Algorithms. ACM Trans. Inf. Syst., Vol. 22, (2004)143-177

An Intelligent Agent-Oriented System for Integrating Network Security Devices and Handling Large Amount of Security Events

Yang-ming Ma, Zhi-tang Li, Jie Lei, Li Wang, and Dong Li

Sch. of Computer Sci. & tech., Huazhong University of Sci. & Tech., Wuhan 430074, China
{mayangming, leeying, leijie, wtwl,lidong}@mail.hust.edu.cn

Abstract. To integrate network security devices to make them act as a battle team and efficiently handle the large amount of security events produced by various network applications, Network Security Intelligent Centralized Management is a basic solution. In this paper, we introduce an intelligent agent-oriented Network Security Intelligent Centralized Management System, and give a description about the system model, mechanism, hierarchy of security events, data flow diagram, filtering and transaction and normalization of security events, clustering and merging algorithm, and correlation algorithm. The experiment shows that the system can significantly reduce false positives and improve the quality of security events. It brings convenience for security administrators to integrate security devices and deal with large security events.

Keywords: network security; agent; intelligence; security event.

1 Introduction

The problem of network security is becoming more and more serious with the increasingly influence of network on people's lives. Network security devices such as firewall, IDS, etc. are widely used which benefit network security management in certain degree, but at the same time, they bring or cause some problems in practice: First, there are little effective cooperation among Security Event Sources (SESs) such as firewall, IDS, important host, server of DNS, and router etc., which typically acts on its own, and they don't function as a team. Second, the large amount of security events produced by SESs turn into security events flooding, they are difficult to analyze, verify and make use of. The security administrators are so tired and fidgety of them.

In recent years, the problem of security events management has been undergoing a great deal of research activity [1],[2],[3]. This paper presents Network Security Intelligent Centralized Management System (NSICMS), in which we make use of characteristics of agent and adopt a global synthetical processing hiberarchy to stepwise reduce amount of security events and improve the quality of security events coming from various SESs. It concentratively analyzes and deals with security events and gives proper responses according to the analytical result. NSICMS handles the following security events: Alerts of IDS, contents about security audit log of Firewall, router etc.

C.C. Yang et al. (Eds.): PAISI 2007, LNCS 4430, pp. 316–317, 2007.

2 NSICMS

NSICMS aims to integrate the SESs to make them (e.g. IDS and Firewall) cooperate with each other like a team and help security administrators handle security events more easily. It is composed of SESs, various agents, two Security Intelligent Management Centers (SIMC) and security administrator. The agents are divided into two major types: subordinate agents and department agents. These two kinds get their name according to a uniform criterion. Subordinate agent's name appears in the form of "post-agent". For example, the relevant agent of IDS is called "IDS-agent". The system contains DNS-agent, Router-agent etc. The department agent's name appears in the form of "function-agent", for example: Correlation-agent, Response-agent etc. The subordinate agent corresponding to SES may be installed in the SES or its network neighbor. SESs can interact among each other via the relevant agents to act as a "security team". The two SIMCs backup information simultaneously, and switch automatically while malfunction occurs.

Like a combatant, the agents in different positions occupy the different power and take the different responsibilities. SIMC is the headquarters of NSICMS. Security administrator is the captain of NSICMS. The alerts from SESs are handled by subordinate agent first. Some are filtered quickly while some are solved at local place. Others that subordinate agent isn't authorized to handle or can't identify are reported to SIMC in uniform format. All criterial-alerts that SIMC has received from subordinate agents and known false negatives of SESs which have been normalized and memorized in SIMC will be clustered. Each cluster is merged as a hyper-alert, and then hyper-alerts are carried on correlation analysis. Hyper-alerts are validated and some become alarms ranked by urgency. Finally, the system presents a global view to security administrator.

3 Experiment and Conclusion

Through gathering real-world network traffic, during a whole week, subordinate agents received 278, 895 raw alerts and reported only a total number of 26,103 criterial-alerts to SIMC. After clustering and merging, there were 452 hyper-alerts. After correlation analysis, 34 alarms were produced. We also found 27 useful rules had been added in cisco firewall and a large amount of malicious data packets were dropped automatically. The results demonstrate that NSICMS can improve the quality of security events and obviously reduce the amount of security events, significantly, which makes SESs cooperate with each other and makes the security administrator manage the large amount of security events of the protected network easily.

References

1. Forte, D. V. "The "Art" of log correlation." Computer Fraud and Security, 2004(8): 15.
2. Chuvakin."Security event analysis through correlation." Information Systems Security,2004(13):13.
3. Debar, H. and Wespi, A.Aggregation and correlation of intrusion-detection alerts. In : RECENT ADVANCES IN INTRUSION DETECTION, 2001.

Link Analysis-Based Detection of Anomalous Communication Patterns

Daniel Zeng[1] and Zan Huang[2]

[1] University of Arizona, Tucson, AZ 85721 USA and Chinese Academy of Sciences, Beijing, China
zeng@email.arizona.edu
[2] Pennsylvania State University, University Park, PA 16802 USA
zanhuang@psu.edu

Detecting anomalous communication patterns is an important security informatics application. Take the example of monitoring email communications. An efficient method that can identify emails that are unusual relative to the common behavior among a network of email originators and recipients can serve many useful functions, one of which is to filter out anomalous email exchanges for further investigation.

We propose an anomalous communication pattern detection method based on the link analysis framework [1]. This method is based on the following observations: (a) observed communications can be viewed as a network with time-stamped links representing communicative acts between nodes (either originators or recipients), and (b) future communications can be predicted through link predictions and anomalous communications can be defined as very unlikely links.

We summarize the major components of our link analysis-based anomalous communication pattern detection method [2]. As the input to our method, we assume that the set of message originators and recipients is known a priori and that all the past communications among them are logged with time stamps. As the output of our method, at any given time, for a given originator-recipient tuple (originator, [recipient1, recipient2, ...]), we assign an anomaly score indicating how unlikely this corresponding originator might communicate with the set of the specified recipients. Note that in real-world security applications, it is more often than not that communications involve one originator and multiple recipients. Our work explicitly considers this type of one-to-many relation.

There are many different ways of formulating and solving the anomalous communication pattern detection problem as a link analysis problem. One simple approach, as adopted in our research, proceeds as follows. First, we construct a communication graph using the historical log data. A communicative act involving multiple recipients is broken down into multiple one-originator-one-recipient links. For instance, an email with the sender-recipient tuple (1, [2, 3]) contributes two links, $1 \rightarrow 2$ and $1 \rightarrow 3$, to the graph. This graph is a weighted and directed graph with the weights capturing multiple occurrences of sender-recipient pairs. Second, link prediction algorithms, which predict possible links based on observed ones, can then be applied to this communication graph to derive likelihood scores for possible links as well as

C.C. Yang et al. (Eds.): PAISI 2007, LNCS 4430, pp. 318–320, 2007.

sender-multiple recipient tuples. Observed links that are extremely unlikely are then interpreted as anomalous communications. Note that, however, most existing link prediction algorithms only work on undirected and un-weighted graphs. Adaptation is needed for these algorithms to handle directed and weighted graphs.

In our approach, we have extended the following set of link prediction methods for anomalous communication pattern detection purposes [2]: preferential attachment, spreading activation, and the generative model. The adapted preferential attachment method computes the sender degree (out-degree) and recipient degree (in-degree) for each node in the observed graph. The likelihood score for a link i → j is given by *Sender_Degree*(i)**Recipient_Degree*(j). The adapted spreading activation method uses a variation of the Hopfield net algorithm which propagates and explores connectedness of a sender-recipient pair within the communication graph. This connectedness measure is defined as the total effect of the weighted paths between the pair. The last method, the generative model uses latent-class variables to explain observed communication patterns. Under this framework, the observed communication graph is modeled as the result of the following probabilistic generation process: (1) selecting a node s as the message originator with probability $P(s)$; (2) choosing a latent class with probability $P(z|s)$; and (3) generating a communication from s to another node r with probability $P(r|z)$. Based on the observed communication graph, all the relevant probabilities and conditional probabilities can be estimated using the Expectation Maximization procedural. Based on these estimated probabilities, $P(s, r)$ provides the needed likelihood scores.

To evaluate the usefulness of our approach, we have conducted a computational study using the publicly-available Enron email corpus. This study is based on more than 40 thousand emails sent from and to 151 Enron employees from May 1999 to June 2002. As a baseline for comparison, in addition to the three link prediction models, we also implemented a random model which states that all links are equally possible. As measured by average likelihood scores, we observe that generally all three link prediction models fit better with the actual email data than the baseline random model. The Spreading Activation model slightly outperforms the Preferential Attachment model in general. The Generative Model provided a significantly better fit with the actual email data than the other two methods. We have also conducted case studies using these link analysis methods to individual email anomaly detection with promising results.

We are currently further evaluating our proposed approach by conducting additional computational experiments. We are also developing methods to explicitly capture hyper-arcs (linking multiple nodes together) and timestamps associated with each link for monitoring and anomaly detection purposes.

Acknowledgement

The reported research was supported in part by an international collaboration grant (2F05NO1) from the Chinese Academy of Sciences, and a 973 program grant (2006CB705500) from the National Natural Science Foundation of China.

References

1. Antonio B. and Kantardzic M.M.: "Link Analysis Tools for Intelligence and Counterterrorism," in Proceedings of the IEEE International Conference on Intelligence and Security Informatics, Atlanta, GA, 2005, pp. 49-59.
2. Huang Z. and Zeng, D.: "A Link Prediction Approach to Anomalous Email Detection," in Proceedings of the IEEE Systems, Man, and Cybernetics 2006 Conference, Taipei, 2006.

Social Modeling and Reasoning for Security Informatics

Wenji Mao[1], Daniel Zeng[1,2], Li Zhang[1], Donghua Wei[1], and Fei-Yue Wang[1]

[1] Institute of Automation, Chinese Academy of Sciences
[2] University of Arizona
{wenji.mao, li.zhang, donghua.wei, feiyue.wang}@ia.ac.cn
zeng@email.arizona.edu

The modeling of human social behavior is central to the design and system development of security-related applications [Liu *et al*, 2006, Wang *et al*, in press]. Social modeling can help identify social relations between entities, leading to better understanding and representation of social information required for ISI system design. Social reasoning provides computational frameworks to facilitate the inference of social knowledge, and in turn, can enhance the social and cognitive functionality of the related analysis. In this paper, we propose an agent-based model to represent social information, and based on the proposed social structure, we discuss the reasoning and analysis techniques to support the design and development of artificial social systems for ISI applications.

Social information includes the social roles and relations of individual agents or actors, and the characteristics of social groups the agents belong to. For example, in a terrorist event monitoring system, a terrorism "society" is composed of terrorism groups, with each group consisting of individual terrorists and connecting to other groups in various ways. The description of an actor includes her personal information (e.g., name, age, gender), her task-related information (i.e., goal and intention), as well as her role and social relationship with other actors. Social groups are interconnected by sub-group and super-group relations, which represent the power structure among different groups and form an organizational structure of the terrorist society. Social groups also have other relations, such as intimacy and trust.

Social structural information is computationally represented as first-order predicates and parameters. For example, superior(x, y) denotes agent x is a *superior* of agent y in power structure. We also describe task-related information for individual and group events. The task model in our system specifies sub-task relations among different tasks, and the responsible agents for task execution. We employ a plan-based approach to represent task knowledge [Mao, 2006]. For example, a "terror bombing" event has the *precondition* "dropping bomb", and has "killing people" as its *effect* to achieve the *goal* "defeating enemy".

To infer social information, we focus on the following key aspects. According to social psychological studies, attribution of intention is essential to people's judgment of behavior. Therefore, one of our focuses is to develop intention detection method for behavior judgment. Our second focus is to analyze important social factors, based on techniques from social network analysis.

- **Intention Detection**

Intentions can be inferred from communication evidence and structural information and features in task representation [Mao & Gratch, 2004]. We have developed a

C.C. Yang et al. (Eds.): PAISI 2007, LNCS 4430, pp. 321–322, 2007.
© Springer-Verlag Berlin Heidelberg 2007

number of commonsense reasoning rules that allow for inferring act intention (i.e., intending an action) and outcome intention (i.e., intending an action outcome). The rules help infer intentions from communicative acts between terrorism groups, such as *order*, *request*, *accept*, *reject* and *counter-propose*. For example, ordering an action shows act intention, and creates an *obligation* for the ordered group to perform the content of the action. In the more general cases, we have developed general intention detection algorithms using probabilistic reasoning and decision-theoretic approach. Based on task representation and action execution of the observed agents, we compute the expected utilities of possible plans in plan library and use maximization of the expected plan utility as the criterion for disambiguation. The computation of expected plan utility is computed using the utilities of outcomes and the probabilities with which different outcomes occur. Although our current work focuses on applying these algorithms to terrorism informatics, it can be applied to other security informatics applications as well.

- **Social Network Analysis**

We have applied social modeling and network analysis to the study of counter-terrorism and public health. In an ongoing effort to develop a monitoring system for China-related terrorism activities called China Dark Net, we collect open-source information and model terrorism groups, terrorists, and terrorism activities. We define them with multi-faceted related factors from the society, and study the relationships and features of the terrorism related to China. Based on the defined social structure and the data we collected, we find contacts among groups, terrorists and activities, and form a network model. We can then conduct a range of network analysis.

To summarize, we identify social modeling and inference as important issues for the design and development of ISI systems and applications. We propose a social structure and task representation, and present our approach to inferring important aspects of social behavior. In our future work, we will fully model the social information in counter-terrorism and public health domains, and conduct case studies to evaluate the automatic reasoning method.

Acknowledgments. This work was supported in part by the Chinese Academy of Sciences Innovative Research International Partnership Project (2F05NO1).

References

1. Liu, L., Yu, E. and Mylopoulos, J. Security Design Based on Social Modeling. Proceedings of the Thirtieth Annual International Computer Software and Applications Conference, 2006.
2. Mao, W. Modeling Social Causality and Social Judgment in Multi-Agent Interactions. Ph.D. Dissertation. Computer Science Department, University of Southern California, 2006.
3. Mao, W. and Gratch, J. Decision-Theoretic Approaches to Plan Recognition. ICT Technical Report ICT-TR-01-2004. USC Institute for Creative Technologies, 2004.
4. Wang, F., Carley, K., Zeng, D. and Mao, W. Social Computing: From Social Informatics to Social Intelligence. IEEE Intelligent Systems, in press.

Detecting Botnets by Analyzing DNS Traffic

Hao Tu, Zhi-tang Li, and Bin Liu

Network and Computing Centre, HuaZhong University of Science & Technology,
1037 Luoyu Road, 430074 WuHan, P.R. China
{tuhao, leeying, bliu}@hust.edu.cn

Motivation. Botnet is a new trend in Internet attacks. Because the propagation of botnets will not cause large traffic like worm, it is often difficult to detect it. Till now, the most common method to detect botnets is to use honeynets. Although previous work has described an active detection technique using DNS hijacking technique[1], there are little information about how to detect the domain names which botnets used. Some researchers also use DNS based method to detect botnets[2,3], but all of them use simple signature or statistical method which require much prior knowledge.

Methodology and Results. The purpose of this paper is to detect the activities of botnets by mining DNS traffic data. We propose a system connected to routers via an optical splitter for filtering all DNS traffic data and storing it to a database for farther analysis. We define the database table as <requestor, nameserver, time, qtype, query> and store the DNS traffic data as figure. 1 shows.

```
mysql>select * from query where requestor = '202.114.0.254' and time = '2006-07-06 12:12:12';
+--------+---------------+---------------+---------------------+-------+------------------------+
| id     | requestor     | nameserver    | time                | qtype | query                  |
+--------+---------------+---------------+---------------------+-------+------------------------+
| 138272 | 202.114.0.254 | 202.114.0.242 | 2006-07-06 12:12:12 | A     | eu5f.kaspersky-labs.com |
+--------+---------------+---------------+---------------------+-------+------------------------+
```

Fig. 1. DNS database table example

After data collecting, we must select a period DNS traffic as training data set. We use some experiential methods to distinguish the suspicious DNS queries from the normal queries. There are two main ways we used:

- Non-local DNS server: When the regular name servers were filtered out, we found out was that a very large number of systems (around 10%) uses several name servers other than the ones provided by the ISP;
- Non-regular query type: There were many lookups for other qtypes than the usual A, quad A and PTR. The qtypes that should require focus are large amount of MX queries and the AXFR/IXFR queries.

Other method such as baseline may be used. By these means, we get a training data set which contain 0.2% suspicious domain in 10 minutes real DNS traffic data.

In our system we decided to use RIPPER[4] -- a fast and effective rule learner. It has been successfully used in intrusion detection as well as related domains, and has proved to produce concise and intuitive rules. RIPPER can produce ordered and unordered rule sets. We decided to use ordered rule sets because they are more

C.C. Yang et al. (Eds.): PAISI 2007, LNCS 4430, pp. 323–324, 2007.
© Springer-Verlag Berlin Heidelberg 2007

compact and easier to interpret. Unfortunately, the standard RIPPER algorithm is not cost-sensitive and does not support incremental learning. We therefore converted it to a cost-sensitive learner by implementing instance weighting. In this way, the learning process is initiated only when it can improve the classification accuracy.

The test data is 1 hour real DNS traffic data captured in the campus network edge and consists of approximately 180,000 records of which approximately 300 are labeled suspicious. Table 1 shows parts of results of the suspicious domain name.

Table 1. Parts of result of the suspicious domain name

Domain name	Type	Number	Comments
fuck.syn-flood.us	A	1789	W32.Spybot.AGEN
ypgw.wallloan.com	A	1573	W32.Esbot.a/b
link.sp4m.info	A	2185	W32.Spybot.AFEW
aaaa.huigezi.org	MX	176	null
botnet.3322.org	A	118	null
con1.dmcast.com	A	611	Adware site
hub4t.sandai.net	A	492	Download software site

Some domains such as "fuck.syn-flood.us" can be clearly distinguished that is used by a botnet for the bot program analysis by virus bulletin, while others can not be found in known botnet lists though they seem very suspicious for using dynamic DNS and not being visited through familiar applications. We also observe that many MX type queries are classified as suspicious domain, the percent is much higher than other type queries. Some domain name with less query times will not be detected by the signature or statistical method. It is possible detect the botnet with small size or in early time.

Conclusion and future work. This paper proposes a technique to detect botnets by mining DNS traffic data. We create a profile defining a suspicious domain by some prior knowledge, and then compare the similarity of a current domain with the created profile using RIPPER to label suspicious domain. Experimental results show this technique can detect not only domain names used by well know botnets, but also domain with less query times which can not detected by the signature or statistical method. As the work is in progress and the results described in this paper are preliminary, we will evaluate our method according to its sensitivities of parameters and the misclassification of the results on the used data set in future work.

References

1. D. Dagon, C. Zou, and W. Lee. Modeling botnet propagation using time zones. In Proceedings of the 13th Annual Network and Distributed System Security Symposium (NDSS '06), 2006.
2. J. Kristoff. Botnets. NANOG 32, October, 2004.
3. Antoine Schonewille, Dirk-Jan van Helmond. The Domain Name Service as an IDS. Master System and Network Engineering at the University of Amsterdam, 2006.
4. Fast effective rule induction. In Armand Prieditis and Stuart Russell, Proceedings of the 12th International Conference on Machine Learning, pages 115-123, Tahoe City, CA, 1995.

HMM-Based Approach for Evaluating Risk Propagation

Young-Gab Kim and Jongin Lim

Center for Information Security Technologies (CIST), Korea University,
1, 5-ga, Anam-dong, SungBuk-gu, 136-701, Seoul, Korea
{always, jilim}@korea.ac.kr

1 Introduction

In order to holistically analyze the scope of risk propagation caused by threats, considering the relationship among the threats, a previous study [1] proposed a probabilistic model for risk propagation based on the Markov process [2]. Using our proposed model, the occurrence probability and occurrence frequency for each threat in an information system can be estimated holistically, and applied to establish countermeasures against those threats. Nevertheless, result gaps between the expected output data evaluated by the proposed Markov process-based, risk propagation model and the real-world observations reported by the Korean Information Security Agency (KISA) [3] can arise due to the unexpected emergence of malicious applications such as Netbus and Subsevens, and new Internet worms. Therefore, the Hidden Markov Model [2] (HMM)-based, probabilistic approach is proposed in this paper to overcome this limitation.

2 HMM-Based Risk Propagation Model

In order to deal dynamically with the unexpected appearance of diverse threats in information systems, a risk propagation model should meet two requirements: valuable information such as the symptoms of any new cyber attack propagated by malicious applications or Internet worms should be extractable from very large historical database, and risk information should be updated automatically against the new cyber attacks. The proposed HMM-based, risk propagation model can meet these two requirements efficiently by using the HMM characteristics.

The HMM-based, risk propagation model is composed of two phases and five important elements: Hidden Threat-State, Threat Transition Matrix, Initial Vector, Observable State and Confusion Matrix. Phase 1 is a process that defines the threat-states, threat transition matrix and initial vector using the historical data of threats from the Markov process-based, risk propagation model. In Phase 1, 'Hidden Threat-State (TS)' is a set of hidden states which can be instigated by threats in the critical infrastructure. 'Threat Transition Matrix' is a square matrix describing the probabilities of moving from one hidden threat-state to another. 'Initial Vector of Hidden Threat-State' is the initial probability of Hidden Threat-States. Phase 1 can be performed with the Markov process-based model proposed in the previous work.

C.C. Yang et al. (Eds.): PAISI 2007, LNCS 4430, pp. 325–326, 2007.

In Phase 2, 'Observable State (*OS*)' is a set of states which can be observed in information systems, and is defined using observable context information (historical data related with threats) such as network traffic and the uncertainty of data items. A very important element is dealing with the unexpected emergence of malicious applications and Internet worms. 'Confusion Matrix' is a square matrix describing the probabilities of observing 'Observable State' from particular 'Hidden Threat-States'. This paper focuses especially on probability estimation, which is the relationship between the 'Hidden Threat-State' and the 'Observable State', as presented in the 'Confusion Matrix' in Phase 2. Fig. 1 depicts the concept of the HMM-based, risk propagation model.

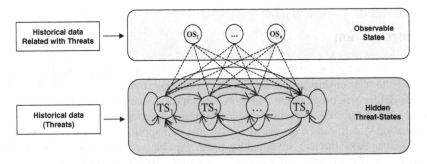

Fig. 1. Concept of the HMM-based risk propagation model

This study extends our previous work on the Markov-based, risk propagation model to incorporate the ability to deal with the unexpected frequency of cyber attacks. The newly proposed HMM-based, risk propagation model can also be applied to diverse threats in critical infrastructure, and promises to overcome the limitation of the Markov process-based, risk propagation model using observable states and confusion matrix in HMM.

Acknowledgement. "This research was supported by the MIC (Ministry of Information and Communication), Korea, under the ITRC (Information Technology Research Center) support program supervised by the IITA (Institute of Information Technology Advancement)" (IITA-2006-(C1090-0603-0025)).

References

1. Y.-G. Kim, T. Lee, H. P. In, Y.-J. Chung, In. Kim, and D.-K. Baik: A Probabilistic Approach to Estimate the Damage Propagation of Cyber Attacks. LNCS, Vol.3935. Springer-Verlag, Berlin Heidelberg (2006) 175-185
2. R. D. Yates, D. J. Goodman: Probability and Stochastic Process. Second Edition, WILEY International Edition (2003)
3. KISA: Statistics and Analysis on Hacking and Virus. http://www.krcert.or.kr

A Symptom-Based Taxonomy for an Early Detection of Network Attacks*

Ki-Yoon Kim and Hyoung-Kee Choi

The School of Information and Communication Engineering,
Sungkyunkwan University, Suwon, Korea, 440-746
{doogysp, hkchoi}@ece.skku.ac.kr

Abstract. We present a symptom-based taxonomy for an early detection of network attacks. Since this taxonomy uses symptoms in the network it is relatively easy to access the information to classify the attack. Accordingly it is quite early to detect an attack as the symptom always appears before the main stage of the attack. Furthermore, we are able to classify unknown attacks if the symptom of unknown attacks is correlated with the one of the already known attacks.

1 Introduction

In order to protect the network against attacks effectively, the attacks must be classified by similar types and patterns, and a proper prevention and defense method for each type of attacks must be selected and applied. To classify attacks with similar patterns, taxonomies which classify attacks using their characteristics have been previously proposed. However, the previously proposed taxonomies show a few weaknesses; 1) taking excessive time to analyze information necessary to classify attacks and hence not being able to respond to newer attacks in a timely manner, 2) being able to trust the consequences of attack classification only when all normal system patterns are identified in advance. Since the weakness in the attack taxonomy directly influences on the selection of a defense method, they may also become the roadblock in the system defense. In order to setup the new taxonomy, we focus on the fact that a network shows symptoms when an attack is prepared and initiated [2][3], and that the variety of information in the network can be collected using the logs from different type of sensors [1]. Based on this fact, we propose the symptom-based taxonomy that uses symptoms in the network to classify attacks.

2 Symptom-Based Taxonomy

The symptom-based taxonomy classifies attacks in two stages; a single flow and aggregated flows. Fig. 1 shows the two-staged classification of the symptom-based

---

* This research was supported by the MIC (Ministry of Information and Communication), Korea, under the ITRC (Information Technology Research Center) support program supervised by the IITA (Institute of Information Technology Assessment).

C.C. Yang et al. (Eds.): PAISI 2007, LNCS 4430, pp. 327–328, 2007.

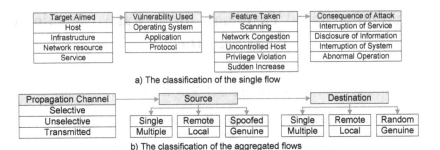

a) The classification of the single flow

b) The classification of the aggregated flows

Fig. 1. Two-staged classifications of symptom-based taxonomy

taxonomy. In the first stage, attacks in a single flow are of interest. A typical example of the first stage attack includes a DoS attack. The classification takes advantages of such information as target (victim) aimed, vulnerability used by attacks, phenomenon shown during attacks, and the consequence of attacks. In the second stage, the aggregated flows are used to judge whether attacks in the form of a single flow are independent to other attacks, and whether they are relevant to form a unified attack. Such an attack as DDoS is the unified attack and occurs simultaneously from various nodes in the aggregated flows. In this case, individual single flows from each node are classified as an attack in the first stage. Then, they are further considered, in the second stage, to check whether the individual attacks are a part of the unified attack. Information used in the second stage is the locations of the attacker and the target. In other words, if a number of attacks in the single flows comes from the same source or passes to the same target or both over a short period of time, then these are the unified attacks by definition. As a result, this taxonomy can resolve problems occurred due to the delayed response to new attack patterns as well as problems occurred due to registering all normal patterns.

3 Conclusion

We present a symptom-based taxonomy for an early detection of network attacks. Only information required to the proposed taxonomy is the distinct symptoms at the scene. The symptoms are available in the convenient and reliable logs from different sensors in the network. As a result, the proposed attack taxonomy is able to classify even unknown attacks without a delay.

References

1. Cristina Abad et al., "Log Correlation for Intrusion Detection: A Proof of Concept", Computer Security Applications Conference, Dec. 2003.
2. Nong Ye, Joseph Giordano and John Feldman, "A Process Control Approach to Cyber Attack Detection," Communications of the ACM, Vol. 44 No 8, pp 76-82, Aug. 2001.
3. Akira Kanamaru et al., "A Simple Packet Aggregation Technique for Fault Detection", International Journal of Network Management 2000, Vol. 10, pp 215-228, Aug. 2000.

Author Index

Lecture Notes in Computer Science

For information about Vols. 1–4332

please contact your bookseller or Springer

Vol. 4381: J. Akiyama, W.Y.C. Chen, M. Kano, X. Li, Q. Yu (Eds.), Discrete Geometry, Combinatorics and Graph Theory. XI, 289 pages. 2007.

Vol. 4380: S. Spaccapietra, P. Atzeni, F. Fages, M.-S. Hacid, M. Kifer, J. Mylopoulos, B. Pernici, P. Shvaiko, J. Trujillo, I. Zaihrayeu (Eds.), Journal on Data Semantics VIII. XV, 219 pages. 2007.

Vol. 4378: I. Virbitskaite, A. Voronkov (Eds.), Perspectives of Systems Informatics. XIV, 496 pages. 2007.

Vol. 4377: M. Abe (Ed.), Topics in Cryptology – CT-RSA 2007. XI, 403 pages. 2006.

Vol. 4376: E. Frachtenberg, U. Schwiegelshohn (Eds.), Job Scheduling Strategies for Parallel Processing. VII, 257 pages. 2007.

Vol. 4374: J.F. Peters, A. Skowron, I. Düntsch, J. Grzymała-Busse, E. Orłowska, L. Polkowski (Eds.), Transactions on Rough Sets VI, Part I. XII, 499 pages. 2007.

Vol. 4373: K. Langendoen, T. Voigt (Eds.), Wireless Sensor Networks. XIII, 358 pages. 2007.

Vol. 4372: M. Kaufmann, D. Wagner (Eds.), Graph Drawing. XIV, 454 pages. 2007.

Vol. 4371: K. Inoue, K. Satoh, F. Toni (Eds.), Computational Logic in Multi-Agent Systems. X, 315 pages. 2007. (Sublibrary LNAI).

Vol. 4370: P.P Lévy, B. Le Grand, F. Poulet, M. Soto, L. Darago, L. Toubiana, J.-F. Vibert (Eds.), Pixelization Paradigm. XV, 279 pages. 2007.

Vol. 4369: M. Umeda, A. Wolf, O. Bartenstein, U. Geske, D. Seipel, O. Takata (Eds.), Declarative Programming for Knowledge Management. X, 229 pages. 2006. (Sublibrary LNAI).

Vol. 4368: T. Erlebach, C. Kaklamanis (Eds.), Approximation and Online Algorithms. X, 345 pages. 2007.

Vol. 4367: K. De Bosschere, D. Kaeli, P. Stenström, D. Whalley, T. Ungerer (Eds.), High Performance Embedded Architectures and Compilers. XI, 307 pages. 2007.

Vol. 4366: K. Tuyls, R. Westra, Y. Saeys, A. Nowé (Eds.), Knowledge Discovery and Emergent Complexity in Bioinformatics. IX, 183 pages. 2007. (Sublibrary LNBI).

Vol. 4364: T. Kühne (Ed.), Models in Software Engineering. XI, 332 pages. 2007.

Vol. 4362: J. van Leeuwen, G.F. Italiano, W. van der Hoek, C. Meinel, H. Sack, F. Plášil (Eds.), SOFSEM 2007: Theory and Practice of Computer Science. XXI, 937 pages. 2007.

Vol. 4361: H.J. Hoogeboom, G. Păun, G. Rozenberg, A. Salomaa (Eds.), Membrane Computing. IX, 555 pages. 2006.

Vol. 4360: W. Dubitzky, A. Schuster, P.M.A. Sloot, M. Schroeder, M. Romberg (Eds.), Distributed, High-Performance and Grid Computing in Computational Biology. X, 192 pages. 2007. (Sublibrary LNBI).

Vol. 4358: R. Vidal, A. Heyden, Y. Ma (Eds.), Dynamical Vision. IX, 329 pages. 2007.

Vol. 4357: L. Buttyán, V. Gligor, D. Westhoff (Eds.), Security and Privacy in Ad-Hoc and Sensor Networks. X, 193 pages. 2006.

Vol. 4355: J. Julliand, O. Kouchnarenko (Eds.), B 2007: Formal Specification and Development in B. XIII, 293 pages. 2006.

Vol. 4354: M. Hanus (Ed.), Practical Aspects of Declarative Languages. X, 335 pages. 2006.

Vol. 4353: T. Schwentick, D. Suciu (Eds.), Database Theory – ICDT 2007. XI, 419 pages. 2006.

Vol. 4352: T.-J. Cham, J. Cai, C. Dorai, D. Rajan, T.-S. Chua, L.-T. Chia (Eds.), Advances in Multimedia Modeling, Part II. XVIII, 743 pages. 2006.

Vol. 4351: T.-J. Cham, J. Cai, C. Dorai, D. Rajan, T.-S. Chua, L.-T. Chia (Eds.), Advances in Multimedia Modeling, Part I. XIX, 797 pages. 2006.

Vol. 4349: B. Cook, A. Podelski (Eds.), Verification, Model Checking, and Abstract Interpretation. XI, 395 pages. 2007.

Vol. 4348: S.T. Taft, R.A. Duff, R.L. Brukardt, E. Ploedereder, P. Leroy (Eds.), Ada 2005 Reference Manual. XXII, 765 pages. 2006.

Vol. 4347: J. Lopez (Ed.), Critical Information Infrastructures Security. X, 286 pages. 2006.

Vol. 4346: L. Brim, B. Haverkort, M. Leucker, J. van de Pol (Eds.), Formal Methods: Applications and Technology. X, 363 pages. 2007.

Vol. 4345: N. Maglaveras, I. Chouvarda, V. Koutkias, R. Brause (Eds.), Biological and Medical Data Analysis. XIII, 496 pages. 2006. (Sublibrary LNBI).

Vol. 4344: V. Gruhn, F. Oquendo (Eds.), Software Architecture. X, 245 pages. 2006.

Vol. 4342: H. de Swart, E. Orłowska, G. Schmidt, M. Roubens (Eds.), Theory and Applications of Relational Structures as Knowledge Instruments II. X, 373 pages. 2006. (Sublibrary LNAI).

Vol. 4341: P.Q. Nguyen (Ed.), Progress in Cryptology - VIETCRYPT 2006. XI, 385 pages. 2006.

Vol. 4340: R. Prodan, T. Fahringer, Grid Computing. XXIII, 317 pages. 2007.

Vol. 4339: E. Ayguadé, G. Baumgartner, J. Ramanujam, P. Sadayappan (Eds.), Languages and Compilers for Parallel Computing. XI, 476 pages. 2006.

Vol. 4338: P. Kalra, S. Peleg (Eds.), Computer Vision, Graphics and Image Processing. XV, 965 pages. 2006.

Vol. 4337: S. Arun-Kumar, N. Garg (Eds.), FSTTCS 2006: Foundations of Software Technology and Theoretical Computer Science. XIII, 430 pages. 2006.

Vol. 4336: V.R. Basili, D. Rombach, K. Schneider, B. Kitchenham, D. Pfahl, R.W. Selby, Empirical Software Engineering Issues. XVII, 193 pages. 2007.

Vol. 4335: S.A. Brueckner, S. Hassas, M. Jelasity, D. Yamins (Eds.), Engineering Self-Organising Systems. XII, 212 pages. 2007. (Sublibrary LNAI).

Vol. 4334: B. Beckert, R. Hähnle, P.H. Schmitt (Eds.), Verification of Object-Oriented Software. XXIX, 658 pages. 2007. (Sublibrary LNAI).

Vol. 4333: U. Reimer, D. Karagiannis (Eds.), Practical Aspects of Knowledge Management. XII, 338 pages. 2006. (Sublibrary LNAI).